MILLS and ROBERTSON

with PRINT and ROWBOTHAM

Fundamentals of Managerial Accounting and Finance

Fourth Edition

Design and Typesetting: Mars Business Associates Ltd

Printed and bound in Great Britain by: Redwood Books Ltd

First reprint: July 2000

LIBRARY OF CONGRESS CATALOGING IN PUBLICATION DATA

Mills, Roger W.

Fundamentals of Managerial Accounting and Finance, 4th Edition

Roger W. Mills   John Robertson

   with Carole F. Print and Sean A. Rowbotham

Included bibliographies and index

ISBN   1 873186 12 6

1. Financial Accounting, Management Accounting, Financial Management

I. Title   II   Robertson, J., Print, C.F., Rowbotham, S.A.

Mars Business Associates Ltd

62 Kingsmead, Lechlade, Glos. GL7 3BW

Tel: + 44 1367 252506   Email: john@marspub.co.uk

Roger W. Mills

Tel: 07070 888888   Email: DrRWMills@aol.com

Preface

This book has been written specifically with the MBA student in mind. Such students we know from our experience need to be financially aware and also to understand the language of accounting for both the MBA course and their career in management, but they do not need to know everything about managerial accounting and finance unless they intend to specialise. We have therefore assumed that the reader of this book will have his or her sights upon general management in the true sense of the word and will seek other sources for purposes of specialisation.

The book is organised in the twelve chapters shown in the following illustration:

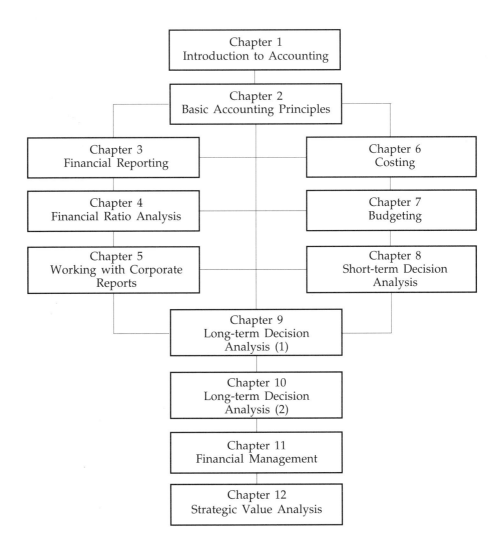

The relationship between the chapters is as follows: Chapters 1 and 2, introduction and basic principles of accounting, assumes that you have had little formal exposure to the main financial statements used within an organisation and the rules and conventions used in drafting them. It will take you through these quite gently. Chapter 2 provides an introduction to many of accounting 'adjustments' such as depreciation, revaluation, goodwill, accruals, prepayments. Also an introduction to bookkeeping through to Trial Balance and the preparation of Trading, Profit and Loss account and Balance Sheet.

On completion of these Chapters there are two alternative routes. First, you can pursue Chapters 3, 4 and 5 which are concerned with the requirements for financial reporting and how to read, interpret and analyse financial reports in the form of published accounts and published information. The UK regulatory framework for financial reporting is discussed in Chapter 3, followed by the principles of financial ratio analysis in Chapter 4, and its practical application including Argenti's failure framework, ratio models and an example, working with published accounts in Chapter 5.

Alternatively, from Chapter 2 you can pursue the route through Chapters 6, 7 and 8. These chapters focus upon internal, as opposed to external and published, managerial accounting and financial issues. Chapter 6 provides an introduction to Costing, including overheads, product cost, marginal/absorption costing and standard costing. The important area of budgeting and budgetary control is discussed in Chapter 7 followed by issues associated with non-routine, but often very important, decisions of a short-term nature in Chapter 8.

Chapters 9 and 10 are concerned with long-term decision analysis. Chapter 9 covers the basic principles through examples dealing with the development of cash flows with a comprehensive example covering the traditional and discounted cash flow techniques associated with capital investment appraisal. Chapter 10 covers additional topics such as mutually exclusive projects, effect of inflation, effect of taxation, sensitivity and risk.

Chapter 11 provides an introduction to financial management and draws together many issues in earlier chapters. Chapter 12 provides an introduction to Strategic Financial Management. Within strategy the financial dimension can be vital in terms of providing an indication about the value of the business and its parts. This chapter discusses the approaches available for undertaking such valuation and you will find it draws upon many areas covered within the book. It is important and in our opinion an appropriate final chapter because it firmly places the value of managerial accounting and finance within a general management context.

Roger W. Mills   John Robertson   August 1999

Contents

CHAPTER 8   SHORT-TERM DECISION ANALYSIS

CHAPTER 9   LONG-TERM DECISION ANALYSIS (1)

CHAPTER 10 LONG-TERM DECISION ANALYSIS (2)

CHAPTER ONE

INTRODUCTION TO ACCOUNTING

LEARNING OBJECTIVES

When you have finished studying this chapter you should be able to:

❏ Understand the relationship between the three main financial statements, Cash Flow Forecast, Profit and Loss Account and Balance Sheet.

❏ Understand the structure of a Balance Sheet both vertical and 'two sided', interpret and show the effect of single transactions.

❏ Prepare Profit and Loss accounts, describe their relationship between the opening and closing Balance Sheets and comment on the differences between profit and cash.

❏ Describe and produce a comprehensive example using the three main financial statements. Interpret the results.

1.1 Introduction

The successful study of accounting and finance is dependent upon the assimilation of a number of basic principles. Rather than deal will all of these by way of a comprehensive introduction, in this chapter, we have selected only those needed for the earlier chapters of the book. In these earlier chapters, the particular focus of attention is upon the principles, content, layout and interpretation of the main financial statements.

This chapter provides an overview of accounting both for those with little or no background in the subject and for those with some background who wish to review some fundamental principles. Specific reference will be made to important terminology and to what financial statements do and do not portray. To know what financial statements do not communicate is just as important as knowing what they do communicate.

Fundamental principles are discussed in the chapter without employing some of the specific accounting techniques (like double entry bookkeeping) and jargon (like debit and credit). It is directed at answering two important questions often asked by managers and other parties with an interest in an organisation: How well did it or will it perform over a given time period? What is, or will be the financial position at a given point of time? The accountant answers these questions with two main financial statements which we shall consider at length in this chapter – the profit and loss account and the balance sheet.

Our focus of attention in the chapter is directed at 'for-profit' organisations and, in particular, limited liability companies. Such organisations typically revolve around a similar, usually regular, cycle of economic activity. For example, retailers and most businesses buy goods and services and modify them by changing their form or by placing them in a convenient location, such that they can be sold at higher prices with the aim of producing a profit. The total amount of profit earned during a particular period heavily depends on the excess of the selling prices over the costs of the goods and services (the mark-up) and the speed of the operating cycle (the turnover). However, as we shall demonstrate, profit is not the only important focus of attention. Cash is equally important and must be carefully monitored as well. Quite how profit, cash and financial position can be monitored and the relationship between them will be demonstrated in this chapter.

Financial statements are used by organisations to summarise aspects of past, present and expected or likely or anticipated future performance. These financial statements are the result of applying certain principles, like double entry bookkeeping and some are reliant upon accounting conventions, a basic knowledge and understanding of which is essential in most of what follows.

One vital feature of the profit and loss account and cash flow statement for you to be aware of is that different principles are applied in drafting each of them. The application of these different principles means that for the same period cash and profit results will rarely be the same, hence the importance of having the two statements to convey the necessary information required for managing a business.

1.2   Introduction to Balance Sheet, Profit and Loss Account and Cash Flow Statement

Our discussion in this chapter will focus on three main financial statements and the difference in the information conveyed by each of them:

1.   The Balance Sheet

2.   The Profit and Loss account

3.   The Cash Flow Statement.

In the rest of this section we will introduce the main components of the Balance Sheet and show its relationship to the Profit and Loss account and Cash Flow Statement. In *Section 1.3* we will show the development of a Balance Sheet over a number of periods; this will include the relationship with the Profit and Loss Account. In *Section 1.4* we will follow a worked example showing how the three main financial statements can be used in a system of forecasting.

1.   Balance Sheet

The balance sheet is the financial statement used to illustrate an organisation's financial position. It can be likened to a snapshot because it is a static representation of an organisation's financial position in the form of its total assets and total liabilities at a particular point in time.

The balance sheet is reliant upon the following simple principle:

TOTAL ASSETS   =   TOTAL LIABILITIES

In developing this principle in this chapter our focus of attention will be upon those liabilities and assets to be found in the balance sheet of a limited liability company. However, in principle, though not the terminology used it is also applicable to most types of organisation. What are assets and liabilities? We provide a short review of each of them.

Total Assets

These are those resources obtained from the sources of finance which are expressed in monetary terms. Assets to be found in a company balance sheet are those in its possession, whether owned or controlled, and which are expected to yield future economic benefits. As shown in *Figure 1.1*, assets are usually referred to as being 'fixed' or 'current'. Fixed assets are those like land and buildings, machinery, vehicles, which are intended for use in the business and are not intended for sale as part of normal trading activity. Current assets form part of the working capital of a business and are instrumental in the generation of profit within the business. The main items of current assets include stock, debtors and cash held for use within the business.

Figure 1.1   Total Assets

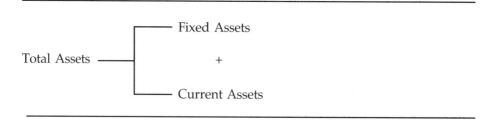

Total Liabilities

These are monetary obligations arising from past events and can be thought of as being the sources of finance used by the business. They include 'liabilities' to the owners, known as shareholders' (owners') funds or equity, which is usually categorised as share capital and reserves (such as retained profit), and liabilities to external sources of finance in the form of long-term loans and short-term sources like trade credit (creditors) and bank overdrafts. The sources of finance and how they may be generally categorised is illustrated in *Figure 1.2.*

Figure 1.2   Total Liabilities

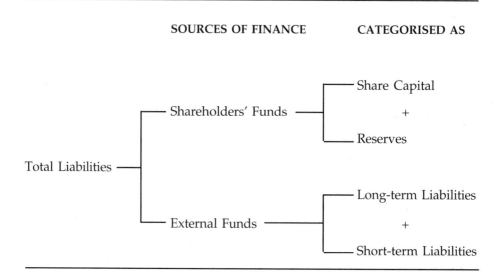

2.   Profit and Loss Account

The profit and loss account summarises the revenue generated and the costs incurred in the trading period between two balance sheet dates. Where the revenue exceeds the cost there is a profit and where the costs exceeds the revenue a loss is incurred.

In a profitable environment the result of recording accounting transactions will be that the assets of the business will increase automatically. On a regular basis, at least annually for publication purposes, companies prepare profit and loss accounts to determine the amount of profit generated by and retained in the business. The amount retained is added to the shareholders' fund under the subheading *Profit and Loss Account*, (please note that Profit and Loss Account in the balance sheet refers to the accumulated profits retained in the business over time, thereby increasing the total liabilities section). In this way the benefit to shareholders from profitable activity is recognised in the form of growth in the assets.

Profit that is retained in the business forms an important link between successive balance sheets. In *Figure 1.3* we show the relationship between the opening balance sheet, the profit and loss account for the period and the closing balance sheet at the end of the period (often a period will relate to one year).

Figure 1.3   Relationship between Balance Sheet and Profit and Loss Account

Balance Sheet	Balance Sheet	Balance Sheet	Balance Sheet
Profit and Loss Account Period 1	Profit and Loss Account Period 2	Profit and Loss Account Period 3	

In *Figure 1.3*, moving from left to right we have:

❏   The Opening Balance Sheet for Period 1, the Profit and Loss account for Period 1 and the Closing Balance Sheet for Period 1.

❏   The next day, the Closing Balance Sheet for Period 1 becomes the Opening Balance Sheet for Period 2 and the process repeats itself.

3. Cash Flow Statement

In its simplest form, the cash flow statement will record sources and uses of funds generated for the period under review. This requires taking:

1. the profit before taxation for the period, adding back non-cash transactions such as depreciation to obtain the profit generated from the operations.

2. the opening and closing balance sheets, extracting the differences between the two and recording them as a source of funds or a use of funds. For example, an increase in an asset is a use of funds while an increase in a liability is a source of funds. This subsidiary statement is known as a Balanced Report. In *Figure 1.4* we show this process.

Figure 1.4   Process for Determining Sources and Uses of Funds

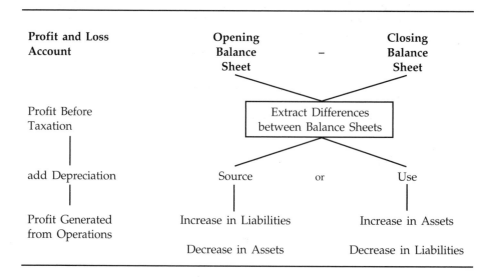

From the figures produced above we can prepare a number of different cash flow statements. One common statement is the Residual Form Report which takes say the Opening cash balance, adds all sources of funds to obtain an interim balance, then deducts all uses of funds; the resulting figure will be the Closing cash balance. This form of statement provides answers to the question 'What has happened to all our cash'?

1.3   Example – Main Financial Statements

In the following example we will show 'snapshots' of a business by comparing two Balance Sheets. To start, we will invest £50,000 in our business. How will this be shown in our opening Balance Sheet?

Balance Sheet 1.

	£		£
Current Assets		**Subscribed Capital**	
Cash	50,000	Share Capital	50,000
	50,000		50,000

In Balance Sheet 1, we show the £50,000 cash under a subheading Current Assets; this is what the company owns. On the Liabilities side of the Balance Sheet we show the £50,000 as Share Capital i.e. owners share capital; this is what the company owes. If the company were to be liquidated, it would simply take the £50,000 cash and pay it back to the owners (shareholders).

Balance Sheet 2.

	£		£
Fixed Assets		**Subscribed Capital**	
Land and Buildings	15,000	Share Capital	50,000
Plant and Machinery	10,000		
Current Assets			
Cash	25,000		
	50,000		50,000

It is now a game! Called 'spot the difference'. You are required to spot the difference between Balance Sheet 1 and Balance Sheet 2. These are the confidence builders!

In this case we can see that the company has bought Land and Buildings for £15,000 and Plant and Machinery for £10,000. We can also see that the Cash has reduced by the same amount i.e. (£15,000 + £10,000). This is a good example of the principles of double entry book keeping; every transaction affects two accounts; in this case Land and Buildings and Cash, and Plant and Machinery and Cash.

Balance Sheet 3.

	£		£
Fixed Assets		**Subscribed Capital**	
Land and Buildings	15,000	Share Capital	50,000
Plant and Machinery	10,000		
Current Assets			
Stock	15,000		
Cash	10,000		
	50,000		50,000

Still with the confidence builders. Now spot the difference between Balance Sheet 2 and Balance Sheet 3. Yes, we have bought Stock and paid for it by Cash. This is typical when companies commence trading since it is unlikely that they will be able to obtain stock on credit. Many small companies find themselves squeezed for cash flow by having to give credit to their customers while their suppliers are reluctant to extend similar credit to them.

Balance Sheet 4.

	£		£
Fixed Assets		**Subscribed Capital**	
Land and Buildings	15,000	Share Capital	50,000
Plant and Machinery	10,000	Profit	4,000
Current Assets			
Stock	7,000		
Debtors	20,000		
Cash	2,000		
	54,000		54,000

Now this is more like it. The difference between Balance Sheet 3 and Balance Sheet 4 shows that some trading has taken place. This is evident by the figure for Debtors. Debtors are our customers to whom we have sold goods on credit. We can also see that there is a figure for Profit i.e. we have 'made' a profit on the sale of the goods. Finally, the Stock and Cash figures have also reduced.

Therefore, Balance Sheet 3 can be viewed as our opening Balance Sheet, we will construct a Profit and Loss Account to show the trading, while Balance Sheet 4 is our closing Balance Sheet for the period. We will now construct a Profit and Loss account (which should explain all the changes from the two Balance Sheets).

Profit and Loss Account for the period ending xx/xx/xx

		£	£
Debtors	Sales (assume all credit)		20,000
Stock	less Materials	8,000	
Cash	less Wages and Overheads	8,000	
	Cost of Sales		16,000
	Profit		4,000

Why is Profit shown as a Liability? It is important to recognise that the physical profit is achieved through trading; i.e. when goods move from Stock and are sold to customers. The profit element is added at this point although it is not physically received until the customer pays for the goods. If we left it at that, the Balance Sheet would not balance. It would have more on the Assets side of the Balance Sheet i.e. the profit. Therefore, we have to put a corresponding entry on the Liabilities side of the Balance Sheet. To whom does the profit belong. The shareholders of the business. If the business were to be liquidated at this point and we obtained book values, the original share capital and the profit would be returned to the shareholders (owner).

We might ask at this point 'how successful is the company, so far'? In pure profit terms, profit as a percentage of sales £4,000 ÷ £20,000 x 100 = 25% which would be considered very good in most cases. However, here we have an example of a company which is selling goods profitably but is running out of cash. Quite simply, it doesn't have enough cash to convert its remaining stock into a saleable state. Furthermore, it is also unable to buy further stock. Is the position the company finds itself in purely the result of selling goods on credit (i.e. its Debtors) or is there other important messages here?

The position is similar to many start–up companies. In this case, we started the company with £50,000 in cash. This should have been sufficient funding until we achieved a foothold in our particular market. However, what did we do? We went out and purchased premises (Land and Buildings) and equipment (Plant and Machinery). This immediately took away half of our cash. What should we have done? Perhaps we should have rented our premises and rented or leased our equipment. This would have conserved our cash which could then have been used in trading.

Balance Sheet 5.

	£		£
Fixed Assets		**Subscribed Capital**	
Land and Buildings	15,000	Share Capital	50,000
Plant and Machinery	10,000	Profit	4,000
Current Assets		**Current Liabilities**	
Stock	17,000	Creditors	10,000
Debtors	20,000		
Cash	2,000		
	64,000		64,000

The difference between Balance Sheet 4 and Balance Sheet 5 introduces Creditors. Creditors are our suppliers who have supplied us goods on credit. In this case, our Stock has increased by £10,000 and we now have Creditors with a £10,000 balance (owing).

We are now relying on our suppliers to supply us goods on credit and our customers to pay their bills.

Balance Sheet 6.

	£		£
Fixed Assets		**Subscribed Capital**	
Land and Buildings	15,000	Share Capital	50,000
Plant and Machinery	10,000	Profit	4,000
Current Assets		**Current Liabilities**	
Stock	17,000	Creditors	10,000
Debtors	10,000		
Cash	12,000		
	64,000		64,000

The difference between Balance Sheet 5 and Balance Sheet 6 shows that we have received £10,000 in cash from our Debtors. Therefore, the Debtors balance has reduced by £10,000 and the Cash balance has increased by £10,000.

We now have the means (cash) to convert further stock for resale.

Balance Sheet 7.

	£		£
Fixed Assets		**Subscribed Capital**	
Land and Buildings	15,000	Share Capital	50,000
Plant and Machinery	10,000	Profit	4,000
Vehicles	5,000		
Current Assets		**Current Liabilities**	
Stock	17,000	Creditors	10,000
Debtors	10,000		
Cash	7,000		
	64,000		64,000

The difference between Balance Sheet 6 and Balance Sheet 7 shows that we have spent £5,000 cash on a Vehicle. At this point in our trading activities this does not seem to be a good idea. Balance Sheet 7 clearly shows that we have taken £5,000 out of our Working Capital Cycle and put it into Fixed Assets i.e. Vehicles. This often occurs when companies make capital investment decisions, either for new plant or vehicles or to acquire another business – in the short-term the company is vulnerable to the reductions in working capital.

The differences between Balance Sheet 7 and Balance Sheet 8 shows a number of movements; Stock, Debtors, no Cash, Bank Overdraft and Profit. In fact we have completed another trading activity. Balance Sheet 7 being the opening Balance Sheet, the trading in the form of a Profit and Loss Account and Balance Sheet 8 being the closing Balance Sheet.

Balance Sheet 8.

	£		£
Fixed Assets		**Subscribed Capital**	
Land and Buildings	15,000	Share Capital	50,000
Plant and Machinery	10,000	Profit	11,000
Vehicles	5,000		
Current Assets		**Current Liabilities**	
Stock	5,000	Creditors	10,000
Debtors	40,000	Bank Overdraft	4,000
	75,000		75,000

In this example, Debtors have moved from £10,000 to £40,000 indicating a sale of £30,000 on credit. Stock has reduced from £17,000 to £5,000 indicating usage of materials of £12,000. Cash has reduced from £7,000 through zero cash into a Bank Overdraft of £4,000 a spending of £11,000 on wages and overheads. Profit has increased from £4,000 to £11,000 indicating a profit on the transaction of £7,000. These movements are now shown in the Profit and Loss Account, below.

Profit and Loss Account for the period ending xx/xx/xx

		£	£
Debtors	Sales		30,000
Stock	less Materials	12,000	
Cash	less Wages and Overheads	11,000	
	Cost of Sales		23,000
	Profit		7,000

Balance Sheet 9.

	£		£
Fixed Assets		**Subscribed Capital**	
Land and Buildings	15,000	Share Capital	50,000
Plant and Machinery	10,000	Profit	8,000
Vehicles	5,000		
Current Assets		**Current Liabilities**	
Stock	5,000	Creditors	10,000
Debtors	40,000	Bank Overdraft	4,000
		Dividend Payable	3,000
	75,000		75,000

The difference between Balance Sheet 8 and Balance Sheet 9 shows that the (retained) profit has reduced from £11,000 to £8,000 while an entry for a (proposed) Dividend payable of £3,000 is shown in the Current Liabilities section. We might be concerned regarding the possible future of this company. So much relies on collecting in amounts owing from its customers. For example, £10,000 of the Debtors figure is outstanding from the previous transaction. How can we obtain more stock from our suppliers? How can we convert stock for resale? How can we pay our creditors? Are we concerned that we have a bank overdraft?

The fact is, this game has been a fairy story. And like all good fairy stories they all start off 'once upon a time' and finish 'they all lived happily ever after'. This is the case for this small company. Wish it were true in practice.

Balance Sheet 10.

	£		£
Fixed Assets		**Subscribed Capital**	
Land and Buildings	15,000	Share Capital	50,000
Plant and Machinery	10,000	Profit	8,000
Vehicles	5,000		
Current Assets		**Current Liabilities**	
Stock	5,000	Creditors	2,000
Debtors	15,000		
Cash	10,000		
	60,000		60,000

We will leave you to make up your own minds regarding the fortunes of this company. What we have shown is the build-up of a Balance Sheet to show the main components. Also the Profit and Loss account and its relationship with the opening and closing balance sheets.

While the two sided Balance Sheet does have an appeal i.e. Total Liabilities equals Total Assets this is not the format used in published accounts throughout the UK and Europe. On the next page, we produce the final Balance Sheet (10), in one of the accepted UK formats. This is a vertical layout where the Assets are followed by the Liabilities rather than shown side by side and the two categories of working capital, Current Assets and Current Liabilities, are placed together within the first section.

Balance Sheet 10 – Vertical format.

	£	£
Fixed Assets		
Land and Buildings		15,000
Plant and Machinery		10,000
Vehicles		5,000
Total Fixed Assets		30,000
Current Assets		
Stock	5,000	
Debtors	15,000	
Cash	10,000	
	30,000	
Creditors: amounts owing within one year		
Creditors	2,000	
Net Working Capital		28,000
Total Assets less Current Liabilities		58,000
Subscribed Capital		
Share Capital		50,000
Profit		8,000
Shareholders' Fund		58,000

Note:

Creditors: amounts owing within one year is the same as Current Liabilities

1.4   Worked example of Financial Statements

1.   Information

MEC Ltd to be formed on 1st July will immediately purchase £250,000 of fixed assets, including land valued at £50,000, using a five year loan. The loan is to be repaid in full at the end of the five year period, but interest on the loan will be paid monthly. In addition, £150,000 of capital will be provided by the injection of shareholders' funds. Its plans for the first six months to 31st December are as follows:

- ❏ Sales for 6 months   £6,000,000

- ❏ Materials used   £2,400,000

- ❏ Materials required to be purchased to
  allow for closing stock of £200,000   £2,600,000

- ❏ Labour in sales   £2,100,000

- ❏ Overheads (including estimated interest charges
  and £20,000 depreciation for the six month period)   £1,400,000

Expected cash receipts and payments for the first six months have been estimated. After making due allowance for credit periods to be allowed to customers and expected to be available from suppliers, the estimates are:

	Cash Receipts from Sales	Cash Payments for Materials
	£'000	£'000
July	430	600
August	600	600
September	600	200
October	800	200
November	1,300	200
December	1,600	200
TOTAL	5,330	2,000

All expenses other than materials are to be paid evenly each month.

2. Cash Flow Forecast

The first statement we will consider is the cash flow forecast, which requires a brief introduction.

Basically, this financial statement is reliant upon principles we apply in everyday life. The cash we have at any point in time is the difference between what we have received and what we have paid out. We can also apply this principle to forecast cash available or required as you will find illustrated for our example in *Table 1.1*. In this table receipts and payments over the six month period are shown for each month. The difference between receipts (part A) and payments (part B) gives cash available or required (part C). The cash available or required for each month can also be viewed in conjunction with previous months in the form of a cumulated cash balance (part D).

Table 1.1 Cash Flow Forecast

	July	Aug	Sept	Oct	Nov	Dec	Total
Part A							
Receipts £'000							
Sales	430	600	600	800	1,300	1,600	5,330
5 year Loan	250						250
Share Capital	150						150
Subtotal A	830	600	600	800	1,300	1,600	5,730
Part B							
Payments £'000							
Materials	600	600	200	200	200	200	2,000
Wages	350	350	350	350	350	350	2,100
Overheads	230	230	230	230	230	230	1,380
Fixed Assets	250						250
Subtotal B	1,430	1,180	780	780	780	780	5,730
Part C							
Balance (A – B)	−600	−580	−180	20	520	820	
Part D							
Balance c/f,							
Cumulative							
Cash Position	−600	−1,180	−1,360	−1,340	−820	0	

The cash flow forecast shows that over the course of the six months there will be an unsatisfactory cash position at the end of each month with the exception of December. The cash flow will be at its worst in September when the shortfall in cumulative cash will reach £1.36 million. That the cash flow position for each month will be unfavourable is indicated by the negative numbers in Part D. *(In accounting and finance, brackets are often used to convey an unfavourable or adverse position).*

The important point to note is that only cash receipts and cash payments are included in the cash flow forecast, irrespective of the time period to which they relate. How could the cash position be improved? Anything which could be done to improve the speed and size of cash inflows and delay the speed and size of cash outflows would doubtless help. The relevant actions would include improving debtor collections, delaying creditor payments and delaying payments for fixed assets. These are all 'levers' which could be pulled to improve the cash position, but cash is only one perspective. Attempts to improve cash flow by pulling such levers will usually also have an impact upon profit and financial position. We consider each of these in what follows.

3. The Profit and Loss Account

Table 1.2 Profit and Loss Account for the six month period

	£	£
Sales		6,000
less Cost of Sales:		
Materials	2,400	
Labour	2,100	4,500
Gross Profit		**1,500**
less Expenses:		
Overheads	1,380	
Depreciation	20	1,400
Net (and Retained) Profit		**100**

The profit and loss account in *Table 1.2* requires cost of sales to be calculated and deducted from sales to yield a gross profit for the period. The cost of sales normally has to be calculated from materials purchased during the period and a stock adjustment. In this case the necessary information has been provided so that a stock adjustment is not required.

Why is a stock adjustment normally required? This adjustment ensures that the sales revenue for a given period is compared with its associated physical cost of sales. The reason for it is best understood if we consider the case of a trader in computers who starts with no stock, buys 2,200 but sells 2,000 in a trading period. In the profit and loss account the profit or loss for the period would be measured by comparing the revenues from 2,000 computers with the costs associated with 2,000, not 2,200. The remaining 200 represent closing stock, the profit or loss on which would be measured in a subsequent profit and loss account when they are sold. Because the 200 items of closing stock are irrelevant to the measurement of profit for this period, it is valued and deducted from the purchase cost of 2,200 items.

The £2.4 million for materials, together with labour costs incurred during the six month period of £2.1 million are deducted from sales. As indicated, the difference between sales and the cost of sales is known as the gross profit from which salaries and expenses are deducted to determine the net (and in this case retained because the illustration does not include taxation or dividend) profit of £100,000 for the 6 months.

One important point about profit illustrated in our example profit and loss account is that there are different 'layers' of profit. These layers we have illustrated in *Figure 1.5*:

Figure 1.5   Profit and Loss Account items

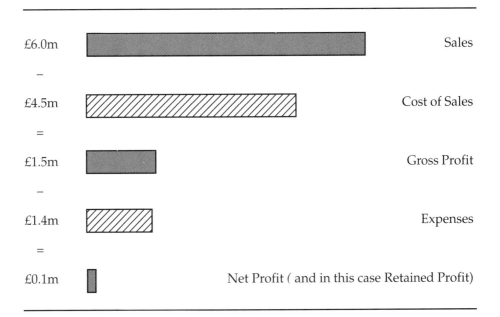

£6.0m		Sales
−		
£4.5m		Cost of Sales
=		
£1.5m		Gross Profit
−		
£1.4m		Expenses
=		
£0.1m		Net Profit (and in this case Retained Profit)

The different layers of profit illustrate the need to be cautious in discussions concerning profit. It is quite possible for communication to be confused by different parties referring to different layers without this being evident.

Whilst the cash flow forecast has been produced on a monthly basis because of limited data, the profit and loss account has been produced for the full six month period. This means that the only cash and profit comparisons for this example can be made for the whole six month period.

If we compare the six monthly totals relating to cash flow and profit, there are some notable differences as illustrated in *Table 1.3*.

Table 1.3 Differences between Cash Flow and Profit

		Column 1 Cash Flow Forecast £'000	Column 2 Profit and Loss Account £'000	Difference £'000
Loan		250	0	−250
Share Capital		150	0	−150
Sales		5,330	6,000	+670
	(A)	5,730	6,000	+270
Materials		2,000	2,400	−400
Wages		2,100	2,100	0
Expenses		1,380	1,380	0
Fixed Assets		250	20	+230
	(B)	5,730	5,900	−170
DIFFERENCE	(A) + (B)	0	100	+100

The differences between the cash flow forecast and the profit and loss account illustrate well how accounting principles affect financial statements differently. First, in calculating profit the legal effect of a transaction is recognised which means that debtors of £670,000 and creditors of £600,000 are included. Second, there is a difference in the treatment of fixed assets. In the profit and loss account the operation of the matching principle means £230,000 less is charged against profit than is the case in the cash flow forecast. In other words the costs of fixed assets are 'packaged' in the profit and loss account over their useful economic lives as a series of annual depreciation charges which is quite different to accounting for cash flows.

This means that there is a depreciation charge for the six months in this example of £20,000, i.e. the useful economic life used in the depreciation calculation was clearly estimated as being five years. (i.e. £200,000 ÷ 5 = £40,000 for a full year, therefore £20,000 for the six month period).

The charging of an annual sum for depreciation against profit and the inclusion of the legal effect of transactions serves to illustrate why there may often be significant differences between the profitability and cash flows of an operation over the same time period.

4.   The balance sheet

The balance sheet in *Table 1.4* is the snapshot of what the financial position is expected to be on 31st December, the last day of the six month financial plan.

Table 1.4 Balance Sheet as at 31st December

	£'000	£000
Fixed Assets:		
Land		50
Other	200	
less: Depreciation	20	180
		230
Current Assets:		
Stock	200	
Debtors	670	870
TOTAL ASSETS		**£1,100**
Shareholders' Funds:		
Share Capital		150
Reserves		100
		250
External Funds:		
Long-Term Loan (5 years)	250	
Creditors	600	850
TOTAL LIABILITIES		**£1,100**

The balance sheet in *Table 1.4* illustrates that on December 31st, six months hence, the value of fixed assets will have diminished such that they will have a net book value of £230,000. In addition to such fixed assets and stocks, both of which have an obvious physical presence, the company will also have debtors of £670,000. This £670,000 represents monies owing to the company which, because of the legal obligation associated with them, are relevant in the calculation of profit, but not cash flow.

The sum of all assets amounts to £1,100,000 which corresponds with the total of all liabilities in the lower part of the balance sheet. Such liabilities comprise the initial injection of share capital of £150,000, the £100,000 of profit to be generated and retained over the six months, the long-term liability in the form of the five year loan, and the current liability in the form of £600,000 of creditors. In common with debtors, the £600,000 owing to creditors is relevant in the calculation of profit because of the legal obligation associated with them. However, they are also irrelevant in calculating cash flow for this six month period because they will involve no movement in cash, as yet.

The outcome of this six month plan can be summarised as being:

❑ a stable cash position as at 31st December, but with potential cash flow difficulties throughout the period;

❑ a profit of £100,000 for the six month period; and,

❑ total assets and total liabilities of £1.1 million as at 31st December.

Any attempt to change the plan will impact upon each of these. Consider, for example, the effect of allowing no credit sales and the collection of £1 million cash per month from sales for each of the six months. This, given the existing position would result in potential cash flow difficulties for July and August as shown in *Table 1.5*.

Table 1.5 Revised Cash Flow Forecast

	July	Aug	Sept	Oct	Nov	Dec	Total
Part A							
Receipts £'000							
Sales	1,000	1,000	1,000	1,000	1,000	1,000	6,000
5 year Loan	250						250
Share Capital	150						150
Subtotal A	1,400	1,000	1,000	1,000	1,000	1,000	6,400
Part B							
Payment £'000							
Subtotal B	1,430	1,180	780	780	780	780	5,730
Part C							
Balance (A–B)	−30	−180	220	220	220	220	670
Part D							
Balance c/f, Cumulative Cash Position	−30	−210	10	230	450	670	

At the end of the six month period the cash flow forecast would show a positive balance of £670,000, reflected in the balance sheet by an entry for cash of the same amount in place of the £670,000 entry for debtors. Would profit be affected? It appears not, but this is not the case. There is one important area that always poses difficulties which we will deal with now. It concerns interest.

If you refer to the basic data used in the example you will see that the £1.4 million for expenses included estimated interest charges. Any action to reduce the potential cash deficit to be financed by borrowing will also reduce the interest charge for the period. Let us see the effect of interest by assuming that the company based its interest charge estimate upon borrowing to cover its worst position of £1.36 million *(Table 1.1:* September) and that the interest rate allowed for the six month period was 10%.

Now with the revised forecast involving no credit sales, the worst position is £210,000. In terms of the interest charge for the period there will be a reduction to be made of £115,000 ((£1,360,000 − £210,000) x 10%). In other words, the interest charge will be £115,000 lower.

If we assume that this interest is all paid by the end of the six month period then the cash balance on December 31st will be:

		£
	Closing Cash Balance [1]	0
+	Extra Income from Sales being forecast	670,000
+	Reduction in Interest Payable	115,000
=	Revised Closing Cash Balance	785,000

1. extracted from *Table 1.1*

You may think this will lead to an imbalance in the balance sheet where total assets will be higher than total liabilities by £115,000. This will not be the case, because of the effect of the reduced interest charge upon profit. As well as a deduction from cash flow, interest payments are a charge against profit. This means that the £1.4 million of expenses charged against profit will be £115,000 lower and hence profit will be:

		£
	Profit Forecast [1]	100,000
+	*Reduction in interest Payable*	115,000
=	Revised Profit Forecast	215,000

1. extracted from *Table 1.2*

What happened to this profit? You will recall that it is retained in the business and shown in the balance sheet in total liabilities under shareholders' funds. Thus, the two parts of the balance sheet, total assets and total liabilities, are kept in balance as illustrated in *Table 1.6*.

Table 1.6   Balance Sheet as at 31st December

	AFTER		BEFORE	
	£,000	£,000	£000	£'000
Fixed Assets:				
Land		50		50
Other	200		200	
less Depreciation	20	180	20	180
		230		230
Current Assets:				
Stock	200		200	
Debtors	0		670	
Cash	785	985	0	870
TOTAL ASSETS		**£1,215**		**£1,100**
Shareholders' Funds:				
Share Capital		1 50		1 50
Reserves		215		100
		365		250
External Funds:				
Long-Term Loan (5 years)	250		250	
Creditors	600	850	600	850
TOTAL LIABILITIES		**£1,215**		**£1,100**

1.5   The Balance Sheet equation and the UK format

One stumbling block often encountered arises because of the variety of layouts encountered in both internal and published balance sheets. If you come into contact with US and other European balance sheets you will often find assets and liabilities illustrated in a different order and sometimes grouped together in different ways. Such grouping differences can be readily dealt with if you recall the reference we made earlier to the balance sheet equation. Whether presented in horizontal or vertical format, the basic balance sheet equation is:

TOTAL ASSETS	=	TOTAL LIABILITIES

We have seen that each of these two can be subdivided

into component assets and liabilities such as:

FIXED ASSETS	SHAREHOLDERS' FUNDS
+	+
CURRENT ASSETS	EXTERNAL FUNDS

In UK published accounts, external funds are typically grouped with total assets as negative items thereby reducing the balance sheet totals. Furthermore in the UK and most EC published accounts a distinction is made between those external funds which fall due within one year and those which fall due after one year. This distinction means that you may often encounter an item referred to as 'net current assets'. Net current assets are the difference between current assets and external funds falling due within one year. Another term used for such assets is 'working capital' because they represent the liquid resources available for use in generating future profit after short term obligations have been met.

The result of grouping external funding with total assets is that you will encounter items of accounting jargon which are summarised in the following illustration, and explained in the next chapter.

Table 1.7 Balance Sheet as at 31 December (UK format)

	£'000	£'000
Fixed Assets:		
Land		50
Other	200	
less Depreciation	20	180
		230
Current Assets:		
Stock	200	
Cash	785	
	985	
less Creditors: amounts falling due within one year	600	385
Total Assets less Current Liabilities		615
less Creditors: amounts falling due after more than one year		250
Net Assets		365
Capital and Reserves		
Share Capital		150
Profit and Loss Account		215
		365

FINANCIAL ACCOUNTING

CHAPTER TWO

When you have finished studying this chapter and completed the exercises you should be able to:

❑ Understand the adjustments made to fixed assets and their affect on the profit and loss account and balance sheet e.g. depreciation, disposal, revaluation, goodwill.

❑ Describe the main components of current assets including stock (valuation), debtors (bad debts written off, provision for doubtful debts) and prepayments.

❑ Describe the main sources of long-term financing.

❑ Prepare final accounts of limited companies from trial balance stage.

2.1   Introduction

In *Chapter 1* we introduced the Balance Sheet from the start-up of a business through a number of transactions. Our aim was to provide an easy entry into the terminology of accounting and show the main sections of the Balance Sheet together with its interrelationship with the Profit and Loss account. We continued with a worked example of the main financial statements and added Cash Flow forecasts to the other two statements.

In this chapter we intend to use the Balance Sheet as our structure. We will take each section and explain the adjustments that have to be made (e.g. Depreciation, Bad Debts, Provision for Doubtful Debts, Accruals, Prepayments) and how they are treated in the accounts. We will also explain some of the other items that find their way onto the Balance Sheet (e.g. Share Premium, Revaluation Reserve, Goodwill, Brands).

We will finish the chapter will an example of the preparation of final accounts incorporating many of the adjustments indicated above. Here we will use the vertical format of the Balance Sheet which is commonly used in the UK.

For those not familiar with double entry bookkeeping we have included a section in *Appendix A* to this chapter.

Table 2.1   Outline Balance Sheet

Fixed Assets	**Share Capital and Reserves**
Land and Buildings	Issued Share Capital
less Depreciation	Share Premium
Plant and Machinery	Revaluation Reserve
less Depreciation	Profit and Loss account
Vehicles	Shareholder's Fund or Equity
less Depreciation	
Other Fixed Assets	
Investments	Long-Term Loans
Current Assets	**Current Liabilities**
Stock	Creditors
Debtors	Accruals
less Provision for Doubtful Debts	Bank Overdraft
Prepayments	Taxation
Short-Term Investments	Dividend
Cash/Bank	

2.2   Fixed Assets and Adjustments

We saw in *Chapter 1*, that fixed assets were those assets that had a life greater than one year. These are the assets that a company acquires before it can carry out trading. They consist of Land and Buildings, Plant and Machinery, Equipment, Vehicles, Furniture and others. There are two main treatments for accounting for fixed assets, these are:

❑   Depreciation. Since the assets extend over an accounting period (normally one year) we have to find a method of attaching a portion of their cost to each accounting period; this is referred to as depreciation i.e. the wearing down of an asset.

❑   Disposal. We also have to recognise that assets will be sold, either at the end of their useful life or part way through their useful lives.

❑   Another asset in the fixed assets section of the balance sheet is Trade Investments. Trade investments normally consist of a portfolio of shares held of companies in the same line of business, major suppliers or major customers. These differ from short-term investments since we cannot say with any certainty that we will be able to sell trade investments (i.e. shares) at the time we might wish to.

We will now deal with:

1.   each of the main classes of fixed assets and the adjustments for depreciation;

2.   the disposal of fixed assets; and,

3.   trade investments.

1.   Depreciation

The purchase a company makes can fall into two categories. The first is as an expense (or cost), for example wages, telephone, electricity. These items are written off in the profit and loss account for the period in which they are incurred. The second is when an asset is bought for use in the business and has an estimated useful life exceeding one year, that is there is an 'unexpired' part of the cost which is reflected in the balance sheet as a fixed asset. These assets are written off in future profit and loss accounts over their estimated useful life by a process known as depreciation.

Depreciation is a measure of the wearing out, consumption or other loss of value of a fixed asset whether arising from use, passage of time or obsolescence through technology and market changes.

The most common methods are, (i) **straight-line** where an fixed amount is taken to the Profit and Loss account each year (ii) **reducing balance** where a fixed percentage is applied to the remaining balance, in this case the amount taken to the Profit and Loss account will start higher than the straight line method but will reduce each year.

The annual figure for depreciation is treated as a deduction of profit in the Profit and Loss account, (thereby reducing the profit for the period) while the accumulated figure for depreciation is shown in the Balance Sheet as a deduction from the asset.

Depreciation Methods

We will now use the following example to demonstrate both the straight-line, the reducing balance and also the sum of the digits methods. The last of these is less common but you may encounter it.

Example

A vehicle bought for £20,000 with an estimated useful life of four years and an estimated residual value £2,592.

1. The Straight-Line Method

The formula for calculating the annual depreciation provision under the straight-line method is as follows:

$$\text{Annual Depreciation Provision} = \frac{(\text{Cost of Asset} - \text{Estimated Residual Value})}{\text{Expected Useful Life in years}}$$

$$= \frac{(£20,000 - £2,592)}{4}$$

$$= £4,352$$

The straight-line method allocates the net cost equally against the profit and loss account, for each year of the estimated useful life of an asset. It is a simple method to apply and understand. However, it takes no account of the fact that an asset will tend to 'lose' a larger proportion of its value in the earlier years.

2. The Reducing Balance Method

With the reducing (or diminishing) balance method a fixed percentage is deducted from the annual balance that exists at the beginning of the accounting period (i.e. cost of asset less any accumulated depreciation). How this approach works can be readily seen using the above example where it is assumed that the relevant rate to apply is 40%. The depreciation for the first year would be £8,000, in the second year it would be (£20,000 – £8,000) x 40% = £4,800, and in the third year it would be (£20,000 – £8,000 – £4,800) x 40% = £2,880. This process would continue for one more year, that is until the end of the estimated useful life of the asset. In this fourth and final year, the depreciation charge would be £1,728 leaving a balance remaining of £2,592 which is the estimated residual value.

The formula used to calculate the percentage to be applied is as follows:

$$r = 1 - \sqrt[n]{\frac{s}{c}}$$

where

r = rate of depreciation

n = estimated useful life in years

s = estimated residual value

c = cost of asset

By applying the formula to the information relating to the example we can see how the rate of 40% is determined.

$$= \quad 1 \; - \; 0.6$$

$$= \quad 0.4 \quad \text{or} \quad 40\%$$

The reducing balance method allocates a higher proportion of the cost of an asset to the earlier years. In the above example, £8,000 was allocated for the first year while only £1,728 was allocated in the fourth and final year.

3. Sum of the Digits

This method is called the 'sum of the digits', or the 'sum of the years digits'. It can be compared to a reducing or diminishing balance method in that it allocates a higher proportion of the cost of an asset to the earlier years. Given the data in the above example, the annual depreciation charge is calculated as follows:

Table 2.2 Calculation of Sum of Digits Depreciation

Year 1	4	4/10	6,963
Year 2	3	3/10	5,222
Year 3	2	2/10	3,482
Year 4	1	1/10	1,741
	10	10/10	£17,408

The basis for determining the annual depreciation charge is found simply by reversing the order of the years, such that for year 1 the depreciation charge is determined from the last year (4 in this case) which is expressed as a fraction of the sum of the digits of the years (4+3+2+1 in this case). Thus, 4/10 of the net depreciation charge of £17,408 (i.e. £20,000 – £2,592), is charged against year 1, and so on for subsequent years.

Table 2.3   Comparison of Depreciation Methods – sum charged each year

	Straight Line	Reducing Balance	Sum of the Digits
	£	£	£
Year 1	4,352	8,000	6,963
Year 2	4,352	4,800	5,222
Year 3	4,352	2,880	3,482
Year 4	4,352	1,728	1,741
Total	17,408	17,408	17,408

UK companies are able to choose any method of depreciation, or even a range of methods for different categories of assets. While most use the straight-line method, care needs to be exercised when making inter-firm comparisons since the use of different methods will affect the reported profits.

Accounting Treatment for Depreciation

Companies must state the method used to calculate depreciation for each major class of fixed asset. This can be found in the Accounting Principles section of the published accounts. The accounting treatment for depreciation of a fixed asset is as follows:

1. Calculate the depreciation provision for each asset. For example, Land and Buildings are normally depreciated over 50 years or for the estimated life of the building if less than 50 years. 'Other fixed assets are depreciated mainly at rates between 5% and 33% per year' (The *Rank Group plc* 1998 report).

2.   The annual provision for depreciation is taken into the Profit and Loss account. This has the result of reducing both the taxable and retained profits for the year and ultimately the Profit and Loss account balance in the liabilities section of the Balance Sheet. (please note that the depreciation written into the Profit and Loss account and the depreciation 'allowed' for taxation purposes can be substantially different in amount).

3.   The final adjustment is on the assets side of the Balance Sheet. Fixed assets are held at cost or realisable value with annual depreciation accumulating over the life of an asset. In published accounts you will typically find a single figure for tangible fixed assets; in a note to the accounts you will find a full page in tabular format providing all the information required i.e. opening balance, additions, disposals together with annual and accumulated depreciation by each major class of fixed asset.

Example – Depreciation of Fixed Assets

We will now show an example of the depreciation of a fixed asset. Assume that this example company has fixed assets of £300,000. They have been replaced at the beginning of the year and are due to be depreciated, straight-line over five years i.e. £60,000 per year. On the liabilities side of the opening balance sheet, our example company has issued share capital of £100,000 and accumulated profits i.e. the profit and loss account opening balance of £200,000. For the purpose of this example, we will assume that the current assets equals the current liabilities at £600,000 each.

We will also assume that the company has a turnover (sales) of £2,000,000, cost of sales of £1,500,000, and administration and distribution costs of £300,000.

The opening balance sheet and profit and loss account and closing balance sheet for the first year are shown in *Table 2.4.*

Table 2.4   *Opening Balance Sheet and Profit and Loss Account and Closing Balance Sheet*

OPENING BALANCE SHEET

ASSETS	£	LIABILITIES	£
Fixed Assets	300,000	Issued Share Capital	100,000
less Depreciation	0	Other Reserves	0
Net Book Value (NBV)	300,000	Profit and Loss Account	200,000
			300,000
Current Assets	600,000	Current Liabilities	600,000
	900,000		900,000

PROFIT AND LOSS ACCOUNT

	£	
Turnover	2,000,000	
less Cost of Sales	1,500,000	(assume all cash items)
Operating Profit	500,000	
less Admin and Distribution	300,000	(assume all cash items)
Net Profit Before Taxation	200,000	

CLOSING BALANCE SHEET

ASSETS	£	LIABILITIES	£
Fixed Assets	300,000	Issued Share Capital	100,000
less Depreciation	0	Other Reserves	0
Net Book Value (NBV)	300,000	Profit and Loss Account	400,000
			500,000
Current Assets	800,000	Current Liabilities	600,000
	1,100,000		1,100,000

If we now assume that at the year end the company decides to provide for depreciation on its fixed assets over five years straight-line. The annual depreciation provision would be £60,000.

In *Table 2.5* we now show the opening balance sheet the profit and loss account and closing balance sheet with depreciation included. (ignore taxation and dividend). You will notice that the annual charge for depreciation is added into the cost of sales (i.e. 1,500,000 + 60,000) which reduces the retained profit. This would result in the Liabilities side of the closing balance sheet being £60,000 less than the Assets side of the balance sheet. To correct this, we deduct the depreciation charge from the Fixed Asset (i.e. 300,000 – 60,000).

Table 2.5   Opening Balance Sheet and Profit and Loss Account and Closing Balance Sheet

OPENING BALANCE SHEET

ASSETS	£	LIABILITIES	£
Fixed Assets	300,000	Issued Share Capital	100,000
less Depreciation	0	Other Reserves	0
Net Book Value (NBV)	300,000	Profit and Loss Account	200,000
			300,000
Current Assets	600,000	Current Liabilities	600,000
	900,000		900,000

PROFIT AND LOSS ACCOUNT

	£
Turnover	2,000,000
less Cost of Sales *	1,560,000
Operating Profit	440,000
less Admin and Distribution	300,000
Net Profit Before Taxation	140,000

* In Chapter 1, we gave a simplified view of cost of sales. In practice, it represents a large number of items including, for example, depreciation.

CLOSING BALANCE SHEET

ASSETS	£	LIABILITIES	£
Fixed Assets	300,000	Issued Share Capital	100,000
less Depreciation	60,000	Other Reserves	0
Net Book Value (NBV)	240,000	Profit and Loss Account	340,000
			440,000
Current Assets	800,000	Current Liabilities	600,000
	1,040,000		1,040,000

Finally, we will show the provision for depreciation for a second year. We will assume that the company has achieved the same turnover, and other costs from the previous year. The closing balance sheet (above), now becomes the opening balance sheet for this period; we will show the profit and loss account for the period and the closing balance sheet in *Table 2.6*.

Table 2.6   Profit and Loss Account and Closing Balance Sheet (end of second year)

PROFIT AND LOSS ACCOUNT

	£
Turnover	2,000,000
less Cost of Sales	1,560,000
Operating Profit	440,000
less Admin and Distribution	300,000
Net Profit Before Taxation	140,000

CLOSING BALANCE SHEET

ASSETS	£	LIABILITIES	£
Fixed Assets	300,000	Issued Share Capital	100,000
less Depreciation	120,000	Other Reserves	0
Net Book Value (NBV)	180,000	Profit and Loss Account	480,000
			580,000
Current Assets	1,000,000	Current Liabilities	600,000
	1,180,000		1,180,000

2.   Disposal of Assets

It is important to note that estimates of the rate of depreciation to be applied, the useful life of the asset and its disposal value may be nothing more than guesswork. The actual outcome may be very different from the estimates and how we deal with differences is explained below.

A company purchased a fixed asset on 1st January 1996 for £47,000. It had an estimated economic life of seven years and an expected disposal value of £5,000. The asset was sold on the 31st December 1999 for £15,000.

The company used the straight-line method for depreciation such that the annual depreciation charge would be found as follows:

$$\text{Straight-Line Depreciation} \quad = \quad \frac{(£47,000 \ - \ £5,000)}{7 \ \text{years}}$$

$$= \quad £6,000 \ \text{per annum}$$

Any loss on the disposal of the asset would be included in the profit and loss account and would result in a reduction of the profit for the period. (Similarly, any profit on the disposal of an asset would result in an increase in the profit for the period).

Had the company known that disposal would take place after four years rather than seven years, with proceeds of £15,000 its annual depreciation charge would have been:

$$\text{Straight-Line Depreciation} \quad = \quad \frac{(£47,000 \ - \ £15,000)}{4 \ \text{years}}$$

$$= \quad £8,000 \ \text{per annum}$$

In other words, by depreciating the asset at £6,000 over four years, now, given perfect knowledge i.e. the life, four years and the disposal value £15,000 we can see that the company has undercharged depreciation over the actual life of the asset. four years at £2,000 per year has not been written off against profit which otherwise would have been. Upon the disposal, any profit or loss needs to be calculated as shown in *Table 2.7*.

Table 2.7   Profit or Loss on Disposal of Asset

	£	£
Sale Price		15,000
Cost of Asset at 1st January 1996	47,000	
less Accumulated Depreciation	24,000	
Net Book Value at 31st December 1999		23,000
Profit or Loss on Disposal of Asset		–8,000

Accounting Treatment for the Disposal of an Asset

The acquisition and disposal of assets becomes a regular activity within most companies. The acquisition of assets is straightforward since it only requires one transaction i.e. opening an account for the asset and reducing the cash/bank balance for the payment. The disposal of an asset requires additional transactions, the aim being to clear out from the accounts all evidence relating to that asset. A typical process would be to:

1. Transfer the cost of the asset being sold into an Asset Disposals account – which clears the asset out of the accounts.

2. Transfer the accumulated Depreciation into an Asset Disposals account – which clears the accumulated depreciation for the asset out of the accounts.

3. Post the remittance received from the sale of the asset. This has the effect of increasing the cash or bank balance. The other entry in the accounts would be in the Asset Disposals account

4. Transfer the balance (i.e. the difference) on the Asset Disposal Account to the Profit and Loss Account.

   ❑ If the net balance on the Disposal Account is greater than the remittance received there is a loss on the sale of the asset and this is taken into the Profit and Loss account as a cost.

   ❑ If the net balance on the Disposal Account is less than the remittance received there is a profit on the sale of the asset and this is taken into the Profit and Loss account as an income.

Example – Disposal of a Fixed Asset

We will continue with the example used in the previous section on depreciation i.e. *Table 2.6*. If we assume that at the end of the second year the company disposed of £100,000 of fixed assets and received a cheque for £50,000. The profit or loss on the disposal would be as follows:

Table 2.8   *Profit or loss on disposal of asset*

	£	£
Sale Price		50,000
Cost of Asset (at beginning of first year)	100,000	
less Accumulated Depreciation	40,000	
Net Book Value at (end of second year)		60,000
Profit or Loss on Disposal of Asset		−10,000

The profit or loss account and balance sheet after the disposal would be as shown in *Table 2.9* – (please note, this is *Table 2.6* adjusted for the disposal).

Table 2.9   *Profit and Loss Account and Closing Balance Sheet after Disposal (end of second year)*

PROFIT AND LOSS ACCOUNT

	£
Turnover	2,000,000
less Cost of Sales	1,560,000
Operating Profit	440,000
less Admin and Distribution	300,000
less Loss of Disposal of Asset	10,000
Net Profit Before Taxation	130,000

CLOSING BALANCE SHEET

ASSETS	£	LIABILITIES	£
Fixed Assets	200,000	Issued Share Capital	100,000
less Depreciation	80,000	Other Reserves	0
Net Book Value (NBV)	120,000	Profit and Loss Account	470,000
			570,000
Current Assets	1,050,000	Current Liabilities	600,000
	1,170,000		1,170,000

Notes to explain the movements following the disposal.

1. We have shown the loss on the disposal of the fixed asset as a separate item in the Profit and Loss account i.e. £10,000. This has the effect of reducing the profit before taxation by £10,000 to £130,000.

2. In the liabilities section of the Balance Sheet we show £130,000 being added to the profit and loss account (balance) to give £470,000.

3. In the fixed assets section of the Balance Sheet we deduct £100,000 from the (cost) of the fixed assets and £40,000 from the (accumulated) depreciation. This leaves a net book value for fixed assets of £120,000.

4. In the current assets section of the Balance Sheet we add the £50,000 received in payment for the fixed asset.

The Balance Sheet now balances at £1,170,000 total assets (i.e. fixed assets £120,000 plus current assets £1,050,000); £1,170,000 total liabilities (i.e. issued share capital £100,000 plus profit and loss account £470,000 plus current liabilities £600,000).

3.   Revaluation of Assets

Not all assets are depreciated. Land, for example often increases in value and such revaluations are commonly seen in the balance sheets of UK companies.

Suppose a professional revaluation has been undertaken on the assets of our example company which has had the effect of increasing the total value from £200,000 to £500,000. This is shown in the balance sheet both as an increase in the fixed asset value from £200,000 to £500,000 and, at the same time, increasing the reserves (under the heading revaluation reserve) by £300,000; thus keeping the balance sheet in balance. Unlike depreciation, however, such revaluations have no impact either on the profit and loss account (since they do not involve an increase in profits from trading) or the cash flow statement (since they do not involve movements of cash).

Table 2.10 shows the impact of a revaluation of fixed assets on the Balance Sheet of our example company.

Table 2.10   Balance Sheet – Impact of Revaluation

BALANCE SHEET (without revaluation)

ASSETS	£	LIABILITIES	£
Fixed Assets	200,000	Issued Share Capital	100,000
less Depreciation	80,000	Other Reserves	0
Net Book Value (NBV)	120,000	Profit and Loss Account	470,000
			570,000
Current Assets	1,050,000	Current Liabilities	600,000
	1,170,000		1,170,000

CLOSING BALANCE SHEET (with revaluation)

ASSETS	£	LIABILITIES	£
Fixed Assets	500,000	Issued Share Capital	100,000
less Depreciation	80,000	Revaluation Reserve	300,000
Net Book Value (NBV)	420,000	Profit and Loss Account	470,000
			870,000
Current Assets	1,050,000	Current Liabilities	600,000
	1,470,000		1,470,000

Many companies now revalue their fixed assets on a regular basis. The outcome is a stronger balance sheet that reflects the current value of the assets and at the same time provides an increase in the equity of the business.

One potential advantage to the company of including current values of assets through revaluations on a regular basis is that it should make the cost of acquiring the company greater should a takeover be considered. The assumption for listed companies is that the revaluation will be incorporated by the market in the company's share price. Revaluations may also improve the ability of the company to borrow funds because the ability to borrow without recourse to the shareholders is usually limited to a percentage of assets. Anything that increases the assets should increase borrowing power.

Our discussion so far has focused upon accounting for tangible fixed assets. However, intangible fixed assets such as brands and goodwill have attracted a good deal of attention in the UK. We propose to deal briefly with the accounting issues associated with just these two categories of intangible asset in the next section.

4. The treatment of goodwill (including brands)

Goodwill is the difference between the value of the business as a whole less the value of the assets less liabilities valued separately. In this case, goodwill can be positive or negative. If goodwill is positive this means that the value of the business as a whole is worth more than the value of the assets less liabilities valued separately. What elements might constitute goodwill? The most obvious is the value of brands, however, the development of a sound supply chain, access to research and development (or know-how), or access to a top-class management team would all contribute to making the value of the business as a whole greater than the value of its assets less liabilities.

At this point it is important to introduce the distinction that is made between tangible fixed assets and intangible fixed assets.

❏ Tangible fixed assets are those physical assets that can be valued such as land and buildings, plant and machinery, equipment, vehicles, furniture and fittings.

❏ Intangible fixed assets are not physical, they are not located in a specific place and will include such items as goodwill and patents and trademarks.

Purchased and non-purchased goodwill

There is also a distinction to be made between purchased goodwill and non-purchased goodwill.

❏ Purchased goodwill is the excess between the amount paid for a company as a whole and the net worth of the tangible assets and liabilities acquired. Since the end of 1998, accounting standards in UK require companies to capitalise goodwill and write it off over a period not greater than 20 years. Where goodwill and intangible assets are regarded as having an indefinite useful economic life, they should not be amortised but be subject to an impairment review.

❏ Non-purchased goodwill relates to the decision by a company to include a value for internally developed brands, supply chain, know-how or human assets onto the balance sheet. *Rank Hovis McDougal* were the first company in the UK to include the value of brands into their balance sheet. They valued their brands at approximately £600 million – this had the effect of nearly doubling the asset value on their balance sheet. Recent accounting standards state that 'except when goodwill is evidenced by a purchase transaction, it is not an accepted practice to recognise it in financial statements'.

Prior to the end of 1998, the accepted practice was to write-off goodwill immediately on acquisition. This was consistent with the practice of not including non-purchased goodwill in the balance sheet. In other words, whether goodwill was purchased or internally developed it would not be included in the accounts.

Goodwill arising on acquisition

On the 30th April 200X, our example company acquired A Bunker for £350,000. The assets and liabilities acquired were as follows:

Fixed Assets	£100,000
Stock	£100,000
Debtors	£200,000
Creditors	£250,000

How much is the goodwill arising on acquisition?

Table 2.11 Calculation of Goodwill

	£'000	£'000
Purchase price		350
Fixed Assets	100	
Stock	100	
Debtors	200	
less Creditors	250	
Net Assets Acquired		150
Goodwill Arising on Acquisition		200

The effect on the balance sheet is shown in *Table 2.12*. We show the first balance sheet after the adjustment for revaluation but before any adjustment for purchased goodwill. We will then show the effect of the acquisition on the balance sheet while capitalising goodwill i.e. entering goodwill on the balance sheet.

Table 2.12 Balance Sheet – Effect of Purchased Goodwill Capitalised

CLOSING BALANCE SHEET (after revaluation taken from *Table 2.10*)

ASSETS	£	LIABILITIES	£
Fixed Assets	500,000	Issued Share Capital	100,000
less depreciation	80,000	Revaluation Reserve	300,000
Net Book Value (NBV)	420,000	Profit and Loss Account	470,000
			870,000
Current Assets	1,050,000	Current Liabilities	600,000
	1,470,000		1,470,000

REVISED CLOSING BALANCE SHEET (with purchase and goodwill)

ASSETS	£	LIABILITIES	£
Fixed Assets:		Issued Share Capital	100,000
Tangible	600,000	Revaluation Reserve	300,000
less depreciation	80,000	Profit and Loss Account	470,000
Net Book Value (NBV)	520,000		870,000
Intangible	200,000		
	720,000		
Current Assets	1,000,000	Current Liabilities	850,000
	1,720,000		1,720,000

Notes:

1. Fixed assets £500,000 + £100,000 = £600,000, therefore the net book value is £520,000.

2. Goodwill is included in the balance sheet (as an intangible asset) and will be written off over the period of its economic useful life. This means that the balance sheet looks stronger but there will be a charge against the profit and loss account each year until written–off.

3. Current assets. We take the opening £1,050,000 balance, add the acquired stock and debtors and deduct the purchase price for the acquisition (assuming that it was paid by cash or cheque) = (£1,050,000 + £100,000 + £200,000 – £350,000) = £1,000,000.

4. No change to the profit and loss account at the time of acquisition.

5. Current liabilities. We take the opening balance of £600,000 and add the acquired creditor balances of £250,000 to give £850,000.

2.3 Current Asset Adjustments

We will concentrate our discussion on two of the main elements which form part of the current assets section of the balance sheet. These are:

1. Stock, including methods of valuation and the effect on the profit and loss account.

2. Debtors, including debtor age analysis, the treatment of bad debts, provision for bad and doubtful debts and sundry debtors or prepayments.

1. Stock

The term stock is used to describe goods available for sale in the normal course of a business. In a manufacturing company it will also include work-in-progress and raw materials. A single value for stock is shown in the current assets section of the balance sheet with a breakdown (if necessary) shown in a note to the accounts. This value represents the closing stock of the business at the end of the accounting period. By default, the closing stock then becomes the opening stock for the next accounting period.

Perhaps the single most contentious issue with stock is the valuation. We will describe a number of the commonly used methods and show the impact a change in the valuation of stock has on the 'apparent' profits of a business. The following methods of valuation will be covered:

1. First in first out (FIFO). Using this method stock is issued at the oldest price. This means that any closing stock will be valued at the latest prices.

2. Last in first out (LIFO). Using this method stock is issued at the latest price. This means that any closing stock will be valued at the earliest prices.

3. Average price. Using this method stock is issued at an average price which will normally be recalculated each time a consignment of stock is received. Average price will tend to value closing stock at latest prices since the 'changing' average will 'drop' earliest prices.

Example – Stock Valuation Methods

A company is considering the method they will use for stock valuation. The following data has been collected:

Sales for the year £116,250,

Purchases in   January   2,000 units at £16.00 per unit

                      June   2,600 units at £20.00 per unit

                      November   1,200 units at £21.00 per unit

There was no opening stock

Closing stock 1,550 units

Table 2.13   Comparison of Stock Valuation Methods

	FIFO		Average		LIFO	
	£	£	£	£	£	£
Sales for Period		116,250		116,250		116,250
Opening Stock	0		0		0	
+ Purchases †	109,200		109,200		109,200	
	109,200		109,200		109,200	
– Closing Stock ‡	32,200		29,187		24,800	
= Cost of Sales		77,000		80,014		84,400
Gross Profit		39,250		36,237		31,850

†   Purchases for the period are calculated as follows:

  (2,000 x £16) + (2,600 x £20) + (1,200 x £21) = **£109,200**

‡   Closing Stock at the end of the period is calculated as follows:

  FIFO   Latest purchase   1,200 x £21.00 =   £25,200
              Next latest purchase   350 x £20.00 =   £7,000   = **£32,200**

  Average Cost £109,200 ÷ 5,800 units = £18.83 x 1,550 units   = **£29,187**

  LIFO   Opening Stock   0   0   0
              Next latest purchase   1,550 x £16.00   £24,800   = **£24,800**

2. Debtors

Trading with customers and allowing credit transactions will inevitably lead to a number of bad debts. However, an effective system of credit control will help to minimise bad debts. In this section we will cover the following:

1. Preparation of and Age Analysis of Debtor accounts.

2. The accounting treatment for writing off Bad Debts.

3. The accounting treatment for making a Provision for Doubtful Debts.

1. Age Analysis of Debtor Accounts

The assessment and control of bad and doubtful debts is an integral part of a credit control system. On a regular basis, and as a routine, debtor balances are assessed against the number of days outstanding. This means allocating part or the whole of the balance of a debtor's account into specific time periods. It is then possible to determine, for example, those accounts over a certain time period with a view to take immediate action. An example is shown in *Table 2.14*.

Table 2.14   Age Analysis of Debtors

	Total	31 – 60	61 – 90	over 90	Action
	£	£	£	£	
A. Able	60,000				
Acorn Partnership	20,000		20,000		Review credit
B. Ball and Co.	150,000	20,000	40,000	30,000	Review credit
Bottle Ltd	10,000			10,000	Court action pending
Bunce Plc	350,000	100,000	100,000		
Calder and Sons	25,000				
Candy Stores Ltd	10,000				
Cookside B.C.	30,000		20,000		Review credit
....					
....					
Total	6,200,000	3,200,000	500,000	140,000	

From the totals above and the comments it might be thought prudent to make a provision of 2.25% of Debtors i.e. £140,000 ÷ £6,200,000 x 100.

2. Bad Debts Written Off

A debt is bad and will be written off when a company considers that it is unlikely to receive payment against the debt. The procedure is as follows:

1. Clear out any outstanding balance on individual debtor accounts into a Bad Debts account. This process will continue throughout the year as debtor accounts are closed and transferred into the Bad Debts account. Should the debt be recovered this process will be reversed.

2. At the end of the accounting period the balance on the Bad Debts account is transferred, as a cost, to the profit and loss account; the effect being to reduce the profit for the period.

3. Also at the year end it may be necessary to write off further Bad Debts. In this case we would have to increase the amount being written off in the profit and loss account and deduct the additional bad debts from the debtor balance in the closing balance sheet.

3. Provision for Doubtful Debts

Throughout the year an assessment is made of each debtor account to consider the actions which must be taken to ensure prompt and timely payment on each account.

At the end of an accounting period an assessment is made of each debtor account to consider the collectability of the remaining balances. A provision for doubtful debts simply recognises the fact that not all debtor balances offer the same opportunity for payment. The provision takes a conservative view of all debtor balances and recognises the accounting principle of prudence.

The provision for doubtful debts will change each year depending on the collectability of the remaining balances and the economic environment, for example, if the economy is booming then there is less likelihood of default from payment of a debt.

Once the amount of the provision has been determined, the increase (or decrease) in the provision (from the previous year) will be taken into the Profit and Loss account, thereby reducing the profit for the period. The new provision will be deducted from the Debtor figure in the current assets section of the balance sheet.

3. Prepayments (paid in advance)

Prepayments, i.e. amounts paid in advance, relate to expenditure incurred on goods or services for future benefit, which is to be charged to future operating periods. Examples include; fire insurance, rent/rates, vehicle taxes paid in advance, payment for goods in advance. At the end of the accounting period prepayments are in effect sundry debtors; they owe the company a product or service which will not be 'received' until (usually) the next account period.

Prepayments are deducted from the expense/cost in the Profit and Loss account and added into the Current Asset section of the balance sheet at the end of the period in which they are incurred.

Example

The Fire Insurance account shows an opening balance of £210, representing fire insurance paid in advance and covering the period 1st Jan 1999 to 31st March 1999. Further payments were made for fire insurance in advance covering six monthly periods as follows, 1st April £480 and 1st October £500.

In this example we have an opening balance, i.e. at the end of the previous year £210 had been paid for a future period. Similarly, at the end of this period £500 of fire insurance has been paid for the period 1st October 1999 to 31st March 2000. Therefore, taking an equal amount, £250 relates to this period while the remaining £250 relates to a future period i.e. 1st January 2000 to 31st March 2000.

From the fire insurance account we would transfer (£210 + £480 + £500 – £250) £940 into the profit and loss account representing the fire insurance for the period. In the fire insurance account there would be a balance remaining of £250 i.e. at the end of the period, the fire insurance company was a sundry debtor to the company for three months of fire insurance.

The net result would mean that the cost of fire insurance would be reduced in the profit and loss account thereby increasing the retained profit. This would mean that the liabilities section of the balance sheet would be greater by the £250 reduction in the cost of fire insurance. We would have to include an item in the current assets section of the balance sheet as a sundry debtor to record the prepayment of fire insurance.

2.4   Long-Term Financing

Share Capital

Share capital relates to various classes of shares that can be offered by a company. Those subscribing to the shares, or buying them on the open market are referred to as shareholders. The various classes of shares can be described as follows:

Preference Shares

Preference shares normally carry an entitlement to dividend at a fixed rate per annum. Cumulative preference shares relate to an entitlement to have the dividend cumulate until the company is able to pay out a dividend on the shares. Convertible preference shares relate to an entitlement to covert the shares into ordinary shares, usually within a given time period and at an agreed conversion. It is possible to have convertible cumulative preference shares. Preference shares may or may not have voting rights. At time of liquidation of a company the preference shareholders will receive payment before the ordinary shareholders.

Ordinary Shares

Ordinary shares are the most common method of shareholder financing. At any given time, a company will have a maximum limit of authorised share capital that the directors can issue. This can be increased following approval at a company's annual general meeting.

Issued share capital relates to the number of shares that have been issued; a monetary value is place on the share by multiplying the number of shares issued times their nominal or par value. Nominal value is the price at which shares were originally issued.

Rights Issues

Rights issues are normally associated with companies who feel they can raise additional share capital from their existing shareholders. The terms of the issue might be that existing shareholders can apply for additional shares, say three shares for every eight held; the offer price will usually be attractive, set at a price that is less than the market price. A rights issue is not available to the general public.

Bonus, Script or Capitalisation Issues

Bonus, script or capitalisation issues are normally associated with a restructuring of the capital of a business. If a business has been successful and built up reserves through profitable trading, revaluation of assets or simply through acquiring an additional premium on shares the directors might be advised to restructure the share capital. A bonus/script/capitalisation issue are free shares offered to existing shareholders, say one bonus share for every share held. An example might be that a company's shares are trading at £4.00. If a shareholder currently held 100 shares they would be worth £400. When a one to one bonus issue is made the shareholder will now have 200 shares but the value of the share will reduce to £2.00 per share, therefore, 200 shares at £2.00 per share – still worth £400. The reality is that the reduction in the share price might not be to £2.00, it might be £2.20; also, more trading tends to be carried out when share prices are lower, therefore, the £2.00 share price should increase at a faster rate than the previous £4.00 share price.

This not the only reason for bonus issues. Perhaps the more pressing reason is the restructuring of the shareholder's fund. By offering a bonus issue (free issue) to existing shareholders the company can transfer amounts from accumulated profits, share premium or revaluations into share capital.

Share Premium

Share premium is the difference between the amount paid for a share and its nominal value. If a company has been successful it will not issue new shares at the nominal (or par) value. It would expect to obtain a premium on the issue. Company law requires that issued share capital is shown at its nominal value and any excess is taken into a share premium account.

Please note, we are not referring here to cash. This side of the balance sheet is the source of funds not the funds themselves. For example, if a company wanted to issue further shares the following might be observed:

Issue 100,000 shares at £3.00; Market Value is £3.50; Nominal Value is £1.00.

The company would receive £300,000 cash (ignoring any issue expenses).

On the liabilities side of the balance sheet we would add 100,000 shares at £1.00 into the issued share capital and 100,000 shares at £2.00 (the premium) into the share premium account.

Revaluation Reserve

Please refer to our discussion on page 41 and 42.

Profit and Loss account

When we refer to the profit and loss account entry in the balance sheet we mean the accumulated profits of the business. Again, they don't represent cash; they only give an indication how some of the assets of the business are financed. It might be better to look at the other way. Instead of retaining and accumulating profits over a period of time a business was to distribute all its profits. The following might be observed see *Table 2.15* if we consider two example companies, say Company A that retains and accumulates profits and Company B who distributes all its profits.

Table 2.15 Comparison of Retaining or Distributing Profits

BALANCE SHEET (Company A – Retains all Profits)

ASSETS	£	LIABILITIES	£
Fixed Assets	300,000	Issued Share Capital	200,000
		Profit and Loss Account	300,000
		Shareholders' Funds	500,000
Current Assets	700,000	Current Liabilities	500,000
	1,000,000		1,000,000

CLOSING BALANCE SHEET (Company B – Distributes all Profits)

ASSETS	£	LIABILITIES	£
Fixed Assets	200,000	Issued Share Capital	200,000
		Profit and Loss Account	0
		Shareholders' Funds	200,000
Current Assets	500,000	Current Liabilities	500,000
	700,000		700,000

In *Table 2.15* it can be seen that Company B has £300,000 less in the profit and loss account and therefore £300,000 less shareholders' fund. This means that £300,000 less has been retained in the company. The balance sheet of Company A looks much healthier than Company B: it has spent an extra £100,000 on fixed assets while retaining an extra £200,000 in current assets.

Shareholders' Funds or Equity

Shareholders' funds or equity is simply the addition of issued share capital plus reserves. If the business were liquidated and received book values for all its assets, paid off all its debts, the remainder would equate to the shareholder's fund or equity.

2.5   Current Liabilities or Creditors: amounts owing within one year

One of the main problems the casual user of published accounts finds is in some of the terminology used. For decades, the accounts prepared in the UK have referred to current liabilities (one of the main sections of the balance sheet). This term is still used in other countries, for example in the US. The 4th EC Directive required harmonisation of accounts across the EC. This resulted in the term – Creditors: amounts owing within one year to be used as the preferred term for current liabilities.

In this section we are only going to discuss the term accruals, which is often one of the components of current liabilities.

Accruals (due, not yet paid)

An amount relating to a period which has not so far been taken into account because they have not yet been invoiced by the supplier, therefore, not included in the accounting system and not paid. Examples would be, wages (due not yet paid), interest (due not yet paid), electricity (due not yet paid). At the end of the accounting period accruals are in effect sundry creditors; the company owes the supplier for a product or service for which no invoice yet recorded, which will not be paid until the next account period.

These amounts are added to the expense/cost in the Profit and Loss account and added to the Current Liabilities section of the balance sheet at the end of the period in which they are incurred.

Example

Wages for October 200X have been paid for the weeks ending the 7th, 14th, 21st and 28th and amount to £36,000. At the end of the period, two days wages are due (30th and 31st October) amounting to £3,500.

In this example, wages paid during the month amount to £36,000. Using accruals and the matching principle the wages for the period are £36,000 plus £3,500 accrued giving £39,500.

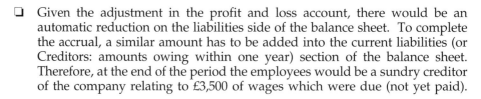

❏   The effect on the profit and loss account would be to increase the expenses for the period thereby reducing the retained profit for the period.

❏   Given the adjustment in the profit and loss account, there would be an automatic reduction on the liabilities side of the balance sheet. To complete the accrual, a similar amount has to be added into the current liabilities (or Creditors: amounts owing within one year) section of the balance sheet. Therefore, at the end of the period the employees would be a sundry creditor of the company relating to £3,500 of wages which were due (not yet paid).

2.6 Final Accounts of Limited Companies

The following example shows the preparation of the final accounts of limited companies. First we will provide a set of rules to determine which items go in which accounts i.e. trading account, profit and loss account, profit and loss appropriation account, balance sheet.

The example starts from the completion of a trial balance. This is simply a listing of all the balances contained in the accounts of the company together with a number of adjustments which have to be included, i.e. notes 1 to 7.

The double entry bookkeeping system is beyond the scope of this book. If you are interested in knowing how it works we suggest that you borrow a basic accounting text from your library.

Example – Final Accounts of Limited Companies

These consist of:

Trading Account;

Profit and Loss Account;

Profit and Loss Appropriation Account;

Balance Sheet.

Rules (what is included in each of the accounts)

When a Trial Balance has been completed, the next stage is to check every item and identify which account it belongs to (i.e. Trading Account, Profit and Loss Account, Profit and Loss Appropriation Account or Balance Sheet). You will find it helpful during your early attempts to refer to the rules which follow, when preparing final accounts.

Trading account

Which takes in the Sales for the accounting period, and deducts the Purchases (adjusted for the difference between opening and closing stock). The output from the Trading Account is the gross profit/loss for the period.

Profit and Loss account

Takes the gross profit/loss and adds any other sources of income (e.g. interest received, rent received, income received), then deducts the expenses and provisions for the period. Expenses will include such things as, wages, rent, rates, lighting and heating, administration, distribution, marketing, computing, interest paid, audit fee etc. Provisions are for those items where the exact amount and the date at which a liability will occur are uncertain; the two main provisions are for depreciation of assets, and for bad and doubtful debts. The output from the Profit and Loss Account is the net profit/loss before taxation for the period.

Profit and Loss Appropriation account

Takes the net profit/loss before taxation and adds any accumulated profits from previous periods (these could be referred to as *Reserves: Revenue:* Profit and Loss account). This gives the amount of profit which can then be appropriated between taxation, shareholders (by way of dividend) and the amount retained in the business (which will be the closing figure for *Reserves: Revenue:* Profit and Loss account).

Balance Sheet

Is a statement (not an account) of the financial position of a company at a given period of time. It records all the fixed assets and current assets (i.e. balances the company OWNS), and all the current liabilities and long term financing from shareholders and other sources (i.e. balances the company OWES).

Examples of the main Balance Sheet items will include:

Fixed Assets	**Share Capital and Reserves**
Land and Buildings	Issued Share Capital
Plant and Machinery	Share Premium
Fixtures and Fittings	Revaluation
Vehicles and others	Profit and Loss account
	Long term Loans/Debentures
Current Assets	**Creditors:** amounts owing within one year
Stock	Creditors
Debtors	Bank Overdraft
Prepayments	Accruals
Short-Term Investments	Taxation Due
Cash and Bank Balances	Dividends Proposed

Example

The Trial Balance of OAK Ltd as at the 31st March 200X was as follows:–

		Dr.	Cr.
BS	Vehicles (at cost)	130,000	
TR	Purchases	720,000	
TR	Sales		1,000,000
BS	Depreciation of vehicles		26,000
TR	Stock at 1st April 200X–1	140,000	
BS	Debtors	85,000	
BS	Creditors		44,000
BS	Long-Term Loans at 10%	60,000	
BS	Share Premium		25,000
BS	Profit and Loss Account		25,000
PL	Wages	35,000	
PL	Rates	2,500	
PL	Heating and Lighting	5,000	
PL	Salaries	20,000	
PL	Administration Expenses	65,000	
BS	Furniture and Fittings (at cost)	18,000	
BS	Depreciation of Furniture and Fittings		9,000
BS	Bank balance	50,000	
PL	Provision for Doubtful Debts		3,000
PL	Loan Interest Paid to 30th Sept 200X–1	3,000	
BS	Freehold Property	200,000	
BS	Issued Share Capital		300,000
PL	Bad Debts Written Off	3,500	
PL	Directors Fees	15,000	
		1,492,000	1,492,000

Prepare a Trading, Profit and Loss Account and Profit and Loss Appropriation account for the year ended 31st March 200X, and a Balance Sheet as at that date.

The following notes are to be taken into account:

1. Stock at 31st March 200X, £150,000

2. Wages outstanding at 31st March 200X, £1,500

3. Rates paid in advance amounting to £500

4. Depreciation of vehicles over 5 years (straight line)

5. Depreciation of furniture and fittings, 5% on cost

6. Provision for bad and doubtful debts, adjust to £3,500

7. Dividend proposed, 50% of profit attributable to shareholders

The notes to the Trial Balance are essentially adjustments which have not been recorded in the accounts. This means that each note affects the Trading Account, OR the Profit and Loss Account, OR the Profit and Loss Appropriation Account AND the Balance Sheet.

OAK Ltd

Trading Account for the year ended 31st March 200X

	£	£
Sales		1,000,000
Opening Stock	140,000	
+ Purchases	720,000	
	860,000	
− Closing stock	150,000	
= Cost of sales		710,000
Gross Profit c/d		290,000

Check the extraction of each item from the Trial Balance and note where they are recorded in the Trading Account. You will notice that the receipts are listed on the right hand side (credit), while the costs are listed on the left hand side (debit). In this example, the receipts are greater than the costs therefore the resulting balance is a gross profit. The double entry is effected by recording the gross profit on the credit side of the Profit and Loss Account.

OAK Ltd

Profit and Loss Account for the year ended 31st March 200X

	Note	£	£
Gross Profit b/d			290,000
Wages	2	36,500	
Rates	3	2,000	
Heating and Lighting		5,000	
Salaries		20,000	
Administrative Expenses		65,000	
Loan Interest	8	6,000	
Bad Debts Written Off		3,500	
Directors Fees		15,000	
Depreciation Vehicles	4	26,000	
Depreciation Furniture and Fittings	5	900	
Provision for Doubtful Debts	6	500	
			180,400
Net Profit Before Taxation c/d			109,600

The entries into the Profit and Loss Account follow a similar pattern to those in the Trading Account. Many of the costs / expenses can simply be recorded, however, those items which are included in the adjustments need special treatment. We will now discuss each adjustment that affects the Profit and Loss Account.

Notes to explain items in the Profit and Loss account

We have allocated an additional note for the interest due on the long–term loans. For an explanation see note 8 below.

2. Wages Outstanding £1,500

To obtain the total wages for the period, we take the wages shown in the Trial Balance and add any wages outstanding (£35,000 + £1,500). This occurs when there are a number of working days at the end of the accounting period where wages have been earned but not paid.

3. Rates Paid in Advance £500

To obtain the rates for the period, we take the rates shown in the Trial Balance and deduct any rates paid in advance. i.e. (£2,500 – £500). This occurs when a company pays rates which includes a proportion that falls into the beginning of the next year.

4. Depreciation of Vehicles

The provision for depreciation of vehicles is calculated using the straight line method over five years. The provision for the year is £130,000 divided by 5 which equals £26,000.

5. Depreciation of Furniture and Fittings

The provision for the depreciation of furniture and fittings is calculated using 5% on cost. The provision for the year is £18,000 times 5 divided by 100 which equals £900.

6. Provision for Doubtful Debts

The entry for the Provision for Doubtful Debts is as follows:

Closing provision required (note 6)		3,500
less Opening provision (from the Trial Balance)		3,000
		500

The balance of £500 represents the additional provision required. The transaction would be; debit the Profit and Loss account and Credit the Provision for Doubtful Debts account. Should the closing provision be less than the opening provision the transaction would be reversed.

8. Long Term Loan: interest at 10%

The entry in the Trial Balance for interest paid represents only six months interest. Therefore the calculation for loan stock interest for the Profit and Loss Account must include interest for the complete accounting period: £60,000 times 10 divided by 100 which equals £6,000.

OAK Ltd

Profit and Loss Appropriation Account for the year ended 31st March 200X

	Note	£
Net Profit Before Taxation b/d		109,600
– Taxation		0
Profit After Taxation		109,600
– Dividend	7	54,800
Retained Profit		54,800

7. Provide for dividend

Dividend is calculated at 50% of profit attributable to shareholders; £109,600 times 50 divided by 100 which equals £54,800.

In published accounts the trading, profit and loss and profit and loss appropriation account would be shown in a single vertical layout with previous year figures also given. It is simply called a Profit and Loss account and requires less detail than shown in this example. However, some of the detail can often be found in the notes to the accounts.

Earnings per share is another figure that is required to be shown in published accounts together with an explanation how it has been calculated. We will introduce earnings per share together with an explanation in *Chapter 4*.

OAK Ltd

Balance Sheet as at 31st March 200X

FIXED ASSETS	Notes	COST	DEPN	N.B.V.
Freehold Property		200,000		200,000
Vehicles	1	130,000	52,000	78,000
Furniture and Fittings	2	18,000	9,900	8,100
		348,000	61,900	286,100

CURRENT ASSETS				
Stock			150,000	
Debtors		85,000		
less Doubtful Debts	3	3,500	81,500	
Prepaid	4		500	
Bank			50,000	
			282,000	

CREDITORS: amounts falling due
within one year

Creditors		44,000		
Accruals	5	4,500		
Dividend Proposed	6	54,800		
			103,300	
				178,700

Total Assets less Current Liabilities				464,800

CREDITORS: amounts falling due
after more than one year | | | | 60,000

Net Assets				404,800

Financed as follows:
SHARE CAPITAL and RESERVES

Issued Share Capital				300,000
Share Premium				25,000
Profit and Loss Account	7			79,800
				404,800

A Balance Sheet is not an account, it is simply a statement which records a true and fair view of the financial position of a company. We will now discuss some of the points which often need clarification.

1. Accumulated Depreciation – Vehicles

Accumulated depreciation shown in the closing balance sheet is calculated by taking the depreciation provision shown in the Trial Balance and adding the depreciation provision for the current year (£26,000 + £26,000) which equals £52,000.

2. Accumulated Depreciation – Furniture and Fittings

Accumulated depreciation shown in the closing balance sheet is calculated by taking the depreciation provision shown in the Trial Balance and adding the depreciation provision for the current year (£9,000 + £900) which equals £9,900.

3. Debtors

Debtors are taken at the value shown in the Trial Balance less the provision for bad and doubtful debts i.e. (£85,000 – £3,500) = £81,500. In published accounts, it is normal just to show the net balance for debtors.

4. Prepayments

Prepayments represent the amounts that have been paid in advance of an accounting period. Prepayments could be listed under a heading 'sundry debtors'. The prepayment in this example is the deduction of £500 from the rates account.

5. Accruals

Accruals represent the amounts due but not paid at the end of an accounting period. They could be listed under a heading 'sundry creditors'. The accruals in this example are the addition of loan interest due plus wages due: (£3,000 + £1,500) which equals £4,500.

6. Dividend Proposed

The dividend proposed was included in the Profit and Loss Appropriation Account and must be recorded in the Balance Sheet as a current liability. The dividend covers the accounting period under review, but will not be paid until it is approved at the shareholder's meeting which could be a number of months into the next accounting period.

7. Profit and Loss Account

This represents the retained profit for the year taken from the profit and loss appropriation account plus the retained profits from previous years taken from the trial balance i.e. £54,800 + £25,000 = £79,800.

Appendix A

An Introduction to Double Entry Bookkeeping

In this appendix we will cover an introduction to double entry bookkeeping. We will do this by means of a number of examples. Should you wish to become proficient in this area we suggest that you work through the same examples until 'the penny drops', yes, while it is a simple process it often takes time before one becomes familiar with the system.

We will start by explaining the basic rules of double entry bookkeeping. A tip, don't try to bring your own logic into these rules – just follow them to the letter and you will achieve. From experience, we know that many students find it difficult to apply these rules without question. We will then take you through a number of examples.

The main aim in providing this appendix is to demonstrate the double entry bookkeeping process from initial transactions through to the preparation of a trial balance. You will note that the trial balance was our starting point for the final accounts example produced in this chapter.

Rules

In accounting, each transaction affects two items (or accounts). The main rules used to determine the actual positions are as follows:

Debit	Credit
IN	OUT
RECEIVER	GIVER

These two rules simply state,

Debit what comes in   Credit what goes out

and/or

Debit the receiver   Credit the giver

Please note, it is possible to mix and match the two basic rules.

Example 1

On the 1st January U.N. Welcome started a business, the first transactions were:

Jan 1   Started a business with £1,000 cash

Jan 2   Purchased goods £250 on credit from G. Ashley & Co

Jan 3   Bought display equipment and paid £200 cash

Jan 5   Sold goods for cash £400

Each transaction affects two accounts. Here we show the two accounts and apply the rules to the above transactions.

	Debit	Credit
Started a business with £1,000 cash	*Cash*	*Capital*
Purchased goods £250 on credit from G. Ashley	*Purchases*	*G. Ashley*
Bought display equipment and paid £200 cash	*Equipment*	*Cash*
Sold goods for cash £400	*Cash*	*Sales*

The first transaction requires us to open an account for cash and for capital. Try to follow the posting. You will see that we have debited the cash account with £1,000. Notice we say capital, this refers to the other side of the transaction. In the capital account we have entered a credit of £1,000, this time it refers to the other side of the transaction which is cash. The posting to the accounts would be: (we have omitted the dates – shortage of space)

	Cash				**Capital**		
Dr.			Cr.	Dr.			Cr.
Capital	1,000	Equipment	200			Cash	1,000
Sales	400						

	Purchases				**G. Ashley & Co**		
Dr.			Cr.	Dr.			Cr.
G. Ashley	250					Purchases	250

	Equipment				**Sales**		
Dr.			Cr.	Dr.			Cr.
Capital	200					Cash	400

Example 2

In this example we have introduced a number of other transactions. We also show the two accounts for each transaction and the rule.

200X	Transactions	Account	Rule
Aug 1	Started business depositing £20,000 into bank	Bank Capital	Debit what comes in Credit the giver
Aug 3	Bought goods on credit from G. Marsh £3,000	Purchases G. Marsh	Debit what comes in Credit the giver
Aug 4	Withdrew £3,000 cash from bank	Cash Bank	Debit what comes in Credit what goes out
Aug 7	Bought Motor Van paying £2,000 cash	Motor Van Cash	Debit what comes in Credit what goes out
Aug 10	Sold goods on credit to T. Barr & Co £500	T. Barr & Co Sales	Debit the receiver Credit the giver
Aug 21	Returned goods to G. Marsh £400	G. Marsh Returns out	Debit the receiver Credit what goes out
Aug 28	T. Barr pays the amount owing by cheque	Bank T. Barr & Co	Debit what comes in Credit the giver
Aug 30	Bought Furniture from B. Wise Ltd £1,500	Furniture B. Wise Ltd	Debit what comes in Credit the giver
Aug 31	Paid £2,500 by cheque to G. Marsh	G. Marsh Bank	Debit the receiver Credit what goes out

We will now post each of the transactions, balance off the accounts and produce a trial balance.

Bank

Dr.			Cr.
Capital	20,000	Cash	3,000
T. Barr	500	G. Marsh	2,500
		Balance c/d	15,000
	20,500		20,500
Balance b/d	15,000		

Capital

Dr.			Cr.
		Bank	20,000

Purchases

Dr.			Cr.
G. Marsh	3,000		

G. Marsh

Dr.			Cr.
Returns Out	400	Purchases	3,000
Bank	2,500		
Balance c/d	100		
	3,000		3,000
		Balance b/d	100

Cash

Dr.			Cr.
Bank	3,000	Motor Van	2,000
		Balance c/d	1,000
	3,000		3,000
Balance b/d	1,000		

Sales

Dr.			Cr.
		Cash	500

T. Barr & Co

Dr.			Cr.
Sales	500	Bank	500

Returns Out

Dr.			Cr.
		G. Marsh	400

Furniture

Dr.			Cr.
B. Wise Ltd	1,500		

B. Wise Ltd

Dr.			Cr.
		Furniture	1,500

We will now show how accounts are balanced using the bank account from the example.

1. If the left side (debit) is greater than the right (credit) we add the left side i.e. £20,000 + £500 to give a total of £20,500.

2. We then take this across to the total on the right side (credit).

3. Deduct any amounts on the right side (credit) from the total i.e. £20,500 – £3,000 – £2,500 to give a balance of £15,000.

4. Take the balance down to the left side (debit)

Bank

Dr.			Cr.
Capital	20,000	Cash	3,000
T. Barr	500	G. Marsh	2,500
		Balance c/d	15,000
	20,500		20,500
Balance b/d	15,000		

If the right side (credit) is greater than the left (debit) we reverse the process.

Finally, we show the trial balance which is simply a listing of all the balances remaining in the accounts.

Trial Balance as at 31st August 200X

	Dr.	Cr.
Bank	15,000	
Cash	1,000	
Motor Van	2,000	
Furniture	1,500	
Purchases	3,000	
Capital		20,000
B. Wise		1,500
Sales		500
G. Marsh		100
Returns Outwards		400
	22,500	22,500

CHAPTER THREE

FINANCIAL REPORTING

When you have finished studying this chapter you should be able to:

❏ Describe the generally accepted accounting concepts, bases and policies.

❏ Have an appreciation of the requirements of company law and corporate governance upon financial reporting.

❏ Understand the regulatory framework which impacts upon financial reporting in the UK.

❏ Outline the main contents of company annual reports including and understanding of the main terms used.

❏ Recognise the importance and in some cases the limitations of the auditors' report.

3.1 Introduction

As well as working with internal financial statements you will need an understanding of published financial statements. Once an entity is established as a limited liability company it has to satisfy the requirements of company law, one of which is the disclosure of information to its shareholders, via published financial statements. These are to be found in the annual reports of companies and are a source of valuable information to competitors, suppliers, employees and other actual or potential stakeholders.

While there are considerable similarities between internal and external published reports, there are differences in the amount of detail included and the timeliness of production. There is also a tension between the willingness of companies to disclose what they might consider sensitive information and the requirements of the UK Companies Acts that set minimum disclosure standards and set out the required format.

In this chapter we will provide an overview of the important influences on financial reporting in the UK, which include:

❑ Accounting Concepts, Bases and Policies;

❑ Company Law;

❑ Accounting Standards;

❑ Stock Exchange and the development of corporate governance issues.

Be warned, you will find some differences from our earlier discussions in terms of both the terminology used and some aspects of the layout of statements. We will highlight important differences and draw your attention to some specific areas where more than a passing familiarity will be required. If you are working outside the UK, or reviewing a set of non UK accounts, you will find that considerable differences in national reporting practices are a fact of life. Although there have been efforts to reduce differences in national practices, such as the development of a set of international accounting standards and efforts to harmonise accounting practices within Europe, caution must be exercised in attempting to analyse and draw conclusions about the published statements and results provided by companies in different countries.

3.2 Accounting Concepts, Bases and Policies

There are a number of generally agreed assumptions and conventions that underlie the way accounts are prepared. These have developed over many years (recognising that the accountancy profession has existed in the UK from the 1850's) from the collective professional experience of those working in the area.

These basic principles are known by a variety of expressions: such as accounting conventions, concepts, methods or postulates. Their importance was recognised in the development of an accounting standard, Standard Statement of Accounting Practice 2 (SSAP 2), which was first published in 1971, and which distinguishes between fundamental accounting concepts, accounting bases and accounting policies. The preface to SSAP 2 states:

> *'It is fundamental to the understanding and interpretation of financial accounts that those who use them should be aware of the main assumptions on which they are based. The purpose of the statement that follows is to assist such understanding by promoting improvement in the quality of information disclosed. It seeks to achieve this by establishing as standard accounting practice, the disclosure in the financial accounts of clear explanations of the accounting policies followed in so far as these are significant for the purpose of giving a true and fair view'.*

1. Accounting Concepts

The following provides an explanation of these generally accepted principles:

❐ **Entity:** An organisation is deemed to have a separate existence from its owners. This means that personal transactions are excluded from business accounts.

❐ **Going concern:** An organisation is assumed to continue in operational existence for the foreseeable future.

❐ **Money measurement:** Accounting only records those events that may be described and measured in money terms.

❐ **Timing of reports:** A time period is fixed as a basis for measurement of profit or loss.

❐ **Realisation:** Accounting recognises only those profits that have been realised in the accounting period. Other than in certain specific situations profit is only accounted for when the earning process is virtually complete.

❐ **Consistency:** The accounting treatment of particular items should be the same from period to period; if changed, the difference should be revealed.

❐ **Prudence or conservatism:** Provision should be made for all potential costs whereas, as indicated, profits should not be accounted for until realised. This means that a far more conservative approach is adopted towards accounting for profit than is the case for costs.

❐ **Accruals/Matching:** Accounts have to ensure that costs are matched with their associated revenues.

❐ **Materiality:** Non standard usage in accounting practice is permissible if the effects are not material.

However, SSAP 2 singles out for special mention four concepts in particular because 'they have such general acceptance that they call for no explanation in published accounts and their observance is presumed unless stated otherwise'. These are; going concern, accruals, consistency and prudence. The four concepts are also identified and recognised in the 1985 Companies Act.

2. Accounting Bases

These are the alternative methods of applying the fundamental accounting concepts to financial transactions and items, which have 'evolved in response to the variety and complexity of types of business and business transactions'. So a business will select the most appropriate accounting base for a particular situation. In practice for example, this means selecting between different methods for depreciating fixed assets e.g. straight-line, reducing balance.

3. Accounting Policies

These are the specific accounting bases selected and consistently applied by a business in the preparation and presentation of their accounts. As there is a choice of accounting policy in many areas, the accounting standard also requires that the business disclose the choice of bases by way of a note to the accounts.

3.3   Company Law

The Companies Acts have been long-standing contributors to the UK regulatory framework. Although their aim has been to protect shareholders and creditors, there has been a growing view that companies also owe duties to other groups in society. In 1975 a significant document called 'The Corporate Report' gave the basic aim of company accounts as being to measure and report on the entity's economic resources and performance. To this end, corporate reports should be 'relevant, understandable, reliable, complete, objective, timely, and comparable'.

While the Corporate report exerted an important influence on financial reporting, the European Community (EC) have had a greater influence. The need for harmonisation between member states has led to the enactment of a succession of Companies Acts which have changed the content of companies' annual reports. The 1948 Act consolidated the accounts of companies with subsidiaries in the form of group accounts while the 1967 Act required companies to disclose total turnover and analyse it by area and business segment. The 1980 Act went much further; creating the split between Ltd and Plc. The latter tend to be companies which offer their shares or loan stock to the general public through the Stock Exchange although some merely seek Plc status without the intention of seeking a Stock Exchange listing. The 1980 Act also introduced new rules restricting the distribution of profits and assets.

The content and format of published accounts produced by companies has been affected significantly by the Companies Act 1981. This Act resulted from the European Community (EC) 4th Directive on company law. It specified in more detail than earlier Acts the items to be shown in published accounts and also the layout of these accounts in 'statutory formats'.

Although the Companies Act of 1981 significantly increased the quantity, and to some extent the comparability, of information to be included in the accounts for shareholders, it also enabled directors of small and medium sized companies to file with the Registrar of Companies accounts containing significantly less information than they had been required to beforehand. Before the 1981 Act the Registrar of Companies received the same accounts as were sent to shareholders. Under the 1981 Act providing a company met certain criteria, it could omit specific information from its published accounts, although a second set of accounts was required to be prepared for shareholders containing all of the statutory information. In essence, the Act made a distinction between small, medium, and large companies. A company qualified for a given status if it satisfied, but did not exceed, at least two from three criteria relating to turnover, balance sheet total and average employees per week, for both the current and the previous year. One important consequence of such classification was that small companies were not required to submit a profit and loss account and medium-sized companies could begin their profit and loss account with the figure for gross profit.

The effect of the 1981 Act was to improve the position of the shareholder analyst, but to disadvantage the non-shareholder analyst. In addition, the apparent benefits of comparability provided by the Act were restricted by the number of options allowed to companies (as permitted by the 4th Directive) on valuation and presentation. (*Appendix A* provides details of alternative formats). The Act was superseded by the 1985 Act which consolidated requirements of earlier acts and specified additional ones. For example, this required companies to prepare a profit and loss account and balance sheet each year in one of the alternative permitted formats illustrating figures for the latest and preceding year. Of vital importance, such published accounts had to show a 'true and fair view' of the profit or loss for the year, and of the company's financial position at the year-end. A 'true and fair view' does not mean that a balance sheet necessarily discloses the 'true worth' of a company. The balance sheet does not attempt to value the business, but is merely a statement of those assets and liabilities recognised by accounting rules. Many significant assets are excluded, especially intangible assets such as business 'know-how' and the value of people. For such reasons the market value of a business often differs widely from the net book value of its assets illustrated in the published accounts.

The 1989 Companies Act that was effective for accounting periods beginning on or after 1 January 1990, is the UK legal instrument used to implement the 7th EC Directive. This concerns the principles to be adopted in preparing consolidated accounts. Its implementation within the UK moves the emphasis away from legal ownership towards the concept of effective control. This is partly intended to curb the use of controlled non-subsidiaries, whereby control could be effected even though the legal requirements constituting a subsidiary were not met. Now, as will be discussed in a later section in this chapter, all undertakings actually controlled by a parent must be consolidated, including partnerships and unincorporated associations carrying on a trade or business (with or without a view to profit).

Two other developments in the 1989 Act were firstly, the introduction of the possibility of companies preparing shorter 'summary financial statements' for their shareholders. These shorter versions would provide a reader with key information concerning the financial performance and position of the company. Companies would still be required to prepare and file a full version of the accounts with the Registrar of Companies. However, they could seek the wishes of their shareholders and supply them with either the full or shorter version.

Secondly, the 1989 Act also gave accounting standards (discussed below) legal force and an enforcement mechanism, while at the same time additions were made to the bodies responsible for accounting standards to complement these changes.

The Companies Acts apply to all limited liability companies in the UK, who are required to produce their accounts for shareholders, and file with the Registrar of Companies, within seven months if a public limited company and within ten months if a private limited company. The following comprise the 'accounts' for a limited company:

❏   A profit and loss account;

❏   A balance sheet;

❏   A report of the directors;

❏   A report of the auditors;

❏   Group accounts, where appropriate.

3.4   Accounting Standards

1. Accounting Standards Committee

The Accounting Standards Committee (ASC) was set up in 1970 by the accounting profession in response to criticisms raised by such events as the *GEC* takeover of *AEI* (£9.5 million of the £14.5 million difference in reported profit was the result of different accounting practices used before and after the takeover). This and other cases highlighted the degree of latitude legally permissible in preparing published accounts.

Statements of Standard Accounting Practice (SSAPs) up to 1st August 1990 were issued by the ASC and are now the responsibility of the Accounting Standards Board (ASB), to be discussed later. Their purpose is to offer both some regulation of disclosure, and to establish the principles by which certain of the figures are calculated. Accounting standards in conjunction with requirements of company law mean that there is a specified minimum amount of information which must be provided.

Accounting standards have been a major source of authority for accountants for the following reasons:

❏ *Comparability*. Those who use financial statements for making investment decisions want to compare the performance of a company with the performance of all other companies. This comparison has serious limitations unless all companies draw up their financial statements on the same basis.

❏ *Trend*. In evaluating a company's performance it is necessary to review the results of a number of years. This review is of dubious value unless a company has drawn up its financial statements on the same basis in each year for which the results are given.

❏ *Public understanding*. Many readers of statements are not experts in the interpretation of accounting information. Standardised information assists the public in gaining an understanding of financial statements.

❏ *Deception*. If any directors wish to mislead investors it is more difficult if companies are required to comply with accounting standards.

❏ *Professional integrity*. The integrity of the accounting profession would suffer if two companies in similar situations could produce quite different results for the same period simply because they were able to use different accounting methods.

Although accounting standards have been properly adopted by the majority of companies, a significant minority have used considerable creativity in their interpretation. This has led to criticism of the accounting profession, particularly in the areas of the treatment of extraordinary items, goodwill and brand valuations where, although the letter of the law has been followed, the spirit of the standards has been breached.

A good illustration of what a UK company could achieve without actually breaching the regulatory framework in the UK was revealed by a review of the suitability of the accounting policies of *Cray Electronics*, which had once been a much-fancied, high-flying, hi-tech 'wonderstock'. The review considered the effect upon Cray's results for the year ended April 29 1989 if brought in line with best accounting practice within the electronics sector. It revealed a pre-tax profit for the year of £5.4 million instead of the £17.03 million that was actually reported. Earnings of 3.3p per share, were calculated; approximately 25% of the figure reported by the company. This review resulted in the publication of a revised annual report incorporating revised published accounts. This was not the end of the story. In August 1990 the Cray Board company comprising a new management team announced that the profit for 1989 would be revised downwards yet again to £1.3 million. In essence then £17.03 million, £5.4 million and £1.3 million all represent a 'true and fair view'!

Situations like the *Cray Electronics* incident should now be a feature of the past. A new system of standard setting following a review process chaired by *Sir Ronald Dearing*, has now been established and an outline of the new structure is shown below.

2. Financial Reporting Council

A new body, the Financial Reporting Council (FRC), was established in 1990 to give a voice to all of those concerned with accounting standards, including users, preparers and auditors. One key characteristic of the FRC is that it represents and involves a wide range of interested parties in the standard setting process. Formerly, the Accounting Standards Committee (ASC), which had responsibility for the setting of accounting standards, was answerable to only one constituency, the six main UK professional accountancy bodies.

Figure 3.1 Financial Reporting Council

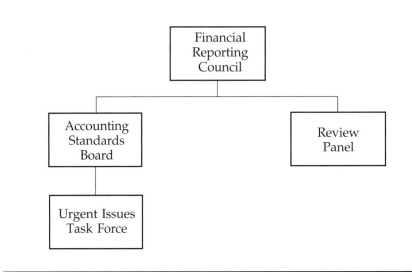

One noteworthy feature of the FRC is that it is jointly funded by the government, the accounting institutes and the city, which together ensure financial support to the standard setting activities of its two subsidiaries, the Accounting Standards Board (ASB) and the Review Panel.

Accounting Standards Board

The ASB, a subsidiary of the FRC, has the responsibility for detailed standard setting. It took over responsibility for accounting standard setting from the ASC on 1st August 1990. It is smaller than the FRC having both a full-time chairman and technical director, together with part-time members which include presence from the non-practising side of the accountancy profession. It issues standards on its own authority, unlike the ASC, and there is now no requirement for the six main UK professional accounting bodies to approve any standards produced. Although the FRC is in a position to give the ASB guidance, it will have no say over the detail of any standard.

The ASB does not need outside approval for its actions, but it does secure support and a consensus in favour of any standards produced. This is achieved by the issuing of a discussion draft for comment and, after the receipt of submissions, a Financial Reporting Exposure Draft (FRED) will be produced. This then forms the basis for the final standard, the Financial Reporting Standard (FRS). A number of Financial Reporting Standards have been issued to date which coexist alongside SSAPs developed under the former ASC. Whilst these SSAPs remain in force, the intention is for the ASB to build up a portfolio of its own. It is intended that new standards will contain a clear statement of underlying principles, why other treatments were rejected and the extent to which they are applicable to small companies.

Urgent Issue Task Force

As illustrated, the ASB is supported by an Urgent Issues Task Force (UITF) whose function will be to tackle urgent matters not covered by existing standards, and for which, given the urgency, the normal standard setting process would not be practicable. It is also the UITF's role to issue UITF Abstracts covering situations where, although a standard is in force, it is not being correctly interpreted. This body, which will be an adjunct of the ASB and not a distinct entity in its own right, represents a new departure for UK practice but is based in principle upon the Emerging Issues Task Force which has existed for some time in the United States.

Review Panel

The second subsidiary of the FRC is the Review Panel, which examines and questions departures from accounting standards by large companies (as defined by the 1985 Companies Act). These should be identified by the requirement to give particulars of departures with reasons, incorporated in the 1989 Companies Act. The Review Panel can act on its own initiative or in response to outside requests. If it believes that the accounts need revising in order to give a 'true and fair view', it will inform the Stock Exchange and any other professional body, such as the one to which the auditors belong, and may publish its findings.

This new system is radically different from that which formerly existed where responsibility lay only with the ASC. In particular the existence and power of the courts have been found to be defective against the test of a 'true and fair view'.

The Review Panel with legislative backing by the 1989 Companies Act was a totally new element in the accounting standards scene. No longer should a company be able to publish accounts which include a material departure from an accounting standard. The Review Panel will be able to apply to the courts and, if the accounts are found not to present a true and fair view, the company may be ordered to prepare revised accounts and circulate them to all persons likely to rely on the previous accounts. The courts may also order that all or part of the costs of the application (by the Review Panel or by the Secretary of State ultimately responsible), and any reasonable expenses shall be borne by such of the directors as they were party to the approval of the defective accounts.

A full list of accounting standards is included at the end of the chapter in *Appendix B*.

3. International Accounting Standards

The standards produced by the ASB apply to the UK and Republic of Ireland group financial statements, and any overseas entities that form part of those statements.

In June 1973 an International Accounting Standards Committee (IASC) was formed. It is an independent body with autonomy in the setting of international accounting statements. The following are its main objectives:

❏ to formulate and publish accounting standards to be observed in the presentation of financial statements and to promote their worldwide acceptance and observance.

❏ to work generally for the improvement and harmonisation of regulations, accounting standards and procedures relating to the presentation of financial statements.

Since its inception the IASC has produced a series of standards which although parallel the topics covered in the UK standards, the approach adopted has not always been the same. It is important to recognise that wherever there may be conflict between an International Accounting Standard (IAS) and the national standard in a country, the latter will prevail.

3.5 The Stock Exchange Requirements

Many of the rules and regulations applying to companies listed on the London Stock Exchange have been incorporated into standards and statute. However, a listed company has to satisfy other demands such as the earlier delivery of accounts to shareholders (six months rather than the seven allowed by the Companies Act), the requirement for interim accounts and the publication of certain information to shareholders in the national press.

Companies with shares or loan stock listed or quoted on the Stock Exchange, are subject to a listing agreement, details of which are set out in the so called 'Yellow Book'. This specifies, among other things, certain information to be disclosed not required by the Companies Acts. The listing agreement is effected when a company's board of directors passes a resolution binding the company to observe the regulations laid down for listed companies. The effect of the listing agreement is evident in its requirements upon the Directors' Report in the annual report. The information required of listed companies includes:

1. The reasons why the trading results shown by the accounts for the period under review differ materially from any published forecast made by the company.

2. A statement by the directors of their reasons for any significant failure to comply with Financial Reporting Standards (FRSs)/Statements of Standard Accounting Practice (SSAPs).

3. A geographical analysis of turnover and of contribution to trading results of trading operations carried on outside the UK (this disclosure is also required by law).

4. The name of the country in which each subsidiary operates.

5. Particulars regarding each company in which the group equity interest is 20% or more of:

   a. the principal country of operation;

   b. detail of its issued share and loan capital and, unless dealt with in the consolidated balance sheet as an associated company, the total of its reserves.

6. Statements of directors' share interests and of other persons' substantial shareholdings.

7. Detailed information regarding company borrowings.

8. Waivers of emoluments by directors and waivers of dividends by shareholders.

9. 'Close' company (controlled by a small number of individuals) and 'investment trust' status.

3.6   Corporate Governance

A requirement for continued listing on the London Stock Exchange for a company is compliance with a Code of Best Practice in Corporate Governance. This Code was produced by the Cadbury Committee that was established in 1991 by the Financial Reporting Council, the Stock Exchange and the accounting profession to report on financial aspects of corporate governance. Two further committees, Greenbury and Hampel, were formed and have produced reports. The former is related to the reporting and disclosure of the remuneration of directors, and the latter provided some 'fine tuning' of the previous reports. In their annual reports ending on or after 31 December 1992, UK listed companies are required to state that they have complied with the Code and to provide an auditor's report confirming this compliance. These requirements for disclosure have significantly added to the amount of information provided in the annual report and accounts of UK listed companies. An overview of the requirements set out by the three committees can be found at the end of this chapter in *Appendix C*. In June 1998 the conclusions of the three committees were published in the 'Combined Code' – a single set of principles of corporate governance. The Turnbull Committee, reporting in 1999, calls for an annual board level review of the effectiveness of a company's internal audit system, and its guidance will become part of the Combined Code.

3.7   Financial Reporting and Accountability in the Public Sector

Public Sector organisations exhibit a wide variety of social, economic, political and legal characteristics. They have different powers and responsibilities and display different patterns of accountability. They have different objectives, are financed in different ways and have different organisational structures. These differences reflect how public sector development has responded to changing pressures over times and also to historical backgrounds and sources.

The powers and responsibilities of all public sector bodies have one feature in common. Their specific powers are derived ultimately from Parliament and their responsibility is ultimately to Parliament.

The way in which public sector bodies are accountable to Parliament takes a variety of forms and here we intend, by way of example, to review how regulation impacts upon such bodies with reference to a specific example. The example we have selected is the *Civil Aviation Authority (CAA)* which is both a public service enterprise and a regulatory body. Its responsibility, expressed in its 1998 annual report and accounts, include:

❑   Air safety, both air worthiness and operational safety, including the licensing of flight crew, aircraft engineers and aerodromes, certificating UK airlines and aircraft and maintaining air traffic services standards.

❏ Economic regulation through licensing of routes, approval of air fares for journeys outside the EU, regulation of certain airport charges and licensing of air travel organisers.

❏ National Air Traffic Services, providing air traffic control services and radio and long-haul aids through a subsidiary company, National Air Traffic Services Ltd. In addition the CAA advises the Government on aviation issues, represents consumer interests, conducts economic and scientific research, produces statistical data and provides specialised services.

The CAA also owns a subsidiary company, Highlands and Islands Airports Limited, which operates eight aerodromes in Scotland.

The Authority has, therefore, some very broad ranging objectives. The main Act relating to the CAA's account is the Civil Aviation Authority (Report) Direction 1998.

This Direction says that "the Secretary of State, in exercise of his powers under 21 (2) (d) of the Civil Aviation Act 1982 hereby specifies that the annual report of the Civil Aviation Authority (the 'Authority') for the year ended 31 March 1998 and for each subsequent accounting year shall include for the Authority and its subsidiaries".

1. The performance of service aims, which have been agreed with the Authority, and the out-turn against these;

2. The main feature of the latest corporate plan of the Authority;

3. A fair and full review of development of business during the year, the significance of the circumstances facing the Authority, and indication of likely future developments. The review should deal separately with the significantly different classes of businesses;

4. A five year summary of the financial results, including and identifying inter alia:

   a. For the historic cost accounts appropriate analysis of income from income and expenditure grants and assets and liabilities;

   b. Profit and Loss Account and Balance Sheet adjustments to current cost accounts;

   c. Assets employed and capital employed;

   d. Profit/loss expressed as a return before interest expressed as a return on average historic cost capital employed and profit before interest expressed as a return on average current cost capital employed, in both cases analysing the results between operations where charges are, and are not controlled by the Authority;

   e. Performance against external financial limits;

5. A section headed 'FINANCIAL COMMENTARY' the contents of which should include:

    a. Comparison results against target including explanations of the relationship between current and historical cost accounts and the significance of returns on assets employed.

    b. Comments on and changes in funding levels and out–turn against the external finance limit.

    c. Significant changes in fixed assets with a brief description of assets involved.

    d. Indication of activities in the fields of research and development.

    e. Comments on other relevant aspects of the financial results.

    f. Summary of significant events since the date of the balance sheet.

The main emphasis of the CAA's annual report is a comprehensive review of performance. This is accompanied by information similar to that produced by a plc in response to various Companies Acts, but with a recognition that differences exist in both funding and accountability.

This means that public bodies respond both to their own regulatory framework established by Parliament and to the requirements of the Companies Act and Stock Exchange rules.

3.8   Financial Reporting and the Regulation of Banks

The overriding principle of regulation is the protection of the providers of funds. In the case of limited liability companies it has long been recognised that there is a need to protect the interests of creditors and, as we have illustrated with reference to the Civil Aviation Authority, there is a similar need to protect the providers of funds to public sector bodies. In the case of banks (and some other financial institutions) there is a particular need to protect the interests of depositors. As a consequence of the Basle Agreement, the amount of business that a bank can conduct is regulated by the relationship between its capital base and a specified requirement. In the case of UK banks, the Bank of England specifies, the amount of business a bank can undertake by specifying some proportion of its capital base. The minimum requirement set by the Bank of England is for its total capital to be 8% of the bank's risk weighted assets (and contingents). What this means is that the assets to be found on the asset side of a bank's balance sheet are weighted according to specified risk categories and the adjusted capital base measured by the total capital and must not be lower than 8%.

For example, a bank when risk weighted with assets of 100 would need an adjusted capital base of 8 to comply with the minimum requirements. If, because of its circumstances, a bank cannot adjust its capital base, this limits its advances to customers. An illustration of a Balance Sheet for a commercial bank is provided at the end of this chapter in *Appendix D*.

3.9   Financial Reporting Practice in the UK

In previous sections in this chapter we identified a number of influences and constraints upon financial reporting. These determine the format, contents and detail of the financial reports produced by different organisations.

Having set the scene and provided the context for financial reporting, we will review what financial reports look like in practice. We will focus in particular upon the main financial statements required of companies with a UK stock exchange listing. You will find that the principles are the same as those discussed in *Chapters 1 and 2*, but there are some differences in detail. In addition, they are supported by a number of other reports, statements and accounts that are reviewed in this chapter.

1. Consolidated/Group Accounts

One important feature of the published financial statements contained in annual reports is that they will often be consolidated to show the results for a group of companies.

What is a group of companies? If two separate companies operate independently of each other, they will maintain separate accounting records and prepare separate financial statements. However, if one company controls the other, the result is a group, comprising the controlling, holding, or parent company and the controlled or subsidiary company. Both parent and subsidiary companies retain their separate legal identity and separate accounting records. Sometimes subsidiaries themselves have sub-subsidiaries, each of which is required to produce its own accounts and, if a UK company, to file them with the Registrar of Companies. The parent company usually produces two sets of accounts contained within the one annual report:

❏   its own accounts in which the subsidiaries will be shown in the balance sheet as an investment and the dividends from them will be shown in the profit and loss account; and,

❏   its group or consolidated accounts. These show the income and expenditure, assets and liabilities of all the companies as a single economic whole and therefore usually give a much clearer and fuller picture.

A company publishing group accounts need not publish its own profit and loss account but must show how much of the group's profit is dealt with in the parent's profit and loss account.

Thus, the position with group accounts is that individual legal identities are retained and, the financial statements are consolidated with the purpose of providing the holders of the parent company with information about the full range of its activities including interests in subsidiaries. The result is a consolidated profit and loss account and a consolidated balance sheet obtained from aggregating the separate profit and loss accounts and balance sheets of the parent and subsidiary companies.

The notional principle of parent and subsidiary companies is straightforward, but their definition is problematic. As a general rule, a subsidiary arises for a company when in any one of the following circumstances:

❏ it holds a majority of the rights to vote at general meetings in any undertaking, including partnerships and unincorporated associations carrying on a trade or business (with or without a view to profit) and any rights held by any nominees;

❏ it has the right to appoint or remove directors holding a majority of the voting rights;

❏ it has the right to exercise a dominant influence (including at least a right to direct the undertaking's operating and financial policies) by virtue of either provisions in the memorandum or articles, or a written contract;

❏ it actually exercises a dominant influence over the undertaking or is managed on a unified basis with it.

These criteria which determine the existence of a subsidiary were the result of the 1989 Companies Act, which extended the meaning of a subsidiary undertaking. Judgement is now required to determine whether a parent actually controls a subsidiary; one test of which might be whether the parent company is in a position to ensure that dividends would always be paid in accordance with its instructions.

2. Annual Reports

Most annual reports for public limited companies (plcs) contain the following:

a. The Chairperson's Statement.

b. The Directors' Report.

c. The Auditors' Report.

d. Accounting Policies.

e. A Profit and Loss Account.

f. A Balance Sheet.

g. A Cash Flow Statement.

h. Notes to the Accounts.

i. Historical Summaries.

The Directors' Report, the Profit and Loss Account and Balance Sheet plus the Notes to the Accounts and the Auditor's Report are all required by law. These should be provided to the shareholders of the company and also filed at Companies House. It is worth repeating that companies and groups that qualify as being Small or Medium Companies are granted disclosure exemptions in respect of the submission to the Registrar of Companies, which mean that the filed accounts for these companies will be less substantial than those provided to the shareholders. The Chairman's Statement is not a legal requirement and is not always provided. The Statement of Cash Flows is a requirement of a Financial Reporting Standard (FRS 1). Historical Summaries are not legally required of companies but have become established practice by most large companies.

a. The Chairperson's (or opening) Statement

According to the Cadbury Report on 'The Financial Aspects of Corporate Governance' (1992), this statement is the most widely read part of company reports. It is generally a review of progress of the company and its business environment over the past year together with some indications of the proposed direction for the company in the forthcoming year. Remarks by the chairperson will generally not be convertible into a forecast of the results for the company for the next year, although usually much of value can be gleaned from the statement in terms, not only of what is included (and excluded), but also from the tone in which information is conveyed.

b. The Directors' Report

In contrast to the Chairperson's Statement, the content of the Directors' Report is laid down by statute and, to a lesser extent, by the requirements of the Stock Exchange for listed companies. Furthermore, the auditors are required to comment in their report if any information given in the Directors' Report is not, in their opinion, consistent with the company's accounts. The main requirements of the Directors' Report is provided in *Table 3.2*.

Table 3.2   Main Requirements of the Directors' Report

❏   Principal activities and business review.

❏   Results and dividends.

❏   Changes in fixed assets.

❏   Changes in share capital

❏   Names of directors, any movements, and details of their shareholdings.

❏   Research and development activities.

❏   A fair review of the year's business, and the end-of-year position.

❏   Likely future developments.

❏   Any important events since the year-end.

❏   Charitable and political contributions.

The Report describes the principal activities of the business and must include a fair review of the development of the business during the year and its position at the end of the year, together with an indication of likely future developments. Details are required of any important events affecting the group since the year end and it should also contain a statement of the directors' interest in the shares of the company, the identity of anyone owning more than 5 per cent of the company in the case of a listed company, and if the company has acquired any of its own shares. Finally, information is required about a number of other matters such as charitable and political donations, research and development, and disabled employees. A point to note, company practices vary such that items may be disclosed in the Directors' Report but alternatively, may be disclosed separately by way of a note to the accounts.

c. Auditors' Report

By law, every limited liability company is required to appoint at each annual general meeting an auditor (or auditors) to hold office from the conclusion of that meeting until the conclusion of the next AGM. The auditors are required to report to the shareholders on the accounts examined and laid before the company in a general meeting. It is important to understand that there is no responsibility as an auditor for the efficiency or otherwise of the business. Specifically, the auditors appointed by the shareholders have historically been required to report to them whether in their opinion:

❏   the balance sheet gives a true and fair view of the company's affairs;

❏ the profit and loss account gives a true and fair view of the profit or loss for the year, and;

❏ the accounts give the information required by the Companies Acts in the manner required.

In addition, there has been a requirement to report to the shareholders when they are not satisfied that:

❏ proper accounting records have been kept;

❏ proper returns, adequate for their purposes, have been received from branches not visited;

❏ the accounts are in agreement with the accounting records and returns received from branches, and;

❏ they have received all the information and explanations required.

An auditors' report will have:

❏ A title identifying the person(s) to whom the report is addressed.

❏ An identification of the financial statements that have been audited.

❏ Two new and significant sections entitled: (1) Statement of Responsibility and (2) Basis of Opinion. These together should clearly indicate the respective responsibilities of directors and auditors; the basis of the auditors' opinion; and the auditors' opinion on the financial statements.

❏ A signature and date.

i. Statement of Responsibility

As can be seen the new auditors report makes a distinction between the accounting responsibilities of the directors. The Cadbury Report on the Financial Aspects of Corporate Governance (1992) recommends that companies will provide a detailed description of the directors responsibilities before the auditors' report so as to provide maximum clarity about the respective responsibilities it is intended to cover. However, if this information is not provided in the financial statements it must be shown in the auditors' report.

In highlighting the responsibilities of the directors specific comment should refer to the need to:

❏ Prepare accounts that give a true and fair view.

❏   Keep all necessary accounting records and to select suitable accounting policies and apply them consistently.

❏   Make reasonable and prudent judgements.

❏   Adhere to Accounting Standards.

Although statutory auditors have normally recognised their own role and responsibilities concerning the audit process, the same degree of understanding has not always been attributed to their clients. The purpose, duties and responsibilities of auditors as perceived by clients often tended to differ dramatically from the work actually performed by auditors leading to what is known as the audit expectation gap.

In an attempt to bridge this gap the UK Auditing Practices Board (APB) came into existence in 1991 with the purpose of improving the standards of auditing, helping to meet the needs of the users of financial information, and enhancing public confidence in the audit process. In May 1993 the APB issued its first Statement of Auditing Standards, 'Auditors Reports on Financial Statements'. The Standard applies to all UK companies whose financial statements are intended to give a 'true and fair' view and whose year end occurs after 30 September 1993. From this date, users of company accounts will have noticed a substantial change in the length and substance of auditors' reports.

The auditors' report is a key independent link in the accountability and communication process between the owners of the business and those officers who control the corporate resources on a daily basis. The auditors' report can be regarded as the very small tip of a rather large financial iceberg because a substantial amount of the underlying audit work is hidden from users of financial statements.

In the past, an auditors' report has consisted of a few lines of narrative which has often been regarded as obscuring more than it revealed. Since many of these users perceived the auditors' report as providing a form of 'financial guarantee' or 'seal of approval', the APB decided to issue its first Standard in an attempt to improve public understanding of reports.

An additional impetus for change has come from a number of large corporate failures over recent years which have occurred shortly after the issue of an unqualified audit report. By failing to fully appreciate the nature, content and implications of the reports, many investors apportioned blame on the auditors for these collapses. The new standards should, in principle, help to diminish some of the underlying and commonly held misconceptions.

The Standard provides a detailed exposition of the revised format and increased content of the new auditors' report. In simple terms, the structure of the new auditors' report will require:

❏ prepare the financial statements on a 'going concern' basis, unless it is inappropriate to do so.

In response to explaining the director's obligations, the auditors will state that their own responsibility is to form an independent opinion on the financial statements and report this opinion to shareholders.

ii. Basis of Opinion

The APB regards it important for auditors to explain why and how they have arrived at their opinion. Therefore, the auditors' report will contain a section entitled 'A Statement of the Basis of Opinion'. In particular it will include:

1. A statement that the company has (not) complied with auditing standards.

2. A statement that the audit process includes an examination, on a test basis, of the evidence which relates to amounts and disclosures in the financial statements.

3. The assessment of any significant estimates and judgments made by the directors.

4. A comment that the company's accounting policies are appropriate, consistently applied and adequately disclosed.

5. A statement that the auditors have planned and performed the audit to obtain a reasonable assurance that the financial statements are free from material misstatement, whether caused through fraud or error.

Finally, the auditors' report must contain a clearly expressed opinion upon the financial statements. Specifically, the auditors are required to comment upon whether these statements provide a true and fair view and have been prepared in accordance with relevant accounting and other requirements. This judgement will include assessing whether:

❏ The financial statements have been drafted by using consistent and appropriate accounting policies.

❏ They have been properly prepared in accordance with legislation.

❏ There is adequate disclosure of all information that is relevant for a proper understanding of the financial statements.

On occasions the auditors' opinion may be qualified. In the past, financial statements which were qualified in the former auditors' report were expressed in a form of coded language and there was a common belief that a large proportion of users simply did not have the necessary skills to understand its significance.

To remedy this situation a qualified opinion in the future will be issued under one of the following clearly defined circumstances:

1. The scope of the auditors' examination has been limited.

2. The auditors disagree with the treatment or disclosure of a matter in the financial statements.

In both these instances the effect of the matter must be so material that the financial statements would not give a true and fair view or comply with other accounting or legal requirements.

Auditors will have to explicitly state that they are giving a qualified opinion and the associated reasons. In most instances a qualified opinion will be clearly prominent and preceded by the phrase 'except for..................' and then followed by the reason for qualification. The former 'subject to..................' qualification which was used frequently in the past is no longer acceptable.

The new Standard also requires auditors to give a special explanation of any fundamental uncertainties where, for example, the uncertainty about the outcome of a future event and its potential consequences is regarded as being of such significance in the context of the financial statements. The ultimate sanction of an auditor disclaiming or giving an adverse opinion will, of course, still remain as an option.

An exemption for small companies for audit requirements was made in the early 1990's. This effectively meant that only UK companies with an annual turnover of in excess of £90,000 would be required by law to file their accounts at Companies House. In 1997 this threshold was raised to £350,000, thereby making a significant reduction in the number of UK companies requiring an auditors' report.

In addition to the requirement for the auditors to report upon the company's financial statements, companies quoted on the London Stock Exchange are required to have an auditors' report on their compliance with the Cadbury Code of Best Practice. The usual form of words in the opinion section of this report of the auditors is:

With respect to the directors' statements on internal financial control and going concern on pages......, in our opinion the directors have provided the disclosures required by the Listing Rules referred to above and such statements are not inconsistent with the information of which we are aware from our audit work on the financial statements.

Based on the enquiry of certain directors and officers of the Company, and examination of relevant documents, in our opinion the directors' statement on page ..... appropriately reflects the Company's compliance with the other aspects of the Code specified for our review of Listing Rule 12.43(j)

d. Accounting Policies

As already discussed, SSAP 2 requires companies to include details of their chosen accounting policies in their statutory report. They will include details of their policies in relation to:

❏ basis of accounting and consolidation;

❏ fixed assets and depreciation;

❏ stocks;

❏ pension contributions;

❏ deferred taxation;

❏ foreign currencies;

❏ goodwill;

❏ leases.

e. Published Profit and Loss Account

We indicated earlier that the format of published profit and loss accounts and balance sheets is prescribed by the UK Companies Acts. The Financial Reporting Standard (FRS 3) 'Reporting Financial Performance' first issued in 1992 introduced changes to the format of the profit and loss account. When you look at UK company accounts you will see these in the form of changes to the profit and loss account, a note of historical cost profits and losses, a statement of total recognised gains and losses and a reconciliation of movements in shareholders' funds. The change to the format of the profit and loss account was to allow a layered approach to 'highlight a number of important components of financial performance'. This allowed for the results of continuing operations (including the results of acquisitions) to be shown separately from the results of discontinued operations. It also allowed for the profits or losses on the sale or termination of an operation, costs of a fundamental reorganisation or restructuring and profits or losses on the disposal of fixed assets to be shown under either continuing or discontinued operations, and for extraordinary items (being outside ordinary activities) to be shown separately.

In the case of the published profit and loss account, companies do have an element of choice as the Act (by virtue of the 4th EC Directive) provides two horizontal and two vertical alternatives. The main difference between the alternatives concerns the way in which costs are analysed. The form frequently encountered is illustrated in the consolidated profit and loss account in *Table 3.3*.

The profit and loss account, in this case consolidated to show the effect on profit for the companies comprising the group, is characterised by 'layers' of profit, similar to those discussed in *Chapter 1*. The last item, the transfer to/(from) reserves is found by using the following 9 steps:

1   Add together all of the companies' revenue to obtain sales (turnover) for the group.

2   Add any other income to sales to obtain total revenue.

3   Add together the companies' costs of sales.

4   Add together the companies' distribution and selling and administrative costs.

5   Subtract the cost of sales and costs in 4. from total revenue to obtain operating profit for the group.

6   Subtract any interest payable by the group (from loans and overdrafts) from operating profit to obtain profit before taxation for the group.

7   Subtract the tax the group has to pay from profit before taxation to obtain group profit after taxation.

8   Subtract any extraordinary item to obtain the profit attributable to shareholders.

9   Subtract dividends to determine the retained profits to transfer to/(from) reserves.

Table 3.3 Published Consolidated Profit and Loss Account

CONSOLIDATED PROFIT AND LOSS ACCOUNT
for the year ended 31st December

	200X £'000	200X–1 £'000
Sales	29,000	26,000
Cost of Sales	–21,000	–20,000
GROSS PROFIT	8,000	6,000
Distribution and Selling Cost	–2,700	–2,000
Administration Expenses	–3,000	–3,000
OPERATING PROFIT	2,300	1,000
Interest Payable	–300	–600
PROFIT/(LOSS) ON ORDINARY ACTIVITIES BEFORE TAX	2,000	400
Taxation	–700	–140
PROFIT/(LOSS) ON ORDINARY ACTIVITIES AFTER TAX	1,300	260
Minority Interests	–10	–10
PROFIT/(LOSS) FOR THE FINANCIAL YEAR	1,290	250
Dividends	–300	–100
TRANSFER TO/(FROM) RESERVES	990	150
EARNINGS PER SHARE	21.7p	4.4p

What exactly is meant by the items included in the profit and loss account are described in the following checklist:

❏ **SALES (TURNOVER):** This is the total sales or operating revenue of the group and can be from goods and or services. Sales exclude VAT which companies have to collect on behalf of governments.

❑ **COST OF SALES:** The cost of sales includes wages and the depreciation of equipment, as well as the value of the materials and services the companies in the group have bought during the year in order to make the goods or provide the services that they sell. These materials and services will include such items as raw materials, components, power for machinery and heating, maintenance bills and fuel for vehicles.

❑ **GROSS PROFIT:** The difference between turnover and cost of sales.

❑ **OTHER COSTS:** Expenses such as distribution and administration expenses are disclosed and deducted from gross profit.

❑ **OTHER INCOME:** Although a company or a group of companies usually has a main trading activity, it may also derive income from other different activities. For example, a company may own property which it lets. The rent it receives will be classed as 'other income'. Share of profits of related companies and income from other investments are also included here.

❑ **OPERATING PROFIT:** This is the profit made when all expenses other than interest payable have been deducted. It is sometimes called 'trading profit'.

❑ **INTEREST PAYABLE:** Interest is payable on loans and is an expense that can be charged against profit, unlike dividends.

❑ **PROFIT/(LOSS) ON ORDINARY ACTIVITIES BEFORE TAXATION:** This represents operating profit less interest payable.

❑ **TAXATION:** This includes UK corporation tax, and overseas taxes for companies operating abroad.

❑ **PROFIT/(LOSS) ON ORDINARY ACTIVITIES AFTER TAXATION:** This represents profit/(loss) on ordinary activities before taxation, less taxation.

❑ **MINORITY INTERESTS:** These refer to the amount of profit attributable to shareholders in subsidiary undertakings which have been included in the consolidated profit and loss account and held by persons other than the parent company and its subsidiaries.

❑ **PROFIT/(LOSS) ATTRIBUTABLE TO SHAREHOLDERS:** This is the amount that can be distributed to shareholders. Subject to any legal constraints, it is up to a company or group of companies how much is distributed and how much is retained for reinvestment and expansion.

❑ **DIVIDENDS:** These are that part of after tax profit to be distributed to shareholders.

❑ **TRANSFER TO/(FROM) RESERVES:** The profit remaining after the deduction of all the above items. It is commonly known as 'Retained' profit.

❑ **EARNINGS PER ORDINARY SHARE (EPS):** You will have observed that at the end of the published profit and loss account illustrated in *Table 3.3* there is an entry for 'Earnings per ordinary share'. In simple terms, this shows how much each of the group's ordinary shares has earned during the year. FRS 14 requires that it is calculated by dividing the profit after tax (less any preference dividends but before extraordinary items), by the average number of issued ordinary shares for the year ranking for a dividend. Where there is another equity share ranking for a dividend in the future, and/or other securities convertible into equity shares in issue, and/or options or warrants exist to subscribe for equity shares what is known as a fully diluted EPS should be disclosed. Such a fully diluted EPS shows how much each of the group's ordinary shares would have earned if the effect of potential change in the financial structure are taken into account. EPS is considered to be an important financial ratio which is frequently related to the market price at which a share is trading, known as the Price Earnings (PE) ratio. Both of these we consider later in *Chapter 4.*

f. Published Balance Sheet

Having considered the published profit and loss account, let us now consider the published balance sheet.

The balance sheet which is shown in *Table 3.4* consists of the following:

1. The sum of all fixed assets within the group.

2. The sum of all current assets within the group.

3. The sum of all group liabilities falling due within one year, usually called current liabilities.

4. Net current assets, which represent the difference between liabilities in 3 and current assets, often called working capital.

5. Total assets less current liabilities, calculated from the sum of fixed assets and net current assets.

6. Net assets, which represent the difference between total assets and all liabilities.

7. Owners equity/shareholders' funds, which is the sum of the share capital and reserves of the group.

Table 3.4   Published balance sheet

CONSOLIDATED BALANCE SHEETS
as at 31st December

	200X £'000	200X–1 £'000
FIXED ASSETS		
Tangible Assets	7,000	5,000
	7,000	5,000
CURRENT ASSETS		
Stocks	8,000	6,000
Debtors	7,000	6,000
Cash	7,000	3,000
	22,000	15,000
CREDITORS: amounts falling due within one year	10,000	6,000
NET CURRENT ASSETS (LIABILITIES)	12,000	9,000
TOTAL ASSETS LESS CURRENT LIABILITIES	19,000	14,000
CREDITORS: amounts falling due after more than one year	7,000	3,000
NET ASSETS	£12,000	£11,000
CAPITAL and RESERVES		
Called up Share Capital (nominal value £1.00)	6,000	5,900
Share Premium Account	4,500	3,900
Profit and Loss Account	1,500	1,200
SHAREHOLDERS' FUNDS	£12,000	£11,000

Please note that the contents illustrated in the consolidated balance sheets *Table 3.4*, may differ from some you will encounter in practice. Apart from differences in the nature of the business, which will affect mix and even types of assets and/or liabilities, there are other reasons, for example, where subsidiaries are not wholly owned, thereby giving rise to what are known as 'minority interests' (external shareholdings outside the group).

You will observe areas of similarity between published and internal balance sheets discussed earlier. However, one key point to note is that whilst the liabilities in published balance sheets are also separated with reference to the length of time of the obligation incurred, the following labels are normally used:

❒ Creditors: amounts falling due within one year;

❒ Creditors: amounts falling due after more than one year.

As indicated in the illustration in *Table 3.4*, the total in the top part of the balance sheet is calculated as follows:

FIXED ASSETS + CURRENT ASSETS − ALL CREDITORS = NET ASSETS

and that

NET ASSETS = OWNERS' EQUITY (SHAREHOLDERS' FUNDS)

The owners' equity/shareholders' funds comprises the sum of capital and reserves and is sometimes also referred to as net worth. This section includes all of the called up share capital of a company. In some company accounts, and indeed in our example company, you will find an item in the reserves called the 'share premium account'. This arises where new shares are offered at an issue price which is more than their nominal or face value. The nominal value of the new shares will be included in Issued Share Capital. The difference between the nominal value and the issue price is the share premium and will be credited to that account.

As with the profit and loss account, more detail about items included in the balance sheet can be found in the notes to the accounts. Notes to the balance sheet would include:

❒ Tangible assets, showing additions, acquisitions, disposals and depreciation by main type of asset.

❒ Shares in subsidiary companies.

❒ Investments, short-term and long-term.

❒ Stocks: showing a breakdown into raw materials, work-in-progress and finished goods, if appropriate.

❒ Debtors, including prepayments.

❒ Creditors: amounts falling due within one year, showing a breakdown into short-term borrowings; trade creditors; other creditors; accruals and deferred income; corporation taxation; other taxation including social security benefits; and proposed dividends.

❐ Creditors: amounts falling due after more than one year, consists mainly of borrowing repayable between one and five years.

❐ Called up share capital.

❐ Reserves, including share premium, revaluation reserve, and other reserves.

❐ Profit and loss account, showing the accumulated profits as at the date of the balance sheet.

Some organisations, including some publicly listed companies, produce balance sheets that may appear to be significantly different in layout to that described. A good example is the balance sheet of a commercial bank, an illustration and explanation of which can be found in *Appendix B.*

g. Cash Flow Statement

This statement is required to be produced by a UK accounting standard (FRS 1) and is also a US reporting requirement. The purpose of the statement is to provide an explanation of the sources from which cash has been generated during the year and how it has been used. The UK approach requires cash flows to be reported using the following standard headings:

❐ Operating activities.

❐ Returns on investment and servicing of finance.

❐ Taxation.

❐ Investing activities.

❐ Financing.

The Accounting Standard classifies cash flows by these standard headings in the following way:

❐ Operating activities: the cash effects of transactions and other events relating to operating or trading activities. A reconciliation between the operating profit reported in the profit and loss account and the net cash flow from operating activities should be given as a note to the cash flow statement.

❐ Returns on investment and servicing of finance: receipts resulting from the ownership of an investment and payments to providers of finance (excluding those reported under operating, investing or financing activities). These would include the receipt and payment of interest and dividends.

❐ Taxation: the cash flows to or from taxation authorities in respect of the reporting entity's revenue and capital profits.

❐ Investing activities: cash flow related to the acquisition or disposal of any assets held; these would include the receipts from the sale or disposal of fixed assets or investment in subsidiaries or other entities, or payments to acquire them.

❐ Financing: receipts from or repayments to external providers of finance, which would include receipts from share issues and loans, and repayment of loans, finance leases.

Table 3.5   Cash Flow Statement

		£'000	£'000
Net cash outflow from operating activities (see note below)	1		2,600
Returns on investments and servicing of finance			
Interest paid			–300
Taxation	2		–700
Capital expenditure and financial investment			
Payments to acquire tangible fixed assets	3	–3,500	
Receipts from sales of tangible fixed assets		1,500	
Net outflow for capital expenditure and financial investment			–2,000
Acquisitions and disposals			
Equity dividends paid	4		–300
Cash outflow before financing			–700
Financing			
Increase in share capital		700	
Increase in borrowing		4,000	
Net cash inflow from financing			4,700
Increase in cash	6		4,000

Notes:

1. Reconciliation of operating profit to net cash inflow from operating activities

Operating profit		2,300
Increase in stock		–2,000
Increase in debtors		–1,000
Increase in creditors		4,000
Loss on disposal of assets	5	–700
Net cash inflow from operating activities		2,600

2. Assumed – taxation paid in current year.

3. Assumed – information not available in *Table 3.3* and *Table 3.4*.

4. Assumed – dividend paid in the year.

5. Assumed – extraordinary item in the Profit and Loss Account.

6. Difference in opening and closing cash position as shown in balance sheet, *Table 3.4*.

In the UK the likely format of the statement of cash flows that will be found in the Report and Accounts is shown in *Table 3.5*, using the data from *Table 3.3* and *Table 3.4*. Please note that this version is for illustrative purposes only. It is based on the information in the tables, but without the detailed notes to provide for depreciation, timing of payments etc.

Although cash flow reporting is used in the UK and in the US, it is important to note that what is known as funds statements continue to be a requirement elsewhere. Consequently, a sound basic understanding of the funds statement may be invaluable in working with annual reports produced outside the UK. You will find the funds statement illustrated and explained in *Appendix E*.

h. Notes to the Accounts

In its published form the profit and loss account is a summarised statement which can only provide a limited indication of how well a business has performed. In working with such a statement you will often want more information to form a more complete view, some of which will be found in supporting notes to the accounts. You will rarely find all of the information you wish because for competitive reasons companies are often reluctant to provide more than the minimum required of them.

Greater detail on all items contained within a profit and loss account are available from the notes to published accounts, the relevant note usually being cross referenced in a separate column in the profit and loss account. What form do such notes take? The following is an illustration of a note that might be found for earnings per share:

> *The Earnings per Ordinary Share are based on the profits after taxation and preference dividend of £1,800,000 (1998, loss £500,000) and 120,000,000 Ordinary Shares (1998, 100,000,000) being the weighted average number of shares in issue during the year.*

Other notes to accounts would typically include:

❏ Turnover and profit or loss for each different type of business.

❏ Turnover for different geographical markets.

❐ Details of net operating costs, including raw materials and consumables, depreciation, staff costs and auditors fees.

❐ Interest payable and receivable.

❐ Details of directors' remuneration, and employees with emoluments over £30,000.

❐ The average number of employees, total wages, social security and pension costs.

❐ Details of tax.

❐ Details of preference and ordinary dividends.

i.   Historical Summaries

Historical Summaries are not a legal requirement, but have been provided by the vast majority of large companies since asked for by the Chairman of the Stock Exchange some 25 years ago. The usual period covered is five years and the more usual items included are:

❐ Turnover.

❐ Profit.

❐ Dividends.

❐ Capital employed.

❐ Various ratios such as earnings per share, return on capital, profit on turnover and assets per share. These have to be interpreted guardedly because, with the exception of earnings per share, there is no commonly accepted standard for any ratio.

3. Interim Reporting

Although the information provided in an annual report may be valuable, it becomes limited with the passage of time. More up-to-date information can be obtained from interim reports.

In addition to a requirement to produce annual reports, the Stock Exchange's Yellow Book, Admission of Securities to Listing, requires as a minimum the following to be provided on an interim basis:

❐ Net turnover.

❐ Profit before tax and extraordinary items.

❐ The taxation charge.

- ❐ Minority interests.

- ❐ Ordinary profit attributable to shareholders.

- ❐ Dividends.

- ❐ Earnings per share.

- ❐ Comparative figures.

- ❐ An explanatory statement to include information on any events and trends during the period as well as details about future prospects.

The whole interim report must be sent to all shareholders, or alternatively, it must appear in two national newspapers. Such reports are not usually audited and thus lack the authority and accuracy which annual reports appear to possess. There are no guidelines on the preparation of interim reports in company law or accounting standards.

Interim reporting has received relatively little attention in the UK. This can be readily understood by comparing UK practice with that in the USA. The New York Stock Exchange has required published information since 1910, the Securities and Exchange Commission (SEC) since 1946 and the American Stock Exchange since 1962. By contrast, the London Stock Exchange did not introduce requirements until 1964.

APPENDIX A – Formats for UK Published Accounts

PROFIT AND LOSS ACCOUNT (Format 1)

Turnover
Cost of Sales
Gross Profit
Distribution Costs
Administration Expenses
Other Operating Income
Interest Receivable
Interest Payable and Similar Charges
Profit on Ordinary Activities before Taxation
Tax on Profit on Ordinary Activities
Profit on Ordinary Activities after Taxation
Profit for the Financial Year
Dividends
Profit Retained for the Year
Earnings per Ordinary Share

PROFIT AND LOSS ACCOUNT (Format 2)

Turnover
Change in Stocks of Finished Goods and Work in Progress
Raw Materials and Consumables
Own Work Capitalised
Other External Charges
Staff Costs
Depreciation
Other Operating Charges
Interest Receivable
Interest Payable and Similar Charges
Profit on Ordinary Activities before Taxation
Tax on Profit on Ordinary Activities
Profit on Ordinary Activities after Taxation
Profit for the Financial Year
Dividends
Profit Retained for the year
Earnings per Ordinary Share

CONSOLIDATED BALANCE SHEET (FORMAT 1)

Fixed Assets

Intangible Assets

Tangible Assets

Investments

Current Assets

Stocks

Debtors

Investments

Cash at Bank and in Hand

Creditors: amounts falling due within one year

Net Current Assets

Total Assets less Current Liabilities

Creditors: amounts falling due after more than one year

Provisions for Liabilities and Charges

Net Assets

Capital and Reserves

Called up Share Capital

Share Premium Account

Revaluation Reserve

Appendix B – Accounting Standards

Standard Statement of Accounting Practice (SSAP)

SSAP 1   Accounting for associated companies

SSAP 2   Disclosure of accounting policies

SSAP 3   Earnings per share

SSAP 4   Accounting for government grants

SSAP 5   Accounting for value added tax

SSAP 8   The treatment of taxation under the imputation system in the accounts of companies

SSAP 9   Stocks and long-term contracts

SSAP 12   Accounting for depreciation

SSAP 13   Accounting for research and development

SSAP 15   Accounting for deferred tax

SSAP 17   Accounting for post balance sheet events

SSAP 18   Accounting for contingencies

SSAP 19   Accounting for investment properties

SSAP 20   Foreign currency translation

SSAP 21   Accounting for leases and hire purchase contracts

SSAP 22   Accounting for goodwill

SSAP 24   Accounting for pension costs

SSAP 25   Segmental reporting

Financial Reporting Statement (FRS)

FRS 1   Cash Flow Statements

FRS 2   Accounting for Subsidiary Undertakings

FRS 3   Reporting Financial Performance

FRS 4   Capital Instruments

FRS 5   Reporting the Substance of Transactions

FRS 6   Acquisitions and Mergers

FRS 7   Fair Values in Acquisition Accounting

FRS 8   Related Party Disclosures

FRS 9   Associates and Joint Ventures

FRS 10   Goodwill and Intangible Assets

FRS 11   Impairment of Fixed Assets and Goodwill

FRS 12   Provisions, Contingent Liabilities and Contingent Assets

FRS 13   Derivatives and Other Financial Instruments: Disclosures

FRS 14   Earnings Per Share

FRS 15   Tangible Fixed Assets (supersedes SSAP 12)

FRS 16   Current Taxation (supersedes SSAP 8)

Appendix C – Corporate Governance

Outcomes of the committees reporting on aspects of Corporate Governance

The Cadbury Code

1 Board of Directors

1. The board should meet regularly, retain full and effective control over the company and monitor the executive management.

2. There should be a clearly accepted division of responsibilities at the head of a company, which will ensure a balance of power and authority, such that no one individual has unfettered powers of decision. Where the chairman is also the chief executive, it is essential that there should be a strong and independent element on the board, with a recognised senior member.

3. The board should include non-executive directors of sufficient calibre and number for their views to carry significant weight in the board's decisions.

4. The board should have a formal schedule of matters specifically reserved to it for decision to ensure that the direction and control of the company is firmly in its hands.

5. There should be an agreed procedure for directors in the furtherance of their duties to take independent professional advice if necessary at the company's expense.

6. All directors should have access to the advice and services of the company secretary, who is responsible to the board for ensuring that board procedures are followed and that applicable rules and regulations are complied with. Any question of the removal of the company secretary should be a matter of the board as a whole.

2 Non-Executive Directors

1. Non-executive directors should bring an independent judgement to bear on issues of strategy, performance, resources, including key appointments, and standards of conduct.

2. The majority should be independent of management and free from any business or other relationship which could materially interfere with the exercise of their independent judgement, apart from their fees and shareholding. Their fees should reflect the time which they commit to the company.

3   Non-executive directors should be appointed for specified terms and reappointment should not be automatic.

4   Non-executive directors should be selected through a formal process and both this process and their appointment should be a matter for the board as a whole.

3   Executive Directors

1   Directors' service contracts should not exceed three years without shareholders' approval.

2   There should be full and clear disclosure of directors' total emoluments and those of the chairman and highest paid UK director, including pension contributions and stock options. Separate figures should be given for salary and performance-related elements and the basis on which performance is measured should be explained.

3   Executive directors' pay should be subject to the recommendations of a remuneration committee made up wholly or mainly of non-executive directors.

4   Reporting and Controls

1   It is the board's duty to present a balanced and understandable assessment of the company's position.

2   The board should ensure that an objective and professional relationship is maintained with the auditors.

3   The board should establish an audit committee with at least three non-executive directors with written terms of reference which deal clearly with its authority and duties.

4   The directors should explain their responsibility for preparing the accounts next to a statement by the auditors about their reporting responsibilities.

5   The directors should report on the effectiveness of the company's system of internal control.

6   The directors should report that the business is a going concern, with supporting assumptions or qualifications as necessary.

Footnote: The company's statement of compliance should be reviewed by the auditors insofar as it relates to paragraphs 1.4, 1.5, 2.3, 2.4., 3.1 to 3.3 and 4.3 to 4.6 of the Code.

The Greenbury Code, Key points:

1. A company should establish a Remuneration Committee of non-executive directors to determine remuneration for executive directors.

2. The committee should be accountable to the shareholders principally via an annual report.

3. The committee should avoid paying more than is necessary to attract, retain and motivate executive directors. It should also take account of what other comparable companies are paying together with the wider employment scene.

4. Periods of notice of more than one year should be avoided wherever possible.

5. The committee should aim to avoid rewarding poor performance and should take a robust line on payment of compensation where performance has been unsatisfactory.

The Hampel Principles of Good Corporate Governance

A   Directors

1. The Board. Every listed company should be headed by an effective board which should lead and control the company.

2. Chairman and CEO. There are two key tasks at the top of every public company – the running of the board and the executive responsibility for the running of the company's business. How these tasks are carried out in each company should be publicly explained.

3. Board balance. The board should include a balance of executive directors and non-executive directors (including independent non-executives) such that no individual or small group of individuals can dominate the board's decision-taking.

4. Supply of information. The board should be supplied in a timely fashion with information in a form and of a quality appropriate to enable it to discharge its duties.

5. Appointments to the board. There should be a formal and transparent procedure for the appointment of new directors to the board.

6. Re-election. All directors should be required to submit themselves for re-election at regular intervals and at least every three years.

B   Directors' Remuneration

1. The level and make-up of remuneration. Levels of remuneration should be sufficient to attract and retain the directors needed to run the company successfully. The component parts of remuneration should be structured so as to link rewards to corporate and individual performance.

2. Procedure. Companies should establish a formal and transparent procedure for developing policy on executive remuneration and for fixing the remuneration packages of individual directors. No director should be involved in fixing his or her own remuneration.

3. Disclosure. The company's annual report should contain a statement of remuneration policy and details of the remuneration of each director.

C   Shareholders

1   Shareholding voting. Institutional shareholders should adopt a considered policy on voting the shares which they control.

2. Dialogue between companies and investors. Companies and institutional shareholders should each be ready, where practicable, to enter into a dialogue based on the mutual understanding of objectives.

3. Evaluation of governance disclosures. When evaluating companies' governance arrangements, particularly those relating to board structure and composition, institutional investors and their advisors should give due weight to all relevant factors drawn to their attention.

4. The AGM. Companies should use the AGM to communicate with private investors and encourage their participation.

D   Accountability and Audit

1. Financial reporting. The board should present a balanced and understandable assessment of the company's position and prospects.

2. Internal control. The board should maintain a sound system of internal control to safeguard shareholders' investments and the company's assets.

3. Relationship with auditors. The board should establish formal and transparent arrangements for maintaining an appropriate relationship with the firm's auditors.

4. External duties. The external auditors should report independently to shareholders in accordance with statutory and professional requirements and independently assure the board on the discharge of their responsibilities under D1 and D2 above in accordance with professional guidance.

Appendix D – Balance Sheet of a Commercial Bank

Balance Sheet as at 31st December

£000's

Liabilities

Share Capital and Reserves

A.	Share Capital	230
B.	Reserves	770
	Shareholder's Funds	1,100
C.	Minority Interests	40
D.	Undated Subordinated Loan Capital	2,000
E.	Permanent Capital Employed	2,040
F.	Dated Subordinated Loan Capital	400
G.	Capital Resources Liabilities	2,440
H.	Current, Deposit, and other Accounts	24,415
I.	Taxation	100
J.	Dividend	45
		£27,000

Assets

K.	Cash and Short-Term Funds	2,000
L.	Bills Discounted	400
M.	Investments	2,000
N.	Advances to Customers	22,000
		26,400
O.	Investments in Associated Undertakings	30
P.	Trade Investments	25
Q.	Premises and Equipment	545
		£27,000

For a conventional commercial company we have already divided the liabilities or sources of finance into:

❏ Owner's Equity, typically referred to as shareholders' funds

❏ External liabilities.

Each of these can be further subdivided for a bank. For example, as you can see in the example balance sheet shareholders' funds *can be subdivided into:*

❏ Share capital, and

❏ Reserves.

and *external liabilities* into:

❏ Minority interests.

❏ Long-term liabilities (creditors falling due after one year) – undated subordinated loan capital, dated subordinated loan capital.

❏ Short-term or current liabilities (creditors falling due within one year) – current, deposit and other accounts, taxation, dividends.

External liabilities – long-term

In addition to the funds provided by the owners (prefixed by **A** and **B**), organisations will receive a proportion of their funding from other investors. This type of funding has more than one year to maturity and may be raised because there is no desire to divide the ownership further, or because such sources are cheaper. As can be seen from the example balance sheet, such funding comes from minority interests (prefixed by **C**) and in particular "undated" and "dated" subordinated loan capital (prefixed by **D** and **F** respectively). That which is dated has a specified redemption period, hence its exclusion from **E**, "Permanent capital employed".

In the example balance sheet, the sum of shareholders' funds and long-term liabilities are referred to as "capital resources" (prefixed by **G**), the term capital in this case reflecting their long-term nature.

You should note that the proportion of shareholders' funds and other long–term funding is an important consideration to all organisations, and banks are no exception to this.

External Liabilities – short-term

Any liability with short-term implications (normally less than one year) has been included under the heading "Liabilities" in the example balance sheet. These liabilities are:

H. Current, Deposit and other Accounts.

I. Taxation.

J. Dividend

You will recall that the assets section of the balance sheet shows how the finance raised by a business is represented at a specific point in time. Such assets range in the ease with which they can be converted into cash from those at one extreme that are already in cash or "near-cash" to those at the other which would normally be difficult to liquidate quickly and are represented by fixed assets like buildings.

K. Cash and short-term funds

All organisations need cash and short-term funds to meet short-term liquidity requirements, for example to pay creditors. Businesses will try to keep just enough cash on hand to satisfy immediate needs and will put as much as possible to use by investing it so that it is "on call", or accessed at very short notice. Banks are no exception to this practice and may often hold more than 50% of their cash and short-term funds in such form. The remainder will be mainly cash in hand and balances with banks, and a fairly small proportion will be negotiable certificates of deposit and cheques in the course of collection.

L. Bills Discounted

A bill, or bill of exchange, is a signed, written, unconditional order addressed by one person directing another person to pay a specified sum of money to the order of a third person.

One way in which banking organisations make money is by discounting bills, that is by buying them at a discount from British and overseas governments, and/or commercial organisations and then profiting from a subsequent selling transaction in which the sum received for them is greater than that paid.

M. Investments

Organisations may look outside the business for profitable investment opportunities other than just to take advantage of a short-term money surplus by investing 'on call' or at very short notice. In the case of banking organisations such investments will be represented by, for example, the securities of, or guarantees by, national governments which may be listed in the UK, or overseas, or be unlisted.

N. Advances to Customers

This is where banks earn a large proportion of their revenue, but their ability to lend is subject to Bank of England restrictions. Often included under this heading are receivables under instalment credit agreements and equipment leased to customers. Also included may be placings with banks for over 30 days, bullion and other metal dealing stocks and other accounts such as interest receivable and assets awaiting sale.

O. Investments in Associated Undertakings

These represent investments in other companies where the bank, has a significant influence over the company, but not overall control. The company is not therefore, classed as a subsidiary. Such a position occurs where the bank holds more than 20% but less than 50% of the company's equity.

P. Trade Investments

Trade investments are the investments in companies where a bank holds less than 20% but more than 10% of the shares, and is holding the investment for long–term strategic purposes.

Q. Premises and Equipment

You may recall that premises and equipment represent fixed assets. These are possessions a business buys or leases and uses to carry out the activities from which it hopes to generate profit. The term "fixed" is used because such assets are not for sale in the normal course of business. Other than premises and equipment they can include such items as motor vehicles and computers.

Appendix E – Statement of Source and Application of Funds

The statement of source and application of funds, usually referred to as the 'funds statement', was a UK requirement prior to the standard (FRS 1) concerning the cash flow statement and is still required in many countries.

The purpose of the funds statement is to explain how the business has managed to generate additional funds during the year, where they have come from, and how they have been used. Information contained in the funds statement is usually no more than an alternative presentation of that already contained in the profit and loss account and balance sheets. This should not be taken to infer that the funds statement cannot provide a further valuable insight into the operation of a business. Indeed, if well presented it can provide a good explanation of the changes in financial strength and standing of the business that have arisen as the result not only of trading, but also of any other major business transactions which have taken place during the year.

The funds statement will often have three identifiable parts of a funds statement as can be seen in *Table 3.6.*

The three sections in the funds statement may be summarised as:

❏ A statement of sources showing where new funds have come from.

❏ A statement of applications, showing what the funds have been used for.

❏ An analysis of the increase or decrease in funds, which corresponds with the difference between the statement of sources and the statement of applications. Funds comprise of changes in the net liquid position (cash and short-term investments) and the other elements of working capital, like stock, debtors and creditors.

Other formats may also be found. For example, three others can be categorised as:

❏ 'balanced' – sources and applications shown separately but with equal totals;

❏ 'remainder'– applications deducted from sources leaving a residual amount;

❏ 'reconciling' – analyses increases/decreases in funds for the period in terms of sources and applications, then reconciles difference with opening and closing fund balances.

Within the source of funds section will be found the cash profit generated during the trading period in question, together with other sources of finance not comprising part of working capital. Similarly the application of funds will also exclude items comprising part of working capital.

Table 3.6 *Source and application of funds statement*

CONSOLIDATED SOURCE AND APPLICATION OF FUNDS
for the year ended 31st December 200X

		£'000	£'000
1.	**SOURCE OF FUNDS**		
	Profit/(loss) on Ordinary Activities before Taxation		2,000
	Adjustment for items not involving the movement of funds:		
	Depreciation		1,000
	Funds Generated from/(Applied to) Operations		3,000
	Net Proceeds of Share Issues	5,300	
	Issue of Loan Notes	8,000	
	Disposal of Tangible Assets	1,500	14,800
	(A)		17,800
2.	**APPLICATION OF FUNDS**		
	Purchase of Tangible Assets	−6,500	
	Dividend Payments	−100	
	Loans repaid	−1,000	
	(B)		−7,600
	(A)−(B)		10,200
3.	**(INCREASE)/DECREASE IN WORKING CAPITAL**		
	Stocks	4,000	
	Debtors	3,000	
	Cash	7,000	
	Creditors	−3,800	
			10,200

[1] *Often two years will be found.*

CHAPTER FOUR

B A S I C
F I N A N C I A L
R A T I O S

LEARNING OBJECTIVES

When you have finished studying this chapter you should be able to:

❑ Describe, calculate and interpret:

- Profitability ratios including return on total assets (ROTA), profit margin% and sales generation.

- Working capital or liquidity ratios, including current ratio and acid test.

- Gearing ratios, including borrowing ratio and income gearing ratio.

- Employee ratios, including sales per employee and profit per employee.

- Investor ratios including earnings per share (EPS) and dividend per share (DPS).

- Corporate ratios including Price Earnings (PE) ratio, Market to Book (MB) ratio and Return on Equity (ROE%).

❑ Describe certain weaknesses in traditional ratios including profitability and liquidity.

4.1   Introduction

Performance measurement is a key issue for all organisations. Management need to measure the results of their actions, not only in comparison to competitor organisations, but in relation to their past performance too. This is a difficult area since the amount, complexity and interpretations placed on data, both published and unpublished, have an infinite variability.

This chapter attempts to show a simplified route through this maze. By explaining the development and use of the most important ratios and the form which they are likely to be presented, you will be equipped with the skill necessary to take a critical view of an important area of company performance measurement.

One major challenge you will have to face in studying for a MBA/DMS or any other postgraduate management qualification, and as your career progresses, is to understand and make sense of internally generated and externally published financial information. In this chapter we will show how the sense of financial information can be achieved using ratio analysis, whereby one piece of financial data (e.g. profit) is expressed in terms of another (e.g. total assets), then the result of which is compared with the same ratio for another time period or another company.

It is possible to calculate any number of ratios and great care has to be exercised to ensure that an approach is adopted whereby only those which are relevant and essential are selected. This can be achieved in assessing profitability by adopting a hierarchical approach involving the calculation of a 'key' ratio and further related ratios. As we will show, the 'key' ratio relates to profit information from the profit and loss account and to the capital employed in the business in terms of assets to be found in the balance sheet. The rationale for its calculation is much the same as that for undertaking personal investment – you need to know how much return or profit will be generated in absolute terms but also how it relates to the amount of money to be tied up.

It is important to apply agreed rules regarding the specification of the various components of any ratio in a consistent manner and to interpret changes in the resulting ratios against previous levels, industry averages or simple benchmarks.

Our discussion of ratio analysis is not restricted to analysing profitability. We will consider other important areas of ratio analysis such as liquidity, financial structure (gearing), employee, investor and corporate performance.

We will reinforce the ratios to be discussed by using examples based upon figures taken from the profit and loss account and balance sheet illustrated in *Table 4.1*, together with some additional information.

Table 4.1 Balance sheet, and profit and loss account

Balance Sheet as at 31st May 200X

	£m		
FIXED ASSETS (Net Book Value)			400
CURRENT ASSETS			
Stock		950	
Debtors		500	
Cash		50	
		1,500	
CURRENT LIABILITIES			
Creditors	425		
Bank Overdraft	675		
		1,100	
NET WORKING CAPITAL			400
TOTAL ASSETS less CURRENT LIABILITIES			800
LONG-TERM LOAN			120
NET ASSETS			£680
CAPITAL and RESERVES			
Issued Share Capital (at £0.25 per share)			130
Profit and Loss Account			550
			680

Profit and Loss Account for the year ended 31st May 1999

	£m
SALES	5,500
Cost of Sales	–2,850
Administrative Costs	–1,800
Selling and Distribution Costs	–600
Interest Payable	–140
NET PROFIT BEFORE TAXATION	110
Taxation	–40
PROFIT ATTRIBUTABLE TO SHAREHOLDERS	70
Dividend	–20
RETAINED PROFIT	50

Notes:		
	Number of Employees	*35,000*
	Market Price of Ordinary Shares	*£1.10*
	Number of Ordinary Shares	*520 million*

4.2   Profitability Ratios

In this section we will illustrate how the key financial ratio, Return on Total Assets (ROTA)% may be used as an analytical tool for gauging profitability performance at the business-level. Providing the necessary financial data is available it can be further subdivided so that more detailed analysis of a number of interrelated ratios can be calculated.

The data required for its calculation is shown in *Table 4.2*, which has been extracted from *Table 4.1*.

Table 4.2   Basic Data for Calculation of Profitability Ratios

	Latest year £'m	Extracted from
Fixed Assets	400	Balance Sheet
Current Assets	1,500	
Profit Before Taxation	110	
Interest Payable	140	
		Profit and Loss Account
Sales	5,500	

1.   Return On Total Assets (ROTA%) – The Key Ratio

Return on total assets ROTA% seeks to provide the answer to a very simple question 'What profit is generated as a percentage of total assets'? It is calculated by expressing Profit Before Interest payable and Taxation (PBIT) as a percentage of total assets. As a general rule, the higher the ratio the better.

For the example company, profit is taken before interest payable and taxation is £250 million (£110m + £140m). Total assets is the sum of fixed assets (excluding intangibles) plus current assets i.e. £400m + £1,500m which gives £1,900 million.

Using this information we can calculate ROTA% to give an indication of the return which a company achieves on its capital employed, sometimes referred to as return on capital employed, or ROCE.

$$\text{ROTA\%} \quad = \quad \frac{\text{Profit Before Interest Payable and Tax}}{\text{Total Assets (excluding Intangibles)}} \quad \text{x} \quad 100$$

$$= \quad \frac{\text{£250 m}}{\text{£1,900 m}} \quad \text{x} \quad 100$$

$$= \quad 13.2\%$$

ROTA% may fall because of a decrease in profits and/or a increase in total assets. ROTA% can be affected by the accounting principles or policies adopted which affect both the profit calculation and total assets. You may recall that we demonstrated the effect upon profit of using different methods for depreciating assets in *Chapter 2*. ROTA% can also be used to show whether or not a company is likely to produce a higher or lower level profit per £ of total assets than it has in the past or relative to their competitors' or industry performance.

But what happens if the ROTA% calculated is lower than that generated in the previous year or by competitors? Is there any way of identifying possible reasons? The answer is yes. ROTA% is the 'key' ratio at the top of a business level ratio hierarchy which can be analysed in more detail by the introduction of sales from the profit and loss account. Introducing sales for the period of £5,500 million enables another level of interrelated ratios within the hierarchy to be calculated which is shown in *Figure 4.1*.

Figure 4.1 Hierarchy of business level profitability ratios

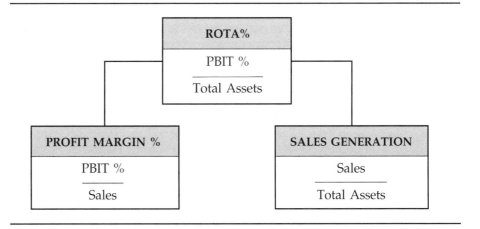

By expanding the key ratio we can see how the level of profitability is being achieved, which could be from a higher or lower PBIT as a percentage of sales, known as the 'profit margin' ratio, from a higher or lower level of sales to total assets, known as the sales generation ratio, or from a combination of the two.

2. Profit Margin

The profit margin ratio gives an indication of the average profit margin achieved by a company. It is calculated by expressing profit before interest payable and taxation as a percentage of sales revenue.

Again profit is taken before interest payable and taxation (PBIT) which for the example company we have already calculated as £250 million. Sales revenue is taken from the profit and loss account in common with PBIT and is £5,500 million.

Using this information we can calculate the ratio to find the profit margin percentage.

$$\text{Profit Margin \%} = \frac{\text{Profit Before Interest Payable and Tax}}{\text{Sales}} \times 100$$

$$= \frac{£250 \text{ m}}{£5,500 \text{ m}} \times 100$$

$$= 4.5\%$$

The ratio of 4.5% shows that the average profit margin across all the lines or products is 4.5% or that 4.5 pence of profit before interest payable and taxation is generated per £ of sales. However, the ratio can hide both high and low margins, and even loss making products. For example, the profit before interest payable and taxation may comprise a profit from product group A of £400m and a loss from product group B of £150m (£400m – £150m = £250m). Clearly, it is desirable to break the profit margin % down as far as possible to reflect the real underlying position, although this may often be difficult.

A lower profit margin% may arise because of a decrease in profits and/or an increase in sales. The expected value of this ratio will differ quite considerably for different types of businesses. A high volume business, such as a retailer, will tend to operate on low margins while a low volume business, such as a contractor, will tend to require much greater margins.

When comparing a profit margin ratio with previous years or against competitors, any significant differences in the profit margin% can be further analysed with a view to identifying likely problem areas. The following headings represent a checklist of areas for further analysis:

❏ Percentage growth in sales.

❏ Product mix from various activities.

❏ Market mix for profit and sales by division and geographical area.

❏ Expansion of activities by merger or acquisition.

❏ Changes in selling prices (usually only available from management accounts and not from published accounts).

❏ Changes in costs (major cost items are shown in published accounts).

The UK accounting standard, *SSAP 25* requires companies to provide an analysis of turnover and contribution to operating profit by principal activities. This information is found in the notes to the accounts as illustrated in *Table 4.3.*

Table 4.3   Analysis of Turnover and Operating Profit

Division (or Principal Activity)	Turnover (Sales)		Profit Before Interest Payable and Tax	
	£'000	%	£'000	%
A	2,200	40	75	30
B	1,320	24	85	34
C	880	16	30	12
D	880	16	40	16
E	220	4	20	8
Total	£5,500	100	£250	100

This table provides useful interpretive information. The overall profit margin we calculated as being 4.5%, and with this information we can readily calculate the PBIT margin made by each division. For a more complete interpretive analysis you should obtain figures for previous years, in this way you will be able to determine trends in turnover and/or PBIT by division (and/or geographic area).

Profit Margin: Analysis by Cost

The main categories of cost from the profit and loss account can be expressed as a percentage of sales, with a view to identifying those costs which require further investigation. The logic behind such investigation is that any cost reduction should, other things being equal, feed through to the profit margin% and therefore improve ROTA%. Do bear in mind that the profit margin% and associated ratios will vary from industry to industry. Low volume businesses are often reliant upon higher margins than high volume businesses such as retailing (e.g. a petrol station), which often operate on low margins such that cost control can be absolutely critical to their success.

In *Figure 4.2* we show how the profit margin% ratio can be broken down into subsidiary ratios such as cost of sales, administration costs and other costs. In practice, these subsidiary ratios would be those appropriate to the analysis being performed.

Figure 4.2   Profit Margin % – Analysis by Cost

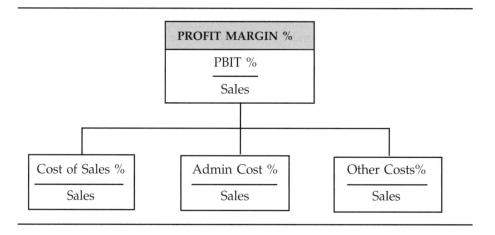

3.   Sales Generation ratio

The sales generation ratio shows the value of sales generated from each £ of total assets. It is calculated by dividing sales revenue by total assets.

$$\text{Generation Ratio} \quad = \quad \frac{\text{Sales}}{\text{Total Assets}}$$

$$= \quad \frac{£5,500 \text{ m}}{£1,900 \text{ m}}$$

$$= \quad 2.89 \text{ to } 1$$

The above ratio indicates that the company has generated £2.89 of sales for each £1.00 of total assets, and can also be calculated by division/principal activity if the information is available.

A low ratio could be due to a decrease in sales and/or a increase in total assets. As a general rule, the higher the ratio the better.

The sales generation ratio can be affected by increases or decreases in fixed assets, current assets and changes in the mix of assets. Increases in this ratio, can be achieved by an increase in sales and/or decrease of the level of total assets.

Sales Generation: Analysis by Asset

Figure 4.3   Sales Generation: Analysis by Asset

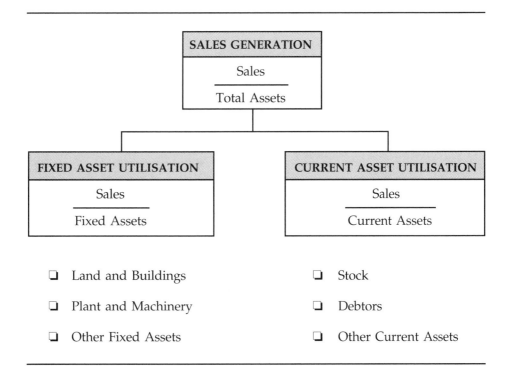

4.   Profitability Ratios, Summary

A summary of the three profitability ratios is given below:

1	Return on Total Assets	13.2%
2	Profit Margin	4.5%
3	Sales Generation ratio	2.89 to 1

Changes in the profit margin % and the sales generation ratio will have direct impact upon ROTA%. Any improvement in either ratio should, other things equal, cause an improvement in the ROTA%

4.3   Liquidity (or Working Capital) Ratios

An analysis of profitability ratios alone is totally inadequate for obtaining a well balanced view of the performance of a company. While profitability is undeniably important, the need to achieve a satisfactory liquidity position is vital for survival. It is a fact that many companies which have failed were profitable but unable to maintain a satisfactory level of liquidity.

The data required for the calculation of liquidity ratios is shown in *Table 4.4*, which has been extracted from *Table 4.1*.

Table 4.4   Basic data for calculation of liquidity ratios

	Latest year £'m	Extracted from
Current Assets	1,500	
Stock	950	
Debtors	500	Balance Sheet
Current Liabilities	1,100	
Cost of Sales	2,850	Profit and Loss
Sales	5,500	Account

In this section we will describe four ratios designed to measure different components of liquidity within the working capital cycle. These are:

1   Current Ratio

2   Liquid (or Acid Test) Ratio

3   Stock Turn

4   Debtor Weeks

Figure 4.4   Working Capital Cycle

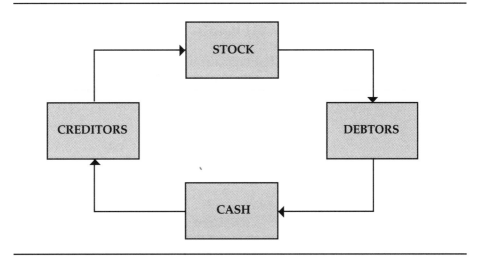

1.   The Current Ratio

The current ratio attempts to measure the ability of a company to meet its financial obligations falling due within one year. It is calculated by dividing current assets by current liabilities.

Current Ratio $=$ $\dfrac{\text{Current Assets}}{\text{Current Liabilities}}$

$=$ $\dfrac{£1{,}500 \text{ m}}{£1{,}100 \text{ m}}$

$=$ 1.36 to 1

For decades, the interpretation of the current ratio has suffered against the unrealistic rule of thumb that current assets should be double that of current liabilities for all companies. This implies that the proportions of current assets and current liabilities should be the same for a fast food company with small stocks and virtually no debtors through to the company undertaking a long term contract with high stocks, high debtors, creditors and bank overdraft.

A very low current ratio indicates potential difficulties, the determination of low varying by the type of business. A high current ratio is not necessarily a good sign; it could mean that a company had idle resources. For example, the current ratio would increase if a company were to increase its stocks or increase its debtors. Similarly, the current ratio would decrease if a company took actions to decrease its stocks or decrease its debtors. We cannot say whether these actions are necessarily good or bad, and care should be taken when attempting to interpret both the size of the current ratio, and the movements year on year.

2. Liquid (or Acid Test) Ratio

The liquid ratio or acid test ratio attempts to measure a company's ability to pay its way in the short-term without having to liquidate stock. Simply it is the 'acid test' – can we pay our way? It is calculated by deducting stock from current assets then dividing the result by current liabilities.

$$\text{Liquid Ratio} \quad = \quad \frac{(\text{Current Assets} \ - \ \text{Stock})}{\text{Current Liabilities}}$$

$$= \quad \frac{(£1,500 \text{ m} \ - \ £950 \text{ m})}{£1,100 \text{ m}}$$

$$= \quad 0.50 \text{ to } 1$$

What do we mean by paying our way in the short-term? For purposes of this ratio, the short-term is considered to be up to 13 weeks, and paying our way to mean that we can pay our debts as and when they fall due. It does not mean that every business needs to maintain the same level to cover all current liabilities.

In common with the current ratio, different liquid ratios apply to different industries. For example, in retailing it has become normal to find a level of around 0.25 to 1 cover for current liabilities. This is possible through cash trading, a high level of commitment from their suppliers and the fact that stock could be liquidated in time to meet maturing debts. Similar to the current ratio, if these companies maintained a higher level of cover for current liabilities there would be idle resources.

3. Stock Turn

The stock turn ratio is a measure showing the number of times stock is 'turned over' on average in a given period (usually one year). It is calculated by dividing the cost of sales by stock.

In published accounts it maybe impossible to obtain a reliable figure for cost of sales. To maintain consistency we suggest that you take sales and deduct profit before tax, interest payable, selling and distribution costs and administration costs. In this example (£5,500m – £110m – £140m – £600m – £1,800m) which gives £2,850 million. Stock is taken from the current assets section of the balance sheet and will include raw materials, work in progress and finished goods. In this example it is £950 million.

Using this information we can calculate the stock turn:

$$\text{Stock Turn} \quad = \quad \frac{\text{Cost of Sales}}{\text{Stock}}$$

$$= \quad \frac{\text{£2,850 m}}{\text{£950 m}}$$

$$= \quad 3.0 \;\; \text{times}$$

A low stock turn ratio indicates that a company may be holding too much stock. The actual size of the ratio will depend upon the mix of stock held and the average holding in the industry. As a general rule, the higher the ratio the better.

If a company holds too much stock then there are potential disadvantages arising from the cost of holding stock, the possibility of obsolescence, and the cost associated with tying up additional working capital, to the detriment of other components within the working capital cycle.

4. Debtor Weeks

The debtor weeks ratio shows the number of weeks on average that debtors take to pay their invoices. It is calculated by multiplying debtors by the number of weeks in the period, then dividing the result by sales revenue for the period.

If we consider calculation of the ratio for our example company, debtors is taken from the current assets section of the balance sheet, i.e. £500 million. Sales revenue is taken from the profit and loss account, i.e. £5,500 million. Using this information we can calculate the debtor weeks as follows:

$$\text{Debtor Weeks} \quad = \quad \frac{\text{Debtors} \times \text{Number of Weeks in the period}}{\text{Sales for the period}}$$

$$= \quad \frac{£500 \text{ m} \times 52}{£5,500 \text{ m}}$$

$$= \quad 4.7 \text{ weeks}$$

The lower the debtor weeks ratio the more effective is the system of credit control and as a general rule, the lower the ratio the better. The actual size of the ratio will depend upon the mix of debtors between large, medium and small customers and the average holding in the industry.

A high debtor weeks ratio means that a company is allowing customers too much time to pay their debts. Other customers might follow by extending the time taken to pay. Furthermore, the cost of financing additional debtors, the possibility of increased bad debts, and tying up additional working capital often lead to detrimental effects on other components within the working capital cycle, e.g. a shortage of funds to finance stock requirements.

In addition to monitoring debtors weeks in aggregate, it is desirable where possible to undertake debtor age analysis to distinguish long outstanding debts from those that are more recent. For example, of the £500m debtors the following breakdown by age may be the case:

Less than 4 weeks,	£200m	40%
More than 4 weeks and less than 8 weeks	£250m	50%
More than 8 weeks	£50m	10%

It is recognised that the longer a debt is outstanding the less likelihood there is that payment will be made at all. For this reason most organisations will aim to decrease the proportion of long term debts outstanding as far as possible.

5. Working Capital Ratios, Summary

A summary of the four working capital ratios is given below:

1	Current Ratio	1.36 to 1
2	Liquid (or Acid Test) Ratio	0.50 to 1
3	Stock Turn	3.0 times
4	Debtor Weeks	4.7 weeks

4.4 Gearing Ratios

Businesses can secure finances from many sources, ranging from shareholders who are owners of the company to those who lend money to the business. One of the key distinctions between these two sources of financing is that, the interest payable on borrowed funds is deductible as an expense in calculating the tax payable. This is known as the 'tax shield'. Imagine a company with a £10m loan on which it is paying interest at 10%. The company's marginal rate of tax, is 25% and because of the deductability of the interest as an expense, the company will pay £750,000 that is 7.5% rather than 10%. The same does not apply, however, for funding from the issues of shares. In that case dividends are paid from after tax income and there is no tax shield.

From this you might be conclude that there is a distinct advantage for a company raising debt as opposed to equity. Depending upon relative rates of interest, this can be the case. By combining debt and equity, it can be shown that a company can lower the cost of its capital. However, there will come a point where increasing the proportion of debt to equity will be perceived as being a risk, first to new borrowers who might doubt the company's potential to service the interest and, second to shareholders who might be concerned at the very high level of debt relative to equity. As a consequence, beyond a certain level, it is generally thought that a company's cost of capital from taking on more debt will actually increase.

Thus, while there is an advantage in holding both equity and debt the relative proportions of each need to be carefully assessed for the risks involved. Hence we calculate 'gearing' ratios to measure the proportion of debt to equity and other measures to assess the firm's ability to service its debts from current profits.

As with other ratios there are different definitions of gearing depending on the interests of the users. In the following section we describe the two most popular measures of gearing: the borrowing ratio and the income gearing ratio.

1. Borrowing Ratio

The borrowing ratio is a very conservative measure showing the number of times total borrowings exceed equity. It is calculated by dividing total borrowings by equity (shareholders' funds).

Total borrowings is the sum of short-term loans (including bank overdraft) and long-term loans, in this example, £795m (£675m + £120m). Equity is the sum of issued share capital plus reserves, £680m (£130m + £550m). Reserves will include such items as share premium, revaluation reserve and profit and loss account.

Using this information we can calculate the borrowings ratio:

$$\text{Borrowing Ratio} = \frac{\text{Total Borrowings}}{\text{Equity}}$$

$$= \frac{£795 \text{ m}}{£680 \text{ m}}$$

$$= 1.17 \text{ to } 1$$

A high borrowing ratio simply indicates that a company has placed a greater reliance upon borrowing than equity to finance its operations. The higher the ratio the more highly geared the company is said to be. Although it should provide a higher return to its shareholders when the economy is experiencing boom conditions, during periods of increased interest rates, economic recession or simply loss of customers the opposite will apply. A company which has high gearing is particularly vulnerable and might find that it cannot continue to finance its borrowings.

2. Income Gearing

The income gearing ratio measures the extent to which interest payable is covered from pre-tax profits plus interest payable. It is calculated by dividing interest payable by profit before interest payable and taxation and expressing the result as a percentage.

Interest payable is taken from the profit and loss account, which for the example company is £140m. Profit before interest payable and taxation (PBIT) is the sum of profit before taxation plus interest payable, £250m (£110m + £140m). Using this information we can calculate the income gearing ratio as follows:

$$\text{Income Gearing} = \frac{\text{Interest Payable}}{\text{Profit Before Interest Payable and Tax}} \times 100$$

$$= \frac{£140 \text{ m}}{£250 \text{ m}} \times 100$$

$$= 56\%$$

The higher the income gearing ratio the greater the amount of available profit a company is liable to pay as interest. The income gearing ratio shows the effect of a company's gearing policy. For example, if a company increased its borrowings this would tend to increase the income gearing ratio. The income gearing ratio also shows the effect on a company of changes in economic circumstances. If interest rates rise or consumer demand fall, other things remaining equal, the income gearing ratio will worsen.

The income gearing ratio provides an indication of the ability to service debt commitments from profit. In the case of the example company, it can 'cover' interest payable just over one and three quarter times, that is the profit before interest payable and tax is 1.79 the size of the interest payable (£250m divided by £140m). When expressed in this form, the ratio is known as the interest cover ratio and is calculated as follows:

$$\text{Interest Cover} = \frac{\text{Profit Before Interest Payable and Tax}}{\text{Interest Payable}}$$

3. Gearing Ratios, Summary

A summary of the two gearing ratios is given below:

1. Borrowing Ratio   1.17 to 1

2. Income Gearing   56%

4.5 Employee Ratios

Organisations of all types try to ensure that they derive as much value as possible from the resources used. In many cases one of the most valuable, but also the most expensive of resources, is that associated with employees.

We illustrate four popular employee ratios used by a number of commercial organisations:

1.   Profit per employee

2.   Sales per employee

3.   Fixed assets per employee

4.   Borrowings per employee

1.   Profit Per Employee

The profit per employee ratio shows the £ value of profit before taxation (PBT) generated by each employee. It is calculated by dividing profit before taxation by the average number of employees.

In the case of the example company, profit before taxation is £110 million. The average number of employees is usually found in the Report of the Directors or in the notes to the accounts, in this example the figure is given, i.e. 35,000. Using this information we can calculate the profit per employee ratio.

$$\text{Profit Per Employee} \quad = \quad \frac{\text{Profit Before Taxation}}{\text{Number of Employees}}$$

$$= \quad \frac{£110 \text{ m}}{35,000}$$

$$= \quad £3,143$$

It is important to ensure that the average number of employees used as the denominator are stated in full time equivalents. In some companies, the average number of employees will include part-time employees working between say 8 and 30 hours per week. If this is the case then you should substitute aggregate remuneration for the denominator and express the result per £1,000 of employee remuneration. With employee remuneration given at £600 million the calculation would be:

$$\text{Profit Per £1,000} = \frac{\text{Profit Before Taxation}}{\text{Employee Remuneration}} \quad x \quad 1,000$$

$$= \frac{\text{£110 m}}{\text{£600 m}} \quad x \quad 1,000$$

$$= \text{£183}$$

In the above example, the result is stated as £183 profit per £1,000 remuneration.

2. Sales Per Employee

The sales per employee ratio shows the £ value of sales generated by each employee. It is calculated by dividing sales, taken from the profit and loss account, by the average number of employees.

$$\text{Sales Per Employee} = \frac{\text{Sales (Turnover)}}{\text{Number of Employees}}$$

$$= \frac{\text{£5,500 m}}{35,000}$$

$$= \text{£157,143}$$

3. Fixed Assets Per Employee

The fixed assets per employee ratio shows the £ value of fixed assets per employee. It is calculated by dividing fixed assets, taken from the balance sheet, by the average number of employees.

$$\text{Fixed Assets Per Employee} = \frac{\text{Fixed Assets}}{\text{Number of Employees}}$$

$$= \frac{\text{£400 m}}{35,000}$$

$$= \text{£11,429}$$

4. Borrowings Per Employee

The borrowings per employee ratio shows the £ value of borrowings attributable to each employee. It is calculated by dividing total borrowings by the average number of employees. Borrowings is the sum of short-term loans including bank overdraft and long-term loans of £795 million.

$$\text{Borrowings Per Employee} \quad = \quad \frac{\text{Total Borrowings}}{\text{Number of Employees}}$$

$$= \quad \frac{£795 \text{ m}}{35,000}$$

$$= \quad £22,714$$

Total borrowing per employee ratios should be compared against trends year-on-year or against competitors/industry figures. A low comparative ratio would indicate that a company was not utilising sufficient financing through debts and/ or it was overstaffed.

5. Employee Ratios, Summary

The strength and popularity of employee ratios is in their simplicity both in calculation and interpretation. A summary of all four ratios is given below.

1.	Profit per employee	£3,143
2.	Sales per employee	£157,143
3.	Fixed assets per employee	£11,429
4.	Borrowings per employee	£22,714

4.6   Investor Ratios

In this section we will demonstrate six ratios which can be used by the investor to assist in investment decisions. The same ratios can also be used by the directors to measure the effect management decisions might have on the future share price and dividends. These ratios are:

1.   Earnings Per Share.

2.   Price Earnings Ratio.

3.   Net Assets Per Share.

4.   Dividend Per Share.

5.   Dividend Yield.

6.   Dividend Cover.

1.   Earnings Per Share

Earnings per share is the only accounting ratio which is required by a financial reporting standard, i.e. FRS 14. The instructions for its calculation given in FRS 14 are an attempt to ensure that the ratio is calculated on a comparable basis as between one company and another.

Earnings per share is calculated by dividing profit attributable to shareholders by the average number of equity shares in issue and ranking for dividend in respect of the period.

Profit attributable to shareholders (earnings) is based on the consolidated profit for the period after taxation and after deducting minority interests and preference dividends, but before the deduction of extraordinary items. In this example £70 million. The number of equity shares is given, i.e. 520 million. Using this information we can calculate earnings per share.

$$\text{Earnings Per Share} = \frac{\text{Profit Attributable To Shareholders}}{\text{Number Of Shares}} \times 100$$

$$= \frac{£70 \text{ m}}{520 \text{ m}} \times 100$$

$$= 13.46 \text{ pence}$$

The earnings per share ratio is the basis for the calculation of a number of other investor ratios. It is also widely used at corporate level as a key measure of performance, i.e. companies are anxious to show that their earnings per share is increasing year-on-year. However, the ratio is not without its problems.

For example, an increase in earnings per share might be due to a decision to finance expansion though debt capital. In this case we would expect the profit attributable to shareholders to increase while the number of equity shares would remain constant. Is this a good sign, or a bad sign? What is the effect on the gearing?

2. Price Earnings (PE) Ratio

The price earnings ratio shows the relationship between the market price of shares and their earnings from the most recent published accounts. It is calculated by dividing the market price of an individual ordinary equity share by the earnings per share.

The market price of an individual equity share for a publicly quoted company is normally available in the financial press. In this example it is given as 110 pence and earnings per share was calculated in the previous section, i.e. 13.46 pence.

Using this information we can calculate the price earnings ratio.

$$\text{Price Earnings Ratio} = \frac{\text{Market Price Of Share}}{\text{Earnings Per Share}}$$

$$= \frac{110 \text{ pence}}{13.46 \text{ pence}}$$

$$= 8.17 \text{ times}$$

The price earnings ratio is expressed as a multiple, with the magnitude of the ratio providing some indication of how the market values the future earnings potential of a share. The emphasis here is upon the word future. The market will form a view about the future quality of earnings which will be expressed in the share price from which a PE ratio may be calculated. However, increases in earnings may not always bring about increases in the share price and, earnings may rise but not be associated with a share price increase.

There is no 'normal' level for price earnings ratios which differ over time, with industry sector and between countries. For example, price earnings ratios in July 1990 for companies classified in Textiles ranged from 3 to 57, but with most falling in the 6 to 13 range, while in the Banks, Hire Purchase and Leasing classification, price earnings ratios ranged from 4 to 50 but with most falling in the 8 to 15 range.

3. Net Assets Per Share

The net assets per share ratio shows the amount which each equity share is covered by the net assets of a company. It is calculated by dividing the net assets by the average number of equity shares in issue and ranking for dividend in respect of the period.

Net assets here is the sum of fixed assets (excluding intangibles) plus current assets minus current liabilities, taken from the Balance Sheet, in this example £800 million. The number of equity shares is given, i.e. 520 million.

Using this information we can calculate the net assets per share ratio.

$$\text{Net Assets Per Share} = \frac{\text{Net Assets}}{\text{Number Of Shares}} \times 100$$

$$= \frac{£800 \text{ m}}{520 \text{ m}} \times 100$$

$$= 153.85 \text{ pence}$$

The net assets per share ratio can produce misleading results because of the discretion that can be exercised in the valuation and depreciation policies to assets.

The net assets per share can be compared against the market price of a share. This usually takes the form of (market price per share ÷ net assets per share) which is known as the Market to Book, or MB ratio, a ratio we will review later within the context of business valuation.

There is benefit to be gained from knowing the amount by which the net assets cover the market share price. At times when a company is experiencing difficulties and the market share price falls, it is useful to identify the 'net asset backing'. As we have seen in the most recent recession, companies may be subject to serious speculation about their ability to generate both profit and cash flow. Such concern may well be expressed by a fall in the share price which can lead to vulnerability from predator companies. If the share price falls too far then a company may appear to be an attractive bargain. One defence against such situations is to monitor and communicate the net assets per share figure to existing shareholders. In such a calculation the directors will have to recognise realism by acknowledging that the values of assets in the Balance Sheet may differ substantially from their realisable value.

4.   Dividend Per Share

The dividend per share ratio shows the amount of gross dividend, in pence, allotted to each equity share. It is calculated by dividing the gross dividend for the period by the average number of equity shares in issue and ranking for dividend in respect of the period.

Dividend for equity shareholders is found in the profit and loss account, in this example £20 million. This is the net dividend i.e. after deduction for taxation. Assuming a personal tax rate of 25%, the gross dividend will be, £26.67m (£20m ÷ 0.75). The number of equity shares is given as follows i.e. 520 million.

Using this information we can calculate the dividend per share ratio.

$$
\text{Dividend Per Share} \quad = \quad \frac{\text{Gross Dividend}}{\text{Number Of Shares}}
$$

$$
= \quad \frac{£26.67 \text{ m}}{520 \text{ m}}
$$

$$
= \quad 5.13 \text{ pence}
$$

Dividend per share is an important indicator of a company performance, particularly to those shareholders who rely upon dividends as an income stream. In their case, an important investment criterion would be annual growth in dividends.

Investors normally expect to obtain either the same level of dividend as in previous years or an increased figure. Should a company reduce the amount of dividend payable per share, the immediate effect is often a substantial reduction in the market price of its shares and therefore its market capitalisation.

The dividend per share ratio can be compared to the earnings per share ratio to find the dividends as a percentage of earnings, known as the 'dividend payout'. In this case we have 13.46 pence available to payout, while the dividend per share indicates that we have 'paid out' 5.13 pence. This represents 38.1%

Dividend per share can also be used to calculate the dividend yield and dividend cover ratios, as we illustrate in 5 and 6 below.

5.   Dividend Yield

The dividend yield ratio shows the dividend payable on an equity share expressed as a percentage of the market price of a share. It is calculated by dividing the dividend per share by the market price of a share. This ratio provides an indication of the return generated on the investment in a share, that is the part of the return that is distributed.

Dividend per share was calculated earlier as being 5.13 pence and the market price of an equity share is given, i.e. 110 pence. Using this information we can calculate the dividend yield ratio.

$$\text{Dividend Yield} \quad = \quad \frac{\text{Dividend Per Share}}{\text{Market Price Of Share}} \quad \text{x} \quad 100$$

$$= \quad \frac{5.13 \text{ pence}}{110 \text{ pence}} \quad \text{x} \quad 100$$

$$= \quad 4.7 \ \%$$

6.   Dividend Cover

The dividend cover ratio shows the number of times dividend is covered by earnings attributable to shareholders. It is calculated by dividing the earnings per share by the dividend per share.

Earnings and dividend per share were calculated earlier as being 13.46 pence and 5.13 pence, respectively. Using this information we can calculate the dividend cover ratio as follows.

$$\text{Dividend Cover} \quad = \quad \frac{\text{Earnings Per Share}}{\text{Dividend Per Share}}$$

$$= \quad \frac{13.46 \text{ pence}}{5.13 \text{ pence}}$$

$$= \quad 2.62$$

7. Investor ratios, summary

1.	Earnings Per Share	13.46 pence
2.	Price Earnings	8.17 times
3.	Net Assets Per Share	153.85 pence
4.	Dividend Per Share	5.13 pence
5.	Dividend Yield	4.7%
6.	Dividend Cover	2.62 times

4.7 Corporate Ratios

In this section we focus upon corporate ratios which are particularly important to potential or actual investors. Our discussion will be based around the following three ratios:

1. Market to Book (MB)%

2. Price Earnings (PE)

3. Return on Equity (ROE)%

Please note that these ratios require the Market Price of an Ordinary Share. This is only available for quoted companies – therefore, not available for the majority of companies (who are not quoted). One other difficulty experienced by those wishing to undertake this analysis is in finding the share price for previous years; also, which share price should you take? year-end, high or low price for the year, an average of the high or low price. We would recommend consistency for example, using year-end prices.

1. Market to Book (MB)%

The MB% ratio shows the extent to which the market value of a company exceeds the book value of equity. Market value of equity (capitalisation) can be obtained by multiplying the market price of a share by the number of shares in issue during the period and the book value of owners' equity (shareholders' funds) is the sum of issued share capital plus reserves.

The MB% ratio is calculated as follows:

$$\text{MB\% Ratio} = \frac{\text{Market Value of Equity}}{\text{Book Value of Equity}}$$

$$= \frac{£572 \text{ m}}{£680 \text{ m}} \quad \text{x} \quad 100$$

$$= 84.1\%$$

This ratio provides an indication of the company's financial position as perceived by the market, but it has to be viewed with caution because book value can be influenced by accounting policy, such as the treatment of intangible assets like goodwill.

How should a MB% ratio be interpreted assuming no concern relating to accounting policy and the book value is realistic? A value of less than 100% would be worthy of attention because, by implication, the acquisition of such a company might be worthwhile simply for the purchase of its assets.

2. Price Earnings (PE) Ratio

The Price Earnings (PE) ratio was covered in *Section 4.6*. We will show the PE ratio calculated using Market Value of Equity divided by Profit Attributable to Shareholders. The only difference between this formulae and the one used in *Section 4.6* is that both the numerator and denominator of the ratio are multiplied by the number of shares in issue, therefore, we obtain the same result.

$$\text{PE Ratio} = \frac{\text{Market Value of Equity}}{\text{Profit Attributable to Shareholders}}$$

$$= \frac{£572 \text{ m}}{£70 \text{ m}}$$

$$= 8.17$$

3. Return On Equity (ROE)%

The Return on Equity ROE% ratio is a measure of shareholder profitability. ROE% ratio can be obtained by expressing the profit attributable to shareholders as a percentage of the book value of equity, where the book value of equity is the sum of issued share capital plus reserves.

The ROE% ratio is calculated as follows:

$$\text{ROE\% Ratio} = \frac{\text{Profit attributable to Shareholders}}{\text{Book Value of Equity}} \times 100$$

In other words, the equity figure used in the calculation is limited to funds provided by ordinary shareholders and excludes those provided from long-term borrowing. In addition, as indicated, the relevant measure of profit is the amount available for ordinary shareholders, after interest on borrowings and any other prior claims have been satisfied. You should be aware that for quoted companies it is possible to use the market value of equity in calculating ROE% which is sometimes referred to as the 'earnings yield'. When calculated in this way we take Earnings per Share (EPS) *(see section 4.6 for a discussion on earnings per share)* and express it as a percentage of the Market Price of a share.

This alternative ROE% ratio is calculated as follows:

$$\text{ROE\% Ratio} = \frac{\text{Earnings Per Share (EPS)}}{\text{Market Price of Share}} \times 100$$

From the information provided in *Table 4.1*, ROE% using **book value** is:

$$\text{ROE\% Ratio} = \frac{\text{Profit Attributable to Shareholders}}{\text{Book Value of Equity}} \times 100$$

$$= \frac{£70 \text{ m}}{£680 \text{ m}} \times 100$$

$$= 10.3\%$$

While ROE% using **market value** is:

$$\text{ROE\% Ratio} = \frac{\text{Earnings Per Share (EPS)}}{\text{Market Price of Share}} \times 100$$

$$= \frac{13.46p}{110p} \times 100$$

$$= 12.2\%$$

We have discussed financial ratios from a profitability, liquidity, gearing, employee, investor and corporate perspective. There is one other important perspective concerned with financial structure that we will consider in this section where we will draw together the ratios discussed so far within a single hierarchical framework. The basic components of this hierarchical framework is illustrated in *Figure 4.5*.

Figure 4.5 ROE%, Profitability and Gearing

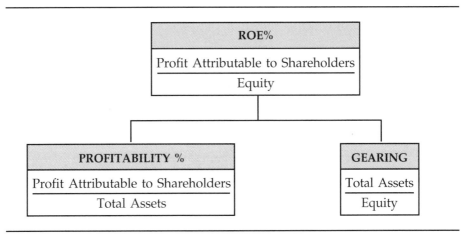

The key ratio in this hierarchical framework is ROE% which we saw earlier is calculated from the profit attributable to shareholders expressed as a percentage of equity. But, at the business level it is usual in the UK to use an appropriate profit figure that equates to operating profit, i.e. profit before any deductions for financing or taxation, rather than profit attributable to shareholders. This means that to include ROTA% in the hierarchy in *Figure 4.5* requires adjustments to be made to profit, as shown in *Figure 4.6*.

Figure 4.6 The Link Between ROE % and ROTA %

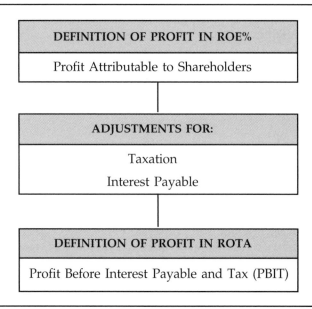

DEFINITION OF PROFIT IN ROE%
Profit Attributable to Shareholders

ADJUSTMENTS FOR:
Taxation
Interest Payable

DEFINITION OF PROFIT IN ROTA
Profit Before Interest Payable and Tax (PBIT)

Profit before interest payable and taxation can be obtained by taking the profit attributable to shareholders and adding back taxation and interest payable, an example of which is shown in *Table 4.5.*

Table 4.5 Adjustments for taxation and interest payable

	£'m
Profit Before Interest Payable and Taxation	250
less Interest Payable	140
Profit Before Taxation	110
less Taxation	40
Profit Attributable to Shareholders	70

Gearing and Gearing Ratios

You will recall that we have discussed ROTA% in *Section 4.2* of this chapter. We have also discussed two popular gearing ratios in *Section 4.4*. However, the ratio framework presented in *Figure 4.5* requires a different specification for a gearing ratio i.e. total assets divided by equity.

The ratio of total assets/equity, is one measure of financial risk known as 'gearing' ('leverage' in the USA). Risk comes from two main sources: business risk and financial risk. Businesses within the same trade may vary in the general volatility of their profits, but the future flow of profits for all businesses which operate in the same sector will often be subject to similar economic influences. The degree of financial risk, on the other hand, is specific and relates to a particular company choice between debt and equity funding. This financial risk is typically measured using gearing ratios which are regarded by the both the stock market and financial directors as being an important indicator of corporate exposure.

Loan financing is preferable to equity because the interest on it is chargeable against pre-tax profit and for this reason is typically cheaper than dividend payments to equity shareholders made from post-tax profits. However, against this benefit there is a disadvantage to be taken into consideration because of increasing financial risk with higher levels of debt financing and gearing. The nature of this financial risk and how to measure gearing we consider in this section.

Gearing can be calculated with reference to one or more of the following:

❑ book values of capital employed and equity from the balance sheet;

❑ book values of borrowings and equity from the balance sheet;

❑ market values of borrowings and equity;

❑ the impact of interest charges upon earnings.

We illustrated the gearing ratio earlier in the ratio framework in *Figure 4.5*, as being represented by total assets divided by equity. The result of calculating the gearing ratio using this approach is:

$$\text{Gearing} = \frac{\text{Total Assets}}{\text{Equity}}$$

$$= \frac{\text{£1,900 m}}{\text{£680 m}}$$

$$= 2.79$$

You may often find this ratio inverted and expressed as a percentage. When calculated in this way the gearing ratio is:

$$= \frac{\text{Equity}}{\text{Total Assets}} \times 100$$

$$= \frac{\text{£680 m}}{\text{£1,900 m}} \times 100$$

$$= 35.8\%$$

Whilst this measure fits well within the ratio framework, it is only one of many, and is less popular in practice than others such as:

$$\frac{\text{Debt}}{\text{Equity}} \times 100$$

and/or,

$$\frac{\text{Total Debt}}{\text{Total Assets}} \times 100$$

The latter of these two, sometimes called the 'debt ratio', measures the percentage of total funds provided by creditors. Debt includes current and long-term liabilities. Creditors will tend to prefer low debt ratios, because the lower the ratio, the greater the cushion against their losses in the event of liquidation. The owners, on the other hand, will may prefer relatively high gearing up to a point because it will result in higher earnings per share or because the alternative of issuing additional equity would mean giving up some degree of control. The debt ratio in this case would be:

$$\text{Debt Ratio} = \frac{\text{Total Debt}}{\text{Total Assets}} \times 100$$

$$= \frac{\text{£1,220 m}}{\text{£1,900 m}} \times 100$$

$$= 64.2\%$$

This measure focuses upon total debt and total assets, whereas concern may often be more directed at the relationship between alternative long term sources of finance. As a consequence you will find debt as a percentage of equity is a widely used measure of gearing. The advantage of this measure is that it is easier to gauge the impact of changes in the balance between debt and equity.

$$\text{Gearing Ratio} = \frac{\text{Long-Term Debt}}{\text{Equity}} \times 100$$

$$= \frac{£120 \text{ m}}{£680 \text{ m}} \times 100$$

$$= 17.6\%$$

A gearing ratio of 17.6% would not be viewed with concern, although the cautious analyst would look further to see whether any disguised debt existed.

Whatever measure of gearing is used, expansion through borrowing can be compared to the risks involved in stretching oneself to buy a new house. There is always a limit to a company's borrowing just as with an individual house purchase. A company's borrowing is typically limited by the value of it's assets and increases above a certain level will require shareholder approval together with the willingness of lenders to provide funds. Such restrictions can sometimes be overcome by regular asset revaluations and the inclusions of intangibles like brands, with the revised total asset base used to determine the amount of debt funding permitted. The inclusion of intangible assets while appearing to increase the total asset base, may not satisfy the shareholders nor the lenders.

4.8   Problems of Applying Financial Ratio Analysis

There are some potential problems of using financial ratio analysis in multi-division companies, which are frequently decentralised into divisions for organisational reasons. Often such divisions are defined as profit or investment centres, each with its own investment responsibility. Such investment responsibility for fixed and current assets and a share of general corporate assets like research laboratories and headquarters buildings, all form the base upon which a division is expected to earn an appropriate return.

For purposes of divisional control the term return on investment or ROI% is used. ROI% is typically expressed as a percentage of some measure of profit in relation to some measure of divisional investment. There is no universal standard for calculating ROI% and there are some factors that need to be taken into consideration. These are:

❑ *Depreciation.* ROI% *is* very sensitive to depreciation policy. If one division is writing off assets at a relatively faster rate than another, then its ROI% will be affected.

❑ *Asset life.* If a division is using assets that have been largely written off, both its current depreciation charge and its investment base will be low. As a consequence, its ROI% will be high in relation to newer divisions.

❑ *Transfer pricing.* The divisions in many multi-division companies trade with one another. Where this happens, the price at which goods are transferred between divisions will have a fundamental effect on divisional profits.

❑ *Divisional projects.* Divisions involved with projects having long gestation periods during which time expenditure is required upon research and development, plant construction, market development and the like, will often suffer an immediate increase in the investment base without an increase in profits for many years. During the life of such projects a divisions' ROI% can be seriously reduced and without proper constraints, its manager may be improperly penalised. If such companies have significant personnel transfers as a matter of course, then it is not difficult to see how the timing problem can keep managers from making long-term investments that are in the best interest of the company.

❑ *Industry conditions.* If one division operates in an industry where conditions are favourable in terms of earning high rates of return, while another is in an industry suffering from excessive competition, the differences may cause one division to look good and the other to look bad, even though the managers in both may be comparable.

Because of these factors, a division's ROI% is usually inadequate for evaluating performance. Some companies analyse comparative growth in sales, profits and market shares and adapt the use of ROI% to recognise the important differences between using ROI% in the measurement of a manager's performance, and in evaluating the worth of a past investment. A manager's performance can only be measured in relation to the assets under his/her control and a manager may have limited control over inherited fixed assets.

Appendix A: Total Assets or Net Assets

Bliss (1924) provides a useful definition of profitability when he writes 'The real measure of the earning power of a business is the operating profits earned on the total capacity used in such operations shown by the asset footing of the balance sheet'. Here it is not clear what he means by operating profits and these can be defined in a number of ways. What is clear, however, is the statement regarding the asset base – he means total assets.

Horngren (1970) confirms this when he states 'The measurement of operating performance (i.e. how profitably assets are employed) should not be influenced by the management's financial decisions (i.e. how assets are obtained). Operating performance is best measured by the rate of return on total assets'. Here again there is no precise definition given for profit, which it is assumed that he means 'rate of return'. While there is some debate regarding profit the use of total assets seems to be widely supported, with Dobson (1967) being one of the earliest writers in the UK to agree with and suggest the use of total assets.

The UK position of using net assets can be traced back to a report in Accountancy in 1956, on the findings of a BIM study group that stated 'It should be understood that capital employed is here regarded in terms of a statement of net operating assets, i.e. gross assets excluding intangible assets such as goodwill, less current liabilities, and this approach is necessary if further examination is to be made into the component parts of employed capital'. This statement has been the basis for the denominator of profitability ratios in the UK since that date.

Parker (1975) gives a fuller definition of the profitability ratio when he states the basis for profit and the basis for what he terms net tangible assets: "Profit is taken before interest and tax in order to separate managerial performance from the effects of different financial structures and from changes in tax rates" and 'Net tangible assets, (defined in his glossary as) Assets except for intangible assets, (goodwill, patents and trademarks), less current liabilities'.

Return On Net Assets (RONA) %

In this chapter we have outlined the calculation for the key profitability using total assets as the denominator i.e. ROTA%. We also showed the breakdown of ROTA% into the profit margin and the sales generation ratio.

In the UK, the ratio most commonly used is return on net assets (RONA)% i.e. profit before taxation and interest payable expressed as a percentage of net assets. Net assets is the sum of total assets minus current liabilities (or fixed assets plus net working capital).

It is important that we offer a word of caution about net assets. If you extract the figures from a published balance sheet you should be able to identify a description "total assets less current liabilities" which is the same as net assets for the purpose of financial ratio analysis. However, we often find the practitioner extracting 'net current assets' which is another name for net working capital and does not include fixed assets, and those described as net assets which, in published accounts, are after the deduction of long-term loans.

In what follows we will compare RONA% with ROTA% discussed earlier in this chapter.

Table 4.6 Basic Data

		Col. 1	Col.2	Col.3
Fixed Assets		5,000	15,000	15,000
+ Current Assets		45,000	45,000	45,000
Total Assets	(A)	50,000	60,000	60,000
Current Liabilities		30,000	40,000	30,000
Net Assets	(B)	20,000	20,000	30,000
PBIT	(C)	6,000	6,000	6,000

Table 4.6 Column 1, contains data extracted from a balance sheet. Column 2 and 3 both show the purchase of a fixed asset for £10,000, but in Column 2, the purchase is financed through short-term borrowings (included in the £40,000) whilst in Column 3 the purchase is financed using a long-term loan therefore, not included in current liabilities.

From the basic data in *Table 4.6*, the RONA% and ROTA% are:

		Col. 1	Col.2	Col.3
RONA%	((C) B (B) x 100	30%	30%	20%
ROTA%	((C) (A) x 100	12%	10%	10%

The most noticeable difference is in the absolute size of the ratios. Is it better to claim that the company is making a return on net assets of 30% or a return on total assets of only 12%.

On closer inspection we find with RONA% that the purchase of the fixed asset when financed through short-term borrowings has produced no increase in the profitability of the company, while with ROTA% there is a slight decrease. However, when long-term borrowings are used (i.e. column 3) there is a significant reduction in RONA% (i.e. 30% to 20%) while ROTA% shows no movement.

This example serves to illustrate that RONA% can be affected significantly by the method of finance used. A company which uses short-term finance to purchase fixed assets and generate the same profits as in the preceding period, RONA % will remain the same (the increase in fixed assets being offset by the increase in short-term borrowings).

Consider the position of a company in poor financial health that uses short-term finance (just to keep things going). Its fixed and current assets are also declining. During the early stages, this company could produce an increase in profitability when using RONA%.

ROTA%, which is the method we recommend, is unaffected by the method of financing assets. This is evident from our example where the same percentage results irrespective of the method of finance used i.e. 10% in column 2 and in column 3.

COMPANY
FINANCIAL
ANALYSIS

When you have finished studying this chapter you should be able to:

❏ Describe and set in context the non-financial approach for recognising corporate financial distress developed by Argenti.

❏ Describe and know when and how to apply Altman's 1968 ratio model.

❏ Describe the development and application of Robertson's 1983 ratio model.

❏ Carry out and analysis of a company using financial and non-financial techniques including:

- ratio analysis;
- ratio models;
- diary of events;
- common-size statements;
- cost analysis statements;
- non-financial indicators.

❏ Identify published sources of company information.

5.1   Introduction

Research by academics over the last 25 years or so has revealed that statistical and non-statistical approaches can be used for analysing financial and non-financial data in order to form a view about corporate financial health. What these approaches are and how they differ are considered in this chapter.

We have shown that a great deal of judgement needs to be used when calculating and applying financial ratios. This is equally true when using 'ready-made' information from data services such as *Datastream* despite their presentation of the ratios as a single score which may be compared against the appropriate benchmarks also supplied.

The combination of ratios and statistical technique has now made it possible to forecast the likelihood of financial failure with some degree of success.

5.2   Argenti's Non-Financial Indicators of Corporate Distress

When companies fail they tend to display non-financial signs of deterioration as well as financial ones. These non-financial indications include some elusive matters like 'bad management' and economic downturn, and others less elusive such as over-trading and excessive inventories.

Many individuals have considered the importance of non-financial factors but *Argenti* (1976) is noteworthy because of his attempt to rank the items in some order of importance.

To summarise the extent of corporate distress, Argenti has proposed an A-score. This is based on the assumption that, as a general rule, most companies fail for broadly similar reasons and in a broadly similar manner. The failure sequence is assumed to take many years, typically five or more, and to fall into three essential stages comprising:

1. Specific *defects* in a company's management and business practices in particularly at the very top.

2. Subsequently, possibly years later, top management makes a major *mistake* because of the specific defects.

3. Ultimately, signs and *symptoms* of failure begin to appear, manifest as financial and non-financial matters.

Argenti has discussed these three stages in more detail which we shall now consider.

1.   The Inherent Defects

The inherent defects identified by *Argenti* relate to:

a. Management.

b. Accountancy systems.

c. Change.

a. Management.

He identifies a major defect as being an autocratic chief executive, particularly where he or she is also the chairperson. Such an individual will tend to be viewed as being 'the company' and will be surrounded by people whose advice he/she has no intention of taking.

The board may consist of passive, non-contributing directors, arguably a desirable situation for an autocratic leader, but not for the company. Secondly, the directors may lack all-round business skills. Thirdly, there may be a lack of strong financial direction. Poor working capital management is often good evidence of this. For example, there may be no substantial cash flow forecasting making it difficult to manage future borrowing. Finally, a lack of management expertise below board level can lead to failure.

b. Accountancy Systems.

Companies that fail are often found to have poor or nonexistent accounting systems, a defect which can be related to poor financial direction. Other than working capital, budgetary control may be a particular problem. Either no budgets are prepared at all or the budgets are prepared but are not followed by adequate variance reports. The consequence is that employees do not know what is required of them or, if they do, they do not know whether they have achieved it.

Within such a defective accounting system costing may be a particular problem. Managers may not know what each product or service costs, and, if they do, they are not likely to be aware of the characteristics of reported costs, i.e. whether they are full costs or not.

c. Change.

Many companies that fail are those which have either not noticed a change in their business environment or have not responded to it. *Argenti* cites signs of such defects as being old-fashioned product, old-fashioned factory, out-of-date marketing, strikes attributable to outmoded attitudes to employees, an ageing board of directors, and no development of information management competencies, such as those associated with computerisation.

2. The Mistakes

Three mistakes are identified by *Argenti* as being responsible for failure.

a. Over-gearing.

b. Over-trading.

c. The 'big' project or contract.

a. Over-Gearing.

Companies dominated by ambitious autocrats and not constrained by a strong finance director are particularly prone to taking on a higher level of gearing than its financial situation should allow.

b. Over-Trading.

Over-trading occurs when a company expands faster than its ability to generate funding. Expanding companies often over-trade and become prone to failure by relying upon loan finance often of a short-term nature.

c. The Big Project.

Some companies are brought down by the failure of a large and over-ambitious project. A 'big project' can be physical, such as launching a major new product or service, but need not necessarily be tangible. The guaranteeing of a loan of a subsidiary company would fall within this category.

3. The Symptoms

Argenti identifies a number of symptoms which can be observed as a company moves toward failure.

a. Financial signs.

b. Creative accounting.

c. Other signs.

a. Financial Signs

Financial signs of failure such as deteriorating ratios were discussed in some detail in the previous chapter. Whilst of doubtless value their major shortcoming relates to their inability to indicate the likelihood of failure in a period of less than two or three years, unlike other non-financial symptoms.

b. Creative Accounting.

The prospect of failure has been known to encourage the accounting system to be used very imaginatively, particularly where financial information is required to be reported to outside parties. Such imagination, when not obviously exercised for reasons other than to mislead, is known as creative accounting. Such creativity may manifest itself in a number of areas. The treatment of depreciation is one example, for which the exercise of creativity is likely to be severely constrained by the role of the auditor.

c. Other Signs.

A company heading for failure may exhibit numerous non-financial signs of distress as well as financial ones. Examples of which are management salaries are frozen, capital expenditure decisions are delayed, product quality or service deteriorates, market share falls, the chief executive is ill, staff turnover rises, morale deteriorates, rumours abound, the dividend is not cut when there would seem to be sound reason for so doing.

At the very end of the process, when failure is imminent, all of the financial and non-financial signs become so severe that even the most casual observer can see them. These are referred to as terminal signs.

The framework developed by Argenti provides a useful checklist for identifying financial distress and potential failure. Argenti's 'A Score' aggregates individual defects to assess a company's failure potential and is shown in *Table 5.1.*

Table 5.1 Argenti's Failure Framework

Defects		
Autocrat		8
Chairman and Chief Executive		4
Passive Board		2
Unbalanced skills		2
Weak Finance Director		2
Poor Management Depth		1
No Budgetary Control		3
No Cash Flow Plans		3
No Costing System		3
Poor Response To Change		15
Total For Defects	**(A)**	43
Mistakes		
High Gearing		15
Over-trading		15
Big Project		15
Total For Mistakes	**(B)**	45
Symptoms		
Financial Signs		4
Creative Accounting		4
Non-Financial Signs		3
Terminal Signs		1
Total For Symptoms	**(C)**	12
Total overall possible score	**(A+B+C)**	**100**
Pass mark		**25**

Argenti recommends that the scores are given only if the observer is confident that an item is clearly visible in the company being studied. Only maximum or nil scores are allowed. This means that, for example, only if the observer is quite sure that the chief executive dominates the suspect company and has deliberately gathered a team of executives whose advice is ignored, a score of eight for 'autocrat' should be given, otherwise the score should be nil.

The overall pass mark according to the system is 25. Scores above that level are considered to show so many of the well-known signs which precede failure that the observer should be profoundly alarmed. Within the overall score, the sub-scores are also noteworthy. If a company scores more than the pass mark of 10 in the defects section, even if it scores less than 25 overall, it is viewed as being indicative of a company in danger of making one of the mistakes that lead to failure.

Argenti's approach to analysing indicators of corporate distress is valuable because it provides a useful checklist of issues and events that have been shown to be common to failing organisations. However, the scoring method he offers is highly subjective.

5.3   Altman's 1968 Ratio Model

In addition to the *Argenti* type approach, a number of researchers have developed financial/mathematical models. The most well known of these is the Z scoring model developed originally by *Professor Altman (1968)*. Using a statistical technique known as multiple discriminant analysis (MDA), long established for distinguishing between life forms in the natural sciences, Altman sought to determine whether any financial characteristics could be found to distinguish those firms that had failed from those which had not.

In developing his 1968 model, Altman selected 33 companies for the failed group. The criteria for selection required each company to be in manufacturing. The asset size ranged from $0.7 million to $25.9 million. The dates of the last set of accounts ranged from 1946 to 1965. The on-going group was selected using a paired sample, each failed company being paired with an on-going company both in terms of industry and size. The *Altman* approach can be summarised as follows:

1. Two matched groups of companies identified in the American manufacturing sector, one group comprising companies that have failed, the other a group of similar companies, known as on-going, that have not.

2. Financial ratios calculated for each group. Data for the failed group being taken from the last set of accounts while data for the on-going group being taken from the same year.

3. The statistical procedure is then designed to produce a single score (Z score) which can be used to classify a company as belonging to the failed group or the on-going group.

4. The intended result is the identification of a set of ratios that can be weighted and summed to give a Score (Z) indicative of potential as distinct from past failure.

From an initial list of 22 financial ratios, the final model consisted of five ratios together with their respective weights and is shown as follows:

$$Z = 1.2 X_1 + 1.4 X_2 + 3.3 X_3 + 0.6 X_4 + 1.0 X_5$$

In this model, Z is the sum of the ratios times the weights, and the individual ratios are defined as:

X_1 = Working Capital ÷ Total Assets

X_2 = Retained Earnings ÷ Total Assets

X_3 = Profit Before Interest and Tax ÷ Total Assets

X_4 = Market Value of Equity ÷ Book Value of Total Debt

X_5 = Sales ÷ Total Assets

In determining the Z score, the failed group and the on-going group are combined and ordered according to their individual Z scores. It is then possible to specify two limits as follows:

❏ an upper limit, where no failed companies are misclassified (none are included in the on-going), and;

❏ a lower limit, where no on-going companies are misclassified (none are included in the failed).

Altman's attempt to discriminate between these two groups of companies was not perfect and misclassifications did occur between the upper and lower limit. The area between the upper and lower limit is what Altman describes as the 'zone of ignorance' or the 'grey area', where a number of failed companies and/ or on-going companies were misclassified. The limits and the zone of ignorance arising from Altman's 1968 model are shown in *Figure 5.1*.

Figure 5.1   Determining the cut-off for Altman's 1968 model

> 2.99		On-Going Companies		
	Failed	2.99		
		2.78	On-Going	*Zone of*
		2.68	On-Going	*Ignorance*
	Failed	2.67		*or*
	Failed	2.10		*Grey*
	Failed	1.98		*Area*
		1.81	On-Going	
< 1.81		Failed Companies		

In order to 'force' a classification, Altman identified a score where the misclassifications would be minimised. This 'cut-off' was between 2.67 and 2.68 which resulted in only one failed company and one on-going company being misclassified. To achieve a single cut-off point Altman selected 2.675 the mid-point.

Example

Ratio models have an appeal since they lend themselves to spreadsheet application to arrive at the total score (in the Altman model, the Z score). They are also much easier to interpret. In the Altman model the Z score is used to classify the company into one of three groups i.e. the on-going group, the 'grey area' or the failed group.

One of the problems with ratio models is trying to determine how each of the ratios are calculated. In the top section of *Table 5.2* we provide the basic data required to calculate Z scores for Altman's model together with capital letters against each item. Please note that you will need to obtain the share price for each year of calculation; be consistent, we suggest that you take year-end prices.

In the bottom section of *Table 5.2* we show how to combine certain of the figures e.g. Working Capital equals Current Assets minus Current Liabilities (B – C).

Table 5.2   Basic data

Basic financial data		200X–1	200X
(A)	Fixed Assets	42,000	44,000
(B)	Current Assets	78,000	79,000
(C)	Current Liabilities	36,000	56,000
(D)	Retained Earnings	59,000	55,000
(E)	Long-Term Loans	25,000	12,000
(F)	Sales	155,000	175,000
(G)	Profit Before Tax	6,000	–3,600
(H)	Interest Payable	3,000	3,000
(I)	Number of Ordinary Shares	48000	48000
(J)	Share Price (pence)	300	180
Combining the figures		200X–1	200X
(K)	Working Capital (B – C)	42,000	23,000
(L)	Total Assets (A + B)	120,000	123,000
(M)	Profit before Tax + Interest Payable (G + H)	9,000	–600
(N)	MV of Equity (I x J ÷ 100)	144,000	86,400
(O)	Total Debt (C + E)	61,000	68,000

In *Table 5.3* below, we show the final calculations to arrive at the Z scores. For ratio X_1 we take the Working Capital figure from row (K) and divide it by Total Assets from row (L); the result is then multiplied by the weight for X_1 i.e. 1.2 to arrive at a figure of 0.42 for 1998. Similar calculations are performed for the remaining ratios X_2 to X_5. The Z score is the sum of ratios X_1 to X_5 giving a total of 4.05 for 1998.

Table 5.3   Altman's 1968 ratio model

		Weight	200X–1	200X
X_1	Working Capital ÷ Total Assets	1.2	0.42	0.22
X_2	Retained Earnings ÷ Total Assets	1.4	0.69	0.63
X_3	PBIT ÷ Total Assets	3.0	0.23	−0.01
X_4	MV of Equity ÷ Total Debt	0.6	1.42	0.76
X_5	Sales ÷ Total Assets	1.0	1.29	1.42
	Z Score		4.05	3.02

Interpretation is against a cut-off, above 2.67 and the company is unlikely to fail in the coming year. In this example the total Z score is above 2.67 for the years 1998 and 1999.

5.4   Application of Corporate Failure Models

1.   Specific Industry Group

Financial ratio models like Z scoring should be developed for specific industry groups only. The model cannot be successfully used across industry boundaries.

In practice it can be difficult to know whether a particular company 'fits' the industry requirement of a model, e.g. a model developed for manufacturing companies can only be used for manufacturing companies. This can be found in *Altman (1982)* where a list of 42 companies included those with names such as:

Allied Supermarkets;

City Stores;

Commonwealth Oil Refining;

General Recreation;

Mays Department Stores;

Murphy Pacific Marine Salvage Co.;

Sambo's Restaurants Inc.;

Shulman Transport Enterprises;

White Motors;

Wilson Freight.

While Altman did not indicate the industry type it seems unlikely, given contemporary industry classifications, that any of the above companies fits the American manufacturing company classification.

Taffler (1980), demonstrated the need to recognise the industry type when he developed a separate distribution model. This means that each industry certainly needs its own model but whether different models should be used for each country is a moot point. Perhaps, in an ideal world, each company would have a model specifically designed for its own peculiar circumstances.

2.   Using a Model to Observe Trends.

Corporate prediction models are developed to operate on a single year's data. This means that the latest year's data is used to predict the possibility of failure. *Barnes (1984)* is particularly critical of the idea of observing Z score trends when he states that "it involves using discriminant coefficients for one period for financial ratios and Z scores for another".

3.   Changing the Specification of the Ratios

The ratios contained in a model are determined at the time when the model is developed. Changing the specification of a ratio requires a complete re-evaluation of the model; perhaps even resulting in another ratio being chosen as doing the best job.

The main reason for wanting to change the specification of a ratio has centred on ratio X_4 in Altman's 1968 model. Ratio X_4 is a short-term gearing ratio and is stated as market value of equity divided by the book value of debt. This ratio effectively restricts the use of the model to those companies that are quoted on a stock exchange. For example, a company not quoted will not have a market value of equity. As a consequence, one might be tempted to substitute the book value, that is shareholders' funds inclusive of reserves. The result is not the same, as *Altman (1983)* has illustrated.

He recalculated the Z score using the book value rather than the market value of equity for the same two groups of companies he used to develop the 1968 model. Changing ratio X_4 to the book value of equity divided by the book value of debt produced the following changes to the weights shown in *Table 5.4*.

Table 5.4   *Change to weights – by adjusting Ratio X₄*

		1968 Model	1983 Revised	% Change
X₁	Working Capital	1.2	0.717	40.3
X₂	Retained Earnings	1.4	0.847	39.5
X₃	Profitability	3.3	3.107	5.8
X₄	Gearing	0.6	0.420	30.0
X₅	Asset Utilisation	1.0	0.998	0.0

From the above it can be seen that a small change to the specification of an individual ratio produces substantial changes to the weights assigned to other ratios in the model. Furthermore, the 1.81 cut-off in the 1968 model is amended to 1.23 as a result of the revision to ratio X_4.

5.5   Robertson's 1983 Ratio Model

In addition to statistically oriented approaches other models have been developed. *Robertson* (1983) has developed a model which measures changes in financial health which:

❏ Suggests key elements (ratio categories) identifiable in failed companies and then constructs ratios to measure each element.

❏ Uses simple weights, to compensate for the natural differences in the individual ratio values, to arrive at a single score.

❏ Interprets the score by measuring changes in financial health from previous periods i.e. measuring changes in the score year-on-year; traditional interpretation follows this procedure.

❏ Identifies changes in financial health and allows examination of the individual ratio movements in order that corrective action can be taken.

The final model comprised of the following ratios each of which have been described in the previous section. The ratios are referred to by using R_1 to denote ratio 1 through to R_5 to denote ratio 5.

$$R_1 = (\text{Sales} - \text{Total Assets}) \div \text{Sales}$$

$$R_2 = \text{Profit before Taxation} \div \text{Total Assets}$$

$$R_3 = (\text{Current Assets} - \text{Total Debt}) \div \text{Current Liabilities}$$

$$R_4 = (\text{Equity} - \text{Total Borrowings}) \div \text{Total Debt}$$

$$R_5 = (\text{Liquid Assets} - \text{Bank Borrowings}) \div \text{Creditors}$$

The financial change model (FCM) takes a similar form to *Altman's* 1968 model where the total score is found:

$$FCM = 0.3R_1 + 3R_2 + 0.6R_3 + 0.3R_4 + 0.3R_5$$

The model was developed using a systems approach. This required a statement of 'key elements' identifiable in failed companies, followed by the development of ratios which have individual meaning and will help to measure each of the elements; finally the provision for feedback (by observing the movements in the scores obtained from the individual ratios) to allow corrective action to be taken if necessary.

1.   Key elements

The identification of the key elements was produced using literature, especially *Argenti's* failure process (discussed earlier) also from a detailed examination of the data already collected for eight failed companies. The 'key elements' identifiable in failed companies were:

❑ **Trading Instability**

Most failing companies experience a fall in sales generated from their asset base. This is true both of the declining product life cycle and the rapid expansion or over-trading company.

❑ **Declining Profits**

The conditions encountered in trading instability can erode a company's profit margins and when combined with other uncontrolled costs can result in substantial losses.

❑ **Declining Working Capital**

If not checked, declining profits can lead to a decline in working capital, accelerating if the company turns into a loss situation. Further reductions in working capital can be caused by continued expansion of fixed assets, especially when financed from short-term borrowings.

❑ **Increase in Borrowings**

Instead of tackling the problem of trading instability and profitability, the failing company increases borrowings to maintain its required level of working capital. This has a double effect in that:

a. It further reduces profits through additional interest payments.

b. It increases the gearing of a company at a time when it is most vulnerable.

The selection of ratios to be included was considered to be the most important factor in the development of the model. Each ratio was selected to reflect the elements that cause changes in a company's financial health.

2.   The Ratios Finally Selected

R_1 (Sales – Total Assets) ÷ Sales

This is a measure of trading stability. It highlights the important relationship between assets and sales. When a company increases it asset base it is looking for a corresponding increase in sales. Companies experiencing trading difficulties are unable to maintain a given level for this ratio. Deterioration indicates a fall in the sales generated from the asset base. If the ratio is maintained it can produce a stabilising effect even for a company that is failing.

R_2 Profit Before Taxation ÷ Total Assets

Profit is taken after interest expense but before tax, because failing companies borrow more and suffer increases in interest payments in the years to failure. Total assets exclude intangibles and are used as the base because they are not influenced by financing policies and tend to remain constant or increase. Failing companies tend to show a decline in profits in the years to failure, often turning into a loss. The deterioration in profit is sufficient to cause this ratio to fall. However many companies are involved in rapid expansion and this, if present, could cause a further decline in the ratio.

R_3 (Current Assets – Total Debt) ÷ Current Liabilities

This is an extension of the net working capital ratio, and requires that long-term debt is also deducted from current assets. It measures a company's ability to repay its current debt without selling fixed assets. When compared over a number of years, failing companies show a marked deterioration in this ratio due to the current assets falling while total debt remains constant or even increases.

R$_4$ (Equity – Total Borrowings) ÷ Total Debt

This is a gearing ratio. A low ratio indicates a high proportion of debt which means high gearing with associated high risk. Failing companies experience a drop in equity through a combination of losses in operations and reorganisation/extraordinary costs, while at the same time borrowings tend to increase. This can turn a healthy balance in favour of equity into a negative balance where borrowings exceed equity. Should a company not borrow but instead obtain additional funds from shareholders, then this will have a stabilising effect and reduce the risk of moving toward high gearing and associated interest payments. It will also help to reduce borrowings and improve liquidity ratios.

R$_5$ (Liquid Assets – Bank Borrowings) ÷ Creditors

This ratio tests changes in immediate liquidity. After deducting bank borrowings from liquid assets it is then possible to measure the immediate cover for creditors. Increasing bank borrowings incurs additional financing costs for current and future periods and might require the company to agree to a fixed and/or floating charge over its assets.

3.   Weights

The weights used were selected to adjust the natural values obtained from certain ratios. For example, the ratio of profit before tax divided by total assets could only, at best, produce a natural score of 0.20 (equivalent to a 20% return on total assets) while a liquidity ratio or a gearing ratio could easily produce a natural score of 1.00 or more. In this case the weights allow the profit ratio to be increased and/or the liquidity or gearing ratios to be reduced. Weights can also be used to increase the effect of one ratio and/or reduce the effect of another.

Each ratio should contribute equally to the overall score and by a series of simple arithmetic calculations a set of weights applicable to a group of companies (or even a single company) was arrived at. The resulting weights should be easy to use and experiments were carried out by changing the weights (for example doubling and halving a ratio weight). This showed, contrary to expectations, that changes in individual ratio weights did not significantly affect the total score when comparing a company year-on-year.

4.   Interpretation of the Score

In traditional ratio analysis, the same ratios are used across 'industries' with ratio values being interpreted by observing the movements from previous periods or from an industry average. Given that the model was developed for use across 'industries', it is appropriate to use similar interpretation, i.e. observing the movements in the total (and individual) scores.

In testing the model it was found that, when the total score fell by approximately 40 percent or more in any year, substantial changes had taken place in the financial health of a company. Immediate steps should be taken to identify the reasons for the change and take remedial action. If the score falls by approximately 40 percent or more for a second year running, the company is unlikely to survive, unless drastic action is taken to stop the decline and restore financial health.

In practice, the model should be used to identify all movements in the total score; further checks should then be carried out on the individual ratios contained in the model in order that action be taken to correct the situation.

5.   Example

In this example we will use the same basic data from the Altman model, please note that there are some additional figures, while others are not required. In the top section of *Table 5.5* we provide the basic data required to calculate the total score for Robertson's model together with capital letters against each item. In the bottom section of *Table 5.5* we show how to combine certain of the figures e.g. Total Assets is the sum of Fixed Assets plus Current Assets (A + B).

Table 5.5   Basic data

Basic Financial data			200X–1	200X
(A)	Fixed Assets		42,000	44,000
(B)	Stock		40,000	45,000
(C)	Current Assets		78,000	79,000
(D)	Bank Overdraft		8,000	26,000
(E)	Creditors		25,000	30,000
(F)	Current Liabilities		36,000	56,000
(G)	Shareholder's Fund		59,000	55,000
(H)	Long-Term Loans		25,000	12,000
(I)	Sales		155,000	175,000
(J)	Profit Before Tax		6,000	-3,600
Combining the figures			200X–1	200X
(K)	Total Assets	(A + B)	120,000	123,000
(L)	Total Debt	(F + H)	61,000	68,000
(M)	Current Assets – Total Debt	(C – L)	17,000	11,000
(N)	Equity (Shareholder's Fund)	(G)	59,000	55,000
(O)	Total Borrowings	(D + H)	33,000	38,000
(P)	Equity – Total Borrowings	(N – O)	26,000	17,000
(Q)	Liquid Assets	(C – B)	38,000	34,000
(R)	Liquid Assets – Bank Borrowings	(Q – D)	30,000	8,000

In *Table 5.6* below, we show the final calculations to arrive at the total scores. For ratio X_1 we take the Sales figure from row (I) and deduct Total Assets from row (K), the result is then divided by Sales from row (I) and multiplied by the weight for X_1 i.e. 0.3 to arrive at a figure of 0.07 for 1998. Similar calculations are performed for the remaining ratios X_2 to X_5. The total score is the sum of ratios X_1 to X_5, giving a value of 0.99 for 1998

Table 5.6   Robertson's 1983 ratio model

		Weight	200X–1	200X
R_1	(Sales – T.Assets) ÷ Sales	0.3	0.07	0.09
R_2	Profit Before Tax ÷ Total Assets	3	0.15	-0.09
R_3	(C.Assets – T.Debt) ÷ C.Liabilities	0.6	0.28	0.12
R_4	(Equity – T.Borrowings) ÷ T.Debt	0.3	0.13	0.08
R_5	(L.Assets – B.Borrowings) ÷ Creditors	0.3	0.36	0.08
	Total Score		0.99	0.28

Interpretation is on the movement in the total score year-on-year. The suggestion is that a fall of more than 40% indicates a significant decline in the financial health of a company. In this case we can see that there is a decline well above the 40%.

The model then allows examination of each of the individual ratio components to identify where the decline has taken place. The analyst should then revert to using traditional ratio analysis to drill down and find the cause(s). In this case we can see that the decline is spread over ratios R_2 to R_5 i.e. profitability, liquidity and gearing.

5.6   Economic Profit, Economic Value Added (EVA®), and Strategic Value Added (SVA)

EVA® has been attracting much attention. It is an approach to assessing performance that analyses a business in terms of the economic profit earned in a given time period after deducting all expenses, including the opportunity cost of capital employed. In other words, a business is only 'truly' profitable in an economic sense if it generates a return in excess of that required by its providers of funds, i.e. shareholders and investors. Economic profit is not a new idea. Alfred Sloan, the patriarch of the *General Motors Corporation* is reckoned to have adopted the principles of economic profit in the 1920s, and the *General Electric Co.* coined the term 'residual income' in the 1950s, which it used to assess the performance of its decentralised divisions [1].

---

[1] McConville, D. J., 'All about EVA', Industry Week, April: 13–14, 1994, pp. 1–3.

Economic profit recognises that the one major cost that the conventional profit and loss account does not take into account is the cost of the capital used in generating profit. Consequently with economic profit, from the net operating profit after tax (NOPAT) a capital charge is deducted based on the product of the capital invested in the business and the cost of capital.

Economic Profit = NOPAT – (Invested Capital x Cost of Capital)

For example, given a NOPAT of £1m, Invested Capital of £10 m and a cost of capital of 5%, the Economic Profit = £1m – £500,000, i.e. £500,000.

What can be the attraction of using economic profit type approaches? There are arguably many, but there is one that seems to be particularly noteworthy and which has not been given a great deal of attention. Many organisations have developed performance assessment approaches that relate the profit generated in a given time period to the asset base, or capital employed in generating it.

As has been illustrated, the Return on Assets approach can be developed as a framework for assessing company performance along a number of dimensions. Relatively poor performance in terms of the Return on Assets generated in a given time period can be viewed in terms of margins (Return on Sales) and asset utilisation (Sales Generation). This Return on Assets can also be linked to capital structure (Gearing) and the markets perception of performance (Price Earnings and Market-Book).

Figure 5.2   Hierarchy of ratios and link with the cost of capital

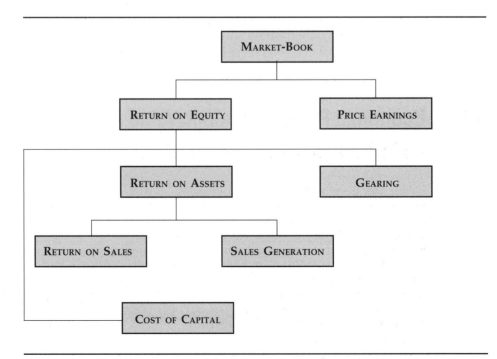

It can take a long time to implement performance assessment measures within companies, a point so often under estimated. As illustrated in *Figure 5.2*, the advantage of economic profit type approaches is that they can be linked to such conventional performance assessment frameworks. We will return to this topic in more detail in *Chapter 12*.

5.6   Working with Published Accounts

We have considered the make-up of corporate reports and the general principles for their analysis using financial ratios in earlier chapters. However, financial ratio analysis is only one tool for interpreting published information much of which may be non-financial in nature.

In this chapter we consider how the published information provided in corporate reports of both a financial and non-financial nature may be analysed in a structured manner to permit useful interpretation. We will use the *Polly Ester Holdings plc* case study which is included in *Appendix A, pages 409–418*. It might be useful to obtain a photocopy of the case study to allow easier access to the material. The following points should be noted:

1. The *Polly Ester* case study is used to demonstrate the strengths and weaknesses of financial ratio analysis. The case is chosen since it provides ideas and allows similar analysis to be undertaken on data for any company.

2. The case also shows the different levels of analysis which can be achieved with the use of the notes to the accounts.

3. Please be aware that the ratios for many companies are stable year-on-year i.e. there is little movement in any of the ratios. This makes it extremely difficult to permit useful interpretation.

4. The sections which address each group of financial ratios include both a description and interpretation. It is not intended that this should be taken as a specimen or suggested answer to the financial analysis of the case.

5. In the early stages of your analysis it is extremely useful to 'build' spreadsheet models. This will allow you to experiment with the data.

6 . Financial ratio analysis is simply one of a number of analysis techniques required for appropriate interpretation. The development of basic strategy models such as SWOT, can be used to identify changes year-on-year.

7. It is also important to collect published and commercial material on your chosen company, as well as those of competitors. This should make it easier to provide realistic explanations of any movements observed in the financial ratios.

1. Diary of Events

Corporate reports do in fact contain much useful information but it may not necessarily be (and is not usually) organised in the most appropriate way to permit analysis. All too often the inexperienced analyst will focus attention upon hard forms of analysis like the calculation of ratios without setting the scene appropriately.

In this section we will consider how to organise the information provided in a useful way via the diary of events. You will find this invaluable for both interpreting corporate reports in practice and for their analysis in business strategy.

A diary of events is a log of significant changes which have taken place in a company during the year under consideration. It should be directed both at financial and non-financial information obtained primarily from published accounts, but which may be supplemented with that from other sources.

What form should the diary of events take? We have provided a basic checklist in *Figure 5.3*.

Figure 5.3   Diary of Events

AUDIT REPORT

Have the accounts been qualified?

DIRECTORS

Have there been any significant movements in key personnel e.g. resignations/appointments?

Are there any non-executive directors?

Who are the non-executive directors?

TRADING STABILITY

Is the company losing its way e.g. unrelated diversification?

Are there any statements on deterioration in the marketplace?

Are there statements referring to "Worst year in company's history"?

Are there signs that the company is over-trading?

BORROWINGS

Is there evidence that the company has agreed to a fixed and/or floating charge on all assets?

How many banks does the company use?

FIXED ASSETS

Is the company selling off key assets?

Is there evidence of over-commitment to a big project which could cause the downfall of the company?

ACCOUNTS

Is there evidence of delay in paying bills, e.g. long creditor days?

Is there evidence of a delay in publishing the annual report?

SALES by activity and PROFIT by activity

Is there any significant movement in sales or profitability by activity?

CAPITAL EXPENDITURE

Is the company expanding from organic growth?

Is there evidence of expansion by acquisition?

ACCOUNTING POLICY AND TREATMENT

Has the company made any significant changes to its accounting policy and the treatment of key items, e.g. goodwill and brands?

Table 5.7   A simplified Diary of Events

Movements in:		1995/96	1996/97	1997/98
Sales	£'000	170,900 to 201,500	201,500 to 252,400	252,400 to 296,600
	%	17.9	25.3	17.5
Fixed Assets	%	22.5	13.5	1.4
Borrowings	%	146	23.3	76.1
No. of Shops		73	74	
Acquisitions		Green & Gillies Pencosmo		Nufurnish. Ind.Inc.
Disposals				Green & Gillies
Other		New textile plant		Franchise – Styleright
Directors				
Resignations		R.J. Somers	P. Peters	A. Moorhouse
Appointments				H. Waterman

Table 5.7 shows a simplified version of the Diary of Events. From the movement in sales it must be asked, how much longer could the company achieve increases in sales in excess of 17% per annum?

The comparison of the percentage increases in fixed assets when compared to the percentage increases in borrowings is stark. Further analysis shows a substantial increase in fixed assets 1995/96 due to an increase in new shops, acquisitions of *Green and Gillies* and *Pencosmo* and the addition of a new textile plant. 1997 was a year of consolidation, or was it? The diary of events does not provide any surprises, except for the resignation of P. Peters towards the end of the year. 1998 saw the purchase of *Nufurnishing Industries Inc*, a franchise deal with *Styleright* and the disposal of *Green and Gillies* having spent considerable cash over the previous two years since its purchase.

From the above it can be seen that the Diary of Events provides useful data and will assist the analyst when undertaking a full interpretation of a company.

2.   Common Size Statement base year = 100

The Common Size Statement (in this case indexing all financial data to a base year 1995) will used to highlight those figures that show extreme movements, or simply those that are out of line with, say, activity.

Table 5.8   *Common Size Statement for Polly Ester Holdings plc*

	1995	1996	1997	1998
Fixed Assets	100	122.5	139.1	141.0
Investments	100	100.0	100.0	140.0
Stock	100	146.8	166.6	230.3
Debtors	100	126.4	173.6	228.1
Current Assets	100	137.0	160.0	212.5
Bank Overdraft	100	432.9	103.8	1084.8
Creditors	100	136.6	197.3	272.1
Current Liabilities	100	184.6	133.5	333.7
Share Capital	100	107.9	116.7	106.6
Long-Term Loans	100	75.9	483.9	33.3
Sales	100	117.9	147.7	173.6
Cost of Sales	100	119.2	164.6	210.4
Profit Before Tax	100	102.7	90.2	–7.1
Interest Payable	100	184.6	384.6	669.2
Retail and Distribution Costs	100	121.0	152.0	184.1
Administration Costs	100	114.1	128.2	177.3
Retail Space (sq mtr)	100	122.2	139.6	153.4

The Common Size Statement in *Table 5.8* shows an increase in Retail space over the period of 53.4%, while retail and distribution costs have increased by 84.1% and bank overdraft by a staggering 1,084.4%.

Stocks, Debtors and Creditors have risen faster than the retail space or sales income. A substantial decline in profit before tax over the period 1997/98 together with an increase in interest payable.

3.   Cost Analysis Statement year-on-year

The Common Size Statement shows that there are many significant changes throughout the period. It will now be useful to consider some in more detail. First we will prepare a Cost Analysis Statement showing changes in income and costs year-on-year. This can be reconciled to the changes in the Profit before tax figures year-on-year.

Table 5.9   Cost Analysis Statement year-on-year

	1995/96 £'000	1996/97 £'000	1997/98 £'000
Sales	30,600	50,900	44,200
Cost of Sales	12,600	29,800	30,000
Retail and Distribution Costs	11,800	17,400	18,000
Administration Costs	3,900	3,900	13,600
Interest Payable	1,100	2,600	3,700
Miscellaneous –Income +Cost	700	0	800
	30,100	**53,700**	**66,100**
	500	–2,800	–21,900
Profit / –Loss before tax	500	–2,800	–21,900
Included in the above:			
Operating Lease/Hire Charges	3,100	1,800	5,100
Staff Costs	11,100	9,700	11,800
Depreciation	4,300	2,300	2,700
Exchange differences –fav +adv	0	–1,100	–5,700
	18,500	**12,700**	**13,900**

In *Table 5.9* above we can see that the incremental sales income for the period 1997/98 was £44.2 million while the incremental increase in costs was £66.1 million which produced a reduction in the Profit before tax of £21.9 million.

When we examine the figures for 1997/98 it can be seen that the cost of sales and retail and distribution cost increases are in line with the previous year even though incremental sales have fallen. Given a similar decrease in costs for both items, cost of sales should be nearer to £25.9 million and retail and distribution costs nearer to £15.1 million. An indication that an additional £7 million was 'consumed' given the pro-rata movement.

Still considering the figures for 1997/98 the most obvious movement is in administration costs, a £13.6 million increase or £9.7 million over the 1996/97 increase. Taking either figure it is difficult to justify these movements.

In the bottom section of the statement we show a breakdown of some of the cost increases included in the top section. An interesting movement is the £11.8 million increase in staff costs of 1997/98. Looking at the three year period we see substantial increases in staff costs, 1995/96; £11.1 million and 1996/97; £9.7 million, some £32.6 million in the three years.

4. Robertson's 1983 Ratio Model

Earlier in this chapter it was seen that *Robertson's 1983 ratio model* measures changes in financial health year-on-year. The model can either be used as the beginning of any analysis to highlight where movements have taken place, then use basic ratio techniques to identify the source(s) of the problem. Similarly, it can be used at the end of a report to substantiate the earlier interpretation. We prefer to use it at the beginning. In this way it can be used as a course screen, say in credit control, to identify those companies that require further analysis.

Table 5.10 Robertson's 1983 Ratio Model

	1995	1996	1997	1998
(Sales – T.Assets) ÷ Sales	0.09	0.07	0.08	0.08
Profit Before Tax ÷ Total Assets	0.56	0.44	0.34	−0.02
(C.Assets – T.Debt) ÷ C.Liabilities	0.20	0.04	0.05	−0.02
(Equity – T.Borrowings) ÷ T.Debt	0.31	0.12	0.09	−0.03
(L.Assets – B.Borrowings) ÷ Creditors	0.16	−0.17	0.14	−0.34
Total Score	1.32	0.50	0.70	−0.33

Early development of the model suggested that a decline in the score in excess of 40% would indicate that substantial changes had taken place in the financial health of a company. This has been modified over the years to examine other movements, especially if they are the result of a change to one of the five component ratios.

In this case, we don't have to use a calculator. We can see that a decline in excess of 40% has occurred in the period 1995/96 and in the period 1997/98. The model punishes any increase in borrowings. Should the subsequent activity of a company benefit from these borrowings then the score will improve. However, many companies do not benefit from an increase in borrowings. We will check this out in a later section when we interpret changes in the gearing ratios. Similarly, in 1997/98 there is a substantial decline in profitability and this will be examined in the next section.

5. Profitability Ratios

In this section we will use the analysis in *Table 5.11* to compare the results obtained by four different specifications for a profitability ratio. These are:

1. Profit before tax (PBT) expressed as a percentage of total assets. This is the preferred method when interpreting changes in profitability ratios year-on-year. It does not allow interest paid to be added back since this should only apply when comparing one company against another i.e. to remove the effect of differences in gearing, one company to another. It also takes total assets as the denominator. In this case an increase in total assets will require, all other things being equal, an increase in profit before tax and vice versa.

2. The second option takes profit before tax expressed as a percentage of total assets less current liabilities. The same numerator as the first option but a different denominator. Total assets less current liabilities is the favoured option in the UK but suffers from its lack of robustness with respect to current liabilities. For example an increase in short-term borrowings will not require any further increase in profits for a company still to be as profitable. Also, a movement from short-term borrowings to long-term borrowings will reduce profitability. It can be seen that the practice of deducting short-term borrowings from total assets severely affects the profitability of a company.

3. The third option takes profit before tax and before the payment of interest (PBIT) expressed as a percentage of total assets less current liabilities. This is the favoured profitability ratio used in the UK. It can be seen that it suffers from, i. adding back interest payable for the numerator and, ii. deducting current liabilities from total assets for the denominator.

4. The fourth option takes profit before tax and before the payment of interest (PBIT) expressed as a percentage of net assets (total assets less current liabilities less long-term loans). This ratio has a number of disagreeable features and will tend to overstate profitability.

In *Table 5.11*, it can be seen that the first option shows a substantial decrease in profitability for the period 1998. It is caused mainly by a decrease in the profit margin (profit before tax expressed as a percentage of sales). What causes a decrease in the profit margin? Either a decrease in income (selling prices) and/or an increase in costs. From the Cost Analysis Statement, *Table 5.9*, it was seen that there was a decrease in the incremental sales (income) for the period and a substantial increase in costs .

The Cost Analysis Statement provides us with the explanations for the decline in profitability. This is backed up with the statement in the case study that the decline in profitability was: 'a loss of margin in overseas core business, substantial start-up losses in *Green and Gillies* and a sharp increase in interest charges. Also:

> *'the reduction in margin can be attributed to the fact that, as sterling based manufacturer, the group has passed the point where they can raise prices to their customers to compensate for the effects on an overvalued pound, particularly in their most important market, North America'.*

While this may be true, it does not explain the substantial increase in staff costs, £11.8 million in 1997/98 nor the increase in operating leases and hire charges of £5.1 million for the similar period.

Table 5.11   Profitability ratios

	1995	1996	1997	1998
First option (preferred):				
Profit Before Tax ÷ Total Assets %	18.6	14.7	11.2	–0.7
Profit Before Tax ÷ Sales %	13.2	11.5	8.0	–0.5
Sales ÷ Total Assets	1.41	1.28	1.39	1.37
Second option:				
Profit Before Tax ÷ (TA – CL) %	28.1	28.2	16.0	–2.0
Profit Before Tax ÷ Sales %	13.2	11.5	8.0	–0.5
Sales ÷ (TA – CL)	2.13	2.46	1.99	3.74
Third option:				
PBIT ÷ (TA – CL) %	29.7	31.2	20.0	9.0
PBIT ÷ Sales %	13.9	12.7	10.0	2.4
Sales ÷ (TA – CL)	2.13	2.46	1.99	3.74
Fourth option:				
PBIT ÷ Net Assets %	33.3	33.9	29.9	9.3
PBIT ÷ Sales %	13.9	12.7	10.0	2.4
Sales ÷ Net Assets	2.39	2.68	2.98	3.88

In *Table 5.11*, it can be seen that second, third and fourth options tend to overstate profitability, especially the fourth option. In the second option, the ratio of sales divided by total assets less current liabilities increases from £1.99 to £3.74 for the period 1997/98. This means that either sales has increased and/or total assets less current liabilities has decreased. Reviewing the basic data shows that sales increased by 17.5% while total assets less current liabilities decreased by 37.4%; the result being an increase from £1.99 to £3.74. This does not make sense. Further examination shows that current liabilities increased from £54.6 million to £136.5 million mainly due to an increase in bank overdraft from £8.2 million to £85.7 million. Here we have a perfect example of changes in short-term financing affecting profitability.

The third option has all the problems just highlighted plus the extra 'benefit' from adding back any interest payments to the profit figure. In this option the company is still 'seen' to be making a profit. How can this be? The calculation requires that the loss before tax of £1.6 million is adjusted by adding back £8.6 million of interest payable; this produces a 'profit figure' for the numerator of £7 million!

The fourth option suffers from much of that contained in option two and option three. However, because it also deducts long-term loans it does not fall into the trap of movements between short-term and long-term borrowing. This meagre benefit does not overcome its major shortcoming of grossly overstating profitability. In the above example it can be seen that profitability was steady for the three years 1995 to 1997.

Here we must return to the real world and agree with Horngren that profitability should be measured on operating assets (i.e. total assets) irrespective of how they have been financed – the first option.

6.   Working Capital Ratios / Liquidity Ratios

Working capital or liquidity ratios attempt to give an indication of a company's ability to pay its way in the short and medium-term. The medium-term is taken to mean up to one year, while short-term is taken to mean up to 13 weeks i.e. 3 months. All working capital ratios should be compared against trends year-on-year and/or industry averages. Working capital ratios correspond to the working capital cycle of a company and represent the flow of goods/services through a business. The main items comprise stock, debtors, cash and creditors. Financial controls should exist for the first three items.

The current ratio, (current assets/ current liabilities) considers the whole of the working capital cycle and gives an indication of a company's ability to pay it way in the medium term.

The liquid ratio or acid test ratio takes current assets, deducts stocks then divides the result by current liabilities. It attempts to give an indication of a company's ability to pay its way in the short-term. Many academic writers suggest that this is a 'more stringent' ratio than the current ratio simply because it deducts stock. In practice, this is not the case. The liquid ratio, in its present form, suffers from movements in bank overdraft. For example, if bank overdraft increases and it is used (correctly) to finance a proportion of current assets, then the ratio is unlikely to change.

The alternative ratio, known as cover for creditors takes current assets, deducts stocks and bank overdraft then divides the result by trade creditors. Research shows this to be more responsive to changes in bank overdraft than the liquid ratio.

The final two ratios examine separate components of the working capital cycle. Cost of sales divided by stock gives the average stock turn. Here, the higher the better. Debtors divided by average weekly (or daily) sales give the average debtor collection period. It would appear that the lower the ratio, the better. However, the simple fact of reducing the amount of credit allowed to its customers might result in a company losing some or many of its customers.

Table 5.12 Working Capital Ratios or Liquidity Ratios

	1995	1996	1997	1998
Current ratio:				
Current Assets ÷ Current Liabilities	1.55	1.15	1.85	0.98
Liquid ratio:				
Liquid Assets ÷ Current Liabilities	0.43	0.26	0.46	0.22
Cover for creditors:				
(LA − BO) ÷ Trade Creditors	0.54	−0.58	0.47	−1.13
Cost of Sales ÷ Stock	1.4	1.2	1.4	1.3
Debtors ÷ Average Weekly Sales	3.7	3.9	4.3	4.8

The working capital cycle ratios for *Polly Ester Holdings plc* are heavily influenced by substantial movements in short and long-term borrowings. In this case, the best way to interpret the current ratio is to ignore the movements in the intervening years, simply take the total movement from 1995 to 1998 i.e. 1.54 to 0.98. A substantial decline in the company's ability to pay its way in the medium term. The main cause of this being the increase in bank overdraft.

In this example, the liquid ratio or acid test seems to follow similar movements to the current ratio. Here the ratio is difficult to interpret. The cover for creditors ratio gives a clear interpretation. It takes current assets, deducts stocks and bank overdraft to show the amount by which trade creditors are covered. In this example, in 1995, trade creditors are covered 54 pence in the pound, while in 1996 the cover for creditors is negative 58 pence in the pound. 1997 another cover for creditors of 47 pence in the pound, then in 1998 a negative of £1.13 in the pound.

The first of the remaining two ratios is known as stock turn, i.e. cost of sales divided by stock. The ideal for the ratio – the higher the better. For *Polly Ester Holding plc* this ratio is fairly stable, between 1.4 and 1.2 times. If we take the 1998 value of 1.3, this means that the company turned its stock over 1.3 times on average per year. Or another way of looking at it, 52 divided by 1.3 gives 40 weeks stockholding (on average). This would be considered very high stockholding, typical stockholding for a retailer might be 10 to 12 weeks. With a stock holding of £104.8 million in 1998 and a revised stock turn of 2.6 weeks this would give 20 weeks stock holding and release £52.4 million from stock for alternative use, perhaps in reducing borrowings.

The final ratio, known as the debtor collection period, debtors divided by average weekly sales shows an increase. The size of this ratio is influenced by the trading environment the company finds itself in i.e. it must provide similar levels of credit to its customers compared to its competitors. For *Polly Ester Holdings plc* the ratio increases from an average 3.7 weeks to 4.8 weeks over the period. This means that the company is allowing its debtors a further 1.1 weeks at average weekly sales i.e. £296.6 divided by 52 times 1.1 gives £6.3 million.

Taking the stock and debtor ratios together it should be possible to reduce the working capital by approximately £60 million and in turn reduce bank overdraft which in turn would reduce interest payable and increase profit before taxation.

7.   Gearing Ratios

There are good gearing ratios but there are gearing ratios that are not sufficiently robust. Quite simply, gearing is the relationship between borrowings (interest bearing debt) and equity (the shareholders interest in the company). In *Table 5.13* we show the good ratios first. These are:

1.   The borrowing ratio. This takes total borrowings and divides the result by equity to produce a ratio. Where the result is less than 0.5 a company would be considered to be low geared. Where the result is greater than 1.0 a company would be considered to be high geared. However, these figures are rather arbitrary. More importantly, the analyst should consider the movements in the ratio year-on-year.

2.   Income gearing. The first gearing ratio gives an indication of the level of gearing. The income gearing ratio gives an indication on whether a company can afford that level of gearing. The ratio takes interest payable and expresses it as a percentage of profit before taxation plus interest payable. In effect it is the mirror of the traditional interest cover ratio. The rule-of-thumb for the interest cover ratio is that interest payments should be covered by profits before taxation and interest, at least four times. For our income gearing ratio this translates to 25% being the benchmark.

And the gearing ratios that are not sufficiently robust:

3. The third gearing ratio, debt expressed as a percentage of equity plus debt is a particularly bad ratio. It ranks with bad computer viruses and should not be used in any commercial system. Debt is taken to mean the total of current liabilities plus long-term loans. Closer examination of the ratio will show that debt is included both in the numerator and the denominator. This means that debt could increase ten thousand fold and the figure would not exceed 100%. This ratio is commonly used in published accounts in their five year summaries (a document which is not subject to audit verification).

4. The fourth gearing ratio suffers again from its construction and is another bad ratio. It takes long-term borrowings and expresses these as a percentage of equity. This might work well for many well managed companies, but for those companies in serious financial difficulties, the results are simply misleading. Companies in difficulty quickly find out that there is no distinction between short-term borrowings and long-term borrowings. When things get tough the majority of long-term borrowings suddenly become short-term bank overdrafts (with the banks taking security on the assets for continued support). With this ratio, which only recognises long-term borrowings for gearing, it could show that a company is low geared when in fact it is at its limits, or has exceeded its limits, at the bank(s).

Table 5.13   Gearing Ratios

	1995	1996	1997	1998
Borrowing ratio:				
Borrowing ÷ Equity	0.24	0.55	0.63	1.22
Income gearing:				
Interest Payable ÷ P.B.I.T. %	5.5	9.4	19.8	122.5
Third gearing ratio:				
Debt ÷ (Equity + Debt) %	42	52.7	54.8	65.7
Fourth gearing ratio:				
LTL ÷ Equity %	12.7	8.9	52.8	4.0

In *Table 5.13* the first two ratios, the borrowing ratio and income gearing ratio show:

1. The borrowing ratio moves from low gearing in 1995 through medium gearing in 1996 and 1997 and into high gearing in 1998. The point here is that the fast movement from low gearing to high gearing is often not accompanied by directors who can 'cope' with the increased requirements/ interest shown by their bank or bankers.

2. The income gearing ratio shows that while gearing was increasing, for the period 1995 to 1997 the company could afford it. However, in 1998 'the roof fell' in when profits were reduced to losses and the income gearing moved

to 122%. Here, the company could not afford this level of gearing. Two options, reduce the level of borrowings to an acceptable level and/or increase the level of profits. Both are extremely difficult to achieve when a company is in such a difficult position.

The *Polly Ester* case provides a good example of the deficiencies in the popular gearing ratios shown below.

3.   A brief examination of the third gearing ratio quickly shows its shortcomings. It does not differentiate to any significant degree, the level of gearing in 1995 compared to that in 1998. Movements from 42% to 65.7% simply fail to provide adequate information on the real movements i.e. total borrowings increasing from £16.6 million in 1995 to £88.6 million in 1997.

4.   The fourth gearing ratio also fails to provide adequate information. If we were to believe the calculated ratios, it actually shows a decrease from 12.7% in 1995 to 4% in 1998.

These results obtained from ratios three and four above compare with other similar companies under research.

8.   Employee Ratios

Employee ratios must rank amongst the easiest of all ratios to calculate and interpret. Many apparently successful companies have used employee ratios to manage their business. This can lead to a number of unsatisfactory decisions e.g. increasing the number of consultants since they do not appear on the denominator of the ratio, but they do cost more than a comparable full-time employee.

The only word of caution when using these type of ratios is to ensure that the number of employees shown in the denominator of the ratio is expressed in terms of full time equivalents. Apart from that, you simply pick a figure, divide it by the number of employees and you have a ratio.

In *Table 5.14* we show examples of five employee based ratios. These ratios are selected in order to verify our analysis so far.

The first two ratios focus on the trading activity i.e. sales per employee and profit per employee. Ideally, we would want to see both ratios increasing at a steady rate. For example, as sales increased we would expect an increase in the number of employees. Similarly, given an increase in sales per employee year-on-year, we would expect to see a corresponding increase in profit per employee – or slightly better.

The next two ratios provide a view to the expansion of a business. Fixed assets per employee show whether or not a company is expanding through the purchase of fixed assets (e.g. purchase of new equipment), or whether it is expanding through the use of more labour (not the favoured approach these days). The second ratio shows the expansion of borrowings and can be viewed as a simple gearing ratio. It also shows whether an expansion in fixed assets is being financed through borrowing.

The last ratio, staff costs per employee highlights one of the major costs in a company. For this ratio we would expect to see a gradual increase perhaps in line with inflation.

Finally, do be aware that the acquisition or disposal of parts of a business can have a substantial affect on employee ratios. For example, if a company made a major acquisition of a high tech business, we would expect staff costs per employee to increase in the year of acquisition and beyond.

Table 5.14 Employee Ratios

	1995 £	1996 £	1997 £	1998 £
Sales per Employee	29,727	29,030	33,998	37,336
Profit per Employee	3,914	3,328	2,734	−201
Fixed Assets per Employee	9,967	10,114	10,735	10,171
Borrowings per Employee	2,887	5,878	6,775	11,153
Staff Costs per Employee	9,062	9,105	9,820	10,662

In *Table 5.14* we can see that the employee ratios are broadly in line with the analysis and interpretation performed so far.

Here we can see that the ratio of sales per employee has increased, though profit per employee has reduced. Action to increase profit per employee would include, an increase in the selling price and/or a reduction in costs e.g. a reduction in the number of employees.

The ratio of fixed assets per employee shows an increase in the first three years followed by a decrease in the final year. The decrease in the final year might be caused by the disposal of *Green and Gillies*, with the fixed assets of that company now removed along with its employees. In this case, the ratio should have remained constant. It failed to do so because the number of employees actually increased. We find that there was a modest increase in fixed assets from £79.7 million to £80.8 with a substantial increase in the number of employees 7,424 to 7,944.

The final ratio shows increases in staff costs per employee above the rate of inflation. Taken together with the increase in the number of employees for the period 1997/98 produces additional staff costs of £11.8 million.

9.   Non-Financial Indicators

We have left the non-financial indicators until last. In practice, they would be firmly embodied during the data collection and analysis phases. Non-financial indicators might include:

1.   Many of the strategy models, for example:

     a.   Strengths, Weaknesses, Opportunities and Threats (SWOT).

     b.   Political, Economic, Social, Technological (PEST).

     c.   Environmental influences (see *Johnson and Scholes)*.

     d.   *Porter's* five forces.

     e.   *Porter's* value chain and competitive advantage.

2.   A diary of events, see *Figure 5.3* and our simplified version in *Table 5.7*.

3.   Argenti's failure framework which has its focus on defects, mistakes and symptoms. Still the best framework around.

4.   The careful use of external material both on the company and it competitors.

The final non-financial indicator is left to the end, simply to make a strong case for the inclusion of such data. In *Table 5.7*, we showed the movement of directors. In this case there was resignation of directors in 1996, 1997 and 1998. It is important to verify the positions of these directors including their replacements.

In the *Polly Ester* case we find that Mr. Philip Peters who was the finance director resigned on the 20th December 1997 (eleven days before the financial year end). During the whole of the period 1998, the company appeared to operate without a finance director. In fact, Mr H. Waterman was not appointed until the 15th April 1999, some 15 months later.

From the analysis and interpretation of the case we have seen that 1998 was a critical year in the life of this company. Substantial over-trading combined with financing expansion mainly through borrowings combined with escalation of basic costs, combined with an inability to pass on costs to customers resulted in a downturn of the companys' fortunes. Would things have been different had there been a finance director in post during this vital period? We think so, but the main point here is to provide a good example on the use and interpretation of non-financial indicators. They do have a bearing.

10. Summary

The analysis and interpretation of the *Polly Ester* case study is based solely on information contained in the published accounts. Depending on the requirements, we would tend to collect other material from a variety of sources on both the company and its competitors.

In the introduction to this chapter we set out to demonstrate the strengths and weaknesses of financial ratios. This has been achieved:

1. With the preparation and interpretation of a simplified Diary of Events, showing movements in sales, fixed assets and directors.

2. With the analysis and interpretation provided by the Common Size Statement and the Cost Analysis Statement. The former providing an easy access to major movements while the latter an explanation of changes in income and costs.

3. In *Robertson's 1983 ratio model* we showed how it can be used to highlight where changes have taken place in the financial health of a company. Basic ratio analysis techniques can then be used to find the root cause.

4. In the sections covering profitability, liquidity and gearing we have provided explanations of each ratio, the strengths and/or weaknesses and our suggestions on which ratios to build satisfactory analysis and interpretation.

5. The employee ratios, follow the practice of Keep It Simple and Straightforward (KISS). Easy to prepare, easy to interpret.

6. Non-financial indicators provide depth and content to any analysis, especially the analysis models used in strategy, *Argenti's* framework and the Diary of Events. We saw the value of this in the movement of directors, especially the resignation of the finance director in December 1997.

Appendix A – Sources of company information

The following are examples of sources of company information which can be found in most university/college libraries, local reference libraries, and in some company libraries. The list of necessity is selective. However, you should experiment by using any library to which you have access to find out details about a particular company or topic.

KOMPASS   (Annual publication in three volumes)

Volumes I Products and Services: Classifies 45,000 UK companies according to their products and services. A useful volume for purchasing, but for the purpose of financial analysis can provide the opportunity to identify companies in a similar industry sector.

Volume II Company Information: Arranges companies by county and town. Most entries give name and address, a list of the directors, share capital, turnover, number of employees and product codes. It also provides some basic financial data for a three year period, together with two financial ratios. This volume is useful in that it often gives entries for a number of limited companies which might form part of a larger group. It is also useful from a geographic point of view.

Volume III Parents and Subsidiaries: Lists over 40,000 parent companies and over 130,000 subsidiaries. Shows their corporate structure. This volume is similar to *Who Owns Whom*.

Kompass is also available for most European countries.

WHO OWN'S WHOM   (annual publication in two volumes)

Volumes are available covering: UK and Ireland, Continental Europe, North and South America and Australasia, Middle East and Africa.

For UK and Ireland two volumes provide the following:

Volume I is in two sections. Both sections show the corporate family trees of parent companies. Section One, the largest section relates to companies registered in the UK while Section Two relates to companies registered in the Republic of Ireland.

Volume II lists subsidiaries in a bold typeface with the parent immediately below (indented and in a normal typeface).

DIRECTORY OF DIRECTORS   (annual publication in two volumes)

Volume I is an alphabetical list of the directors of the principal public and private companies in the UK, giving the names of the companies with which they are directors.

Volume II is an alphabetical list of the principal public and private companies in the UK, giving the names of their directors, together with limited financial data for some companies.

STOCK EXCHANGE YEARBOOK   (annual publication)

London and Dublin stock exchange companies are listed in some detail in this publication. Information provided includes: address of registered office, registrars, names of directors, secretary, auditors, solicitors, principal bankers, and brokers. Details of registration, including registered number, a statement of the principal activities of the company and principal subsidiaries.

Limited financial data is provided for two years including employee details. Sections also show recent dividends, capital structure, substantial shareholdings and registrars. A final section, in some entries, gives a brief five year summary.

FT McCARTHY (included in the FT DISCOVERY package)

FT McCarthy sheets (now renamed European Business Intelligence) are produced for quoted and unquoted UK registered companies. The service represent a collection of press cuttings which are accumulated for each company, covering write–ups in relevant newspapers and magazines. There is also an Industry Service which is based on subjects. This makes it possible to compare the performance and development of individual companies in their field of operation. The service is also included in the new FT Discovery package.

THE HEMSCOTT COMPANY GUIDE

Produced by Hemmington Scott who advertise it as "The No 1 information source on UK stockmarket companies". Basic company entries are six to a page. This gives a brief statement of principal activities, head office with full contact details, announcements, and limited financial data for five years. Companies can subscribe to have a larger entry, up to one page. These entries will give details of directors, registrars, brokers, auditors, financial advisers, and solicitors. In addition, extracts from Chairperson's or Chief Executive's statements are also included.

A large section in the back of the guide provides references to Actuaries, Auditors, Financial Advisers, Financial PR Advisers, Foreign Banks, Investment Managers, International Lawyers, Pension Fund Managers, Property Advisers, Registrars, Solicitors, Stockbrokers and Venture Capital Companies.

COMPANY REGISTRATION OFFICE

The Company Registration Office, Crown Way, Maindy, Cardiff telephone 01222 380801 holds certain information on companies on microfiche. Public limited companies are required to lodge their annual return not later than 7 months after their year end, limited companies 10 months.

The contents in a packet of microfiche contains general information about the company, including details of its incorporation, articles of association and memorandum of association; also details of movements of directors. It also includes financial information for a number of years which includes profit and loss account, balance sheet, source and application of funds, notes to the accounts, director's report and the auditor's report.

To obtain microfiche for a company, it is important to have the correct company name; better still to have the registered number of the company. Access can be gained through, visiting the Companies Registration Office at Cardiff or Companies House, London search room, (Edinburgh in Scotland), by post, or by using a company search agent.

One company search agent is *Company Formations Ltd*, 82 Whitchurch Road, Cardiff CF4 3LX telephone 01222 66 65 64 who provide an additional range of company related services all separately priced. These include, Director's Report and Accounts, Annual Return, Liquidation search, Directors database search, Company microfiche, through to a full Credit Status report. Should you wish to use this type of service contact the company for their current fees.

FAME (financial analysis made easy)

'A database containing company information. It contains detailed information on 500,000 UK and Irish companies, and summarised information on an additional 1.2 million companies. (1.7 million companies in total)

For each company there is up to 10 years of historical information. A company record typically contains: profit and loss account, balance sheet, cash flow statement, ratios and trends, SIC codes and activity information, credit score and rating, lists of directors, shareholders, subsidiaries and holding companies, registered and trading addresses and details of miscellaneous information that has been filed at Companies House.

The software allows you to search for companies that fulfil your criteria (by over 100 criteria). You can also compare companies against each other and present your results in graphs and tables. The integral analysis software is very sophisticated. Information can be downloaded for further analysis or marketing. You can also use "Addin" functionality to access FAME from within Excel or export data directly into tailor-made templates.

FAME is widely used for all types of financial analysis as well as sales and marketing projects. It is available on CD-ROM, DVD-ROM and the Internet and is updated weekly and monthly'.

SHAREFINDER COMPANY REPORTS

These reports are available by telephone, 0870 601 4600 and currently cost £8.95. The reports are aimed at investors and include a summary page, usually with a recommendation to buy, hold or sell the shares. Other sections of the report include ratings and earnings analysis, key financials at a glance, summary key financials, stock market performance, sector performance overview, corporate details, latest directors' share dealings and latest company announcements.

ICC BUSINESS RATIOS *plus*

'140 Business Ratios *plus* titles are published covering the whole of UK industry. In each report, company data is presented alphabetically with a two page spread for each showing address, trading activity, directors, subsidiaries and other company details, *plus* Profit and Loss, Balance Sheet, ICC Ratio Analysis and League Table Positions'.

Other sections of the report give Performance League Tables where companies are ranked by Size, Profitability, Efficiency, Liquidity, Gearing, Employee Performance and Growth. Also an Industry Profile i.e. an Industry Profit and Loss Account and Industry Balance Sheet. A final section Industry Comment which is a summary of the report findings, put into context of recent industry developments. Reports are typically 400 pages in length.

INTERNET

There are many good sites on the internet providing UK company information. By its very nature the internet is continually changing and evolving therefore many links no longer work. We will continue to operate our company web site **http://www.marspub.co.uk/** and post amendments/updates from time to time. We now list a few useful sites, some included just for their links.

http://profiles.wisi.com/ Historical share prices.

http://www.corporateinformation.com/ukcorp.html

http://www.bloomberg.com/uk/ukhome.html

http://finance.uk.yahoo.com/

http://www.bized.ac.uk/

http://www.northcote.co.uk/   Annual reports

http://www.icaew.co.uk/

http://www.researchindex.co.uk/

http://www.icbinc.com/   The ultimate Annual Reports service

CHAPTER SIX

COST ACCOUNTING AND COST MANAGEMENT

LEARNING OBJECTIVES

When you have finished studying this chapter you should be able to:

❑ Describe the main elements of costs and the various classifications of costs.

❑ Calculate overhead recovery rates and prepare product costs using absorption costing techniques.

❑ Describe and understand the differences between Absorption costing and Marginal costing.

❑ Describe the process of Standard costing, calculate and interpret variances.

❑ Describe and calculate costs using Activity Based Costing.

❑ Understand the use of internal Service Level Agreements to achieve value for money when goods and services are provided internally.

6.1   Introduction

Costs may often represent a significant proportion of an organisation's income and, therefore, are a very important area to be able to manage. For example, from an examination of the 1997 Report and Accounts of the *Standard Chartered Bank* it can be seen that 82% of the Group's net revenue is accounted for by operating expenses (in 1998, 94% of *Tesco's* revenue is accounted for by operating expenses).

Cost management is a declared priority of the Group, a point made in repeated Chairman's Statements. It is particularly important because profit depends upon knowing the cost of doing business. However, there is a major problem in knowing whether the costs incurred are really warranted. Are they really necessary? Could they be avoided? How can we tell?

Cost management is associated with cost accounting. The management of costs within an organisation may well be influenced by the way in which they have been accounted for. At its simplest the concern with cost accounting is to determine what it costs to produce a good or provide a service. This can be very straightforward in a one product or one service organisation where all costs can be clearly identified with the product/service being provided. However, very few such organisations exist and in a multi-product or multi-service environment procedures have to be found and used if costs are to be identified with that which is produced or provided.

If you refer to most cost accounting texts you will discover that procedures have been developed primarily in manufacturing organisations to deal with the cost accounting problems of different types of operation. Thus, you will encounter descriptions and discussions about cost accounting techniques and approaches for organisations producing bespoke one-off products, and those dealing with batch operations, process operations and long-term contracts. These techniques will focus upon the various elements of cost like labour and materials and the problems of accounting for raw materials, work in progress and finished goods.

What is important for you to understand about cost accounting is that it is not a science, and that considerable judgement is typically employed. In accounting for costs, particularly overheads, considerable judgement is employed in allocating and apportioning them to products and/or services. How such judgement based allocation and apportionment is applied we review in the next section. Thereafter, we will consider one important development in cost accounting, and more importantly cost management known as Activity Based Costing, or ABC. This approach has a claimed advantage over traditional methods because it attempts to relate the costs of an organisation to those activities responsible for generating them.

Whilst ABC provides one means of encouraging cost control, there are some costs in very large organisations that are notoriously difficult to control. This is because they are incurred centrally and distributed throughout the organisation. Management informations systems costs are a good example of such internally transferred costs. How these can be managed using what are known as service level agreements we consider in the last section.

6.2   Elements of Cost

Originally cost accounting methods were developed to provide ways of accumulating costs and charging these to units of product or service in order to establish stock valuations. These were principally related to historical calculations, but the advantages of using these methods for planning were soon realised and cost accounting was extended to the areas of budgeting and decision analysis.

Almost every decision made by management has an affect on cost, and a good understanding of the types of costs and how they are used for cost control and cost management is important for sound financial management.

Total costs of a product or service comprise three main elements:

1.   materials – the cost of materials consumed in making the product or providing the service;

2.   labour – the cost of wages and salaries of employees, who are involved in producing the product or providing the service;

3.   expenses – the cost of other expenses; which will include occupancy costs, power, depreciation, interest charges, telecoms. etc.

As we shall see later in this chapter there are different possible treatments of these three basic elements, arising from differing views of how they should be analysed and reported, which allow for alternative views of the 'cost' of a product or service.

6.3   Classifications of Cost

This expression covers the way in which costs can be grouped, or classified, for analysis and reporting. A very common usage is the grouping of costs by function, e.g. splitting the costs of the organisation into production, selling, distribution, administration. These can be further subdivided into, say, departmental costs within each function, and is a system commonly used in the budgeting process.

Two other important classifications of cost are:

1.   Direct/indirect costs,

2.   Variable/fixed costs,

and an understanding of these is important as they are linked to two methods of costing, absorption costing and marginal costing, which you will meet later in this chapter.

1   Direct/Indirect Costs

A direct cost is a cost that can be traced in full to the product, service or function etc. that is being costed, whereas an indirect cost is a cost that has been incurred in the making of a product, providing a service, etc., but that cannot be traced in full to the product, service or function.

As an illustration, if a management consultant is currently working for three clients, the actual time spent on each client can be identified and charged directly to the individual client's account, but the cost of the administrative facilities, such as, say, occupancy costs cannot be traced directly to each client, These are indirect costs, which have to be shared on some basis between the clients to arrive at a total client cost.

Materials costs, labour costs and expenses can be classified as a direct cost or an indirect cost. When the three basic elements of cost are classified in this way the total of the direct costs is known as prime cost and the total of the indirect costs is known as overhead. Total cost is the sum of prime cost and overhead.

2   Variable/Fixed Costs

This classification is based on a basic principle of cost behaviour, which assumes that as activity increases so usually will cost. It will usually cost more to send 10 faxes than to send 5. It will usually cost more to produce 150 cars than to produce 120. However, not all costs will increase in the same way or by the same amount. A definition of cost behaviour is:

> "The way in which costs of output are affected by fluctuations in the level of activity". (CIMA Official Terminology)

Costs which tend to vary directly with the volume of output are variable costs. The most obvious of these is direct materials, and the relationship between cost and volume can be shown graphically as follows:

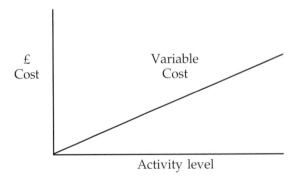

Costs which tend to be unaffected by increases or decreases in volume of output, and as such will be incurred regardless of output volume, are fixed costs. Examples of these would be rent and salaries. Of course in the long term all costs are likely to change – the rent of the premises and employees' salaries would inevitably rise, but they do not alter as a direct result of making one more item. Graphically, a fixed cost would look like this:

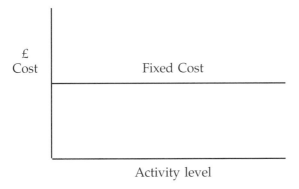

However, many items of a fixed cost nature are fixed within a particular activity level. For example, it could be that a number of administrators could handle a certain level of purchase orders, but beyond that certain level another administrator would have to be employed. This type of situation gives rise to what are called stepped fixed costs, and also introduces the concept of the 'relevant range', that is the activity level over which the cost is fixed. A stepped fixed cost situation such as that described would appear graphically as follows:

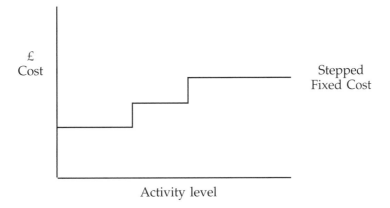

Some costs include parts that are variable and fixed. Such costs are usually called mixed, semi-variable or semi-fixed costs. Common examples are telephone and electricity charges, where there is a fixed rental element and a variable portion depending upon usage.

6.4   Techniques of Costing

Costing is undertaken in organisations with the purpose of providing management with the information they need to be able to plan, control and make the necessary decisions. As such it has evolved, and continues to evolve, providing a 'toolkit' of methods and techniques that can be selected by management to suit their analytical and reporting purposes. There is no 'regulatory framework' requiring companies to produce costing statements etc., but some requirements of the accounting standards do demand that organisations prepare figures for their statutory accounts using particular techniques. For example, organisations are required to value their stocks at 'full production cost' which means that for their annual accounts they must use absorption costing techniques. However, internally, they are free to choose the most relevant and valuable for their type of operation. In the following section we will review the main costing techniques.

1. Overhead Absorption Costing

Overhead absorption costing is concerned with the process of charging indirect costs – overhead – to products or services. It is concerned principally with the charging of indirect production costs, i.e. not non-production costs such as selling, distribution and administration overhead. In determining the cost of a product or service it is not usually the direct costs which are difficult to charge to products or services. It is finding an equitable way of apportioning overheads to products or services to enable an understanding of product/service cost and profitability which poses the challenge. The following section looks at the process of allocation and apportionment of overhead, and the ways in which overhead can be 'absorbed' into product/service cost.

Overheads, Allocation and Apportionment

Organisations of all types incur overhead costs in the form of those costs that cannot readily be identified with individual products or services. Given that such costs may well be a very significant proportion of total costs, some means has to be found for distributing them across products and services if the full cost of products and services is to be determined. 'Cost plus' pricing remains a common method of pricing products and services, of course bearing in mind key market considerations.

The way that costs are distributed traditionally is by a process known as 'allocation and apportionment' whereby, for example, an overhead like rent would be apportioned typically according to area occupied and allocated to parts of the business on that basis. This process can be most readily understood from the following example.

1.   Example

The PVY Company has two production departments and a raw material and finished goods store.

The budgeted costs for the last quarter of 200X are as follows:

	£
Rent	12,000
Maintenance to Plant	4,000
Depreciation of Plant	12,000
Lighting and Heating	4,000
Supervision	9,500
Fire Insurance	500
Power	10,000
Personnel Services	12,000
General Expenses	8,000

Additional information has been collected for use in allocating and/or apportioning the budgeted costs to departments.

	Dept. A	Dept. B	Store	Total
Number of Employees	10	7	2	19
Area (square metres)	1,700	300	400	2,400
Machine Hours (for quarter)	17,500	3,400	0	20,900
Direct Labour Hours (weekly)	440	300	80	820
Plant Value	£564,000	£100,000	0	£664,000
Value of Stock Used	£10,200	£1,800	0	£12,000
kW Hours, metered	160,000	25,600	0	185,600

The Factory Manager has given an estimate for supervision costs being the time spent in the two departments.

Department A	£7,500
Department B	£2,000

Complete an overhead analysis sheet showing clearly the basis used for apportionment. (Round all figures to the nearest hundred)

Table 6.1   *Overhead Analysis Sheet*

Budgeted costs	Basis of Apportionment	Total £	Dept A £	Dept B £	Store £
Rent	Floor Area	12,000	8,500	1,500	2,000
Maintenance to Plant	Mach. Hours	4,000	3,300	700	0
Depreciation of Plant	Plant Value	12,000	10,200	1,800	0
Lighting and Heating	Floor Area	4,000	2,800	500	800
Supervision	Tech.Estimate	9,500	7,500	2,000	0
Fire Insurance	Floor Area	500	300	100	100
Power	kW Hours	10,000	8,600	1,400	0
Personnel Services	No. Employees	12,000	6,300	4,400	1,300
General Expenses	Labour Hours	8,000	4,300	2,900	800
		72,000	51,800	15,300	4,900
Service Dept (Store)	Stock Value	0	4,200	700	–4,900
		72,000	56,000	16,000	0

Example for the apportionment of rent to Department A:

$$\text{Department A} \quad = \quad \frac{£12,000}{2,400} \quad \times \quad 1,700$$

$$= \quad £8,500$$

The bases for apportionment shown in *Table 6.1* are used simply to illustrate the process. Apportionment is an art. It is possible to question the use of floor area as a means for apportioning the costs of items such as rent, lighting, heating and fire insurance, in fact it is possible to present a good case against any apportionment base.

Consider the case of using floor area for lighting and heating, clearly, there is a requirement for different forms of lighting and heating in a variety of work situations few of which would correspond to floor area.

Similarly, consider the case of using machine hours to apportion the maintenance of plant. This suggests that the more a machine is used the more maintenance will be required and vice versa. Therefore, if we use a machine infrequently it will not require much maintenance! It also assumes that all machines cost the same and are of similar age.

COST ACCOUNTING AND COST MANAGEMENT   201

2.   Overheads, Absorption Rates

Once the overhead allocation and apportionment process has been completed the total overhead cost for a part of the business can be calculated by simple addition. For example, the total overhead for Department B we calculated as being £16,000. We can now use this figure to determine a future unit charge out rate by absorbing it over a number of bases. One common base is labour hours, such that if labour hours were 2,000 we would have an overhead absorption rate of £8 per labour hour (£16,000 ÷ 2,000). In costing future products we would charge overhead to them according to the number of labour hours. Therefore, if a product required two hours of labour, a charge of £16 for overhead (£8 x 2) would be made.

How this approach can be applied using different bases and the effect of different methods of absorption we illustrate in the following example:

The PVY Company has prepared a Production Cost Budget for the last quarter of 200X as follows:

	£	£
Direct Materials		24,000
Direct Labour – Department A	32,000	
– Department B	16,000	
		48,000
Prime Cost		72,000
Overheads – Department A	56,000	
– Department B	16,000	
		72,000
Production Cost		144,000

Department A is a machine based department with a total of 1,750 machine hours budgeted during the quarter. The labour rate in the department has been set at £6.00 per hour.

Department B is a labour based department with a total of 4,000 labour hours budgeted during the quarter. The labour rate in the department has been set at £4.00 per hour.

We will calculate an overhead absorption rate using each of the following bases:

a.   Percentage on Direct Materials.

b.   Percentage on Direct Labour   –   Whole Company

c.   Percentage on Direct Labour   –   Department A

d.   Percentage on Direct Labour   –   Department B

e.   Machine Hour Rate   –   Department A

f.   Labour Hour Rate   –   Department B

The calculation of absorption rates (also known as overhead recovery rates) requires that an overhead cost is divided by an agreed absorption base. We will now show the calculations for the most popular methods and comment on each one.

a. Percentage on Direct Materials

$$\frac{\text{Overheads}}{\text{Material Costs}} \times 100 = \frac{£72,000}{£24,000} \times 100 = 300\%$$

The percentage on direct materials is a simple method. However, it is difficult to find a situation in which to use the method. The problem is that it can only be used in a single (including single quality) material environment. If it were used in a mixed material environment, products would absorb overheads on the basis of their material cost.

b. Percentage on Direct Labour – Whole Company

$$\frac{\text{Overheads}}{\text{Labour Costs}} \times 100 = \frac{£72,000}{£48,000} \times 100 = 150\%$$

The percentage on direct labour is also a simple method but unlike materials is widely used. In this example, overheads would be absorbed at 150% of the total labour cost for each product or service. The major problem with this method arises when there are different levels of labour costs in different departments or cost centres. In order to address this problem most companies calculate separate absorption rates for each department or cost centre.

An example is shown in c, and d below. It can be seen that instead of using 150% for the whole company, we would now use 175% absorption rate to recover overheads in Department A and 100% absorption rate to recover overheads in Department B.

c. Percentage on Direct Labour – Department A

$$\frac{\text{Overheads}}{\text{Labour Costs}} \times 100 = \frac{£56,000}{£32,000} \times 100 = 175\%$$

d. Percentage on Direct Labour – Department B

$$\frac{\text{Overheads}}{\text{Labour Costs}} \times 100 = \frac{£16,000}{£16,000} \times 100 = 100\%$$

One of the most popular methods to absorb overheads is using the hourly rate. This method also requires that separate absorption rates are calculated for each department or cost centre. In this example, we would absorb overheads for Department A based on the number of machine hours required times the rate of £32 per machine hour. Similarly, if the product used labour hours in Department B, there would be an absorption of overheads based on the number of labour hours required times the rate of £4 per machine hour. See calculations below.

e. Machine Hour Rate – Department A

$$\frac{\text{Overheads}}{\text{Machine Hours}} = \frac{£56,000}{1,750} = £32.00 \text{ per machine hour}$$

f. Labour Hour Rate – Department B

$$\frac{\text{Overheads}}{\text{Labour Hours}} = \frac{£16,000}{4,000} = £4.00 \text{ per labour hour}$$

3. Overheads, Comparison of Absorption Methods

We have described the calculation of absorption rates and commented on each. However, there still remains the question 'What absorption method should we use'? We will complete this example by showing the effect of using each of the absorption methods on the production costs of two products. Each product comprises different proportions of materials and labour. The example will use the following data:

❑ The executives of the PVY Company are trying to agree the method to be used for absorbing overheads to products.

❑ The following information is available to calculate the prime costs for Products 101 and 102.

	Product 101 per unit	Product 102 per unit
Direct Material Cost	£14	£28
Direct Labour Hours – Department A	4 hours	1 hour
– Department B	3 hours	4 hours

For convenience, we now restate the direct labour rate which was used in the previous section.

Direct Labour Rate	– Department A	£6.00 per hour
	– Department B	£4.00 per hour

An estimate of machine hours for both products is as follows:

Machine Hours (per 100 units)	Product 101	47 hours
	Product 102	15 hours

Using the information for Products 101 and 102, we will prepare a table to show the effect of using absorption methods based on materials, direct labour and hourly rates. Costs will be calculated, per 100 units.

In *Table 6.2* we have taken the direct material cost for Product 101 and multiplied it by 100 (£14 x 100) to give £1,400. The direct labour cost is found by multiplying the direct labour hours per unit for Product 101 spent in Department A by 100 (4 hours x 100) to give 400 hours, then multiplying the hours by the direct labour hourly rate (400 hours x £6) to give £2,400. A similar calculation is performed for Department B. Finally, the direct material costs and the direct labour costs are added (£1,400 + £3,600) to give the prime cost for Product 101. Now check the calculations for Product 102.

COST ACCOUNTING AND COST MANAGEMENT

Table 6.2   Comparison of Absorption Methods

		Product 101		Product 102	
		£	£	£	£
Direct Material			1,400		2,800
Direct Labour:					
Dept. A (£6 p.h.)	400 hrs	2,400		100 hrs 600	
Dept. B (£4 p.h.)	300 hrs	1,200		400 hrs 1,600	
			3,600		2,200
Prime Cost			5,000		5,000
1. 300 % on Direct Materials			4,200		8,400
			9,200		13,400

In this first example we have multiplied the direct materials for each product by 300%. For Product 101 (£1,400 x 300%) to give the overheads of £4,200. Finally, we added the overhead to the prime cost (£4,200 + £5,000) to give the total production cost of £9,200. Similar calculations for Product 102 gives a total production cost of £13,400. Both costs are arithmetically accurate, but they are heavily influenced by the material cost and subsequent overhead absorption using materials.

2. 150% on Total Labour	5,400	3,300
	10,400	8,300

When using a percentage on total labour the calculations are similar. In this case we use the total labour cost for Product 101, £3,600 x 150% to give the overheads of £5,400 and £3,300 for Product 102. You will notice the difference between the two methods, with Product 102 now lower, due to the direct labour costs.

3. 175% on Labour Dept. A	4,200	1,050
4. 100% on Labour Dept. B	1,200	1,600
	5,400	2,650
	10,400	7,650

When using individual absorption rates we take the rate and multiply it by the direct labour cost for a department. For example for Product 101 we take the direct labour cost of £2,400 x 175% to give £4,200 of overheads for Department A, then add the direct labour cost of £1,200 x 100% to give £1,200 of overheads for Department B. Total absorbed overheads for both departments amounting to £5,400. Similar calculations for Product 101 produce total absorbed overheads of £2,650. We discussed the problem of using a percentage on total labour in the previous section. We can now see the effect of using individual absorption rates for each department or cost centre.

5.	£32 M.Hour Dept. A	47 hrs	1,504	15 hrs	480	
6.	£4 L.Hour Dept. B	300 hrs	1,200	400 hrs	1,600	
			2,704		2,080	
			7,704		7,080	

In the final section we have used the hourly rate method. If Product 101 requires 47 machine hours in Department A, the absorbed overhead is (47 hours x £32) which gives £1,504. Overheads are absorbed in Department B using direct labour hours, the overhead is (300 hours x £4) which gives £1,200. To complete the calculations we add the two overhead figures to give £2,704, then add in the prime cost of £5,000 to give £7,704.

The purpose of the above example is to demonstrate the differing ways in which the overhead <u>could</u> be attributed to products. The method applied should be that which most closely aligns overhead and product. Most commonly used are time-based methods, (i.e. labour hour, machine hour) although there is growing interest in using 'an activity base'. This is discussed in more detail in *Section 6.5*.

Before moving on to consider other techniques of costing, we will now look at the construction of a quotation for an order, which is based on absorption costing principles.

Example – Quotation for an Order

Mouldit Ltd makes a range of products in expanded polystyrene (cups, trays, DIY materials etc.). The budget for the six months to 31st October 200X is as follows:

	£	£	£
Sales			780,000
Polystyrene (5,000 kg)	200,000		
Direct Labour (10,000 hours)	50,000		
Variable Overhead	150,000		
Total Variable Costs		400,000	
Fixed Overhead		250,000	
Total Cost			650,000
Budgeted Profit			130,000

You have been asked to quote for an order which is estimated to require 100 kg of polystyrene and 240 hours of direct labour.

The order is from a regular customer. The company applies normal absorption costing principles. Variable overhead is assumed to be related to direct labour hours, and fixed overhead and profit are based on a loading of total variable cost and total cost respectively.

Table 6.3   Calculation of Quote Price

		£
Materials	100kg at £40 per kg	4,000
Labour	240 hours at £5.00 per hour	1,200
Variable Overhead	240 hours at £15.00 per hour	3,600
Total Variable Costs		8,800
Fixed Overhead	£8,800 x 62.5 ÷ 100	5,500
Total Cost		14,300
Budgeted Profit	£14,300 x 20 ÷ 100	2,860
Quote Price		17,160

The steps to be taken in the calculation of the product cost/quote price are shown below:

1. Materials: Calculate the price per kilogram, i.e. £200,000 ÷ 5,000 kg = £40.00 per kg.

2. Labour: Calculate the labour hour rate, i.e. £50,000 ÷ 10,000 hours = £5.00 per labour hour.

3. Variable Overhead: Calculate the variable overheads on a labour hour basis i.e. variable overheads divided by labour hours = £150,000 ÷ 10,000 hours = £15.00 per labour hour.

    Please note, in 2. above we have found that the labour hour rate is £5.00 per labour hour, while in 3. above we have found that the variable overhead rate is £15.00 per labour hour. Therefore for each hour worked we have to recover £5.00 to pay the wages plus £15.00 to cover our variable overheads.

4. Total variable cost is the sum of materials + labour + variable overheads i.e. £4,000 + £1,200 + £3,600 = £8,800.

5. Fixed Overhead: We are told that this will be recovered as a percentage of total variable cost, therefore we have to calculate this percentage i.e. £250,000 ÷ £400,000 x 100 = 62.5%.

6.   Total cost is the sum of total variable cost plus fixed overhead i.e. £8,800 + £5,500 = £14,300.

7.   Budgeted Profit: We are told that budgeted profit will be added as a percentage of total cost, therefore we have to calculate this percentage. Budgeted profit is £130,000 and total cost is (£250,000 + £400,000) £650,000. Therefore the percentage is £130,000 ÷ £650,000 x 100 = 20%.

8.   The price to quote is the total cost plus the budgeted profit i.e. £14,300 + £2,860 = £17,160.

In summary, in determining the cost of a product or service it is not usually the direct costs that are difficult. It is the apportionment of overheads that provides the challenge. Overhead absorption costing is a mechanism to enable the total production cost, including overheads, to be identified with a product or service to enable management to more fully understand and appreciate the determinants of product/service cost and profitability. However, it does have its opponents. Concern about the 'traditional' methods of apportioning and absorbing overhead accurately led to the original development of activity based costing (which is reviewed later in this chapter). Concern about the validity of apportioning fixed costs over products/services and including fixed costs in stock valuations led to the development of an alternative method of costing. This is marginal costing and will be reviewed in the next section.

2. Marginal Costing

Marginal costing is an alternative costing system of accounting for costs and profit, and is also known as variable costing and direct costing (in the US). Although marginal costing is the most used term, theoretically, it can be argued that the most correct expression is variable costing as it is the distinction between variable and fixed costs that is fundamental to the technique. The expression 'marginal cost' has its roots in economics where it is considered to be the incremental cost of producing one more unit, and although in marginal costing the terms marginal cost and variable cost are often used interchangeably, a variable cost in accounting terms is not necessarily a marginal cost. In accounting terms, variable cost is the average variable unit cost of production within the relevant range of activity. The expression 'direct costing' is really quite confusing, because marginal costing is not concerned with the classification of direct and indirect costs. However do be aware that organisations will use many different expressions for costing techniques and an understanding of the underlying principles is important to help you to appreciate what is being used! In what follows where the expression 'marginal cost' is used it is taking the accountant's interpretation, i.e. the same as variable cost.

The following is CIMA's definitions of marginal costing, and marginal cost:

"Marginal costing – the accounting system in which variable costs are charged to cost units and fixed costs of the period are written off in full against the aggregate contribution."

"Marginal cost – the cost of one unit of product or service which would be avoided if that unit were not produced or provided."

In marginal costing, costs are segregated between variable and fixed. The variable costs are deducted from revenue for the period to provide a new measure of performance – contribution. This is a key concept in the technique. *Table 6.3* shows that having deducted the variable costs from the sales, what is left is the amount that contributes towards covering the fixed costs and providing profit.

Table 6.3 Marginal Cost Statement

	£
Sales	100,000
less Variable Costs	50,000
Contribution	50,000
less Fixed Costs	30,000
Profit	20,000

In using the marginal costing technique there is no attempt to apportion fixed costs to products. Here we can calculate the contribution each product makes towards covering the fixed costs and profit. The fixed costs are controlled through the budgeting system and are written off to the profit and loss account as a cost of the accounting period. *Table 6.4* illustrates a marginal cost statement for products.

Table 6.4 Marginal Cost Statement – Products A and B

	Product A £	Product B £	Total £
Sales	60,000	40,000	100,000
less Variable Costs	33,000	17,000	50,000
Contribution	27,000	23,000	50,000
less Fixed Costs			30,000
Profit			20,000

Those in favour of marginal costing argue that looking at the contribution offered by an individual product/service, without considering the sometimes arbitrary apportionment of fixed costs provides a fairer assessment of that product or service's worth. We will not expand on this here because this type of situation and others where the use of such analysis can be helpful for decision-making are addressed in *Chapter 8*, but there are implications in terms of assessing cost and profit using this technique compared to using absorption costing which need to be considered.

Marginal/Absorption Costing

In marginal costing, only variable costs are charged as a cost of sale, the difference between these and sales providing a contribution. Closing stocks of finished goods or work in progress are valued at marginal production cost. The fixed costs are treated as a period cost, being written off in full in the period in which they are incurred.

In absorption costing, all production costs are charged as a cost of sale, the difference between these and sales providing a gross or operating margin. Closing stocks of finished goods or work in progress are valued at full production cost. The fixed production costs incorporated in the closing stock valuations are carried forward to the balance sheet, the cost only being taken to the profit and loss account when these stocks are sold.

Therefore, in a period when there is no difference between sales and production, i.e. no stock, there will be no difference between reported costs and profits using the marginal or absorption costing techniques. However, when there is a difference between sales and production, the profit reported using the marginal costing technique will differ from that reported using the absorption costing technique.

Example – Profit Calculations using Marginal and Absorption Costing

A company makes and sells a single product. At the beginning of the first period, there are no opening stocks of the product.

Variable Cost	=	£8 per unit
Selling Price	=	£20 per unit
Fixed Cost	=	£15,000 for the period,
		of which £9,600 are fixed production costs.
Sales	=	3,200 units
Production	=	3,200 units
Planned Output Level	=	3,200 units

Table 6.5   Profit Calculations using Marginal and Absorption Costing

---

a. Marginal Costing

	£
Sales	64,000
less Variable Costs	25,600
Contribution	38,400
less Fixed Costs	15,000
Net Profit	23,400

b. Absorption Costing

	£
Sales	64,000
less Cost of Sales [1]	35,200
Gross Profit	28,800
less Other Fixed Costs	5,400
Net Profit	23,400

[1]   The absorption rate for the fixed production overhead is £9,600 ÷ 3,200 = £3. Therefore total production cost per unit = variable cost of £8 + fixed production overhead of £3 = £11. Total production cost for 3,200 units = (3,200 x £11) £35,200.

It can be seen that where there are no closing stocks, levels of calculated net profit are the same. All that differs is the presentation of the information. *Table 6.6* shows that this will not be the case where there are units of stock.

Let us now assume that instead of sales of 3,200 units, only 2,700 units are sold, 500 being left in stock:

Table 6.6   *Profit calculations using marginal and absorption costing – with stock*

---

a. Marginal costing

	£	£
Sales		54,000
less Variable Cost of Sales:		
Production Costs	25,600	
less Closing Stock (1)	4,000	
		21,600
Contribution		32,400
less Fixed Costs		15,000
Net Profit		17,400

(1) 500 units valued at variable cost of £8

b. Absorption costing

	£	£
Sales		54,000
less Cost of Sales:		
Production Costs	35,200	
less Closing Stock (2)	5,500	
		29,700
Gross Profit		24,300
less Other Fixed Costs		5,400
Net Profit		18,900

(2) 500 units valued at full production cost, i.e. £11

This illustrates the differing levels of profit calculated using the different methods. Here, where production exceeds sales, the absorption costing profit is higher by £1,500 than that calculated using marginal costing. This difference relates to the fixed production cost of £3 per unit being carried forward in the valuation of the 500 units of stock: here the fixed production cost is treated as a product cost, rather than being charged as a period cost to the profit and loss account as is the case with marginal costing.

It should be noted that the differences in profit are related to timing and in the long run total profit will be the same whichever technique is used. In *Table 6.7* we will assume in the following period that costs stay the same, 2,700 units are produced and 3,200 units are sold utilising the stock.

Table 6.7   Profit Calculations using Marginal and Absorption Costing – with Stock

a.   Marginal Costing

	Period 1		Period 2	
	£	£	£	£
Sales		54,000		64,000
less Variable Cost of Sales:				
Opening Stock	0		4,000	
Production Costs	25,600		21,600	
less Closing Stock	4,000		0	
		21,600		25,600
Contribution		32,400		38,400
less Fixed Costs		15,000		15,000
Net Profit		17,400		23,400

b.   Absorption Costing

	Period 1		Period 2	
	£	£	£	£
Sales		54,000		64,000
less Cost of Sales:				
Opening Stock	0		5,500	
Production Costs	35,200		29,700	
less Closing Stock	5,500		0	
		29,700		35,200
Gross Profit		24,300		28,800
less Other Fixed Costs		5,400		5,400
Underabsorbed Overhead [1]				1,500
Net Profit		18,900		21,900

[1]   in period 2 only 2,700 units are produced, absorbing fixed production overhead of 2,700 x £3 = £8,100. The planned output level upon which the calculation of the fixed production overhead per unit was based was 3,200 units. There has been an underabsorption of overhead of 500 units x £3, which has to be charged to the profit and loss account.

It can be seen in *Table 6.8* that the total profit over the two periods is the same for marginal and absorption costing:

Table 6.8   Profit Comparisons using Marginal and Absorption Costing

Profit	Marginal Costing £	Absorption Costing £
Period 1	17,400	18,900
Period 2	23,400	21,900
Period 1 and 2	40,800	40,800

We have considered alternative techniques, identifying that the use of marginal or absorption costing will produce different levels of profit, cost and stock valuation. The choice between the two methods depends upon situation and purpose. Internally, organisations are free to choose the techniques which suit their purpose best. Externally, however, there is a need for organisations to report consistently, and the requirement of Statement of Standard Accounting Practice 9 is for companies to use absorption costing for external reporting. You will meet marginal costing principles again in *Chapter 8* where you will see how the use of the variable/fixed cost classification can be very valuable in certain types of short-term decision analysis.

3.   Standard Costing

1. Introduction

An early CIMA definition for standard costing states:

> *"A standard cost is a predetermined cost calculated in relation to a prescribed set of working conditions, correlating technical specification and scientific measurement of materials and labour to the prices and wage rates expected to apply during the period to which the standard cost is expected to relate with an addition of an appropriate share of budgeted overhead."*

That being said, we all practice the basic techniques of standard costing in our daily lives. For example, driving to work – we normally have a standard time in mind that can be used to compare our actual time taken, the difference being the variance from the standard time (allowed). When setting our standard time we would have to take into account, the likely road conditions, the performance of the car and the abilities of the driver. If we completed the journey in less time (or more time) we could explain the reason(s) why.

Driving to work is a repetitive activity, therefore, it lends itself to the development of a standard. In business, standard costing is applied to the planning and control of direct materials and direct labour, although it can be used to develop a full standard cost and price for a product or service.

2. Setting the Standards

Who Would Set the Standards for Materials?

An engineer, designer, chemist or similar person would prepare a specification of material required, both quality and quantity. The recipe in a cookery book is a good example. It not only gives a listing of the ingredients and quantities but also specifies the method to be used.

The method to be used would dictate the prescribed set of working conditions (the driving to work example), in terms of location, equipment and people.

Standard prices are determined for each material. These will be prepared by the appropriate purchasing specialist and will apply throughout the period to which the standards have been developed, normally in line with the budget period.

Who Would Set the Standards for Labour?

An industrial engineer will determine the best working method (using method study) and will then carry out timings to find out the time taken to complete each part of the process including the number of people and their grades.

It is important to recognise that should the working method change then the standard times will change. Often the labour standards have been reduced in the standard costs, in anticipation of the revision to the working method – normally a saving in labour through increased mechanisation.

Standard labour rates are determined for each grade of labour. The Personnel Director would be responsible for setting a base labour rate from which all other rates would be adjusted. When setting standard labour rates it is important to take into account holiday pay, normal bonus payments, normal overtime working and the mix of labour grades for each process.

What is a Normal Standard?

A normal standard is one that considers normal working conditions and a normal (achievable) level of activity. It is a standard that a worker can achieve without resorting to changes in working methods. If a standard is set too tight and is not achievable, it is unlikely that the workforce will recognise the standard and will not produce the desired result.

3. Variance Analysis

In budgeting systems, budget holders develop their budgets for the coming year. Once approved, these are used to compare actual expenditure and identify variances from budget. The same principle applies in standard costing systems where standard costs are developed for each product or service. Once approved, these are used to compare actual costs and identify variances from standard costs.

In standard costing these variances are used to determine who is responsible for each variance. For example, the material cost variance is split into a material usage variance and a material price variance. The former would be the responsibility of the production manager/supervisor, while the latter would be the responsibility of the purchasing specialist.

Standard Costing – Example

A company manufactures a component with the following specification for direct labour:

Standard Direct Labour Hours   20 hours

Standard Direct Labour Rate   £5.00 per hour

During the month 250 components were produced, and the actual wages paid amounted to £30,800 for 5,600 hours worked.

Table 6.9   Calculation of Standard Costing Variances – Labour

Column A			Column B			Column C		
Standard Hours times Standard Rate			Actual Hours times Standard Rate			Actual Hours times Actual Rate		
Hours	Rate	£	Hours	Rate	£	Hours	Rate	£
5,000	5.00	25,000	5,600	5.00	28,000	5,600	5.50	30,800

£3,000 adverse   £2,800 adverse
Labour Efficiency Variance   Labour Rate Variance

£5,800 adverse
Labour Cost Variance

The steps to be taken in the calculation of the labour variances are shown below:

1. Enter actual hours and actual wages paid in Column C, i.e. 5,600 hours and £30,800. Optional, divide the actual wages paid by the actual hours to arrive at the actual rate, i.e. £30,800 ÷ 5,600 hours = £5.50. *We will use this actual rate when interpretating the labour rate variance, see below.*

2. Enter actual hours in Column B.

3. Enter standard labour rate in Column B, then multiply the actual hours by the standard rate, i.e. 5,600 hours x £5.00 = £28,000.

4. Calculate the standard labour hours (number of components multiplied by the standard hour per component), i.e. 250 components x 5 hours = 5,000 hours. Enter the result in Column A.

5. Multiply the standard hours by the standard rate, i.e. 5,000 hours x £5.00 = £25,000. Enter the result in Column A.

6. Calculate and interpret the variances:

    Labour Cost Variance. This is the total variance and is calculated by taking Column A minus Column C, i.e. £25,000 − £30,800 = £5,800 adverse. Interpretation; we were 'allowed' £25,000 to produce the 250 components. We actually paid £30,800 in wages, therefore, the adverse variance of £5,800. Interpretation; it is not possible to say much about this variance other than it is favourable or in this case adverse. We must look at the two subsidiary variance, labour efficiency and labour rate, to find out the causes.

    Labour Efficiency Variance. This is a sub-variance of the labour cost variance and is found by taking Column A minus Column B i.e. £25,000 − £28,000 = £3,000 adverse. Interpretation; we were 'allowed' 5,000 hours to produce the 250 components. We actually took 5,600 hours, i.e. 600 hours more at the standard labour rate of £5.00 per hour = 600 hours x £5.00 = £3,000 adverse. Consider reasons for the labour efficiency variance between the standard hours 'allowed' and the actual hours taken; could be caused by using incorrect skill of labour.

    Labour Rate Variance. This is a sub-variance of the labour cost variance and is found by taking Column B minus Column C i.e. £28,000 − £30,800 = £2,800 adverse. Interpretation; for 5,600 hours worked, we were 'allowed' £28,000 at the standard labour rate. The actual wages paid were £30,800. This can be checked by taking the actual hours worked and multiplying by the difference between the standard labour hour rate and the actual labour hour rate, i.e. 5,600 hours x (£5.00 − £5.50) = £2,800 adverse. Consider reasons for the labour rate variance; increase in actual labour rates above those incorporated into the standard labour rate, similar with overtime rates; could have used a different (more expensive) grade of labour.

In the next chapter on budgeting, you will find illustrations of the calculation of material and labour variances, where these are linked to the variances identified when a budget is flexed to take into account the actual level of activity achieved in a budget period.

6.5 Activity Based (Costing) Analysis and Reasons for its Development

1. Introduction

Traditionally the costing of products was associated with manufacturing organisations. Costing systems decades ago were required by companies which manufactured a narrow range of products where direct labour and materials were the dominant factory costs. For such organisations overhead costs were relatively small and the distortions arising from overhead allocations were not significant.

We have illustrated how costs are allocated to cost centres by applying judgement, for example rent and rates on the basis of floor space occupied. Once all such overheads have been allocated, they could then be apportioned to products or services on the basis of labour hours.

Although such cost allocation and apportionment methods have been developed in manufacturing organisations they are not readily transferrable to the growing service sector. In services the relationship between costs and the activities from which costs arise is more problematic. It is this background which has led to the development of Activity Based Costing (ABC).

For financial service providers, like banks, activity-based costing has particular attractions because such organisations operate in a highly competitive environment and they incur a large amount of support overhead costs that cannot be directly assigned to specific cost objects. Furthermore, their products and customers differ significantly in terms of consuming overhead resources.

ABC systems assume that activities cause costs to be incurred and that products (or other selected cost objects, such as customers and branches in the case of a bank) consume activities in varying amounts. A link is made between activities and products by assigning the cost of activities to products based on an individual product's demand for each activity.

The development of an ABC system will involve the following:

❑ The identification of the key activities that take place in the organisation.

❑ The creation of a cost pool for each major activity.

❏   The assignment of costs to activity cost pools.

❏   The determination of the cost driver for each activity cost pool.

❏   The determination of the unit cost for each activity.

❏   The assignment of the costs of activities to selected cost objects (for example, products) according to the cost object's demand for each activity.

Stage 1 identifies the major activities performed in the enterprise. Activities are simply the tasks that people or machines perform in order to provide a product or service. For example, in retail banking this would correspond with processing a deposit, issuing a credit card, processing a cheque, setting up a loan, opening an account or processing monthly statements, and so on. In a support activity like a personnel department, activities would be recruitment, remuneration, training, union negotiation, personnel administration, and staff welfare.

Stage 2 creates a cost pool for each activity, and then in stage 3 costs are analysed and assigned to the appropriate activity pool. For example, the total cost of processing a deposit might constitute one activity cost pool in a retail bank for all deposit processing related costs, with separate cost pools being created for each type of deposit account if different types of deposits consume resources differently. In a personnel department, recruitment may constitute an activity pool for recruitment related costs like advertising, interviewing, contracts, and induction.

Stage 4 then identifies the factors that influence the cost of a particular activity. The term 'cost driver' is used to describe the events or forces that are the significant determinants of the cost of the activities. For example, if the cost of processing deposits is generated by the number of deposits processed then the number of deposits processed would represent the cost driver for deposit processing activities. In the case of a personnel department the cost drivers would be staff recruited, staff retired, staff on roll.

The cost driver selected for each cost pool should be the one that, as closely as possible, mirrors the consumption of the activities represented by the cost centre. Examples of cost drivers that might be appropriate for other retail banking activities include:

❏   Number of applications processed for setting up a loan;

❏   Number of statements mailed for processing monthly statements;

❏   Number of mortgage payments past due date for processing activities relating to mortgage arrears.

The next stage divides the cost traced to each activity cost pool by the total number of driver units in order to calculate a cost per unit of activity.

Finally, the cost of specific activities is traced to products (or services) according to their demand for the activities by multiplying unit activity costs by the quantity of each activity that a product consumes.

The total cost of a product or service is then found by adding the individual costs of the activities that are required to deliver the product or service. In other words, a product or service can be viewed as a bundle of activities. ABC focuses on the costing of these activities and the bundling of them into products, customers or any other cost objects.

ABC seeks to measure as accurately as possible those resources consumed by products or services, whereas traditional costing systems just allocate and apportion costs to products or services. The ABC approach seems to offer considerable advantages as can be seen if we reconsider our retail banking example. The traditional approach might allocate deposit transaction processing costs to customers, or different types of deposit accounts, on the basis of the number of customer accounts. This would distort product costs if deposit processing costs are driven by the number of transactions processed. Allocating cost according to the number of customers will lead to low value deposit accounts that involve numerous 'over-the-counter' transactions being under-costed, whereas high value long-term savings accounts requiring very few transactions will be over-costed. In contrast, an ABC system would establish a separate cost centre for deposit processing activities, ascertain what causes the costs (that is, determine the appropriate cost driver, such as the number of transactions processed) and assign costs to products on the basis of a product's demand for the activity.

ABC Example

The following provides an illustration of the assignment of costs on an activity base compared with the more 'traditional' view. Here we consider an estate agency, where there are three 'lines of business', Residential, Commercial and Letting.

Total overheads are £750,000, which have, in the past, been allocated to products on the basis of sales commission. Sales commission for the past year was:

	£
Residential	350,000
Commercial	750,000
Letting	150,000

An ABC analysis has been undertaken and the following costs drivers and overhead costs by activity identified:

Overhead costs:

	£
Occupancy (4,000 sq. ft in total)	200,000
Salaries	360,000
Advertising	190,000

Cost drivers:

	Residential	Commercial	Letting
Floor space - sq. ft.	1,000	2,000	1,000
No. staff	3	5	4
No. advertisements	8	5	6

Table 6.10 Calculation of Overheads to 'Lines of Business'

Original basis:

	£
Residential	210,000
Commercial	450,000
Letting	90,000
Total overheads	750,000

Using ABC:

	Occupancy	Salaries	Advertising	Total
Calculated on the basis of:	Floor Area	No. Staff	No Adverts	
	£	£	£	£
Residential	50,000	90,000	80,000	220,000
Commercial	100,000	150,000	50,000	300,000
Letting	50,000	120,000	60,000	230,000
Total Overheads	200,000	360,000	190,000	750,000

This simple illustration serves to show that using a more comprehensive basis for apportioning the overhead relative to the 'consumption' for each activity will provide a more realistic basis for determining the overhead for each 'line of business'.

2.   How is ABC Applied?

Activity-based profitability analysis is best thought of in hierarchical terms. First, the costs of undertaking the various activities should be listed, and those that can be analysed by products should be deducted from revenues, so that a contribution to profits can be derived for each product. Products in our retail banking example are deposit accounts and loans and an example of a specific cost would be an advertising campaign aimed at one specific type of loan.

The next level is the product line or product group. For example, deposit accounts and loans may represent some of the individual products within the product line. Although some expenses can be traced to them individually, some of those incurred are common to all products within the product line and are not identifiable with individual products. These expenses are function, or product-line-sustaining, expenses and are traced to product lines but not to individual products within the line.

Not all costs can be readily assigned to products. Some costs are common and joint to all products. These costs are called business or facility-sustaining expenses and include such items as top management salaries. When deducted as a lump sum from the total of all the profit margins from all the individual products lines yield the overall profit of the enterprise or a particular strategic business unit.

3.   How ABC can Help in Managing Costs

ABC has attracted a considerable amount of interest because it provides not only a basis for more accurately determining the cost and profitability of individual products, product lines, customers and branches, but also a mechanism for managing costs. It is in the area of cost management and cost control that ABC could have its greatest potential.

As we have shown, traditional accounting control systems are not particularly helpful for controlling overhead costs. Activity based costing concentrates on managing the business on the basis of activities that make up the organisation. By collecting and reporting the costs consumed by the significant activities of a business, it is possible to understand and manage costs (including overhead costs) more effectively.

With an ABC system, costs are managed in the long-term by controlling the activities that drive them. In other words, the aim is to manage the activities rather than the costs. By managing the forces that cause the activities (that is, the cost drivers), cost will be managed in the long-term.

It is claimed that ABC results in organisations reaching a better understanding of costs and their causes. This opens up opportunities to reduce or eliminate activities that do not add value.

Because traditional management accounting reports may not be able to show how much activities cost, charting the flow of activities and estimating the activities' costs should enable management to see the costs being incurred and the waste that has been tolerated in the past. Managers are frequently surprised at how many activities are performed within their organisation that do not add value to any product or service but consume significant resources. These non-value added activities are often repeatedly incurred because they have been hidden by traditional cost systems. ABC makes them visible so that steps can be made to eliminate them. Furthermore, by merely knowing the costs of activities, potential non-value added activities are highlighted so that steps can be taken to improve profitability.

Consider a situation where loans staff, as a result of costing activities, are informed that it costs £100 to process and maintain loans of less than £500. They become aware that it is questionable to provide loans of less than £500 unless more cost effective ways can be found of undertaking this activity. Similarly, if the cost of processing and maintaining low value and high value mortgages is the same, management is made aware that it is more profitable to focus on high value rather than low value mortgages.

It is important to note, however, that process improvements should lead to actions that reduce resource spending or the creation of extra resources that lead to higher profits.

Problems Associated with Managing Internally Transferred Costs and Achieving Value for Money

Most organisations are very conscious of the problems of overhead cost control, but there are some types of cost that require particular attention because they may not arise to the recipient as a consequence of an 'arms length' decision to incur them in that form specifically. For example, the decision may have been made at some time in the past to purchase a computer system that all within the organisation will be required to use and pay for. In such circumstances, where there is an internal rather than an external market, there is a challenge to ensure that value for money is achieved.

'Value-for-money' could mean getting the same goods or services for less expenditure (that is, a cost reduction) or it could mean obtaining better quality goods or services for the same expenditure. Value-for-money exercises involve management in detailed considerations of all the organisation's overheads. Each overhead cost centre must ask, 'Is this cost really necessary'? and, 'What is the maximum amount of value that can be achieved for the minimum amount of expenditure'?

6.6   Service Level Agreements

Within many organisations the question of whether value for money is being received where one profit/cost centre provides a service to another is currently under consideration with reference to what are known as 'Service Level Agreements'. These agreements are drawn up to set out an agreed basis in terms of service and costs and should cover:

❏ The nature of the service provided.

❏ Service usage/volume expectations.

❏ Quality standards and performance measures for the provision of the service.

❏ The charging basis for the service provided.

❏ The arrangements to be applied if either side fails to meet its 'contractual' commitments, including details of any transfer charging implications.

The nature of the 'service' provided from one profit/cost centre to another will vary from centre to centre and the service level agreement should therefore reflect the specific nature and complexity of the relationship between the centres.

CHAPTER SEVEN

BUDGETING
AND
BUDGETARY
CONTROL

When you have finished studying this chapter you should be able to:

❏ Identify the diverse range of organisations to which budgeting is appropriate.

❏ Outline the activities which can be identified as being an integral part of the budgeting process.

❏ Describe the main budgeting techniques including flexible budgets, zero based budgeting and rolling budgets.

❏ Explain the key elements in administrating a budget.

❏ Prepare and interpret cash budgets.

❏ Prepare and interpret the main budget financial statements including cash budget, profit and loss and balance sheet.

7.1   Introduction

In *Chapter 1* we reviewed the main financial statements together with the accounting principles and policies important in drafting them. Here we place these financial statements into context by reviewing business planning, its links with budgeting, and how the main financial statements can be used effectively in business planning.

In common with earlier chapters it is important to stress that the purpose of this chapter is *not* to make you into a financial specialist. Although the output from the budgeting process may be expressed in financial terms, the purpose underlying budgeting is to ensure that scarce resources are allocated as efficiently and effectively as possible. In other words, budgeting is a *managerial process*.

The result of budgeting we will illustrate as being a set of financial statements in the form of a profit and loss account, balance sheet and cash flow forecast. These statements are prepared and approved prior to a defined future period, for the purpose of attaining specific objectives.

Budgeting is used in organisations of all types to help in the development and co-ordination of plans, to communicate those plans to the people who are responsible for carrying them out, to secure co-operation of managers at all levels and as a standard against which actual results can be compared. You will find budgeting used in a diverse range of organisations and activities including:

❏   Central and local government.

❏   The health service.

❏   Education.

❏   Large companies.

❏   Small businesses (such as the local garage).

❏   Churches.

❏   Charities.

❏   Television and radio networks.

❏   Local clubs.

❏   The family.

The analogy of our discussions with the family budget may be helpful. For example, a budget could be compared with the preparation of a shopping list. In its preparation we would be able to make changes to the list to ensure that personal objectives were met both for the goods obtained and money spent.

During the actual shopping activity, regular comparisons of actual spend against budget could be undertaken and, if necessary, changes could be made to attain our objectives.

Why budget? Consider the alternative of shopping without making a mental or written list. The outcome might be that many of the important items would not be bought and/or a situation of overspend reached, a feature of many bankrupt companies!

7.2   Planning the Business through Budgets

Organisations plan for the future in a number of ways. One useful way of looking at the process is to consider it in relation to the planning horizon – that is, the time span to be covered. One straightforward framework considers planning in the following three phases:

–   Long-term.

–   Medium-term.

–   Short-term.

There is no universally accepted definition of the period of time for which each plan should apply; it very much depends on the type of business – its markets, product life cycles, etc. However, the purpose of each phase in the planning process is quite clear.

Long-term planning is essentially a strategic exercise aimed at assessing trends and identifying and choosing between alternative courses of action over a period of many years.

Medium-term planning, is a more practical exercise aimed at optimising the use of resources over a manageable future period, bearing in mind the strategies identified in the long-term planning process.

Short-term planning, or budgeting, is a much more detailed process in which the medium-term objectives can be modified and adapted in response to immediate pressures and constraints. The short-term plan or budget normally covers periods of up to one year. It is this document (or set of documents) with which we will be most concerned in this chapter.

7.3 Budget Environment

Successful budgeting is difficult, particularly in large complex organisations. To achieve success attention has to be paid to a number of activities which can be identified as being an integral part of the budgeting process. These are:

❏   Defining Objectives.

❏   Planning.

❏   Organising.

❏   Controlling.

❏   Co-ordinating.

❏   Communicating.

❏   Motivating.

1. Defining Objectives

A budget must relate to and support the achievement of an organisation's financial objectives. Rational financial objectives should be set, bearing in mind the risk associated with them and the uncertainty of the future in relation to the return which shareholders expect from their investment.

Budget objectives or targets have two further characteristics. They should be capable of:

❏   Attainment by the managers concerned, and

❏   Objective measurement.

The budgeting process cannot be seriously undertaken until top management has defined in measurable terms the objectives of the business to be achieved during the period of the budget. Objectives might include:

❏   The achievement of a specified percentage return on capital employed.

❏   The reduction of borrowing by a specified amount.

❏   An increase in market share by a specified percentage.

❏   The introduction of a specified number of new products.

❏   The reduction of labour turnover by a specified figure.

A good framework is captured in the acronym S.M.A.R.T. which stands for the following; Specific, Measurable, Achieveable, Realistic and Time banded.

Whether the objectives set are acceptable will depend on:

❑ What has been achieved in the current and recent years

❑ Comparison with the performance of other business units working in similar business environments

❑ Management's opinion of what can be achieved in the business environment of the near future

The above are only a few examples of possible business objectives. They will usually relate to a range of activities within a company and not necessarily be restricted to purely financial or profit orientated objectives.

One key issue in defining objectives concerns those factors which limit the ability of an organisation to do exactly as it would wish. These are known as *limiting factors* and can be broken down into two types:

1. External factors over which an organisation has no direct control. The *external factors* might be the availability of:

   ❑ Sales demand in the marketplace.

   ❑ Raw materials.

   ❑ Scarce and specialised equipment.

   ❑ Skilled employees.

   In many cases external limiting factors can be related to the economic climate.

2. Internal factors over which it has a considerable amount of control. The factors which may limit the firm *internally* could include the following:

   ❑ Productive capacity of the company.

   ❑ Capacity and skill of the work force.

   ❑ Availability of cash.

All organisations will encounter constraints which limit their ability to do exactly as they wish. Some of these will be obvious, others not so obvious. The attainment of budgetary goals is limited by the capacity and commitments of the organisation as it currently exists. It is vital to identify and monitor closely the more important limiting factors in an organisation in order to set realistically attainable targets and budgets.

Limiting factors are identified in the external environment by the use of subjective judgement. Consideration of the social, technological, economic and political domains together with the competitive environment are a key part of strategic analysis and decision making which can be used to inform the budgeting process.

The limiting factors internal to the organisation are much less problematic. Objective measurements can be made of skills, capacities and other resources available which may limit the provision of goods or services to the market.

Careful and systematic consideration of both external and internal constraints may lead to the identification of previously unknown limiting factors, thus alerting management to problems likely to occur during implementation of a particular strategy.

Once top management has agreed overall company objectives then particular areas of responsibility can be assigned to lower levels of management and the budgetary process can commence.

2. Planning

Planning within the budgeting process takes place by the expression of departmental, functional or cost centre activities for the forthcoming year within individual budgets. These budgets will relate to the business objectives set by or agreed with top management for the year and will usually be a part of the overall budget, commonly called the 'master budget'.

Good planning provides the opportunity to evaluate alternative courses of action so that resources may be used effectively under conditions of minimum risk.

There are many different types of plans which will need to be developed into budgets, examples of which are:

❑ Sales plans.

❑ Purchasing plans.

❑ Manpower plans.

❑ Research and development plans.

❑ Capital expenditure plans.

❑ Marketing plans and business plans.

How are these plans linked and drawn together as budgets? As indicated in the last section, most organisations should have some idea of which aspects of the business limit their ability to generate profits; that is, where their major limiting factors are to be found. This should be the point at which they enter the budgeting process.

Very often, demand and the availability of the resources to meet it will be major constraints. For example, in times of buoyant sales prospects, actual sales may be limited by the maximum physical productive capacity of the organisation. On the other hand, where forecast sales demand is below the productive capacity of the business, the projected budget for the use of resources will be based on those sales forecasts.

Figure 7.1   Master Budget and Financial Objectives

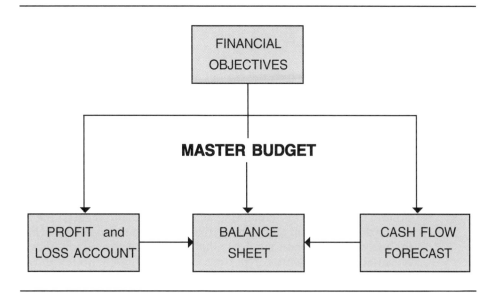

Theoretically, once the limiting factors have been identified the budgeting process should be simple to complete. In practice, however, the process is rather more complex, since the tendency is for the various budgets to be prepared in a predetermined sequence, each budget feeding information to the next. As problems of incompatibility between budgets occur, these are solved by going back through the process and re-budgeting as necessary. The entire exercise becomes one of negotiation and agreement between the various parties to the process.

Alternative scenarios can be analysed through a master budget which is illustrated in *Figure 7.1*. This consists of a profit and loss account, balance sheet and cash flow forecast. Once approved the master budget allows management to plan and co-ordinate the future direction of the business.

3. Organising

A budget will not happen on its own. The more physical and human resources that are involved the less likely is it to be conceived or achieved without good organisation.

Organising necessitates an understanding of the organisational structure, the tasks, the processes and systems, and the people involved if any agreed budget is to have any chance of success. In particular its success requires the following characteristics:

❑   The definition of the organisation structure so that possible areas of overlap can be identified and removed or at least reduced.

❑   The identification of tasks, responsibilities and the methods by which individuals will be measured.

❑   The means by which the budgeting activities will take place, including any training and/or documentation required.

❑   The recognition that budgeting can only be achieved through people and that they are an integral part of the process and any systems developed.

4. Controlling

Control is achieved by monitoring actual performance against the budget plan, noting deviations and taking corrective action where necessary. This is done by the analysis of variances similar to that of standard costing (discussed in *Chapter 6*). In addition, exception reporting is used to highlight only those deviations from the plan which warrant management attention.

The reporting of variances may be made before expenditure occurs where proposed spending is set against the budget or after the event when actual spending is compared to the plan. The former allows management to modify spending (for example, by seeking a cheaper source of supply) while the latter enables management to adjust future spending or ask for extra resources to conform to the plan.

5. Co-ordinating

Co-ordinating is an integral part of the budgeting process. Having organised, as discussed earlier, there is the need to look at the sequencing and interrelationships of the individual budget components.

As with limiting factors, it is difficult to view any process without considering its effect on other processes. Co-ordinating can be seen as a balancing activity which seeks to allocate priorities by predetermined agreement and also to unite a number of individual activities into a whole.

The different viewpoints of the co-ordinating process are usually apparent when agreeing company objectives. The activities will take into account the overall balance within the company, also such things as competitors and customers, economic political and social change, and if there is a need to change the future direction of the company.

6. Communicating

Within any budgeting system communication is important. Everyone concerned needs to know about:

❏ Objectives;

❏ Guidelines;

❏ Completed budgets and revisions;

❏ Actual results;

❏ Deviations from budget;

❏ Corrective action to be taken; and,

❏ Revisions to be included into forecasts which are provided to relevant management in an appropriate form.

7. Motivating

The budgeting process is often considered as a purely mechanical exercise. It is argued, however, that the process is just as much a political as a mechanical process. Any system which seeks to allocate scarce resources through a decision making hierarchy which is characterised by its unequal distribution of power, is bound to be influenced by internal politics. This may tend to upset the objective calculations of the designers.

Problems caused by political influences include the pursuit of personal or group objectives at the expense of the whole organisation (lack of goal congruence), built-in slack in budget estimates, where targets tend to be imposed from above and the adoption of short-term perspectives at the expense of long-term profit optimisation.

The problem is how can we know that if we take certain actions, then individuals will respond in a particular manner? For example, why do some managers like the budgeting process? Is it the challenge? Is it the power that information gives? Is it the 'games' they can play? Is it because they understand the system? Is it because they can see the purpose of the budgeting system? Is it because they are winning?

7.4   Budgetary Control

Of equal importance to planning in the budgeting process is the need to establish a monitoring system to ensure that budget targets are met. Such a system is concerned with the:

❑   Comparison of actual results against budget;

❑   Identification, recording and communication of controllable differences; and,

❑   Taking of corrective action either to maintain budget levels or to replan to meet recent developments.

The comparison of actual against budgeted performance requires that the budget is divided into monthly/four weekly periods against which actual results for each period may be compared.

To facilitate the control process, organisations may adopt approaches like flexible budgeting and/or rolling budgets. In the first case, differences in volume between the budget and actual performance are incorporated in a revised budget. In the second case, a re-forecasting process is used to update the original budget.

7.5   Budgeting Techniques

1. Fixed/Flexible Budgets

A fixed budget is one designed to remain unchanged irrespective of the level of activity. However, in most companies, levels of activity and operating conditions vary from month to month. Controlling against a fixed budget will lead to significant variances when activity levels are not as planned. To aid the control process, differences in volume between budget and actual performance are incorporated in a revised, or flexible, budget.

It is important to ensure that the comparison of budgeted and actual performances matches like with like. For example, if actual sales volumes are higher than budgeted, then certain items in the budget which are volume related should be increased. If this process was omitted a simple comparison would show an overspending on variable cost items, the result of which would be to record an unrealistic difference from budget. This is illustrated in *Table 7.1* below where the planned level of activity was the production and sale of 48,000 meals, whereas the reality was that 60,000 meals were produced and sold.

Table 7.1   Comparison of Budget and Actual

Budget Activity Level: 48,000 meals
Actual Activity Level: 60,000 meals

	Unit Cost per Meal £	Variable Cost 48,000 Meals £	Fixed Cost 48,000 Meals £	Total Budget 48,000 Meals £	Total Actual 60,000 Meals £	Variance £
Sales	1.75			84,000	103,200	19,200
Ingredients	0.35	16,800		16,800	20,280	–3,480
Wages	0.55	26,400		26,400	33,000	–6,600
Electricity	0.10	4,800	1,000	5,800	6,750	–950
Administration			12,000	12,000	11,500	500
Depreciation			9,000	9,000	9,000	0
Total Costs		48,000	22,000	70,000	80,530	–10,530
Profit				14,000	22,670	8,670

It can be seen that there are significant negative cost variances, which result in actual level of total cost being £10,530 higher than budget. However, this is offset by higher actual sales – £19,200 higher than budget – resulting in £8,670 profit greater than budget. On a line by line basis this is not very helpful for control purposes. For example, wage costs are significantly higher than planned, but they were for a different level of operation. What is needed is an understanding of how they match what should have been the level of cost at the level of actual activity. A flexible budget can be used to show this. Cost and revenues at the actual level of activity are recorded and matched against actual costs and revenues to identify the variances that are not related to differences in volume.

Obviously any variation in profit as a result of volume change is also important to know, but for control purposes, knowledge of variances due to efficiency and expenditure differences are vital. To produce the flexible budget a knowledge of those costs that change as activity levels change, as opposed to those that are fixed in the period is essential. *Table 7.2* illustrates the variances when actual performance (costs and revenues) is matched against the budget for the actual level of activity, i.e. actual costs and revenues for 60,000 meals and the budget for the 60,000 meals. It can be seen that the high unfavourable total cost variance of £10,500 when actual is compared to original budget, is more realistically reported as £1,470 favourable when the budget is flexed to represent the actual level of activity. However, because of the unfavourable sales variance, when the volume increase is taken into account the profit variance reported of £8,670 against the original budget becomes £330 unfavourable.

Table 7.2   Flexed Budget v Actual

Flexed Budget Activity Level: 60,000 meals
Actual Activity Level: 60,000 meals

	Unit Cost per Meal	Variable Cost 60,000 Meals	Fixed Cost 60,000 Meals	Total Flexed Budget 60,000 Meals	Total Actual 60,000 Meals	Variance
	£	£	£	£	£	£
Sales	1.75			105,000	103,200	−1,800
Ingredients	0.35	21,000		21,000	20,280	720
Wages	0.55	33,000		33,000	33,000	0
Electricity	0.10	6,000	1,000	7,000	6,750	250
Administration			12,000	12,000	11,500	500
Depreciation			9,000	9,000	9,000	0
Total Costs		60,000	22,000	**82,000**	**80,530**	**1,470**
Profit				23,000	22,670	−330

In summary, using flexible budgeting allows separation of the causes of variance between those that are volume related and those that are related to efficiency or expenditure. In the previous example the difference between the planned outcome of £14,000 and the actual outcome of £22,670 of £8,670 is accounted for by differences in profit because of:

Changes in Volume [1]	£9,000	Favourable
Cost Expenditure and Efficiency Variances	£1,470	Favourable
Selling Performance	£1,800	Adverse
	£8,670	Favourable

[1]   Contribution margin x Volume increase = (1.75 – 1.00) x 12,000 = £9,000

The planned performance was exceeded because of the increased volume and cost efficiencies, but diluted because of the lower sales revenue achieved.

The previous examples provide illustrations of the use of flexible budgeting retrospectively in considering the variances between performance at actual level and budgeted performance at that level. However, as well as providing information about past performance preparing flexible budgets at varying levels of activity can be valuable in planning in considering the effects of changes in volume on future performance. An organisation might well consider not only the performance at its planned level, but also apply some sensitivity and consider the impact of a 5%, 10% and 15% increase or decrease from that level.

The use of variance analysis is a central part of the budgeting process. It is also used in a technique of costing, known as standard costing, in which variances are used to compare performance, assessed on predetermined costs and revenues, with actual results. By this means deviations from budget can be analysed in detail, enabling understanding and better cost control.

This technique is appropriate in situations where there are a series of repetitive operations, and in *Chapter 6, section 6.3* you will have read about this type of costing and the setting of standard costs.

Organisations using standard costing are likely to calculate variances for materials, labour, overheads and selling prices and volumes. As an illustration, variances for material and labour will be calculated using the information from the flexible budgeting example. The purpose of this illustration is to demonstrate how further analysis of the variances can be helpful for cost control.

2. Material Variances

In setting the material standard, quality, quantity and price data will be required. Let us assume that the material standard for the ingredients for one meal is calculated to be 500 g. at £0.70 per kg., i.e. £0.35. The total variance between the budgeted and actual ingredients cost of 60,000 meals is the total material (ingredients) cost variance:

Ingredients	£	
Actual Cost of Actual Production	20,280	
Standard Cost of Actual Production	21,000	
Total Material Cost Variance	720	Favourable

This total material cost variance has been caused by a number of factors, such as a change in the price from the original budget, a change from the budgeted amount of ingredient used in the production of each meal. The change could also be caused by a change in the mix and yield of ingredients. The total material cost variance can be broken down into two main variances – price and usage:

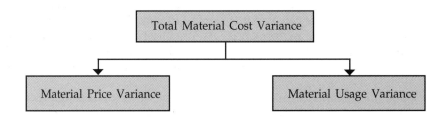

In our illustration the actual material cost for 60,000 meals was £20,280. This represents the cost of 31,200 kgs. at a cost of £0.65 per kg.

To calculate the **material price variance**, the difference between the standard (budgeted) price (SP) per kg. and the actual price (AP) per kg. is multiplied by the actual number of kilograms purchased i.e. actual quantity (AQ):

(SP – AP) AQ   (£0.70 – £0.65) 31,200 kgs.   =   £1,560 Favourable

To calculate the **material usage variance**, the difference between the standard quantity (SQ) to be used for the actual production and the actual quantity (AQ) is multiplied by the standard price (SP) per kg:

(SQ – AQ) SP   (30,000 kgs [†]. – 31,200 kgs.) £0.70   =   £ 840 Adverse

[†] 60,000 meals at 500 g per meal

The total of these two variances equals the total material cost variance, and provide the organisation with a clearer understanding of where divergences from the plan are occurring and so that the appropriate action can be taken:

	£	
Material Price Variance	1,560	Favourable
Material Usage Variance	840	Adverse
Total Material Cost Variance	720	Favourable

3. Labour Variances

In a similar way the standards for labour will be set using quality, quantity and price data, considering the level of skill required, the number of hours required for each meal and the cost of the labour per hour. Let us assume that the labour standard for one meal is calculated to be 10 minutes at £3.3 per hour, i.e. £0.55. The total variance between the budgeted and actual labour cost of 60,000 meals is the total labour cost variance:

Labour	£
Actual Cost of Actual Production	33,000
Standard Cost of Actual Production	33,000
Total Labour Cost Variance	0

This would imply that there is no deviation from the plan. However, further analysis is necessary to ensure that there has been no change in the rate paid to the workforce, or the time taken per meal. The two main labour variances are very similar to the material cost variances, but different terms are used. The labour rate variance is very similar to the material price variance, and the labour efficiency variance is very similar to the material usage variance. The total labour cost variance can be broken down into:

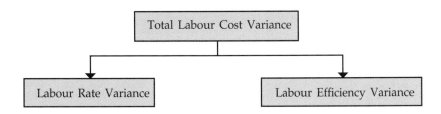

In our illustration the actual labour cost for 60,000 meals was £33,000. This represents 12,000 hours at £2.75 per hour.

To calculate the **labour rate variance**, the difference between the standard (budgeted) rate (SR) per hour and the actual rate (AR) per hour is multiplied by the actual hours (AH):

$$(SR - AR) \, AH \qquad (£3.30 - £2.75) \, 12,000 \qquad = \qquad £6,600 \text{ Favourable}$$

To calculate the **labour efficiency variance,** the difference between the standard hours (SH) to be worked for the actual production and the actual hours (AH) taken is multiplied by the standard rate (SR) per hour:

$$(SH - AH) \, SR \qquad (10,000^\dagger - 12,000) \, £3.30 = \qquad £6,600 \text{ Adverse}$$

† 60,000 meals at 10 mins. per meal

The total of these two variances equals the total labour cost variance, and provides a useful illustration of the value of exploring more deeply areas of performance. Using the total labour cost variance without the further analysis would not provide the necessary information to understand and manage the operation:

	£	
Labour Rate Variance	6,600	Favourable
Labour Efficiency Variance	6,600	Adverse
Total Labour Cost Variance	0	

Organisations using standard costing will expand their analysis to look at variances in variable and fixed overheads, as well as variances caused by changes in price and volume of sales. There is a need to ensure that the large amount of data that it is possible to produce is managed successfully. The use of exception reporting, where only variances of say over or under 5% are required to be reported upon, can aid this. There is also an important requirement to ensure that the standards are regularly reviewed to ensure that they are up to date so that confidence is maintained.

4. Incremental/Zero-Base Budgeting (ZBB)

In preparing a budget it is important to establish the base or starting point. One way, incremental budgeting, is to take the current levels as base data and to adjust for changes expected to occur during the budget period. For example, if salaries of a department are currently £100,000, with no increase in numbers expected, inflation is anticipated at 3%, the new budget figure would be £103,000. Although this may be an appropriate way of proceeding in such situations, the disadvantage of this approach is that it may allow past inefficiencies to become part of the new period's budget.

An alternative approach is the use of zero-base budgeting, which is also sometimes known as priority-based budgeting (PBB). The essence of a zero-base approach is to allow an organisation to actively search for, learn from and adapt to changing environments[1]. The Chartered Institute of Management Accountants' Official Terminology defines Zero-Base Budgeting as:

> *A method of budgeting whereby all activities are re-evaluated each time a budget is set. Discrete levels of each activity are valued and a combination chosen to match funds available.*

In practice this would mean that each manager has to budget ignoring the past, acting as though he were preparing a budget for the first time, and preparing a justification for the proposed spend. A decision package is prepared for each activity showing costs, purposes, alternatives, performance measurements and benefits. These packages are then screened and judged in a review process to determine benefits and the allocation of resources and funding. Advocates of this method claim that allocation of resources are more closely linked to need and benefit and it encourages an attitude which questions the status quo. However, it has to be said that it can take significant resourcing to undertake the activity, and as with all such areas of management there is a need to consider cost-benefit.

5. Rolling Budgets/Years Forecast or Out-Turn

Companies may choose to complement their annual budget with a regular (usually monthly) rolling or continuous forecast. This is intended to reflect changing circumstances and targets and aids in identifying corrective action. How is this achieved?

Assume that a company compares actual against budget every four week period. At the end of the first period a comparison is made against budget. Budget holders are required to forecast the effect any deviations from budget will have on the year end position and this is incorporated into a years forecast or out-turn. At the end of period six, budget holders will have sufficient actual results to be asked to forecast for the remaining six or seven periods. As the number of actual periods increase the importance of the original budget is reduced and the years forecast takes on a higher level of significance.

6. Activity-Based Budgeting

In *Chapter 6*, the development of activity-based costing was considered. Organisations that have adopted this approach may well extend their use of the activity-based concepts, combining them with elements of priority-based budgeting to budget on an 'activity-base'. Such a budget will involve a form of matrix calculation of costs for major activities and the resource inputs (e.g. salaries, telecoms.) for each activity, with identification of the cost driver activity. We provide an illustration of an Activity-budget schedule in *Table 7.3*.

Table 7.3   *Illustration of an Activity-Budget Schedule*

	Receiving Purchase Requests	Vetting Supplies	Ordering Items	Expediting Delivery	Approving Payment	Supervising Dept. Work
Salaries						
Occupancy						
Telecoms						
Travel						
Training						
Stationery						
Total Cost						
Activity Cost Driver	No. of Requests	No. of Suppliers	No. of Items	No. of Deliveries	No. of Deliveries	No.of

7.6   Budget administration

What are the key elements in administering a budget? We recommend that you review those we provide and compare them with practice in your own organisation. See if you can identify possible areas for improvement.

1. Budget Guidelines

Budget guidelines are a means of conveying important budget assumptions to budget holders. They should be prepared at least annually and should include various percentages for budget holders to apply to expense items. They might also include information relating to overall movements in sales volumes, the increase/reduction in certain sectors of the business, or the requirement to implement a particular aspect of health and safety.

2. Budget Manual

A budget manual should contain sufficient information to enable managers to operate the budgeting system within a particular business, division or department. It should explain all the terms which are used in the budgeting system and provide worked examples of the main documents. A budget manual should not only deal effectively with the detail that a budget holder requires but also provide an overview of the total system.

3. Budget Period

The main budget period within business is usually one year. However, many companies consider their three year plan to operate within the budgeting system. The usual method of operating such a three year plan is that the annual budget forms the first year of a three year plan. The second year is usually shown in less detail, with the third year simply taking a broad overview.

4. Budget Factor

In any business there can be a number of factors which restrict its potential growth, a common one being sales volume. Whatever the factor that restricts potential growth it should be identified and made explicit. For example, if sales are considered to be such a factor then all other budgets should be prepared in an attempt to maximise sales. Other budget factors could include shortage of skilled labour, shortage of materials, storage of material, storage space or a specific item of plant within the manufacturing process.

5. Budget Timetable

In many large organisations budget preparation will often extend over the six months prior to the budget period. The complex nature of budget preparation demands that a detailed timetable be produced to ensure that each component within the overall activity will be completed in time for input into other components of the system.

Budget timetables should be produced to meet a number of key dates which relate to divisional and group board meetings.

6. Budget Training

If the budgeting system is to succeed it is important that the budget administration should include management training in the processes and techniques appropriate to a particular business. Such training should involve guided in-company instruction by staff familiar with the system and the specific responsibilities. It is not desirable to leave an individual with the manual and the responsibility – the training should precede the responsibility.

We have now set the scene for budgeting and budgetary control which is a vital area for all managers to understand. Budgeting is far more than simply working with numbers, as we have sought to illustrate with our review of key considerations within the budget environment, budgetary control and budget administration.

In the following sections we will take you through the preparation of key budget statements.

❏ *Section 7.7* provides an illustration of the cash budget, a vital document for assessing the future liquidity of the business. It will identify the need for action to secure additional funding or indicate if surpluses of cash are likely.

❏ *Section 7.8* provides a comprehensive example of the preparation of monthly trading accounts, cash budget, profit and loss statement for the budget period and a balance sheet at the end of the budget period. Consideration is also given to the viability of the budgets prepared.

7.7   Preparation of Cash Budget

From the following information prepare a cash budget for the six months to 30th June 200X. The estimated cash balance at 1st January 200X is £4,000

	Sales	Purchases	Wages
200X–1	£	£	£
November	40,600	24,500	
December	48,000	23,200	
200X			
January	34,200	16,600	5,600
February	36,400	18,900	6,200
March	38,500	20,300	6,350
April	42,500	22,100	6,500
May	43,400	24,400	6,650
June	47,100	27,200	6,800

a.   Credit allowed to customers   60% pay in one month
                                      40% pay in two months

b.   Suppliers are paid one month in arrears

c.   Other payments:

		£
January	Taxation	20,000
March	Equipment	40,000
June	Dividend	10,000

The steps to be taken in the preparation of a cash budget are shown below:

1   Enter the opening cash balance in January which is given i.e. £4,000

2.   Calculate the receipts from Debtors, 60% pay in one month, 40% pay in two months following the month of sale, therefore:

Cash Received	60% of Sales in	40% of Sales in
January	December	November
February	January	December
March	February	January
April	March	February
May	April	March
June	May	April

3. Payment to creditors is delayed by one month. Therefore purchases in December will not be paid until January.

4. Complete the cash budget by entering the remaining figures and then calculate the monthly and cumulative balances to establish the cash flow picture.

Table 7.4   *Monthly Cash Budget – for the Six Months Ending 30th June 200X*

	Jan £'000	Feb £'000	Mar £'000	Apr £'000	May £'000	Jun £'000
Part A Receipts						
Sales	45,040	39,720	35,520	37,660	40,900	43,040
Subtotal A	45,040	39,720	35,520	37,660	40,900	43,040
Part B Payments						
Purchases	23,200	16,600	18,900	20,300	22,100	24,400
Wages	5,600	6,200	6,350	6,500	6,650	6,800
Taxation	20,000					
Equipment			40,000			
Dividend						10,000
Subtotal B	48,800	22,800	65,250	26,800	28,750	41,200
Part C						
Cash Flow (A–B)	–3,760	16,920	–29,730	10,860	12,150	1,840
Part D						
Balance b/f	4,000	240	17,160	–12,570	–1,710	10,440
Balance c/f (C+D)	240	17,160	–12,570	–1,710	10,440	12,280

In this case there will be a shortage of cash in March and April and we can use the statement to help identify the problem areas and possible courses of action. The main problem is the purchase of the capital equipment in March. As an alternative we could:

❏ delay the purchase of the capital equipment;

❏ negotiate terms for delayed payment;

❏ negotiate finance for the capital equipment;

❏ arrange hire or lease;

❏ obtain additional bank finance;

❏ reduce credit period allowed to customers, and/or;

❏ increase credit period taken (allowed) from suppliers.

Each course of action involves the consideration of an additional set of variables before arriving at a decision. For example, the last two items on the list above both affect the trading environment. If a company attempts either, it could lose customers and/or suppliers.

In February, May and June the statement show that there will be a surplus of cash. In this case a company should take steps to transfer funds into other activities which will generate interest. These include:

❏ bank deposit or building society;

❏ short-term money market. (Many large companies have departments whose function is to forecast closing cash positions on a daily basis and then negotiate terms on the overnight market).

7.8   Mechanics of Budgeting

In this example we start with an opening balance sheet and a number of budget assumptions and show the preparation of monthly trading accounts, monthly cash budget, budgeted profit and loss account for the period and a closing balance sheet.

Estimated Balance Sheet as at 30th June 200X

	Cost £'000	Depn £'000	£'000
FIXED ASSETS			
Land and Buildings	650		650
Plant and Machinery	1,760	500	1,260
	2,410	500	1,910
CURRENT ASSETS			
Stock – Goods for Resale		950	
Debtors		1,650	
Cash		70	
		2,670	
less CURRENT LIABILITIES			
Creditors	650		
Bank Overdraft	1,100		
		1,750	
Working Capital			920
Net Assets			**£2,830**
Financed as follows:			
Issued Share Capital			400
Profit and Loss Account			930
Shareholders' Fund			1,330
Long-Term Loan (12% per annum)			1,500
			£2,830

The executives of Rusty and Dusty Musty Ltd are preparing budgets for the six months July to December 200X. They have produced two financial objectives as guidelines for the assessment of the budget:

❏ To increase working capital by £150,000.

❏ To reduce borrowings (overdraft and long-term loans) by £300,000.

The following transactions should be incorporated:

a. The board has approved the purchase of a new machine in August 200X costing £250,000.

b. Wages, assumed to be 10% of monthly sales.
   Fixed costs estimated at £60,000 per month (all cash payments).

c. Depreciation to be charged at £24,000 per month.

d. Interim dividend of £50,000 payable 15th July 200X.

e. Sales and closing stock estimates:

	July £'000	Aug £'000	Sept £'000	Oct £'000	Nov £'000	Dec £'000
Sales	600	760	840	1,000	680	520
Closing Stock	1,000	900	800	800	700	650

f. Creditors at 30th June 200X are for purchases:

May	£270,000
June	£380,000

Debtors at 30th June 200X are for sales:

April	£500,000
May	£600,000
June	£550,000

Assume the same credit periods will continue, i.e. two months for creditors and three months for debtors.

g. Gross profit to sales is budgeted at 30%.

Assume purchases to be the balancing figure for the preparation of the monthly trading accounts.

1. Monthly Trading Accounts

The monthly trading accounts record the physical transactions and balances. In this example we have been given a gross profit percentage and monthly forecast of closing stock. Purchases, are the balancing figure. Later we will use the summary when preparing the budgeted profit and loss account.

The following steps should be taken during the preparation of the monthly trading accounts. You can check the results in *Table 7.5*.

Step

1. Enter the Sales and Closing Stock from note (e), then calculate the Gross Profit i.e. 30% of Sales (30% of £600,000 in July).

2. Enter the Opening Stock for July (£950,000) which is taken from the opening balance sheet, then enter the remaining Opening Stock figures, i.e. previous month's Closing Stock.

3. Cost of Sales is the sum of Sales less Gross Profit, e.g. for July: (£600,000 – £180,000) = £420,000.

4. Purchases will be the balancing figures and calculated as follows: Cost of Sales + Closing Stock – Opening Stock, e.g. for July: (£420,000 + £1,000,000 – £950,000) = £470,000.

Table 7.5   Monthly Trading Accounts for the Six Months Ending 31st December 200X

	July £000	Aug £000	Sept £000	Oct £000	Nov £000	Dec £000	Summary £000
Sales	600	760	840	1,000	680	520	4,400
Opening Stock	950	1,000	900	800	800	700	950
Purchases	470	432	488	700	376	314	2,780
	1,420	1,432	1,388	1,500	1,176	1,014	3,730
Closing Stock	1,000	900	800	800	700	650	650
Cost of Sales	420	532	588	700	476	364	3,080
Gross Profit	**180**	**228**	**252**	**300**	**204**	**156**	**1,320**

2. Monthly Cash Budget

At each stage, check the figures against *Table 7.6.*

Step

1. Enter the opening cash balance which is taken from the opening balance sheet.

2. Income from debtors. The example states a three month delay, therefore:

Sales	Cash Received
April	July
May	August
June	September
July	October
August	November
September	December
October ⎫ November ⎬ December ⎭	Closing Debtor Figure

3. Payments to creditors are delayed for two months. Therefore purchases from May to October will be paid for in July through to December. November and December purchases will remain unpaid and represent the closing creditors figure.

4. Complete the cash budget by entering the remaining figures then extract the monthly balances.

Table 7.6   *Monthly Cash Budget – for the Six Months Ending 31st December 200X*

	July £'000	Aug £'000	Sept £'000	Oct £'000	Nov £'000	Dec £'000	Total £'000
Part A Receipts							
Sales	500	600	550	600	760	840	3,850
Subtotal A	500	600	550	600	760	840	3,850
Part B Payments							
Purchases	270	380	470	432	488	700	2,740
Wages	60	76	84	100	68	52	440
Dividend	50						50
Machines		250					250
Fixed Costs	60	60	60	60	60	60	360
Subtotal B	440	766	614	592	616	812	3,840
Part C							
Cash Flow (A–B)	60	–166	–64	8	144	28	10
Part D							
Balance b/f		70	130	–36	–100	–92	52	70
Balance c/f (C+D)	130	–36	–100	–92	52	80	80

3. Budgeted Profit and Loss Account

Key points:

1. The figures for the first section of the profit and loss account (from Sales down to Gross Profit) are taken from the summary column of the monthly trading accounts, *Table 7.5*.

2. There is no delay in the payment of Wages or Fixed Costs therefore the totals can be taken from the total column of the monthly cash budget, *Table 7.6*.

3. Calculate the loan interest due for the six months
    i.e. (£1,500,000 x 12% ÷ 2).

4. Enter Depreciation then add Salaries, Fixed Costs, Interest Payable and
    Depreciation the sum of which should be deducted from gross profit to find
    the profit for the period i.e. (£1,320,000 – £1,034,000 = £286,000).

Table 7.7   Budgeted Profit and Loss Account for the Six Months Ending 31st December 200X

	£'000	£'000
Sales		4,400
Opening Stock	950	
Purchases	2,780	
	3,730	
Closing Stock	650	
Cost of Sales		3,080
Gross Profit		1,320
Wages	440	
Fixed Costs	360	
Interest Payable	90	
Depreciation	144	
		1034
Profit for the Period		286
Dividend		50
Retained Profit		236

4. Budgeted Closing Balance Sheet

The simplest way to prepare the closing balance sheet is to take each figure in
turn from the opening balance sheet and

❏   if no change has occurred then enter the same figure in the closing balance
    sheet, or

❏   if change has occurred make the necessary adjustment then enter the revised
    figure in the closing balance sheet.

You will find that the preparation of the closing balance sheet helps to 'tie up' a number of figures which, until now had apparently been forgotten. At each stage check the source of all figures and the end result in the closing balance sheet as illustrated in *Table 7.8* and the figures included there were calculated as follows:

Table 7.8   Budgeted Closing Balance Sheet as at 31st December 200X

	£'000	£'000	£'000
FIXED ASSETS	Cost	Depn	
Land and Buildings	650		650
Plant and Machinery	2,010	644	1,366
	2,660	644	2,016
CURRENT ASSETS			
Stock – Goods for Resale		650	
Debtors		2,200	
Cash		80	
		2,930	
less CURRENT LIABILITIES			
Creditors	690		
Bank Overdraft	1,100		
Interest Payable	90		
		1,880	
Working Capital			1,050
Net Assets			3,066
Financed as follows:			
Issued Share Capital			400
Profit and Loss Account			1,166
Shareholders' Fund			1,566
Loan-Term Loan (12% per annum)			1,500
			3,066

Key points:

1. Land and Buildings: No change.

2. Plant and Machinery: In this case additional capital has been spent and the provision for depreciation increased. Therefore the calculation is (£1,260,000 + £250,000 − £144,000 = £1,366,000).

3. Stock: This is the closing stock at December, i.e. £650,000.

4. Debtors: Sales for October, November and December will remain unpaid at the end of the period, therefore (£1,000,000 + £680,000 + £520,000 = £2,200,000).

5. Cash: This is the closing cash position at December, i.e. £80,000.

6. Creditors: Purchases for November and December will remain unpaid at the end of the period, therefore (£376,000 + £314,000 = £690,000).

7. Bank Overdraft: No change.

8. Interest Payable: We calculated the interest payable and entered £90,000 into the profit and loss account. A similar entry is required in the closing balance sheet to recognise the liability.

9. Share Capital: No change.

10. Profit and loss account: This is found by taking the figure from the opening balance sheet and adding the profit for the period (£930,000 + £236,000 = £1,166,000).

11. Loan-Term Loan: No change.

5. Interpretation of Budget Statements

The cash budget, *Table 7.6* produces a satisfactory result if taken for the whole six month period. However, there is a period in the middle when the company will not be able to meet its cash commitments. The main problem is the purchase of capital equipment in August and we considered possible courses of action when reviewing the cash budget.

6. What About the Two Financial Objectives Set?

1. To increase working capital by £150,000

    An examination of the net working capital position between the opening and closing balance sheets clearly shows an increase in working capital of £130,000 which does not meet this particular budget objective.

2. Reduce borrowing by £300,000

    The assumptions contained in this budget revision do not meet this budget objective. There is no change in short-term or long-term debt financing.

As a consequence the likely result in practice would be at least another round of budgeting to meet the objectives.

CHAPTER EIGHT

SHORT-TERM DECISION ANALYSIS

LEARNING OBJECTIVES

When you have finished studying this chapter you should be able to:

❏ Describe the main differences between fixed and variable costs, relevant and irrelevant costs.

❏ Use cost, volume and profit (CVP) analysis and understand the advantages and disadvantages of its application.

❏ Prepare statements to show whether a company should continue with apparently unprofitable products, divisions, branches.

❏ Apply the concept of relevant costs to:

- identify the best use of scarce resources;
- the make our buy decision;
- competitive tendering.
- the decision to accept or reject a special order.

❏ Use a framework to aid the structuring of decisions.

8.1   Introduction

Not all managerial action can be preplanned and handled within a budgetary context. The reality of management is that periodically events will arise on a non-routine or adhoc basis which require a decision to be taken. What tends to make such events difficult to deal with is that rarely are they the same. However, there are some guidelines that are generally applicable which can be summarised as:

❒   Establish the exact nature of the issues requiring a decision to be taken.

❒   Identify the alternative courses of action.

❒   Identify the most appropriate data, irrespective of its source.

❒   Measure data correctly and logically analyse it.

❒   Ensure that financial and non financial data is presented well to facilitate information sharing and its correct interpretation.

In this chapter we are primarily concerned with decisions directed towards the short-term, which is frequently defined as one year or less, and the accounting information required to make these decisions. Decisions with implications greater than one year are discussed in the next chapter, however, it must be emphasised that much of the discussion about organising and analysing short-term decisions is relevant to dealing with long-term decisions.

As we will illustrate, dealing with short-term decisions requires a sound understanding of the economic issues of each situation to ensure an appropriate action is taken. In particular, use of the right data in the right way for each decision is critical for making good decisions. Unfortunately, there can often be confusion concerning the correct data to use because of a temptation to rely upon systems developed and currently operating to provide data for routine accounting purposes, such as budgetary control. Such systems will often have been developed for specific purposes relating to the control of activities and the information provided by it is often inadequate for answering the key question for managing decisions which is:

> *'How do costs and revenues differ if one*
>
> *course of action is adopted rather than another?'*

Answering this key question requires the ability to identify costs and revenues which are likely to change as a consequence of the decision, irrespective of their source. For example, in a decision whether to discontinue an operation or not, the historical cost of the stock from the accounting system may often be irrelevant. The crucial question is what alternative uses are there for the stock. If the only alternative is to sell the stock, the relevant information is its resale value which may be totally different from its historical cost. It also should not be ignored that there will often be non-financial information to be taken into consideration which may have a significant impact upon a particular situation, such as the effect on labour relations in the case of discontinuing an operation. Once all relevant points have been considered, it is critical that the resulting information is presented in the most appropriate form to ensure it is interpreted and correctly acted upon by the parties involved.

In this chapter we will consider the evaluation of non-routine decisions with the aid of a number of illustrations which represent the subtle differences in emphasis as to the type of data required. We first focus upon those decisions which require the analysis of cost behaviour and its application in what is now popularly called *cost-volume-profit* analysis. This type of approach can be useful for studying such issues as what is the effect on profit when a new product range is introduced. It is also relevant to managers in not-for-profit organisations, mainly because knowledge of how costs fluctuate in response to changes in volume is valuable regardless of whether profit is an objective. No organisation ever has unlimited resources!

8.2 Cost-Volume-Profit Relationships

A good understanding of how cost, volume and profit relate to one another can be invaluable in dealing with certain types of short-term decisions. Consider for example a request by a customer to provide a large consignment of standard product at a substantial discount. In order to establish the viability of such a request one issue likely to be of importance is the profitability that will result. We will illustrate how using Cost-Volume-Profit (CVP) analysis such a request can be readily evaluated but before then, it is important to be aware of some basic terminology associated with its use.

1. Fixed and Variable Costs

You have already met this classification of costs in *Chapter 6* – but it is worth repeating the distinction here. At its simplest, cost-volume-profit analysis is reliant upon a classification of costs in which fixed and variable costs are separated from one another. Fixed costs are those which are generally time related and are not influenced by the level of activity. For example, the rent payable by a manufacturer for factory space will not be related to the number of items produced. Whether times are good or bad the cost will have to be incurred and the same will apply to any other costs which are contractually incurred. Of course if activity is to be increased beyond the capacity of the premises additional rent would have to be incurred, but within what is known as the 'relevant range' of activity the cost is fixed. Variable costs on the other hand are directly related to the level of activity; if activity increases variable costs will increase and vice versa if activity decreases.

Fixed and variable costs can be readily understood when portrayed graphically as illustrated in *Figure 8.1.*

Figure 8.1 Illustration of Fixed and Variable Costs

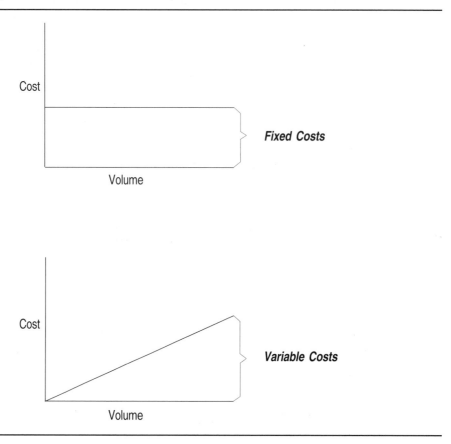

Fixed costs are shown to be constant for all levels of activity within the relevant range, whilst variable costs can be seen to increase in proportion to the level of activity. The sum of the fixed and the variable costs equals the total costs to be incurred over the level of activity within the relevant range.

In considering cost-volume-profit relationships it is usual to consider cost behaviour within the context of a model comprising only straight lines. This assumption can, of course, be relaxed to accommodate non-linear relationships, but it does make the analysis more difficult and in considering whether so to do, it is important to determine whether the benefit derived from greater accuracy of the input data will warrant the effort required to be expended.

Finally, you should not ignore the fact that costs may be simultaneously affected by more than one activity base. For example, labour costs associated with road haulage may be affected by both the weight and the number of units handled.

4.   Uses of Cost-Volume-Profit Analysis

The ability to analyse and use cost-volume-profit relationships is an important management tool. The knowledge of patterns of cost behaviour offers insights valuable in planning and controlling short and long run operations. The example of increasing capacity is a good illustration of the power of the technique in planning. The implications of making changes upon profit can be determined as well as the requirements to achieve a given level of profit. The technique can be used to work forwards or backwards and, as should be only too obvious, it is ideal for spreadsheet analysis, whereby the effects of all sorts of modifications and assumptions can be evaluated.

The technique is also useful within the context of control. The implications of changes in the level of activity can be measured by flexing a budget using knowledge of cost behaviour, thereby permitting comparison to be made of actual and budgeted performance for any of activity.

8.3   An Example of Cost-Volume-Profit Analysis

The following data relates to a new product due to be launched on the 1st May:

Selling Price	£20.00 per unit
Forecast Volume	120,000 units
Variable Costs	£16.00 per unit
Fixed Costs	£300.000

In the following we will apply the principles to CVP analysis to the following five situations in which each has been treated as being independent of the other

1   Break even point in units.

2   Break even point in units if variable costs per unit increase to £17.00.

3   Break even point in £ sterling if the fixed costs increase to £336,000.

4   Minimum selling price to meet a profit target of £120,000.

5   Volume of sales required at a selling price of £19.00 per unit.

Finally, we will prepare a break even chart using the original data.

The first step in tackling such a problem is to calculate the total contribution and the contribution per unit.

	£	£ per unit
Sales	2,400,000	20.00
less Variable Costs	1,920,000	16.00
CONTRIBUTION	480,000	4.00
less Fixed Costs	300,000	
Profit	180,000	

1. Using this information we calculate the breakeven point by dividing the costs to be incurred irrespective of the level of activity (i.e. fixed costs) by the contribution each unit will generate.

$$\text{Break Even Point (units)} = \frac{\text{Fixed Costs}}{\text{Contribution Per Unit}}$$

$$= \frac{£300,000}{£4.00}$$

$$= 75,000 \text{ units}$$

2. Where the variable costs per unit change, so too will the contribution per unit:

	£ per unit
Sales	20.00
Variable Costs	17.00
Contribution	3.00

With an unchanged £20.00 selling price and a revised variable cost of £17.00 a contribution per unit of £3.00 will result. Assuming that the fixed costs remain unchanged at £300,000, the break even point in units is 100,000 (£300,000 ÷ £3).

3. Break even always arises where total cost equals total revenue. To find the break even point in value rather than volume, we first calculate the break even point in units and then multiply it by the selling price.

    In this case where fixed costs are £336,000 (with no other changes), the break even point in units will be £336,000 divided by £4.00, which equals 84,000 units. Break even in value can be found by multiplying 84,000 by £20.00, which equals £1,680,000.

4. The minimum selling price to meet a target profit is found from the sum of the contribution per unit plus the variable cost per unit. The contribution per unit in this situation can be found by dividing the required units into the sum of the fixed costs and the profit target. For example, we are told that the profit target is £120,000 which added to the fixed costs of £300,000 gives £420,000 (i.e. the contribution in value). The contribution per unit can now be found by dividing £420,000 by 120,000 units to give £3.50. Therefore, the minimum selling price is £3.50 plus the unit variable cost of £16.00 which equals £19.50.

5. The calculation of total volume to cover fixed costs and meet the target profit is similar to the approach used to determine the break even volume. The only difference is that the profit target is added to the fixed costs in order to calculate the number of units (volume) required to cover fixed costs and to cover the profit target from a given contribution per unit.

    In this case the requirement is to identify the volume to cover fixed costs and profit assuming that the selling price per unit is decreased to £19.00. Where the selling price is £19.00, the unit contribution falls to £3.00, i.e.

	£ per unit
Sales	19.00
Variable Costs	16.00
Contribution	3.00

The volume of sales under those circumstances is found by adding the fixed costs of £300,000 to the profit target of £180,000 and then dividing the result by £3.00, to give 160,000 units.

Break even analysis can also be plotted on a graph. The basic data required is total forecast volume, total sales revenue, total fixed costs and total variable costs. A break even graph, using the original data from the previous example is shown in *Figure 8.2.*

Figure 8.2   Break Even Graph

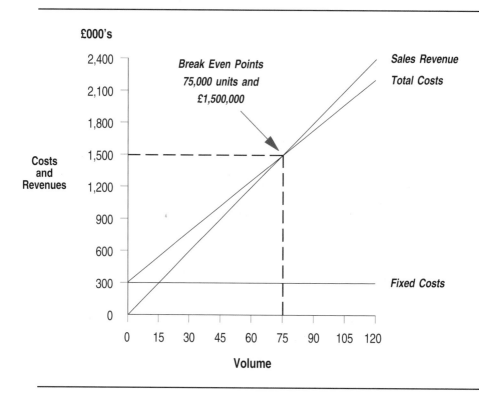

One of the most difficult tasks when preparing a break even chart is to determine the intervals between the values (e.g. units of 15 for the volume). You must also consider the overall size of the graph, its position on the page and give it a suitable heading.

In the above graph,

1.   First, plot the total fixed costs i.e. £300,000, a straight line across the page.

2.   Next, plot the total variable costs i.e. £1,920,000, from £300,000 at zero units to £2,220,000 (£1,920,000 + £300,000) at 120,000 units.

3.   Finally, plot the total sales revenue i.e. £2,400,000, from £0 at zero units to £2,400,000 at 120,000 units.

Break even is the point where total costs equal total revenues. Also at this point, the total cost per unit equals the selling price per unit. To the left of the break even point the total costs exceed the total revenues and represents the loss segment, while to the right of the break even point the total revenues exceed the total costs and represents the profit segment.

Breakeven is shown to be 75,000 units in terms of volume and £1,500,000 costs and revenues. It can be seen that the only values to affect break even are any change in:

1. Total fixed cost. For example, should total fixed costs increase then break even will also increase.

2. Variable costs which in turn will affect total costs. For example, an increase in variable costs will increase the break even volume.

3. Selling prices which in turn will affect the total sales revenue line. For example a decrease in selling prices will increase the break even volume.

Contribution Margin and Gross Margin

We have shown the contribution margin to be the excess of sales over all variable costs. It can be expressed as a total amount, a unit amount, and a percentage.

You should be aware of the potential for confusion about the difference between contribution and gross profit. Gross profit is a widely used concept, particularly in the retailing industry and is the excess of sales over the cost of goods sold. However, the cost of goods sold will usually be very different in nature and amount from the contribution. The cost of goods sold relates solely to the direct costs associated with those items sold and any attributed overhead. It, therefore, usually contains elements of both fixed and variable costs unlike the contribution margin which is calculated with sole reference to variable costs.

Wagner plc manufactures an instrument which has a variable cost structure as follows:

	£
Materials	54.00
Labour	13.50
Variable Costs	5.40
	72.90

The instrument sells at £121.50 each and the company expects a sales revenue from this product in the current year of £1,822,500 and fixed overhead expense attributable to this product is budgeted at £189,000. A wage agreement with the employees states that a 10% increase will be paid to labour in the forthcoming year, whilst the managing director believes that from the beginning of the new financial year material prices will rise by 7.5%, variable overhead by 5% and fixed overheads by 3%.

Required

1. Calculate the new selling price if the contribution/sales ratio is to be maintained.

2. Calculate the sales volume required in the forthcoming year if the price remains the same and the profit level is to be maintained. (The selling price is to remain at £121.50 in spite of the increase in costs).

	Existing Variable cost		Revised Variable cost
	£	%	£
Materials	54.00	7.5	58.05
Labour	13.50	10.0	14.85
Variable Costs	5.40	5.0	5.67
	72.90		78.57

1. Revised selling price

$$\text{Contribution to Sales Ratio} = \frac{(121.50 - 72.90) \times 100}{121.50}$$

$$= \quad 40\%$$

Thus, to maintain the current contribution to sales ratio, the revised variable cost must equal 60% of the selling price.

$$\text{Revised Selling Price} = \frac{£78.57 \times 100}{60}$$

$$= \quad £130.95$$

2. Alternative sales volume required:

$$\text{Existing Sales Volume} = \frac{£1,822,500}{£121.50}$$

$$= \quad 15,000$$

Existing profit level:

Contribution (15,000 x £48.60)		729,000
less Fixed Costs		189,000
		540,000

$$\text{Revised Fixed Costs} = \frac{£189,000 \times 103}{100}$$

$$= £194,670$$

Existing Profit Level	540,000
Revised Fixed Costs	194,670
Contribution Required	734,670

$$\text{Sales Volume Required} = \frac{£734,670}{(£121.50 - £78.57)}$$

$$= 17,113$$

5. Limitations of Cost-Volume-Profit (CVP) Analysis

A major limitation of conventional CVP analysis that we have already identified is the assumption and use of linear relationships. Yet another limitation relates to the difficulty of dividing fixed costs among many products and/or services. Whilst variable costs can usually be identified with production services, most fixed costs usually can only be divided by allocation and apportionment methods reliant upon a good deal of judgement (covered in *Chapter 6*). However, perhaps the major limitation of the technique relates to the initial separation of fixed and variable costs. This can often be difficult to achieve with any sort of precision because many costs do not fall neatly into one or other of the two categories, and methods for separating fixed and variable costs may be required for the technique to be used. If this is the case, then you should be particularly mindful about applying a great deal of sophistication to any analysis because this may serve to cloud the key topic which is the quality of the data input.

The quality of input data is an important point and one you will find we often emphasise. In our opinion too much emphasis has been placed upon how to make techniques more sophisticated without sufficient consideration of the quality of the data to which such sophisticated techniques will be applied. With this in mind let us consider briefly how fixed and variable costs can be separated.

First, judgement can be applied to the data in an attempt to separate those costs which can be considered as being wholly fixed or wholly variable. Bearing in mind that we are considering a defined range of activity, examples of fixed costs would be salaried staff and occupancy costs, such as rents and rates, whilst materials costs and sales commissions are illustrative of typical variable costs to a commercial oriented manufacturing operation.

Of course, the likelihood of separating a substantial proportion of total costs in this way is often very low and the remainder will fall somewhere between the two extremes of wholly fixed and wholly variable costs. This remainder, known as semi-fixed, or semi-variable costs, need to be separated in order to make cost-volume-profit analysis operable.

A number of methods are available to make such a separation possible ranging from comparing costs at high and low levels of activity, to regression analysis, whereby using statistical analysis a line of best fit is found from available cost data. Irrespective of the method applied, the result will only be an approximation! Yes, it is possible to minimise the approximation but you should weigh the cost of so doing against the relative likely benefit that will be achieved.

8.4 Contribution Analysis

We have introduced the characteristics of financial information required for short-term decision making which must be differential as between alternative choices and relate to the future. We will reinforce these two requirements and, where appropriate, apply the principles of CVP analysis with reference to five common applications of short-term decision techniques.

❏ Whether to continue with apparently unprofitable products, divisions, branches.

❏ How to make the best use of available scarce resources.

❏ Whether to make/use internal resources or buy from outside.

❏ Whether or not to use competitive tendering.

❏ Whether or not to accept a special order.

8.5 Relevant Costs

The application of the principles of CVP analysis does suffer one major limitation for many decisions, other than those discussed earlier. In situations where there are different potential courses of action, relevant data for evaluating the alternatives is required and the cost behaviour information used in CVP analysis is unlikely to meet all of its requirements. What must be identified in such circumstances is the amount by which costs will change if one course of action is taken rather than another.

Surely, you must be thinking, this is simply an extension of cost-volume-profit analysis, but this need not be so. In discussing and applying cost-volume-profit analysis we did not question the relevance of the input data used to the decision in question. Questioning cost relevance is an important part of choosing between alternative courses of action.

As a manager, you must avoid using irrelevant information for evaluating alternatives no matter how impressive it may appear to be. The problem is, how do you avoid the use of irrelevant information and identify that which is relevant?

First, the accounting information used in any decision must relate to the future, not the past. It is essential that only costs and revenues yet to be incurred are used for purposes of decision making. This is because they alone will be incurred as a result of taking the decision in question. Past costs and revenues, which are often referred to as 'sunk' costs and revenues, are irrelevant to decision making, apart from their use in helping to forecast the future.

Second, where you are faced with a decision, the only relevant costs or revenues are those which are different under the alternative courses of action. Such costs are often referred to as *differential or incremental* costs. An understanding of how to use differential costs is important because most decisions will require at least two courses of action to be considered, given that one course of action may merely be to confirm current practice!

1. Cost Relevance in Action

E. Tee, an aspiring manager, recently hit by the increase in interest rates upon his newly acquired mortgage, has a problem with the financial arrangements for his golf. He can either pay £9.00 every time he plays or £140.00 for a non-refundable season ticket plus £2.00 for every round played. Which should he choose? This you should immediately recognise as being similar in principle to the earlier discussion of cost-volume-profit analysis. In order to make a decision between these two alternatives we can work out how many times E. Tee would have to play so that he is indifferent between either of the two. This point of indifference where he is no better or worse off is like the break even point discussed earlier. It is found by taking the cost of the annual season ticket and dividing it by the savings (the differential cost/benefit) achieved each time E. Tee would play.

$$
=\ \frac{\text{Annual Season Ticket}}{\text{Saving on Each Round}}
$$

$$
=\ \frac{\text{£140.00}}{\text{£ 7.00}}
$$

$$
=\ \text{20 times}
$$

E. Tee would have to play more than 20 times in the year before a season ticket and £2 payment for each round would be a worthwhile decision. Because E. Tee likes golf and intends to play twice a week for the whole year he purchases an annual season ticket for £140.

Simple so far, but true to life complications arise. One month later, he identifies another problem which he cannot solve. He has visited another golf club which is nearer to his home. There is a single payment of £360.00 for membership with no additional green fees. The course is not heavily used, and it takes approximately three hours to complete a round compared to the four hours at the present club. What should he do? What about the £140.00 he has recently paid for his annual season ticket? The £140.00 is not relevant to this decision. It has already been paid, is not refundable and it will be the same irrespective of the decision he takes. Only the additional costs (incremental costs) and the additional savings (incremental receipts) are relevant to this new decision, i.e. those costs which will change as a result of making the decision.

The incremental costs in this case would be the £360.00 membership fee, and the incremental savings would be the £2.00 per round he has to pay at the present club.

$$
=\ \frac{\text{Incremental Costs}}{\text{Incremental Savings}}
$$

$$
=\ \frac{\text{£360.00}}{\text{£ 2.00}}
$$

$$
=\ \text{180 times}
$$

Therefore, E. Tee would have to play four times a week in order for it to be financially worth his while joining the other golf club. If, on the other hand, E. Tee could save £1.00 on travel by joining the other golf club (which is nearer to his home), breakeven would be achieved after 120 rounds (£360 divided by [£2 + £1]). However, there are a number of other aspects not necessarily of a financial nature which should be considered in making a decision to change to another club. Examples are:

- ❑ The time taken to play and travel.

- ❑ The possibility of sharing travelling.

- ❑ Who else plays.

- ❑ The amenities and social aspects.

- ❑ The quality of the facilities.

2. Cost Relevance – An Example

A firm of boat builders has just had an order for a luxury yacht cancelled after it has been finished. The only potential buyer is Mr Apostolides; who said that he might buy the yacht on the following conditions:

1. that the price to him was no more than £37,500

2. that certain specified conversion work was undertaken

3. that he could take delivery within one month.

The firm's accountant submits the following price estimate to help management decide whether a sale to Mr Apostolides would be worthwhile and to decide the minimum price that could be charged.

Table 8.1 Cost of Building the Yacht – Price Estimate

		£
Materials at Cost		21,000
Labour		18,000
		39,000
Variable Costs (100% on Direct Cost)		39,000
		78,000
less Deposit, retained when order cancelled		22,500
		55,500
Add, conversion work:		
Materials at Cost	4,500	
Labour	1,500	
	6,000	
Fixed Costs (100% on Direct Cost)	6,000	
Administration (25% on Production Cost)	1,500	
		13,500
Total Cost		69,000
Add, Profit Mark-up (5%)		3,450
Suggested Price to Mr. Apostolides		72,450

The following information is available:

1. Three types of materials were used in the original building of the yacht:

    a. Type one cost £10,500; but it could now only be sold to a scrap merchant for £3,000 but to put it in a suitable form for sale it would take 20 hours of labour at £5 per hour. This work would be undertaken by the firm's maintenance department which is very slack at this time.

    b. Type two cost £7,500 and it could now be sold as scrap for £3,000, again after 20 hours of labour had been spent on it by the maintenance department. Alternatively it could be kept for use next year as a substitute for a material which is expected to cost £4,500, but an additional 40 hours of highly skilled labour over and above that spent to make the material suitable for resale would then have to be hired at £7.50 per hour.

    c. Type three cost £3,000; it could now be sold for £2,250. Alternatively it could be kept until next year as a substitute for a material which is expected to cost £3,000, but because of its special nature would have to be stored at an additional cost of £300.

2. There are two further types of materials to be used for the conversion:

    a. Type four was ordered last year at a price of £3,000, delivery was delayed and its realisable value has fallen to £1,500. In recognition of this the suppliers have given the firm a discount of £900. The material could be used only for this one job.

    b. Type five has been in stock some time and originally cost £1,500. Because of its high content of precious metal it could now be sold for £3,750, but metal brokers would charge 10% commission for selling it.

3. Of the £1,500 conversion labour charge, £1,350 represents the skilled men that would have to be specially hired, the other £150 represents the time spent by the foreman who is a permanent employee.

4. The plans and specifications for the yacht could be sold for £3,750 if it is scrapped.

The accountants cost statement indicates that Apostolides's offer of £37,500 would be significantly below the cost of £72,450. Is that the right conclusion? If you think it necessary, redraft the original schedule in the way you think might be more helpful to management. Your answer should include any assumptions you have made.

Table 8.2   Value of Yacht, as is

			£
Material Type 1	Note 1		3,000
Material Type 2	Note 2		4,200
Material Type 3	Note 3		2,700
Value in Current State			9,900
Plans			3,750
		(A)	13,650
Conversion Cost:			
Material Type 4	Note 4		1,500
Material Type 5	Note 5		3,375
Labour			1,350
		(B)	6,225
Apostolides's Offer			37,500
Minimum Price if Co		(A – B)	19,875
Additional Contribution if Converted and Sold to Apostolides			17,625

Notes:

1. Realisable scrap value no labour charge as maintenance department over (under) capacity.

2. Replacement list value of £4,500 less skilled labour charge £300 (40 hours x 7.50 per hour). No maintenance labour as in Note 1.

3. Replacement cost less storage cost.

4. Realisable value.

5. Realisable value.

6. Foreman, fixed cost.

8.6   Whether to Continue with Apparently Unprofitable Products, Divisions, Branches.

This application of short-term decision making techniques will consider using the following example:

> T.O. Wood Ltd manufactures and sells three products, X, Y and Z. The internally prepared product profitability statement for the company is shown in *Table 8.3*. Fixed overhead costs are absorbed as a percentage of labour costs and have been rounded to the nearest £100,000. Products X and Z are machine intensive while Product Y is labour intensive. Management is considering whether to drop Product Y because it is making a loss, the assumption being that they could increase the total profit of the company by £100,000 by dropping Product Y. Do you agree?

Table 8.3   T.O. Wood Ltd – Product Profitability Statement

		X £'000	Y £'000	Z £'000	Total £'000
(a)	Sales	1,500	1,600	800	3,900
(b)	Material Costs	500	400	100	1,000
(c)	Labour Costs	400	800	300	1,500
(d)	Fixed Costs	300	500	200	1,000
(e)	Total Costs	1,200	1,700	600	3,500
(f)	**Profit/(Loss)**	**300**	**–100**	**200**	**400**

With reference to line (d) Product Y is absorbing 50% of the total fixed costs many of which may not be avoided even if the company were to drop Product Y. In such a situation where there is a limited differential effect upon fixed costs in continuing or dropping Product Y, they are not relevant in making the decision.

On the assumption that fixed costs are not avoidable in the short-term we have re-arranged the contents of *Table 8.3* to show a distinction between those costs likely to be avoidable and those that are not:

Table 8.4 T.O. Wood Ltd – Product Contribution and Profitability Statement

	X £'000	Y £'000	Z £'000	Total £'000
Sales	1,500	1,600	800	3,900
Material Costs	500	400	100	1,000
Labour Costs [1]	400	800	300	1,500
Total Variable Costs	900	1,200	400	2,500
Contribution	600	400	400	1,400
Fixed Costs				1,000
Profit				400
CONTRIBUTION/SALES %	40	25	50	

[1] *Labour costs are usually considered to be variable costs because they do respond to changes in the level of activity, albeit that this response may not be immediate.*

In the re-arranged *Table 8.4* the value of retaining Product Y is shown assuming that no fixed costs are avoidable. Product Y can be seen to contribute £400,000 towards the fixed costs. If dropped, T.O. Wood Ltd would lose this contribution, with the result being a reduction in the total contribution by £400,000. Furthermore, this £400,000 reduction in contribution would completely wipe out the £400,000 profit currently obtained from making all three products.

This example illustrates one issue which must be considered in short-term decision analysis that arises from the allocation of fixed costs. Where fixed costs have been identified with products, as in this example, it is tempting but usually wrong to assume that they will necessarily disappear when a product is dropped. In fact, in many organisations all that is known with any certainty is the total fixed costs likely to be incurred, their allocation across products or services is frequently heavily dependent upon judgement.

T.O. Wood Ltd is a useful illustration of CVP analysis. This technique can frequently be usefully extended by relating the contribution per product to the sales revenue to produce what is known as the contribution to sales (C/S) ratio. The contribution to sales ratio is potentially useful when costs have been separated into fixed and variable categories. This is because the effect on total profit of a given volume change for any product(s) can be assessed using knowledge of the contribution to sales ratio. Let us consider the calculation and application of the C/S ratio.

The contribution to sales ratios for X,Y and Z, are found by expressing the contributions of £600,000, £400,000 and £400,000 as a percentage of the sales revenues of £1,500,000, £1,600,000 and £800,000, respectively. The resulting contribution to sales ratios are 40%, 25% and 50%. The effect on profit of an extra £1,000,000 of sales revenue being generated by each of the products assuming that fixed costs would remain the same would be £400,000, £250,000 and £500,000, for X, Y and Z, respectively. Therefore, given the potential to increase sales revenue by £1,000,000 the first product to be selected would be Product Z which has the highest contribution to sales ratio. Thus the assumption that fixed costs are time related and remain unchanged for such an increase in activity, and, that there is no differential effect between products, then the highest profit will be generated from increasing sales of Product Z.

You will note that we have been able to consider the potential financial benefits of an increase in sales revenue by considering the C/S ratio alone. Given that the relationships in the model are understood it is not necessary to undertake lengthy calculations to gauge the benefit.

Of course we have assumed no resource constraints. Where these exist the contribution to sales ratio is not a useful distinguishing mechanism between alternative products, as we will see in the next section.

8.7   How to Best Use Available Scarce Resources

In some production and distribution decisions, management may be confronted with the question of how best to allocate the firm's limited resources. Where demand for the product is greater than the production or distribution capabilities available, a company should seek to maximise its total contribution margin from these limited resources.

Limited resources can arise from one, or a combination of the following:

❑   Shortages of raw materials or purchased goods.

❑   Shortage of certain labour skills.

❑   Restricted space for production, in the warehouse or in a retailing outlet.

❑   Maximum machine capacities.

It may not only be on the supply side that limitations prevail. It is also quite possible that a firm will face limitations upon the amount it can produce and/or sell because of:

❑   Customer demand for one or more products or services.

❑   Government restrictions.

In such circumstances the challenge is to obtain the maximum possible benefit from the market opportunities and the resources available.

Where there is one single constraint, it is possible to carry out an analysis to determine the best mix of products to maximise total contribution margin. At its simplest the analysis requires the contribution margin for a product to be divided by the unit of scarce resource i.e. limiting factor. That product or service with the highest contribution per unit of the scarce resource is the most desirable whilst the resource constraint operates. The application of the contribution per unit of scarce resource will be demonstrated with reference to T.O. Wood Ltd, where management is considering the most desirable mix of products to incorporate into their annual budget.

Market research information has produced the estimated sales of T.O. Wood's present products together with further estimates of two new products, P and Q. There is no sales constraint, but there is a constraint on machine capacity of 4,800 hours and, given this constraint, management needs to know the mix of products which should be produced so as to maximise total profit margin. The product data which has been summarised in *Table 8.5* is available:

Table 8.5   T.O. Wood Ltd – Possible Alternative Products

	Existing Products			New Products	
	X	Y	Z	P	Q
Machine Hours	2,000	800	2,000	800	1,000
	£'000	£'000	£'000	£'000	£'000
Sales	1,500	1,600	800	700	1,000
Material Costs	500	400	100	200	400
Labour Costs	400	800	300	200	200
Total Variable Costs	900	1,200	400	400	600
Contribution	600	400	400	300	400
Contribution to Sales Ratio	40%	25%	50%	43%	40%

Unfortunately, as we will illustrate, the current product analysis is inadequate for selecting the appropriate product mix to maximise profit. What is required is an analysis of the contribution yielded per machine hour for each product. This we have provided in *Table 8.6* which has been used to rank the products from those which show the highest contribution per machine hour through to the lowest.

Table 8.6   *Best Use of Scarce Resources – Ranking*

| | Existing Products | | | New Products | |
	X	Y	Z	P	Q
(a) Machine Hours	2,000	800	2,000	800	1,000
	£,000	£,000	£,000	£,000	£'000
(b) Contribution	600	400	400	300	400
Contribution Per Machine Hour [(b) ÷ (a)]	£ 300	£ 500	£ 200	£ 375	£ 400
Ranking	4	1	5	3	2

The analysis shows that Product Y ranked first, provides the highest contribution per machine hour. Each unit requires less of the scarce resource than the other products, and it contributes £500 per machine hour.

The ranking illustrated in the table provides the order which will result in the best use of scarce machine hours. Given the total constraint of 4,800 hours and the selection of Product Y which requires 800 hours, the remaining 4,000 hours would be allocated to products Q, P and X. This allocation to the four products does not exhaust the 4,800 hours available and 200 hours still remain unused. This 200 hours spare capacity could be used to ease production scheduling, or it might be used to produce a proportion of Product Z.

You will have doubtless noted by selecting the product mix using contribution per machine hour, Product Z with the highest contribution sales ratio is the least desirable. Whilst it may produce the largest effect on contribution for a given increase in sales, it suffers from being inefficient in terms of machine hour use. Hopefully, you will be thinking why not buy or lease a new machine or investigate sub-contracting production. This line of thinking is entirely appropriate as is questioning whether T.O.Wood should focus more heavily on Product Y. However, your attention would not have been so readily directed at these questions in the absence of the analysis we have outlined.

Assuming that the 200 hours are retained to ease production scheduling, the following revised product income statement shows the results of maximising total contribution per machine hour available.

Table 8.7 Product Contribution and Total profit Statement

	Y	Q	P	X	Total
Machine Hours	800	1,000	800	2,000	4,600
	£'000	£'000	£'000	£'000	£'000
Sales	1,600	1,000	700	1,500	4,800
Material Costs	400	400	200	500	1,500
Labour Costs	800	200	200	400	1,600
Total Variable Costs	1,200	600	400	900	3,100
Contribution	400	400	300	600	1,700
Fixed Costs					1,000
Profit					700

Where more than one constraint exists the problem will be reliant upon operations research methods like linear programming for its solution. Such techniques are beyond the scope of this book.

8.8   The Decision to Make or Buy

If you are not involved in a manufacturing environment, you may be tempted to skip this section on the grounds that make or buy decisions will be irrelevant to you. Nothing could be further from the truth! This we will demonstrate in the next section which is concerned with the evaluation of providing internal services against the use of outside contractors, and represents a good illustration of an application of make or buy principles.

Stated very simply, in a make or buy decision, buying is preferable on economic grounds when the relevant costs for making are greater than the price quoted by the supplier. As with many decisions, what often confuses the analysis is the distinction between those costs that are relevant to making the decision and those that are not. The distinction between relevant and non-relevant costs for make or buy decisions is exactly the same as described earlier insofar as relevant costs are future orientated and differential. However, to aid your understanding of their applications to make or buy decisions we will relate it to the following example.

The purchasing manager of T.O. Wood Ltd has been investigating the possibility of buying a certain component from an outside supplier. L. Driver Ltd is prepared to sign a one year contract to deliver 10,000 top quality units as needed during the year at a price of £5.00 per unit. This price of £5.00 is lower than the estimated manufacturing cost per component of £6.00, which is made up as follows:

Table 8.8   Product Cost Statement

	Unit cost £.00
Direct Material Costs	1.20
Direct Labour Costs	1.80
Factory Variable Cost	0.60
Annual Machine Rental	0.40
Factory Fixed Cost – Allocated	0.50
– Apportioned	1.50
	£6.00

It appears at first sight that it will make better economic sense to buy rather than to make, however, let us consider whether all of the items within the product cost breakdown are relevant, i.e. 'If the decision is made to buy, which of the costs will be avoided?' An investigation of the components reveals that direct materials, direct labour, factory variable costs, annual machine rental and factory fixed costs – specific would all be avoided. As the total of these relevant costs amounts to £4.50, which is less than the price of £5 quoted by the supplier, the decision should be to continue making the component. The remaining £1.50 of costs relating to apportioned fixed costs would presumably have to be borne elsewhere in the company and because they do not differ, irrespective of the course of action, are irrelevant.

Even if the analysis had indicated it to be more desirable to buy on economic grounds, there would still be factors to be considered other than purely the financial ones. For example loss of know-how in producing this component, the loss of certain skilled labour, not being able to control future cost increases and, therefore, final product prices, the ability to fill up capacity in slack times, and the possibility of finding it difficult to obtain supplies at a reasonable price during boom times, which must all be taken into consideration.

8.9   Competitive Tendering

As indicated, the principles used in the make or buy decision can also be applied to an evaluation of services to answer the question 'Do we provide service using our own resources or do we invite outside suppliers to compete to provide the service?'

There are many examples of organisations using competitive tendering in an attempt to obtain savings in the services they provide. These include, local authorities with refuse collection, health authorities with domestic, catering and building maintenance services, and even the Royal Navy with ship repair.

What is the basis used to determine whether an organisation should provide a service in-house or accept an offer from an outside supplier? The financial criteria are exactly the same as the make or buy decision, such that an organisation should provide an in-house service when the relevant costs associated with its provision are less than the price quoted by outside suppliers. These relevant costs are once again those costs which would be avoided if the provision of the service were to cease, and would tend to include materials consumed and wages. However, you must be constantly aware of irrelevant costs like historical as opposed to future values of stocks and other assets, and allocated costs which can often cloud a decision. A thorough review of all costs associated with such a service must be undertaken.

Once again please do note that our discussion has been concerned with financial criteria only. As we have emphasised on a number of occasions there will always be non-financial issues often of equal importance to take into consideration before a decision can realistically be taken.

8.10   The Decision to Accept/Reject a Special Order

One issue likely to be appropriate to all managers at some time in their careers is whether to accept what we will refer to as a special order. By this we mean 'Are there circumstances in which it might make sense in financial terms to sell products or services at a lower price than normal, or, alternatively to provide a service internally at less than its full cost?'

In considering such decisions it is most important to be quite clear about the meaning of the term *full cost*. In many organisations external and internal prices for products and services are generated with reference to the full or total cost of its provision plus a percentage margin, a practice known as *cost-plus pricing*. Within the full cost there will usually be allocated and apportioned fixed overheads required to be covered irrespective of whether a special order is accepted. Such irrelevant costs must be ignored such that the criterion for accepting a special order must only consider whether the direct benefits which result exceed those costs that could be avoided by not taking it.

Such evidence as exists from surveys of pricing reveals that some organisations do accept special orders using some form of the contribution analysis, although the bias towards its use is not as significant as many textbooks would imply.

You should be aware that the acceptance of a special order with reference to direct costs and benefits can be problematic if it generates a special order 'culture'. If all orders are priced as special how will fixed overheads ever be recovered!

There are also other considerations to be taken into account that may have financial consequences. For example, if it became widely known that special orders were negotiable then the subsequent marketing and selling of products, or services, may be far more difficult, and require a good deal more effort to be expended than currently.

As a general guideline then, in these types of decisions a company must consider:

1   Whether the acceptance of a special order will tie up capacity which could be used for profitable orders at some time in the future. If it does so then it should avoid the special contract.

2   Whether the acceptance of a contract will affect the regular sales of the product and ultimately the future pricing structure of that product. Generally speaking a special contract should not be accepted if it will affect consumer behaviour adversely within the same market place. General knowledge of the availability of special orders may well lead to consumer games with the supplier.

8.11   Structuring Decision Analysis

Clear thought and the application of certain key principles is critical for making sound decisions. We have offered these key principles by way of a number of applications which you may be able to apply to your own circumstances. All too often a major barrier to decision making is a lack of structure and we offer the following as a guideline:

❏   Clearly define exactly what the problem is for which a solution is sought.

❏   Consider all possible alternative courses of action which could lead to a solution.

❏   Discard those alternatives which on a common sense appraisal are 'non-starters' for one reason or another.

❏   Evaluate the cost and benefit differences between each of the remaining courses of action.

❏   Weigh up the non–financial factors related to each course of action.

❏   Take into account both financial and non-financial factors important to the decision, make the necessary trade-offs and decide.

All common sense you might be thinking? We would agree, but in our experience it is all too easy to overlook, underestimate, or evaluate incorrectly one or more of the steps.

CHAPTER NINE

LONG-TERM DECISION ANALYSIS 1

When you have finished studying this chapter you should be able to:

❏ Understand the need of organisations to identify and invest in high quality capital projects.

❏ Prepare a list of the main financial variables required for project appraisal.

❏ Identify the main points to consider when assessing the quality of input data.

❏ Calculate project cash flows.

❏ Appreciate the importance of project monitoring, control and post audit.

❏ Evaluate capital projects using traditional methods of investment appraisal such as:

Simple Payback and Accounting Rate of Return (ARR);

Net Present Value (NPV) and Profitability Index (PI);

Internal Rate of Return (IRR).

9.1   Introduction

Growing a business by internal development, as opposed to external investment in other organisations, requires sound commercial judgement. Such growth only occurs when the future returns from internal investment exceed the present costs; this means that managers must test their judgement against the difficulties presented by a highly unpredictable and uncertain future.

In considering this problem we ask:

❑   Are there any tools or techniques available from the realms of accounting and finance to help assess the desirability of particular investments?

❑   What are the differences between these tools and techniques?

We will consider these questions and other important issues in this chapter in relation to the evaluation of investments within the business. Such evaluations are similar to those made by private individuals when say, buying a car. The decision needs first to be weighed against other spending priorities. Various models would then be considered evaluating the costs and benefits of each before the actual choice is made. After the purchase a conscious or perhaps sub-conscious evaluation would be undertaken on the quality of the decision.

The process is roughly the same for commercial decisions except that the financing of capital expenditure projects is treated separately.

9.2   Organising Investment Decisions

A major stimulus for much investment is often the concern about the future performance of the business if investment does not take place. However, in practice many businesses actually consider investment requirements according to the particular needs to be addressed. Let us consider such needs with reference to the following four categories of investment:

1. Asset replacement.

2. Cost saving.

3. Expansion.

4. Reactive.

1.   Asset Replacement

If a company fails to replace those assets which currently generate its cash flow and profit, then in the absence of any other investment, its performance will decline, whether quickly or slowly. If the current profile of activities are appropriate to future long-term plans then, in order to continue to generate adequate cash flows and profit, the business must replace assets as they become worn out or obsolete.

2.   Cost Saving

Cost saving projects are critical to companies which have products or services where sales revenues have reached the maximum level that can be sustained by the market. Irrespective of whether this maximum is temporary because of depressed economic conditions, or more permanent because the maximum achievable share of a mature market has been reached, a reduction in the firm's costs is possible by improving the efficiency of existing asset use. Sales generation ratios (described in *Chapter 4*) can be used to identify possible areas for improvement, such as the automation of a previously labour intensive production system. This usually involves the substitution of an avoidable variable cost with an unavoidable fixed cost in order to secure forecast savings.

Finally, cost saving projects may be important to the not-for-profit organisation in which there may be no revenues associated with a project. The analysis of cost savings enables comparisons to be made with existing practice and between alternatives.

3.   Expansion

Business growth can result from internal or organic expansion or by focusing upon external targets via an acquisitive strategy. Much investment activity can be related to the desire to achieve growth which many organisations (particularly smaller ones) will attempt to achieve internally. Successful internal growth will eventually permit an organisation to contemplate external expansion, particularly where its shares may be traded publicly. However, even companies with a successful track record of acquisitions will undertake internal investment resulting in business expansion to achieve growth.

4.   Reactive Investment

Reactive investment covers two particular types of capital expenditure. The first is that which is required as a defensive response to threatening changes in the commercial environment. For example, some of the changes which can be observed in the major U.K. clearing banks services are the result of substantial investment caused by threats from previously dormant players in the financial services sector, such as Building Societies, in recent years. The second embraces that imposed upon the business because of legislative or other reasons where the benefits of the expenditure are not always readily measurable. It is perhaps, best illustrated by the following examples;

❏ As a result of new legislation, the U.K. furniture industry was required to undertake substantial investment in fire resistant foam filling.

❏ Following the Piper Alpha disaster, North Sea Oil companies have been required to undertake safety modifications to offshore installations estimated to cost hundreds of millions of pounds.

5. Managerial Responsibility for Investment

In larger organisations managerial responsibility for investment is usually delegated from top management to lower levels of management. This delegation will usually exclude the raising of finance other than from short-term sources. Decisions about sources of finance with long-term implications are usually taken by top management who will try to balance proportions of debt and equity so as to minimise the cost of capital to the business.

The delegation of managerial responsibility for the evaluation of capital expenditure can be achieved by specifying cut-off levels, the amount of which corresponds with given levels of seniority. For example, senior divisional management may be responsible for capital expenditure up to an agreed cut-off sum, and approval would have to be obtained from top management for capital expenditure above the agreed cut-off. In addition, such senior divisional management may also be required to approve submissions for capital expenditure from its divisional management, where the capital expenditure required exceeds the level of delegated responsibility.

9.3 Appraising Investment Opportunities

In this section we provide a background to the financial appraisal of potential investment opportunities. In common with many areas of accounting and finance, numerous terms are used to describe the financial appraisal process of which investment appraisal, project appraisal and capital budgeting are common. To avoid confusion and to reinforce the point that our concern is not with investing in securities of other organisations, we will adopt the term *project appraisal* to refer to the evaluation of capital expenditure.

You may find it easy to become lost in the detail of the financial issues associated with project appraisal, so let us take stock of the key financial requirements to be met:

❏ only those projects which meet the objectives of the business should be selected, i.e. those which provide what the business regards as a satisfactory return for the risks involved;

❏ the return to be expected from a project must exceed the financing cost that the capital expenditure will necessitate, and;

❏ the most financially desirable project must be selected from the range of opportunities available (assuming, as is normally the case, that resources are limited and that not all projects can be undertaken).

In addition to these financial requirements it is important to stress that for many investments non-financial factors may be very important. Therefore account must also be taken of these so that both financial and non-financial considerations are given appropriate weight.

With these points in mind and before we consider individual techniques for gauging the financial benefit, let us consider the main financial variables of a project appraisal. A definitive list is impossible, but the following items will usually occur in one form or another:

❏ The initial capital outlay including the cost of fixed assets, working capital and, if appropriate, deliberate start-up losses.

❏ The expected useful economic life of the project.

❏ An estimate of the residual value of assets remaining at the end of the project's useful economic life.

❏ The amounts and timing of all cost and revenue components associated with the project.

❏ Expected price level changes for each cost and revenue component.

❏ Taxation assumptions and any regional grants likely to affect the corporate position.

❏ The relevant cost of financing the project (cost of capital).

❏ Likely estimates of variation for each of the above variables.

Many of these financial variables will be discussed in the next section outlining the major project appraisal techniques, and the remainder are considered in the next chapter. Before considering the techniques, let us review certain key points discussed in the previous chapter concerning the requirements of data for purposes of decision making. It is all to easy to focus upon the mechanics of the techniques themselves whilst losing sight of their limitations in the absence of good quality input data. It cannot be over-stressed that the benefit to be derived from any technique used for appraising a project can be no better than the quality of the input data employed.

9.4 Assessing the Quality of Input Data

The main points to consider in assessing the quality of input data are:

1. Future Orientation

The only capital outlay, operating costs and revenues relevant to a proposed capital project are those that concern the future. Sunk, past costs are irrelevant even though there may be a temptation to treat them otherwise, as are costs to be found in a company's cost or management accounting system. This is the case whether they are past or present and they are useful only as a guide in forecasting future cost levels.

It is not only the costs themselves that are irrelevant but also the patterns of cost behaviour. Such patterns may be appropriate to the routine accounting functions of budgeting and variance analysis, but may not be suitable for decisions where the relevant time span is longer than that required for effective control. Assumptions which ordinarily permit different costs to be described as fixed, variable or semi-variable in their behaviour may need to be adapted when five or ten year time scales are involved, since at the time a capital project decision is being made all costs relevant to the decision are variable. It is only when the project is accepted and implemented that project associated costs become fixed.

2. Attributable Costs and Revenues

The costs and revenues relevant to a capital project are only those which can be legitimately attributed to it rather than any other source. Whilst this notion is simple and manageable in principle at the level of the individual project, difficulties can be encountered in practice when the cumulative effects of several proposed capital projects need to be anticipated.

3. Differential Costs and Revenues

Where decisions require more than one course of action to be examined, the only costs and revenues to be considered are those that will differ under the alternative courses of action. Common costs and revenues may be ignored, provided they are expected to behave identically in each of the alternatives under consideration.

4. Opportunity Costs and Benefits

These costs and benefits are usually the most difficult of all to deal with. Nevertheless, opportunity costs and benefits must be included in any project decision. For example, if a consequence of introducing a new model of a product currently sold at a profit is that sales of the existing product will be lost, then the lost contribution on the existing product is an opportunity cost of the new model which must be included in the appraisal.

5.   Financing Costs

It is often tempting, but incorrect, during a project appraisal to include the financing costs associated with a proposal within the estimated operating costs. As we will show in the next section, how the financing costs are compared with the financial benefits does vary according to the appraisal techniques used, but they should not be included with the estimated operating costs.

6.   Uncertainty and Inflation

It is important that the risk and uncertainty associated with projects is incorporated within any appraisal, together with expectations about changes in costs and prices. Any failure to make appropriate allowances for risk, uncertainty and inflation can result in an appraisal of questionable value.

7.   Qualitative Issues

A serious limitation of conventional project appraisal is the omission of non-financial issues, such as improvements in product quality for corporate image, or a lower susceptibility to adverse social pressures. Whilst such benefits are often extremely difficult to assess, they should not be ignored.

9.5   Determining the Cash Flows

Very often, for convenience, the input data for an investment appraisal is assumed to be available. In practice, the determination of the cash flows is a very demanding task. Here we will consider how a cash flow profile may be built up by drawing upon information from a wide range of sources.

1.   Example Using Capital Outlay and Savings

The cost of the equipment is relatively easy to obtain. Perhaps a quote from a number of suppliers. The other items are also important, for example in certain projects the cost of services could be quite large if it meant laying a mains cable or an access road.

Table 9.1   Determining the Capital Outlay

	£'000
Equipment – Web offset press	£1,700
Services	£50
Contingency	£35
Expenses	£15
	£1,800

From the following list it can be seen that the basic data required to determine savings must be obtained from a number of sources. The sales forecast, expected selling price and average page count of the manuals could be obtained from the marketing department, while the technical data concerning pages per impression and run speed would be obtained from the equipment manual, and the average run length and set up could be obtained from past experience.

Table 9.2   Basic Data for Calculation of Annual Cash Flows

Sales Forecast per annum	£6,000,000
Average Selling Price per Book	£2.00
Average Page Count	352 pages
Pages Per Impression	16 pages
Run Speed	20,000 impressions per hour
Average Run Length per job	6,000 books
Set-up	30 minutes

Table 9.3   Calculation of Forecast Annual Volumes

Total Books	(£6,000,000 ÷ £2.00)	3,000,000 books
Total Impressions	(3,000,000 x 352 ÷ 16)	66,000,000 impressions
Total Print Jobs	(3,000,000 ÷ 6,000)	500 jobs

We now require data concerning the time taken to prepare, print, bind and warehouse. This will be obtained from work study records and hourly rates to produce the following:

Table 9.4   Additional Data to Establish Annual Costs

Preparation	30 hours (per average run length job) £25 per hour
Paper and materials	£4,200 per job
Printing:	
Setup	£100 per hour
Text	£100 per hour
Covers	7 hours, rate £70 per hour (per average run length job)
Binding	150 minutes per 1,000, rate £140 per hour
Warehousing	£100,000

Table 9.5   Calculation of the Annual Costs

			£
Preparation		(500 x 30 hours x £25)	375,000
Printing	Setup	(66 m x 30 ÷ 60 ÷ 6,000 x £100)	550,000
	Text	(66 m ÷ 20,000 x £100)	330,000
	Covers	(500 x 7 hours x £70)	245,000
Binding		(3 m x 150 ÷ 60 ÷ 1,000 x £140)	1,050,000
Warehousing			100,000
			2,650,000

The annual cash flows can now be established using the sales forecast as the income then deducting materials and the costs of printing, binding and warehousing. The results are shown in *Table 9.6*.

Table 9.6   Annual cash flows

		£
Income	(Sales Forecast)	6,000,000
less:	Materials (£4,200 x 500)	2,100,000
	Printing, Binding, Warehousing	2,650,000
Annual Cash Flow		1,250,000

2. Example – Forecasting Cash Flows Using 'Drivers'

The example we have just reviewed considered a situation involving capital expenditure and potential savings. However, as we indicated at the beginning of this chapter, there are cases where the purpose of the investment is to expand. In such circumstances, an alternative approach to deriving the cash flows is by the use of a number of 'cash flow' drivers. Using this approach, the implications of an expansion can be mapped out by their impact upon the business which we illustrate with a simple example.

Imagine a business which has achieved a sales revenue of £10 million from, for the sake of simplicity, a single product. With the usual forecasting difficulty it estimates 'an expansion' potential of 10% in the market in which it operates. What does the firm need to consider?

Assuming it has the production capacity, it will receive cash revenues from the increased sales after deducting operating expenses (excluding depreciation) and taxation. To take advantage of such a market it may also incur cash expenses from increases in working capital; increased debtors as a result of more aggressive marketing and more stock to provide a better service to customers. If the firm does not have the capacity it must provide for increased production by incurring capital expenditure; another drain on its cash.

To see how the cash flow driver approach works our example will now assume the following:

❑   Depreciation of £40,000

❑   Sales growth rate of 10%

❑   Operating profit margin of 20%

❑   Tax rate of 25%

❑   Additional fixed capital requirement of 5%

❑   Additional working capital requirement of 10%

Table 9.7   First Year Cash Flow

	£000's
Sales Revenue (£10m increased by 10% sales growth rate)	11.00
Operating Profit Margin Before Tax (£11m x 20%)	2.20
less Tax at 25%	0.55
Operating Profit Margin	1.65
add Depreciation	0.04
Operating Cash Flow	1.69
Replacement Capital Expenditure	–0.04
Additional Fixed Capital Expenditure (£1m x 5%)	–0.05
Additional Working Capital (£1m x 10%)	–0.10
Free Cash Flow	1.50

Using this approach cash flow can be readily estimated. Different assumptions about the growth rate potential, the operating profit margin, the tax rate, the fixed and working capital needs can be readily built in so as to build up a profile cash flows for a given time period. As with any matter concerning cash, depreciation has to be taken into consideration and added back to the profit margin. In this example, the simplified assumption has been made that depreciation is a reasonable proxy for what would be required to maintain the quality of existing assets in terms of their replacement as they wear out. This is what we have referred to as 'Replacement Capital Expenditure'.

The most difficult part of this exercise is actually determining the percentages and there is no easy solution to this. Historical records and competitor analysis will be required in order to produce an accurate picture. For example, the ability to achieve sales growth will be dependent upon internal resourcing and any limiting factors, as well as the action of competitors. A major advantage of the approach is that is does force trade-offs to be considered; to achieve future cash inflows by expansion, additional fixed and working capital expenditure will be necessary.

9.6   Project Monitoring, Control and Post Audit

Considerable emphasis is often given to the appraisal process and, although this is important it is not the 'be all and end all' in making sound investment decisions. Appropriate monitoring and control procedures ensure that funds committed to a particular project are used effectively. These may involve ongoing procedures to monitor expenditure regularly and/or the use of what is known as the 'post audit'. Typically, this is focused upon apportioning blame, although this need not necessarily be so. An increasing number of companies (usually very large companies) have developed procedures at varying stages of a projects development, with a terminal evaluation sometime after project completion. Companies with such procedures have used them as part of a learning process.

It would be rare for all projects to be post audited. More often, on a regular basis, a sample of completed capital projects are submitted for post audit. For those selected there is a thorough investigation of all aspects of each project from the original idea through to eventual implementation. The main purpose of post audit being to provide a feedback mechanism to benefit future projects. It should cover:

❏   How does each project fit into the present and future resource requirements?

❏   What improvements might be made in the collection of better data for each project?

❏   To what extent have savings been overestimated and capital requirements underestimated?

❏   Were projects properly evaluated, including sensitivity and risk?

❏   Did all projects produce the forecast savings? Have the necessary standards been amended?

❏   What are the main recommendations for improvement to future capital projects?

❏   Should the procedures for capital projects be amended?

9.7   Project Appraisal Techniques

We have now set the scene for project appraisal in our discussions of the financial variables required and important issues associated with the quality of cost and revenue inputs. The important issue for consideration now is how such data is organised for purposes of appraising a project. This we will illustrate with reference to the four major project appraisal techniques. Where we have deliberately omitted issues such as inflation and taxation which sit more comfortably with the discussions which follow in the next chapter.

1.   Payback period.

2.   Accounting rate of return.

3.   Net Present Value (NPV) and Profitability Index.

4.   Internal Rate of Return (IRR).

The distinguishing characteristics of these four project appraisal techniques and their respective advantages and disadvantages are best illustrated with financial data. Accordingly we will use data for an imaginary organisation contemplating the following four alternative projects which are summarised in *Table 9.8* below.

Table 9.8   Basic Data for Four Projects

	Project A £'000	Project B £'000	Project C £'000	Project D £'000
Capital Outlay	−15,000	−18,000	−10,000	−18,000
Net Cash Inflows:				
Year 1	7,000	6,000	5,000	4,000
Year 2	4,000	6,000	5,000	5,000
Year 3	3,000	6,000		6,000
Year 4	2,000	6,000		7,000
Year 5	1,000	6,000		8,000

1.   Payback Period

The payback period is calculated with reference to cash flow data. It is expressed in terms of a number of years (or years and months) and summarises the time required for a project to recover its capital outlay from cash inflows. For example, for Project B which has a capital outlay of £18 million and cash inflows of £6 million for each year of its five year expected economic life, the payback is exactly three years:

$$\frac{\text{Capital Outlay}}{\text{Net Cash Inflow}} = \frac{\text{£18 million}}{\text{£ 6 million}} = 3 \text{ years}$$

Project B is straightforward because the payback period occurs exactly at the end of year three, but this is not usually the case. For example, if you try to calculate the payback period for projects A and D you will find that it does not occur at the end of a single year. Let us see how this can be dealt with using the data for Project A. The first step is to accumulate the cash flows as follows:

Table 9.9   Calculation of Payback Period – Project A

	£'000		
Capital Outlay	−15,000		
Net Cash Inflows:	(i)	(ii)	(iii)
	Annual £'000	Annual to Payback £'000	Cumulative to Payback £'000
Year 1	7,000	7,000	7,000
Year 2	4,000	4,000	11,000
Year 3	3,000	3,000	14,000
Year 4	2,000	1,000	15,000

The figures in column (iii) show that in each of the first three years the whole of the net cash inflows are used to accumulate to £14 million. In the fourth year, only £1 million of the net cash flows are required to make the accumulated net cash flows equal to the capital outlay. Therefore, the payback period takes place in three and one half years i.e. three years, plus £1 million out of £2 million.

The results for all four projects may be summarised as:

	Project A	Project B	Project C	Project D
Payback Period (years)	3.5	3.0	2.0	3.4

The main aim in using any project appraisal technique is to find out which project should be selected from a number of competing projects. A simple ranking, this case based on the project offering the shortest payback period, would reveal that Project C is the best project. However, some companies will evaluate the payback period in relation to the project's useful economic life. This means that Project B which pays back after three years of its estimated five year life may be viewed far more favourably than Project C, which pays back at the end of its useful economic life. The relationship between the payback period and the useful economic life for each of the projects may be summarised as:

	Project A	Project B	Project C	Project D
Payback Period (years)	3.5	3.0	2.0	3.4
Useful Economic Life (years)	5	5	2	5
Payback ÷ Economic Life	0.70	0.60	1.00	0.68

Payback period has a major advantage over other methods because it is simple to calculate, understand and implement. Against this, the payback period focuses upon time taken to recover the capital outlay but cash flows generated after the payback period may not be taken into consideration. One other major shortcoming, the substance and importance of which will become evident shortly in our discussion of the discounting principle, is that unless the cash flows are specifically adjusted, the time value of money is ignored.

2.   Accounting Rate of Return

The accounting rate of return differs from the payback period since its calculation draws on data relating to the whole life of a project. You must be aware, however, that it is calculated using a project's profit, rather than cash flows and thus suffers, as we saw earlier, from the ambiguity of the definition of profit. Once profit is defined the accounting rate of return is relatively straightforward to calculate. Take note that different users may arrive at different accounting rates of return using the same input data, and what is even more confusing is that none of the resulting calculations are necessarily incorrect!

The first step in calculating the rate of return is to add the estimated annual profit flows to establish the total profit of the proposed project. If only cash flow information is available then the annual cash flows must be added together to find the total cash flows, which in our example are £17 million, £30 million, £10 million and £30 million for Projects A, B, C and D, respectively. From this total the capital outlay (the total depreciation) is deducted to give the total profit. The average annual profit required for the calculation is found by dividing the total profit by the life of the project. This is illustrated for our four example projects in *Table 9.10*.

Table 9.10 Calculation of Accounting Rate of Return

		Project A £'000	Project B £'000	Project C £'000	Project D £'000
Total Net Cash Inflow	(A)	17,000	30,000	10,000	30,000
Capital Outlay	(B)	−15,000	−18,000	−10,000	−18,000
Total Profit	(C)=(A)−(B)	£2,000	£12,000	0	£12,000
Life (years)	(D)	5	5	2	5
Average Annual Profit	(C)÷(D)	£400	£2,400	0	£2,400

The accounting rate of return is then calculated by dividing the average annual profit by the capital outlay. For Project A, the calculation is:

$$\text{Accounting Rate of Return (\%)} = \frac{\text{Average Annual Profit}}{\text{Capital Outlay}} \times 100$$

$$= \frac{£0.4 \text{ million}}{£15 \text{ million}} \times 100$$

$$= 2.7\%$$

Similar calculations for Projects B, C and D produce accounting rates of return of 13.3%, 0% and 13.3% respectively. A simple ranking from highest to lowest rate of return shows that Projects B and D are ranked equal.

	Project A	Project B	Project C	Project D
Accounting Rate of Return %	2.7	13.3	0	13.3
Ranking	3	1 =	4	1 =

It was indicated earlier that using the same input data, different accounting rates of return can be produced. How can this happen? It is conceivable that one might use some notion of average capital outlay rather than the total capital outlay adopted in our example and, indeed, some organisations do just this. As you will appreciate, anything which has the effect of reducing the capital outlay in the calculation will increase the accounting rate of return. Consider for example the effect on Project B if the average capital outlay was calculated as being £9 million. The rate of return percentage would double!

The potential ambiguity in accounting rate of return results is sometimes presented as being a shortcoming. Nevertheless, the technique is used and with some success particularly where manuals of capital expenditure procedure provide a specific definition of the items to be used in accounting rate of return calculations.

3.   The principle of discounting

The two remaining techniques for discussion, the net present value (NPV), and the internal rate of return (IRR) are both reliant upon a principle which involves discounting, or scaling-down, future cash flows. In order to appreciate the principle involved we will compare discounting with the more familiar but related technique of compounding.

Compounding is applied to a sum of money so that its value in future may be calculated given a required rate of interest. Discounting is the reverse. Future cash inflows are discounted at a given rate of interest so that they may be directly compared to the present outlay of cash.

Figure 9.1   Compounding and Discounting Cash Flows

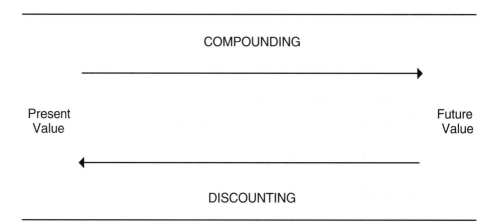

How is this discounting achieved? Cash flows can be discounted using factors which are readily available in statistical tables. The basis for their calculation is similar to the principles used in calculating compound interest. We will use the information in *Table 9.11* to show the relationship between compounding and discounting. There we make specific reference to the factors used to compound and discount cash at a 10% rate.

Table 9.11   Compound Interest and Discounted Cash Flow Factors

	Compound interest factors 10%	Discounted cash flow factors (DCF) 10%
Year 0	1.000	1.000
Year 1	1.100	0.909
Year 2	1.210	0.826
Year 3	1.331	0.751
Year 4	1.464	0.683
Year 5	1.611	0.621

Using the factors in *Table 9.11*, £1,000 invested today at 10% compound interest would yield £1,210 at the end of year two i.e. £1,000 x 1.21. The reverse can be seen if we assume a forecast cash flow of £1,210 at the end of year two, discounted at 10% back to a present value would produce £1,000 i.e. £1,210 x 0.826. The principle of discounting thus operates by scaling down future cash flows to produce a present value. In this way future cash flows can be readily compared with the present value of capital outlays. The reduction in the value of future cash flows using the discounting process is dependent upon the rate of interest. The higher the rate of interest, the more severely the cash flows will be scaled down. The technique of adjusting cash flows might seem tedious but the discount factor tables are readily available at the end of the book. In this table the present value of £1 has been calculated for a wide range of interest rates.

4.   Determining the Relevant Discount Rate

In order to calculate the net present value technique (and other discounting techniques such as, the profitability index, or the discounted payback period that we will discuss), the relevant discount factor must be known. This discount factor should be the company's required rate of return (sometimes known as the hurdle rate from the sporting analogy where hurdles have to be jumped to even stand a chance of being successful). This rate as represented by the company's cost of capital, is the projects' break even point. Projects undertaken yielding a return above this *hurdle* rate will increase the value of the business whilst those below will decrease value.

The components involved in the determination of a company's cost of capital have been the subject of much academic research and debate. However, there does seem to be some agreement that the appropriate rate should comprise the weighted average of the after tax cost of debt capital and the equity cost of capital. In the case of debt capital the after tax cost is used because, interest is deductible before tax thus providing a reduced real cost. This is unlike dividend payments which have to be met from after tax profits. How this cost of capital is arrived at is best understood from the following example: *A company has an after tax cost of debt of 6 per cent, an estimated cost of equity of 16 per cent and future gearing comprising 20 per cent debt and 80 per cent equity. In this simple* case, the company's weighted average cost of capital is 14%, and the basis for the calculation is illustrated in *Table 9.12*.

Table 9.12   *Weighted average cost of capital   (WACC)*

	Weight A (%)	Cost B (%)	Weighted cost A x B % (%)
Debt	20	6	1.2
Equity	80	16	12.8
			14.0

This cost of capital includes the returns demanded by both debt-holders and shareholders because pre-interest cash flows are those to be discounted. Given that both debt-holders and shareholders have claims against these, the appropriate cost of capital will be one that incorporates the relative capital contribution of each group. Thus, total pre-interest cash flows which are attributable to both lenders and shareholders are discounted by a weighted cost of capital to yield a value to the business.

It is important to realise that the relative weights attached to debt and equity within the calculation should be based on the relative proportions of each estimated for the future. This is because the concern of a capital project appraisal is with the future and not with the past. Thus, the present or previous debt to equity proportions are irrelevant, unless they apply to the future. There is also a useful analogy with the matching principle discussed in relation to accounting in *Chapter 1*. The objective is to compare like with like, hence the use of a future orientated gearing ratio for establishing the cost of capital at which to discount future cash flows.

The determination of the relevant discount factor is important not only to project appraisal. In recognition of its importance it is discussed more fully in a later chapter.

5.   Net Present Value   (NPV)

We will now illustrate the application of the net present value (NPV) technique, where for a given rate of interest, future cash flows are discounted using the principle discussed in the previous section. The sum total of these discounted future cash flows is compared with the capital outlay and where it is greater than that outlay, the NPV is said to be positive and the project is acceptable on economic grounds. Conversely, if a negative NPV results (capital outlay is greater than the sum of discounted future cash flows) the project is not acceptable on economic grounds.

Using basic data for the four proposed projects illustrated earlier, and assuming a 10% cost of capital, the following NPV analysis can be carried out for Project B.

Table 9.13   Calculation of Net Present Value – Project B

Year	Column 1 Discount Factor 10%	Column 2 Cash Flows £000	Column 3 (Col. 1 x Col. 2) Present Value £000
1	0.909	6,000	5,454
2	0.826	6,000	4,956
3	0.751	6,000	4,506
4	0.683	6,000	4,098
5	0.621	6,000	3,726
Present Value of Cash Inflows			22,740
less Capital Outlay			18,000
Net Present Value			£4,740

The annual net cash flows shown in column 2 are multiplied by the 10% discount factors in column 1 to produce the annual present value of the cash flows in column 3. These annual present values are then added together to give the total present value of the cash inflows of £22.740 million. The net present value is calculated by deducting the capital outlay from the total present values of the cash inflows (i.e. £22.740 million – £18.000 million) giving £4.740 million. The effect of discounting the cash flows is also illustrated in *Figure 9.2.*

Figure 9.2   Comparison of Cash Flows – Project B

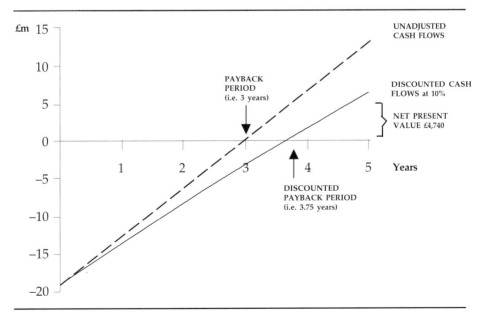

The capital outlay of £18 million is the starting point of the upper diagonal which is constructed from accumulating the annual net cash inflows of £6 million. The result is a cumulative cash inflow of £30 million at the end of year five. When these annual cash inflows of £6 million are discounted at 10% and plotted in the diagram, the lower diagonal results. The application of the 10% discount factor can be seen to cause a scaling-down which results in a net present value of £4.740 million. Raising the discount factor would scale-down the cash flows even further, thereby resulting in a lower net present value. One other observation from the diagram is the effect upon the payback period when discounted rather than undiscounted annual net cash inflows are used. You will see from the diagram that the *discounted payback period* is 3.75 years rather than the original three years when the net cash inflows are discounted at 10%. Furthermore, should the discount factor be increased resulting in a greater scaling down of cash flows, the discounted payback period becomes even longer.

We will consider the discounted payback and profitability index once we have reviewed the net present value calculations for all four projects.

Table 9.14 Comparison of Net Present Values

	Project A £000	Project B £000	Project C £000	Project D £000
Present Value of Cash Inflows	13,907	22,740	8,675	22,021
Capital Outlay	15,000	18,000	10,000	18,000
Net Present Value	–£1,093	£4,740	–£1,325	£4,021

The results show that only Projects B and D produce a positive net present value and on economic grounds would be acceptable because they:

❑ exceed the required rate of return (cost of capital) of 10%;

❑ cover the capital outlay; and,

❑ produce a sum in excess of the capital outlay which is referred to as the net present value.

Discounted Payback

The discounted payback period is similar in principle to the simple payback period, the only difference being that we use the discounted annual flows, and accumulate them until their sum equals the capital outlay.

In *Figure 9.2* we illustrated the discounted payback period for Project B of 3.75 years, but how is this calculated? Using the discounted annual cash flows for Project B, the discounted payback period can be calculated in a similar manner to simple payback:

Table 9.15   Calculation of Discounted Payback – Project B

	£'000		
Capital Outlay	−18,000		
Discounted Cash Flows:	**(i)** **Annual**	**(ii)** **Annual to Payback**	**(iii)** **Cumulative to Payback**
	£'000	**£'000**	**£'000**
Year 1	5,454	5,454	5,454
Year 2	4,956	4,956	10,410
Year 3	4,506	4,506	14,916
Year 4	4,098	3,084	18,000

Note. The adjusted cash flows shown in column (i) have been extracted from Table 9.13

The discounted cash flows to achieve the £18 million capital outlay can be monitored from column (iii). At the end of Year three £14.916 million will be recovered, leaving £3.084 million to be recovered in Year four. Given that £4.098 million will be recovered from Year four, the proportion of a year represented by £3.084 million can be readily calculated. Thus discounted payback is achieved in three years plus £3.084 million divided by £4.098 million, which equals approximately 3.75 years.

Similar calculations for the discounted payback can be performed for Projects A, C and D to produce the following results:

Table 9.16   Comparison of Discounted Payback

	Project A	Project B	Project C	Project D
Discounted Payback (years)	n/a	3.75	n/a	4.19

Profitability Index

Where the capital outlay differs from project to project the *profitability index* is calculated and provides useful information to assist in the decision making process. The profitability index is a ratio which relates the present value of the cash inflows from a project to its capital outlay. For Project A this would be £13.907 million divided by £15 million which gives 0.93 and for Projects B, C and D it is 1.26, 0.87 and 1.22, respectively. It is now possible to rank all projects competing for limited funds using the profitability index – all other things being equal, the higher the profitability index the better.

Table 9.17 Calculation of Profitability Index

		Project A £000	Project B £000	Project C £000	Project D £000
Present value of Cash net Inflows	(A)	13,907	22,740	8,675	22,021
Capital Outlay	(B)	15,000	18,000	10,000	18,000
Profitability Index (A) ÷ (B)		0.93	1.26	0.87	1.22

The index of 1.26 for Project B means that the capital outlay is covered once plus an additional 26% and that where capital is restricted, should be preferred to the other alternatives on economic grounds. Where the profitability index is less than 1, e.g. Project A, this means that the project does not cover its capital outlay, therefore, does not provide the minimum return i.e. company's cost of capital. However, before drawing any further conclusions let us consider the internal rate of return.

6.   Internal Rate of Return (IRR)

The net present value, the profitability index and the discounted payback calculations require knowledge of the company's cost of capital as necessary data input for their calculation, but internal rate of return (IRR) does not.

The IRR is a discounted cash flow method which seeks to find the discount rate at which the present value of net cash inflows from a capital project exactly equal the capital outlay, in other words at the IRR the net present value is zero.

The IRR can best be understood with reference to *Figure 9.3* in which you can see that the lowest line corresponds with a NPV of £0. This is achieved by scaling-down the net cash inflows by applying a discount factor corresponding with the IRR percentage. Thus the percentage which when converted to a discount factor and multiplied by the net cash inflows gives a present value equal to the capital outlay is the internal rate of return.

Figure 9.3   Graph Showing Internal Rate of Return   (IRR)

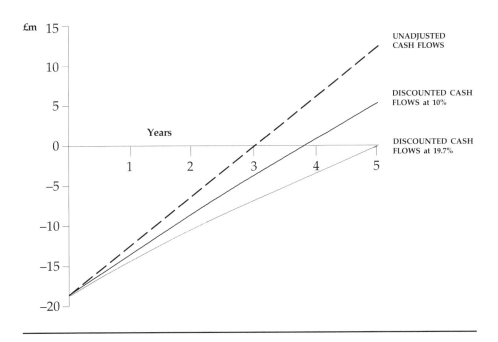

Once determined the IRR percentage should then be compared with the company's cost of capital in order to establish the economic acceptability of a project. The principle is that if the IRR exceeds the cost of capital then a project is acceptable on economic grounds. On the other hand, if the IRR from a project is lower than the cost of capital the project is not acceptable on economic grounds.

The calculation of the IRR is based on trial and error to find the discount rate corresponding to a zero net present value. As such several calculations may need to be made and are best facilitated with the aid of a computer. The calculations necessary to find the IRR for Project B are based upon data summarised in *Table 9.18.*

Table 9.18 Trial and Error Calculation of Internal Rate of Return (IRR) – Project B

Year	Cash Inflows £'000	DCF factor 18%	Present value £'000	DCF factor 21%	Present value £'000
1	6,000	0.847	5,082	0.826	4,956
2	6,000	0.718	4,308	0.683	4,098
3	6,000	0.609	3,654	0.564	3,384
4	6,000	0.516	3,096	0.467	2,802
5	6,000	0.437	2,622	0.386	2,316
Present Value of Net Cash Inflows			18,762		17,556
less Capital Outlay			18,000		18,000
Net Present Value			£762		–£444

Table 9.18 shows that cash flows for Project B when discounted at 18% provide a net present value of £0.762 million. To find the IRR (where the net present value is zero), in this case a higher discount is required. The result of increasing the rate to 21% shows that the net present value is negative at –£0.444 million. The internal rate of return must therefore fall between 18% and 21% and can be found approximately by linear interpolation.

$$IRR = d_1 + [n_1 \div (n_1 + n_2) \times s]$$

Where: d_1 = lower dcf; d_2 = higher dcf; n_1 = NPV at lower dcf; n_2 = NPV at higher dcf; $s = d_2 - d_1$

Therefore the IRR for Project B is calculated as follows:

$$IRR = 18 + (762 \div 1,206 \times 3)$$

$$= 18 + 1.9$$

$$= 19.9\%$$

Similar calculations carried out for Projects A, C and D produce the following results shown alongside that for Project B:

	Project A	Project B	Project C	Project D
Internal Rate of Return %	6.1	19.9	0	17.5

The approximations of the IRR% in this case are fairly accurate and in fact those obtained from using both a computer and a programmable calculator were 6%, 19.9%, 0% and 17.4% for Projects A, B, C and D respectively.

The results achieved from using manual calculations for the IRR produce satisfactory results provided that the difference between the two discount rates is not too large (e.g. greater than 5%). However, it is preferable to use a computer or programmable calculator which allow the user to change any of the figures with relative ease.

One major problem with the IRR is that it may be impossible to provide a clear cut solution to projects that have irregular cash flows. In such a situation there may not be an internal rate of return, or if there is, it may not be unique.

9.8   Using Annuity Tables

In addition to the arithmetical tables which provide a stream of discount factors it is also possible to obtain arithmetical tables which give cumulative discount factors over a specific period of time. These tables which are included in *pages 425 and 426*, are referred to as annuity tables because they convert a lump sum into a stream of equal annual payments. To find out the total present value of £100 over 10 years we could undertake 10 individual calculations in a similar manner to that illustrated in the last chapter. Alternatively, we can achieve the same result from a single calculation by multiplying £100 by the cumulative discount factor found from the annuity tables.

Before we go any further it might help to consider the benefit of using cumulative discount factors in appraising potential investment opportunities. From *Table 9.19* we can identify the cumulative discount factors for any period between one and five years. If we return to Project B we can calculate the present value of the net cash inflows at 10% in one operation:

    £6 million   x   3.790   =   £22.740 million

This is a quicker method than that used before, see *Table 9.13*, where five multiplications were required! However, this method can only be used where the annual cash flows are equal.

Table 9.19   Discount Factors at 10%

Period	Discount Factors at 10%	Cumulative Discount Factors at 10%
1	0.909	0.909
2	0.826	1.735
3	0.751	2.486
4	0.683	3.169
5	0.621	3.790

A final point regarding the cumulative discount factors. Compare the figures we have just used in *Table 9.19* above with the corresponding figures in *Appendix B*. The slight difference is due to rounding and for the calculation of further examples we will use the figures from *Appendix B*.

Example – Using Annuity Tables

We will continue to make use of Project B, (as we already know the answer) and use the cumulative discount factors to calculate the following:

1. The internal rate of return given a capital outlay of £18 million, annual savings of £6 million and a five year life.

2. The minimum annual savings for the project to be acceptable on economic grounds, given a cost of capital (discount rate) of 20%, a capital outlay of £18 million and a five year life.

3. The maximum capital outlay worth expending on such a project, given only that the cost of capital is 20%, annual savings are £6 million, and the expected life is five years.

1.   Calculate the Internal Rate of Return

First, we calculate the cumulative discount factor as follows:

Capital Outlay ÷   Annual Savings

£18 million ÷   £6 million   =   3.000

Second, we use the table in *Appendix B* and check the cumulative discount factors on the line for a five year life until we obtain a value which is close to the 3.000. In this case we will see that a figure of 2.991 is the closest and this represents the cumulative discount factors at 20%. With the use of interpolation, say between 19% and 20% it is possible to arrive at rates correct to one decimal place.

2. Calculate the Minimum Annual Savings

We are given a cost of capital and the life of the project therefore we refer to *Appendix B* and extract the cumulative discount factors at 20% for a period of five years which give 2.991. The minimum annual savings is found from:

Capital Outlay   ÷   Cumulative Discount Factor

£18 million   ÷   2.991   =   £6.018 million

In this case, we conclude that if the capital outlay is expected to be £18 million and the company's cost of capital is 20% then the project will need to provide a minimum annual savings of £6.018 million for five years.

3. Calculate the Maximum Capital Outlay

We follow the same procedure as in 2. above and obtain a cumulative discount factor of 2.991. The maximum capital outlay is found from:

Annual Savings   x   Cumulative Discount Factor

£6 million   x   2.991   =   £17.946 million

Here we conclude that if the annual savings for five years are expected to be £6 million and the company's cost of capital is 20% then a maximum capital outlay of £17.946 million can be spent.

9.9 Project Appraisal in Practice

Many studies of project appraisal practice have been undertaken. Most have been orientated towards the practices of large organisations to which the following general observations apply:

1 The most frequently used technique is the payback period. This is often in conjunction with other techniques, but it may be used on its own for smaller projects.

2 When a discounted cash flow technique is used it is more likely to be the internal rate of return method rather than the net present value method.

3 Qualitative judgement is regarded as important.

4 The accounting rate of return is used despite potential ambiguities in definition.

5 The use of techniques is guided by standard procedures, usually in the form of a capital budgeting manual of practice.

In addition to these five observations relating to the techniques, three others are noteworthy and will be dealt with in detail in *Chapter 10*.

❑ Inflation adjustments are made in appraising projects using rates applicable to specific inputs although the use of a single general rate is also practised.

❑ Adjustments for taxation are made to take account of the tax benefits i.e. allowances on capital projects and the tax liabilities i.e. payments due on any savings (profits).

❑ A formal analysis of risk is a standard pre-decision control procedure in many organisations, most often in the form of testing the sensitivity of key inputs and underlying economic assumptions.

One important question which emerges from the observations from the studies of practice is – 'Why the IRR is far more popular than the theoretically preferred NPV technique'? This has been attributed to a number of reasons, such as the appeal of a percentage to managers who, apparently, would be far less comfortable with interpreting a NPV calculation. Using IRR calculations a ranking of projects can be obtained without the need for knowledge of the company's required rate of return although, as indicated in the last section, this ranking may be inferior to that provided by NPV calculations. Associated with there being no need for a predetermined cut-off rate is the political appeal of the IRR. One recognised feature of the appraisal process is the potential for playing the system by ensuring that projects which have acquired the personal commitment of management always meet or exceed the prescribed hurdle rate. If the hurdle is not formally communicated then perhaps this problem can be removed. Certainly our observations of practice have found some confirmation of this view in some organisations. In such cases, the IRR usually in conjunction with other techniques, is prescribed for use below corporate level. At corporate level, however, where the desired hurdle is known the NPV technique may play a more significant role.

LONG-TERM DECISION ANALYSIS 2

When you have finished studying this chapter you should be able to:

❏ Illustrate the important differences which can arise in evaluating projects when using net present value (NPV) and internal rate of return (IRR).

❏ Apply inflation and taxation adjustments to capital projects.

❏ Describe the three stages for managing risk and uncertainty in the evaluation of projects.

❏ Explain the impact that risk has on strategic decision making.

❏ Undertake sensitivity analysis on capital projects.

❏ Put together a business case for a project.

10.1   Introduction

The successful introduction of a new product will attract competing products. This competition may force a reduction in price to a level which renders further investment non-economic. Although first entrants to a market may establish competitive advantage through the experience curve or product protection by trade marks or patents, cash flow projections should recognise market developments and competitor reactions.

To make an assessment of competitor reactions existing managerial knowledge and judgement needs to be used in conjunction with expert systems specially designed to model cash flows in a dynamic environment. This will avoid an over–reliance on projections of sales and cost of sales which, although internally consistent, do not reflect the real world.

In summary, sound financial management of capital projects should ensure that:

❑   Individual requests are in harmony with the plan for corporate growth and development, and the risks of accepting 'no hope' capital projects should be minimised.

❑   An appropriate hierarchical structure exists for authorising capital expenditure, which should encourage all good projects, even those proposed at low levels of authority.

❑   The numbers used in appraisal calculations are complete and valid in light of the circumstances surrounding a project request.

❑   Any method used to provide a measure of the relative desirability of projects is valid.

❑   Actual expenditures are compared to planned capital outlays, and that there is an appropriate control system to prevent a waste of resources.

❑   A post completion audit of selected major projects should be conducted to identify both good practice and mistakes to feed forward into new projects.

❑   A balance is maintained between those projects acquired on economic grounds and those which are a matter of necessity.

❑   A balance is maintained between high risk/high return projects and low risk/low return projects in order to prevent suffering the consequences of being at either end of the scale.

With the developments in personal computers and pre-programmable calculators, no technical barrier should exist to the widespread use of discounting procedures for evaluating proposed capital projects. However, in spite of the extensive experience of many companies with the techniques, problems still arise with the use and interpretation of project appraisal techniques. These problems arise when:

1. Payback is required over time periods far too short for certain types of capital projects.

2. Inappropriately high discount rates are used.

3. New capital projects are compared with unrealistic alternatives.

4. Capital projects selected are biased towards incremental opportunities.

5. Evaluations ignore important capital project costs and benefits.

1. Payback is Required Over Time Periods Far Too Short for Certain Types of Capital Projects

Considerable judgement is required in appraising certain types of capital project, particularly those in new untested process technologies. Many companies have been known to impose very short payback periods, such as two or three years, on all types of capital projects.

Some types of capital project, particularly those involving process technology like Flexible Manufacturing Systems (FMS) or Computer-Integrated-Manufacturing (CIM) are difficult to justify when subjected to such payback criteria in the face of more traditional alternative projects. Given that the benefits from such projects will arise several years in the future, when major renovation or replacement of traditional automated machines would be required, discounted cash flow analysis is far more appropriate. However, there are problems associated with quantifying the costs and benefits of such projects which makes the practical use of discounted cash flow techniques very difficult.

2. Inappropriately High Discount Rates are Used

It is not uncommon to find companies using excessive discount rates for appraising capital projects. The use of an excessively high discount rate in appraising a long-lived capital project has as many drawbacks as using an arbitrarily short appraisal time. This is because discount rates compound geometrically every time period penalising cash flows received five or more years in the future.

3. New Capital Projects are Compared with Unrealistic Alternatives

We indicated earlier in *Chapter 5* that making a decision may require a comparison to be made against an alternative involving doing nothing. Where an evaluation is made with the status quo, it is quite incorrect to assume that present cash flows can be maintained.

When a new technology becomes available and requires a substantial investment of funds, it will probably also be available to others. This means that a likely alternative to adopting the technology will be vulnerable market share and gross margins, with the possible consequence of declining cash flows in the future.

4. Capital Projects Selected are Biased Towards Incremental Opportunities

The project approval process for many companies specifies different levels of authorisation for different levels of management. Such a procedure can create an incentive for managers to propose a sequence of small projects that fall just below the cut-off point for higher level approval.

A consequence of this approach is that the company can become less efficient because a division never receives the full benefit from a completely redesigned and re-equipped plant that can exploit the latest technology.

5. Evaluations Ignore Important Capital Project Costs and Benefits

It is not uncommon for capital project proposals to underestimate costs quite significantly. This is particularly the case for projects that embody revolutionary new technological features. Computer software and the training of staff may be significant costs associated with the project which can be easily overlooked.

While some costs are readily identified, but overlooked, others are more difficult to measure. Innovative technologies provide benefits in reduced stocks, improved quality and reduced floor space which can be estimated but other returns such as improved flexibility, faster response times to changing market conditions, reductions in lead times and opportunities to learn innovate and grow from new technology use will be much more difficult to quantify.

The inadequacy of the information provided by costing systems in relation to the complex characteristics of new processes is a major source of the problem. Very simply, procedures used within companies may not be updated to respond to such complexities in the required time-frame.

Shorter product life cycles and more flexible technologies means that plant is now being installed which may last for several product life cycles, and may also be used to produce several products simultaneously. The result is that the relationship between plant life and product life has changed, with the consequence that the basis for investment must also be changed, as must the costing systems to permit an allocation of capital and running costs over a range of products.

Thus, the key problem with the conventional application of project appraisal techniques is that they are unable to quantify the technological benefits of a new investment, many of which are seen as being unquantifiable and intangible. Such intangible benefits (apparently) almost invariably appear in a different department from that where the investment is made. Furthermore, because they were not forecast or quantified, when they do appear they are recorded as an unplanned variance which is not attributed to the project.

There are no simple solutions to these problems. Current experience with such new technologies is limited such that the benefits of flexibility, reduced throughput time and lead time, organisational learning, and technology options are difficult to estimate. This does not mean however that they need necessarily be assigned a zero value when conducting a financial appraisal. As with all projects, there will be those factors difficult to quantify but which must be taken into consideration if a real view is to be formed. These are no exception.

10.2   Differences Between NPV and IRR

IRR seems to be preferred by non-financial managers. One reason for its appeal is that it is simple because the output from its calculation produces a percentage figure which can be compared against a company's hurdle rate. If the IRR is above the hurdle rate then the project is acceptable, if it is below the hurdle rate the project is not acceptable.

NPV and IRR will provide the same accept/reject for the majority of capital projects. However there are a number of situations where this is not the case and it will be seen that the use of IRR will produce an incorrect decision. These are because:

1. The output from an IRR calculation is a percentage return rather than the physical size of the earnings.

2. There are differences in the reinvestment assumptions.

3. The IRR can give more than one rate of return.

4. The IRR can incorrectly rank mutually exclusive projects.

1.   The Output From an IRR Calculation is a Percentage

This is best understood with reference to the following example:

	Project X	Project Y
Capital Outlay	£18,000	£60,000
Annual Savings (5 years)	£ 8,000	£20,000
IRR	34.2%	19.9%
NPV (at 10% Cost of Capital)	£12,328	£15,820

Project X has an IRR of 34.2% compared to only 19.9% for Project Y but this does not take into account the difference in the absolute size of the earnings. Project Y is clearly preferable in terms of the NPV it generates despite its lower IRR.

2. Differences in the reinvestment assumptions

In using the NPV and IRR approaches there is an assumption that future cash flows from projects are available for reinvestment. However there are major differences in the way in which these reinvestment assumptions are made.

NPV assumes that annual cash flows are reinvested at the company's cost of capital. On the other hand, IRR assumes that annual cash flows are reinvested at the percentage IRR obtained from each project.

For Project X, NPV assumes that the £8,000 annual cash flow is reinvested at the cost of capital of 10%. IRR assumes that it is reinvested at 34.2%.

The reality is that the company has determined that the return it expects from reinvestment is its stated cost of capital. IRR requires that the reinvestment is often much higher and as such is not theoretically correct.

3. IRR can Produce More Than One Rate of Return

In capital projects where the cash flows are irregular, i.e. not consistently positive, it is possible to find that the IRR method produces more than one rate of return.

		Project Z
Capital Outlay		£5,387
Cash Inflows	Year 1	£7,575
	Year 2	£5,353
	Year 3	–£8,000

Figure 10.1   Calculation of NPV's from 14 to 28%

Discount Factor %	14	16	18	20	22	24	26	28
Net Present Value £000's	−27	−8	0	6	14	6	0	−22

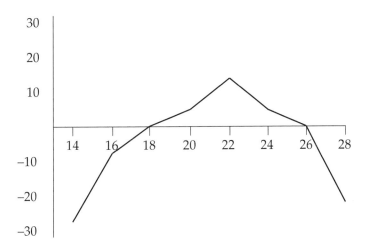

Note: We have used discount factors correct to three decimal places.

4.   IRR can Incorrectly Rank Mutually Exclusive Projects

Mutually exclusive projects exist where there are two or more projects, any of which is acceptable in technical terms, but only one is required to perform the task demanded. In this case the decision rule is that the most acceptable in economic terms should be selected first. The question is what decision rule do we use? Should we use internal rate of return (IRR), or net present value (NPV)? Does the IRR and NPV methods always produce the same results? To answer these questions we will use the following example.

A company is considering which of two mutually exclusive projects it should undertake. The company anticipates a cost of capital of 10% and the net cash inflows for the projects are as follows:

	Project X £	Project Y £
Capital Outlay	120,000	120,000
Net Cash Inflows:		
Year 1	21,000	130,000
Year 2	48,000	6,000
Year 3	54,000	6,000
Year 4	45,000	2,000
Year 5	12,000	2,000
NPV at 10%	+17,478	+10,240

1. Draw a graph to show the relationship between the net present value and the discount rate for the two projects. You should use discount rates at 10, 14, 18 and 22%.

2. Use the graph to estimate the internal rate of return for each project. State with reasons the project you would recommend. Would your advice change if the company's cost of capital was 15%?

The first stage is to calculate the net present value for each project. These are shown in *Table 10.2*.

Table 10.2   Net Present Value for Project X and Y

	Discount Rate %	Project X NPV £	Project Y NPV £	Incremental NPV (X–Y)
(a)	10	+17,478	+10,240	+7,238
(b)	14	+4,647	+4,896	–249
(c)	18	–6,399	–22	–6,377
(d)	22	–16,035	–4,420	–11,615

In the final column of *Table 10.2* we show the incremental net present values which are simply the net present value for Project X less the net present value for Project Y. We will return to the incremental approach in a later section.

Figure 10.2 Comparison of Mutually Exclusive Projects

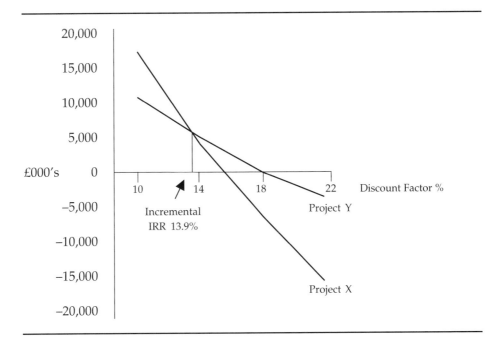

The second part of our example asks for an estimate of the IRR for each project. From the graph, we can see that the line for Project X cuts the horizontal axis at 15.5% approximately while for Project Y the IRR is 18% approximately. We have also shown the incremental IRR (this shows the point where there is no preference for Project X or Project Y).

The decision rule is that we should choose the project with the highest net present value provided that the company's cost of capital is less than the incremental IRR. In this case if the cost of capital is less than the incremental IRR i.e. between 0 to 13.9% then we would choose Project X, if the cost of capital was greater than 13.9% but less than 18% we would choose Project Y provided that it produced a positive net present value.

A summary of the results produces the following:

	Project X	Project Y	Incremental
NPV at 10%	+17,478	+10,240	
IRR	15.5%	18.0%	13.9%

10.3 Effect of Inflation

In our discussion of discounting, we assumed that the discounting process simply reflects the opportunity cost of money. Perhaps the easiest way to understand this opportunity cost is that in a world with no change in prices, individuals would still have preference for cash now versus cash later. This is understood by considering whether if you sought to borrow money from a bank in a world with zero inflation it would still require you to pay interest. The answer is undoubtedly, yes! What happens in an inflationary environment is that the rate of interest is increased to compensate for the loss of the purchasing power of money. For example, Brazil has had an inflation rate in excess of 1,000% per annum for a three year period. In such an environment, investors require returns far in excess of 1,000% to compensate for the loss of purchasing power, as well as to reflect the opportunity cost of money. This has implications for undertaking an investment appraisal.

If the rate at which a project is discounted incorporates expectations about inflation, then similar expectations need to be incorporated in the cash flows.

If we refer back to examples in previous sections, you will see that we have made no allowance for inflation in the cash flows. This is a problem if inflation is seen to be present in the cost of capital. If not, then there is no problem because the rule in dealing with inflation is:

1. If cash flows and the cost of capital are in real terms, such that no inflation expectations have been built into either, then the real cash flows can be discounted to reflect the real cost of capital.

2. If inflation expectations are present in either the cash flows or the cost of capital, then an adjustment must be made to ensure that the two are matched. In other words, inflated cash flows should be discounted by a cost of capital which includes inflationary expectations.

An adjustment can be made for inflation in the discount rate by rearranging the formula as in the following example:

$$(1+m) = (1+i) \ (1+r) \ .$$

where

m = the money or nominal rate

i = the expected rate of inflation, and

r = the real rate

Using this formula, we can adjust the cost of capital expressed in real terms to one that incorporates inflation and vice versa. For example, if the cost of capital in real terms (r) is 10% and the expected rate of inflation is 10%, then the money rate is 21%, i.e.

$(1+m) = (1.10) (1.10) = 1.21$, and

$m = 1.21 - 1 = 0.21$, or 21%

Or, if we know the money rate, quoted by a financial institution like a bank is 21%, and the expected rate of inflation is 10% then we can find the real rate of 10% by rearranging the formula, i.e. $(1 + r) = (1 + m) \div (1 + i)$. This type of adjustment we will demonstrate shortly.

Alternatively, as we will illustrate, if the cost of capital available incorporates the expected rate of inflation then this can be left and adjustments can be made to the cash flows. The advantage of this approach is that inflation does not necessarily impact on all sectors of the economy evenly and it may, therefore, be necessary to take into account the differential effects of inflation. For example we know that on occasion retail prices and wage rates have moved at differential rates.

An Example

Consider the following example where there is a capital outlay of £90,000 which will result in annual savings of £30,000 for five years and a cost of capital of 10%.

We will now show the effect of inflation on a capital project on which no adjustments have been made for inflation (i.e. *Table 10.3*). In what follows we will illustrate:

❑ adjustments are made to the cash flows and discount rate to allow for inflation at 6%.

❑ different inflation factors are applied to revenues, costs and the discount rate.

Table 10.3 Net Present Value of Capital Project with no Inflation

	£
Present Value of Cash Inflows (£30,000 x 3.791)	113,730
less Capital Outlay	90,000
Net Present Value (NPV)	23,730

1.   Adjustments to Cash Flows and Discount Rate.

First, we must adjust the cash flows to increase them by 6% per annum, compound.

Table 10.4   *Adjustment of Cash Flow/Savings*

Year	£	Factor	Adjusted Cash Flows £
1	30,000	1.06	31,800
2	31,800	1.06	33,708
3	33,708	1.06	35,730
4	35,730	1.06	37,874
5	37,874	1.06	40,146

Next we adjust the discount rate to include 6% inflation, as follows:

$$(1 + rate) \quad x \quad (1 + inflation)$$

$$1.10 \ x \ 1.06 \quad = \quad 1.166\%$$

Therefore the new discount rate is 16.6%. To obtain discount factors at 16.6% you could take a point between 16% and 17%. However, it is possible to obtain discount factors with the aid of a calculator. In simple terms, we need to divide 1 by 1.166 which will give 0.858 for year 1. We then carry out successive divisions by 1.166 until we have the required number of factors. Test you calculator to find out how the constant works. For example, on many calculators you can enter say 1.166 then press divide divide (yes twice), then equals equals; this should give 0.858 rounded to three decimal places. For the remaining factors keep pressing the equals button. The long method is now shown in *Table 10.5*:

Table 10.5   *Calculation of Discount Factors at 16.6%*

1	1 ÷ 1.166	=	0.85763	0.858
2.	0.85763 ÷ 1.166	=	0.73553	0.736
3.	0.73553 ÷ 1.166	=	0.63081	0.631
4.	0.63081 ÷ 1.166	=	0.54100	0.541
5.	0.54100 ÷ 1.166	=	0.46400	0.464

Table 10.6   Net Present Value – With Inflation

Year	A Cash Flow	B DCF Factor 16.6%	Present Value
	£		£
1	31,800	0.858	27,284
2	33,708	0.736	24,809
3	35,730	0.631	22,546
4	37,874	0.541	20,490
5	40,146	0.464	18,628
Present Value of Net Cash Inflows			113,757
less Capital Outlay			90,000
Net Present Value (NPV)			£23,757

You will notice that the net present value is the same in *Table 10.3 and 10.6*. (the slight difference is due to rounding). This result shows that if inflation is ignored, or that inflation is applied equally to the cash flows and the discount factors the result is the same. In this case, *Table 10.6*, we have increased the cash flows by 6% and increased the discount factors by 6% – therefore, we are discounting higher cash flows at higher discount rates.

2.   Differential Inflation

Differential inflation adjustments need to be made where the cash inflows and cash outflows inflate at different rates. Different inflation assumptions need to be incorporated in each of the components which make up the total cash flow and within the discount rate.

In this example we will assume that the discount rate includes expected inflation of 6% per annum, while the components making up the annual cash flows are affected as follows:

Cash Inflows   £130,000   + 5% per annum

Cash Outflows   £100,000   + 7% per annum.

Table 10.7 Adjusting Revenues and Costs for Inflation

Year	Cash Inflows 1.05 £	Cash Outflows 1.07 £	Net Cash Inflows £
0	130,000	100,000	n/a
1	136,500	107,000	29,500
2	143,325	114,490	28,835
3	150,491	122,504	27,987
4	158,016	131,079	26,937
5	165,917	140,255	25,662

In *Table 10.7*, we have adjusted the revenues by 5% per annum and the costs by 7% per annum. The third column shows the net cash flows which now show a decline over the lifetime of the project.

Table 10.8 Net Present Value – With Differential Inflation

Year	A Cash flow £	B DCF factor 16.6%	C Present value £
1	29,500	0.858	25,311
2	28,835	0.736	21,223
3	27,987	0.631	17,660
4	26,937	0.541	14,573
5	25,662	0.464	11,907
Present Value of Net Cash Inflows			90,674
less Capital Outlay			90,000
Net Present Value (NPV)			£674

In *Table 10.6*, with a single inflation rate applied to the individual cash flows and the discount rate, the net present value was +£23,757. This meant that the project was viable and could be considered for selection.

However, in *Table 10.8*, with differential inflation, the net present value is now £674. This shows the effect of a small change in the inflation assumptions; in this case, we reduced the revenue inflation from 6% to 5% while we increased the cost inflation from 6% to 7%.

It is possible to show that the arithmetic effect of applying the same inflation rate to the individual cash flows and to the discount rate produces the same net present value. It is tempting to conclude that it is possible to ignore inflation in the cash flows and the discount rate. The application of different inflation assumptions to individual components of the cash flows and to the discount rate, however, can have a significant effect on the accept/reject of a project. You will also find that the issue becomes even more complex when both taxation and inflation have to be taken into consideration.

10.4   The Treatment of Taxation

Taxation will have an impact on both cash and profit streams used in project appraisal. Although taxation is beyond the scope of this book the general principle to follow in project appraisal is similar to that of inflation discussed earlier in this chapter. This means that in addition to cash flows being discounted using an interest rate allowing for inflation, the discount rate must also allow for taxation.

In reality the detail of taxation as applied to project appraisal is beyond the concern of most non-financial managers. Provided you have understood the principle of comparing 'like' cash flows with a 'like' discount rate discussed with regard to inflation, that is sufficient. It is then time to involve a taxation specialist!

1.   The Effect of Taxation on Cash Flows

In this section it is assumed that the capital projects that are being appraised relate to companies which operate in a profit making environment, and that these companies purchase capital assets which qualify for capital allowances and are subject to the payment of corporation tax.

There are three areas for consideration when applying tax adjustments to capital project cash flows. These are:

❏   The timing of tax receipts/payments. *

❏   Tax payable on project savings.

❏   Capital allowance.

---

*   Please note, the timing of tax receipts and payments will reflect the tax laws of a specific country. For example, in the UK companies whose profits exceed £1.5 million will have to pay their corporation tax, quarterly, in advance.

The Timing of Tax Receipts/Payments

When appraising capital projects, companies assume that:

a.   tax will be paid in the year following the one in which taxable profits (i.e. project savings/revenues) are made.

b.   tax will be recovered in the year following the one in which tax allowance are available.

Tax Payable on Project Savings

It is often not appreciated that any financial benefits (i.e. savings) resulting from a capital project will have tax consequences. Other things equal, greater savings will produce higher profits, not all of which will be of benefit to the project initiator – the tax authorities will demand their share less, of course, any capital allowances (discussed in the next section).

Capital Allowances

In certain circumstances the expenditure incurred on the capital outlay for a project can be deducted from the profit generated by a company in the form of a capital allowance.

These capital allowances reduce future tax payments according to the amount of allowance available, the tax rate in operation and the economic life of each project.

Capital allowances can be likened to a personal tax allowance in so far as they reduce the amount of earnings subject to assessment for tax. A company can normally   reduce its taxable profits by the amount of capital allowances available.

2.   An Example *

If we take the same example we used for inflation where there is a capital outlay of £90,000 which will result in annual savings of £30,000 for five years. We will now assume:

1.   A cost of capital of 10%.

2.   Capital allowances, calculated on a 25% reducing balance, apply.

3.   Corporation tax at the rate of 35%

4.   A one year delay in the effect of taxation on receipts and payments

5.   Sufficient profits available to offset capital allowances.

---

*   This example is provided to show how tax can be incorporated into cash flows and assumes companies in the UK with annual profits less than £1.5 million.

Table 10.9 Calculation of After Tax Capital Allowances

Year	A Reducing Balance	B Capital Allowance (at 25%)	C Tax Saved Using Capital Allowance
	£	£	£
1	90,000	22,500	7,875
2	67,500	16,875	5,906
3	50,625	12,656	4,430
4	37,969	9,492	3,322
5	28,477	7,119	2,492
6	21,358	21,358	7,475

The £90,000 shown in year 1 is the original capital outlay. The availability of the 25% capital allowance means that we are allowed 25% of this amount that can be offset against taxable profits, hence the £22,500 in column B. However, the net tax effect is 35% of the £22,500 which equals £7,875. In year 2, the reduced balance (i.e. from £90,000) is £67,500 (£90,000 – £22,500), and the process continues. In year 6, the reduced balance is £21,358. We have assumed that the project ends in year 5, therefore the whole of the remaining balance is taken and offset against our taxable profits.

The tax payable on the annual savings is simply 35% of £30,000 which equals £10,500. For project appraisal we assume that tax will be payable one year later, i.e. from year 2 through to year 6.

A full appraisal incorporating tax is given in *Table 10.10.*

Table 10.10 Project Appraisal Incorporating Taxation

Year	A Tax saved using capital allowances £	B Savings £	C Tax on savings at 35% £	D Cash flow (A+B+C) £	E DCF 10 % factor	F Net present value £
1	7,875	30,000		37,875	0.909	34,428
2	5,906	30,000	−10,500	25,406	0.826	20,985
3	4,430	30,000	−10,500	23,930	0.751	17,971
4	3,322	30,000	−10,500	22,822	0.683	15,587
5	2,492	30,000	−10,500	21,992	0.621	13,657
6	7,475		−10,500	−3,025	0.564	−1,706

Present Value of Net Cash Inflows	100,922
less Capital Outlay	90,000
Net Present Value (NPV)	£10,922

The tax saved by claiming capital allowances, column A, is shown above in *Table 10.10.* The savings for the project are shown in years 1 through to 5, whilst the tax due on the savings is shown in column C. This is delayed one year with the final tax being due in year 6. The cash flow in column D is the sum of columns A plus B plus C.

The individual cash flows can then be adjusted by the company's cost of capital to find their present value. Finally, these are aggregated and the capital outlay is deducted to give the net present value of £10,922. Compare this with the result of the project without any adjustment for taxation, *Table 10.3* shows a net present value of £23,757. In *Table 10.10* it can be seen in Column D that the cash flows are greater in year 1 by decline steadily over the life of the project, compared to the without tax cash flows which were £30,000 per year.

10.5   Managing Risk and Uncertainty

In everyday terms we often think of risk as the 'What can go wrong with something we are committed to doing?' Such a view just looks at the downside aspect of risk. Risk can also be viewed as an upside opportunity which needs to be managed e.g. developing new products and services to push forward the frontiers of customers experiences and so get ahead of the competition. So, risk arises as much from the likelihood that something good won't happen as it does from the threat that something bad will happen.

Typically risk and uncertainty are viewed synonymously and the words are often used inter-changeably. However, there is a useful distinction, when we take a risk we are betting on an outcome that will result from the a decision we have made, in that for the risk we take there exists some basis upon which to estimate outcomes whilst for uncertainty there is very little basis. So, the distinction is one of the level of information and/or knowledge we have to estimate possible outcomes and our degree of commitment to those outcomes.

There are three stages to any risk management process:

1.   Risk identification.

2.   Risk assessment.

3.   Risk management actions.

1.   Risk Identification

Critical to any project evaluation is the identification of the risks that will affect it. In identifying risks it is useful to take a number of different perspectives:

❑   internal versus external risks e.g. risk from lack of skilled people versus competitor risk.

❑   risks as threats and as opportunities e.g. risk of explosion and risk of developing new competitive advantages.

❑   soft versus hard risks e.g. risk from cultural change versus interest rate risk.

In the identification of risk it can be useful to use a checklist such as the one shown in *Figure 10.3*. However, one must bear in mind that risks are by their very nature a function of the particular situation being looked at.

Figure 10.3   Risk Identification Checklist

Environmental Risks

Product risk, market risk, industry risk, competitor risk, technological risk, regulatory risk, legal risk, political risk, social risk, financial market risk etc.

Operational Risks

Supplier risk, input price risk, capacity risk, health and safety risks etc.

Financial Risks

Interest rate risk, foreign currency risk, liquidity risk, credit risk etc.

People Risks

Risks arising from; employee and management fraud, leadership and management capability, employee competence and skills, authority limits etc.

Technology Risk

Design risk, completion risk, infrastructure risk, engineering risk etc.

Organisational Risk

Risks arising from culture, structure, processes etc.

---

2.   Risk Assessment

This stage may usefully be thought of as comprising two parts:

a.   First, tracing project risks through to the project cash flows; and,

b.   Second, risk prioritisation by assessing the significance of each risk using the likelihood versus impact matrix.

a.   Tracing Project Risks

By using a typical Profit and Loss account, one can trace each risk identified for a project to the appropriate cash flow line of the project and hence assess the impact of each risk. This is show in *Table 10.11.*

Table 10.11 Examples of Risk Impacting on Cash Flows

Calculation of Cash Flows for a Project	Examples of Risks Impacting Cash Flow Line Items
Revenue	Competitor, Foreign currency and Regulatory risks
less: Cost of Sales	Operating, Supply and management risks
Gross Margin	
less Other Operating Costs	Operating and Environmental risks
Profit Before Interest and Tax (PBIT)	
less Interest	Financing and Project Completion risks
Profit Before Tax (PBT)	
less Cash Tax	Political risks
Profit after tax (PAT)	
add back: Depreciation	
add back: Interest	Political and Project Completion risks
Operating Cash Flow After Tax	
less Capital Investment	Design and Regulatory risks
less Working Capital Investment	Supply risks
Free cash flow to the Firm (FCFF)	
less Interest After Tax	
less Debt Repaid/Raised	Financing and Project Completion risks
Free Cash Flow to Equity (FCFE)	

Note 1: See *Chapter 12* for an explanation of calculation of FCFF and FCFE.

b. Risk Prioritisation

Prioritisation of each project risk into one of four categories using the matrix, shown in *Figure 10.3*, to assess the significance of the risk in terms of its likelihod of occurrence and the severity of its impact should it occur. In this way the matrix enables a management team to focus on the vital few risks that must be managed.

Figure 10.3   Project Risk Categories

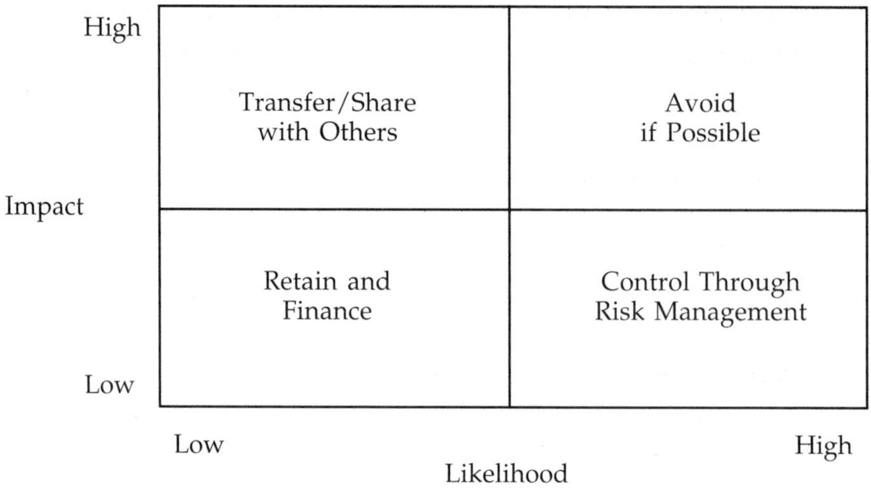

	Low ← Likelihood → High	
High Impact	Transfer/Share with Others	Avoid if Possible
Low	Retain and Finance	Control Through Risk Management

3.   Risk Management Actions

Each quadrant in the above matrix has an associated implication in terms of the management actions that may be taken to manage the risk.   With each management action there are a number of key issues to be addressed:

❏   Retain and Finance: Retain the risks and finance them as and when they arise using the firms own internal resources. Key issue: How much should be set aside as a contingency for these risks?

❏   Control: Control risks through organisation wide risk management processes. Key issues: Who will be responsible and accountable for risk management within the organisation and how will the risk management process be implemented?

❏   Transfer and/or share: Transfer and or share the risks with other parties who are willing to take on the risks for a price. Issue: Need to identify who will take all or part of the risk and at what cost?

❏   Avoid: Avoid the risk in its entirety. Issue: Is it possible to completely avoid the risk?

A common rule of thumb in risk management practice is that the person, organisation or group most able to handle and manage a risk is the one who should bear it.

4. Approaches for the Treatment of Risk in the Appraisal Process

In general we have two main approaches open to us for the treatment of risk within the project appraisal process.

❑ First, is to test the robustness of the analysis and evaluation by changing the assumptions and examining the effects of these changes on the conclusions. Techniques for doing this include sensitivity analysis, scenario analysis and simulation analysis each of which is summarised below.

- **Sensitivity Analysis**: Examines the sensitivity of the decision rule e.g. NPV, IRR etc. to changes, one at a time, in the assumptions of the key variables underlying the project.

- **Scenario Analysis**: Specific scenarios are developed for the future of the project and the viability of the project is examined under each scenario. These scenarios tend to be based on macroeconomic and industry factors.

- **Simulation Analysis**: Applies statistical sampling in an attempt to use the information in the entire distribution of the variables rather than just the expected value, to arrive at a decision.

❑ Second, is to factor the risks into the discount rate or the expected cash flows and see the impact on the performance measures such as NPV and IRR used to evaluate the project.

As regards the second approach we need to separate the total risks of a project into two parts, namely the risks specific to the project itself and the macroeconomic risks affecting the project. Specific risks are best dealt with through the cash flows of the project which are adjusted to take account of the impact of such risks whilst macroeconomic risks which affect all projects are best dealt with by adjusting the discount rate. *Figure 10.4* summarises this distinction and the treatment of risks within the appraisal process.

Figure 10.4   Distinction and Treatment of Risks within the Appraisal Process

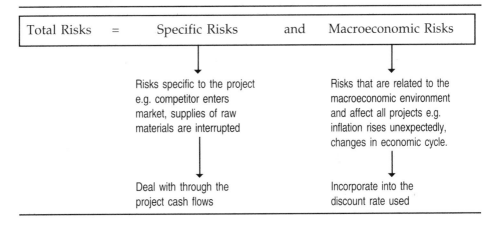

| Total Risks | = | Specific Risks | and | Macroeconomic Risks |

Risks specific to the project e.g. competitor enters market, supplies of raw materials are interrupted

Risks that are related to the macroeconomic environment and affect all projects e.g. inflation rises unexpectedly, changes in economic cycle.

Deal with through the project cash flows

Incorporate into the discount rate used

5. Risk and Strategic Decision Making

One aspect that is often missed from any risk assessment exercise is that of the decision maker themselves and the impact they have in terms of their role as the decision maker. *Figure 10.5* shows the pivotal role played by the decision maker between external and the internal environment of a firm for which a project decision is about to be made.

Figure 10.5   *External and Internal Environment of a Firm*

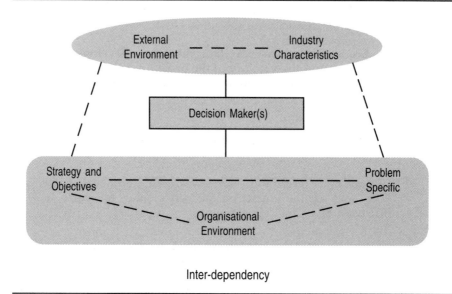

Inter-dependency

The areas of risk not covered so far relate to:

Problem Specific Risks.

These arise from the organisations ability or otherwise to formulate and resolve a specific strategic problem or issue. For example the following issues may prove difficult and expose the organisation to risk:

❏ Identification of the problem and its consequential effects.

❏ Structuring the problem, understanding the key variables and their interrelationship.

❏· Identifying alternative solutions to the problem and their respective implications.

❏ Complexity of the decision task.

Risks Arising From the Decision Maker

These risks relate to:

❏ Experience of previous problems and projects and their solutions.

❏ Degree of aversion to taking risk.

❏ Bias in decision making resulting from level of knowledge, political allegiance, incentives, beliefs and values.

10.6   Sensitivity Analysis

One important management tool available for questioning both potential benefits and risks associated with a project is sensitivity analysis. In essence, the assumptions surrounding a project can be input to computer software or a programmable calculator to produce a base case net present value and internal rate of return, from which changes in assumption can easily be made to gauge the effect upon them. The mechanics of such an application are now considered within the context of a simple example. The data to be used in our example concerns a project with the following features:

❏ Capital Outlay   £5,000,000

❏ Life   10 years

❏ Sales Volume   80,000 units

❏ Selling Price   £85 per unit

❏ Labour Costs   £22 per unit

❏ Material Costs   £40 per unit

❏ Fixed Costs   £660,000 per annum

❏ Cost of Capital   12%

In practice the data would be far more detailed and important factors like taxation and inflation should be included if the resulting net present value is to be calculated at a company cost of capital. However, we have deliberately made the example as simple as possible to show the advantages of such an application.

Steps:

1. Determine the cash flow and calculate the net present value before making any adjustments to the input variables.

2. Adjust each of the input variables adversely by a fixed percentage, in this case we will use 10%.

3. Determine the alternative cash flows and calculate revised net present values.

4. Rank each of the input variables according to the sensitivity of the net present value.

1.   Determine the Cash Flow and Calculate Net Present Value (NPV)

a.   Determine the Cash Flow

(Sales volume x Contribution per unit) – specific fixed costs

=   (80,000 x £23.00) – £660,000

=   £1,180,000

Calculation of Contribution Per Unit:

	£
Selling price	85.00
– Labour cost	22.00
– Material cost	40.00
Contribution per unit	23.00

b.   Calculate the net present value

(Cash flow x Annuity factor) – Capital cost

=   (£1,180,000 x 5.630) – £5,000,000

=   £1,667,000

2.   Adjust the Input Variables Adversely by 10%

Table 10.12   Input Variables Varied Adversely by 10%

	Original Estimate	Factor	Varied Adversely by 10%
Capital Outlay	£5,000,000	x 1.10	£5,500,000
Life (years)	10	less 1	9
Sales Volume (units)	80,000	÷ 1.10	72,727
Selling Price	£85.00	÷ 1.10	£77.27
Labour Costs per unit	£22.00	x 1.10	£24.20
Material Costs per unit	£40.00	x 1.10	£44.00
Fixed Costs per annum	£660,000	x 1.10	£726,000
Cost of Capital	12%	x 1.10	13.2%

Calculation of the sales volume and selling price is as follows:

a.   Vary the sales volume adversely by 10%:

  80,000 units divided by (1 plus 0.10) = 72,727 units

b.   Vary the selling price adversely by 10%:

  £85.00 divided by (1 plus 0.10) = £77.27

Alternative calculation of sales volume and selling price:

For simplicity, it is possible to take 10% of the sales volume, i.e. 80,000 times 10% which equals 8,000 units. The net figure would be 72,000 units. Similarly, the selling price would be reduced by £8.50 to give a net of £76.50. It is important to realise that this method is not technically correct and will not produce a consistent movement in each of the variables.

3.   Determine Alternative Cash Flows and Calculate Revised NPVs

Table 10.13 Determine the Alternative Cash FLows

	A Sales Volume Units	B Contri- bution P.Unit £	C Fixed Costs £	D Cash Flow (A*B–C) £
Capital Outlay	80,000	23.00	660,000	1,180,000
Life (years)	80,000	23.00	660,000	1,180,000
Sales Volume (units)	72,727	23.00	660,000	1,012,721
Selling Price	80,000	15.27	660,000	561,600
Labour Costs per unit	80,000	20.80	660,000	1,004,000
Material Costs per unit	80,000	19.00	660,000	860,000
Fixed Costs per annum	80,000	23.00	726,000	1,114,000

Calculation of contribution per unit:

	Selling Price £	Labour Cost £	Material Cost £
Selling price	77.27	85.00	85.00
– Labour cost	22.00	24.20	22.00
– Material cost	40.00	40.00	44.00
Contribution per unit	15.27	20.80	19.00

Notes for calculations in *Table 10.13*.

1. Column A. For each variable must determine the volume; these are all at 80,000 units except for the reduction in sales volume to 72,727 units.

2. Column B. For each variable must determine the contribution per unit. These are all at £23.00 per unit except for the adverse changes in selling price, labour costs and material costs; revised calculations are shown above i.e. £15.27, £20.80 and £19.00.

3. Column C. These are the fixed costs and are all at £660,000 per annum except for the increase in fixed costs line to £726,000.

4. Column D. Shows the revised cash flows for each of the elements within the project. The calculation is Column A times Column B minus Column C.

In Table 10.4 we calculate the revised net present values using annuity tables, (see pages 422 to 423).

Table 10.14 Calculate NPVs (Using Annuity Tables)

	A Cash Flow £	B Annuity Factor	C Present Value of Cash Flow (A x B) £	D Capital Outlay £	E Net Present Value (C – D) £
Capital Outlay	1,180,000	5.650	6,667,000	5,500,000	1,167,000
Life (years)	1,180,000	5.328	6,287,040	5,000,000	1,287,040
Sales Volume	1,012,721	5.650	5,721,874	5,000,000	721,874
Selling Price	561,600	5.650	3,173,040	5,000,000	–1,826,960
Labour Costs p.u.	1,004,000	5.650	5,672,600	5,000,000	672,600
Material Costs p.u.	860,000	5.650	4,859,000	5,000,000	–141,000
Fixed Costs p.a.	1,114,000	5.650	6,294,100	5,000,000	1,294,100
Cost of capital	1,180,000	5.382	6,351,940	5,000,000	1,351,940

Notes for calculations in *Table 10.14*.

1. Column A. We take the revised cash flows from Table 10.13, Column D.

2. Column B. For ease of calculation we are using annuity factors to arrive at the present value of the cash flows. For most of the elements we will use the annuity factor for a 10 year life at 12% i.e. 5.650. The second element, the life, we use the annuity factor for a 9 year life at 12% i.e. 5.328. The last element, the cost of capital, we use the annuity factor for a 10 year life at 13.2% i.e. 5.382. For this last annuity factor we used a standard spreadsheet program to determine the value of 5.382.

3. Column C. Column A (revised cash flow) times Column B (annuity factor).

4. Column D. This is the capital outlay. For most of the elements the capital outlay is £5,000,000. The only exception is the capital outlay element which is adversely adjusted by 10% to £5,500,000.

5. Column E. Column C (present value of cash flows) minus Column D (capital outlay).

4.   Rank Each of the Input Variables

The final stage in the sensitivity analysis is to rank each of the elements of the project in descending order based on the revised net present values. Here we take the output from Table 10.14, Column E starting with selling price with a negative net present value of –£1,826,960 through to fixed costs with a net present value of £1,294,100.

Table 10.15   *Input Variables in Decreasing Order of Sensitivity*

	NPV
	£
Selling Price	–1,826,960
Material Costs	–141,000
Labour Costs	672,600
Sales Volume	721,874
Capital Outlay	1,167,000
Life	1,287,000
Fixed Costs	1,294,100
Cost of Capital	1,351,940

The analysis highlights the variables which will have the greatest impact on the net present values of a project. By amending the original data by 10% negative, two sensitive variables to the project are found i.e. the selling price and the material costs. If the selling price were not £85.00 per unit but only achieved £77.27 per unit, then the project would generate a negative NPV of £1,826,960, while a 10% increase in material costs would generate a negative NPV of £141,000.

Given that the company's cost of capital is 12% then a £7.73 reduction in selling price could be a potential disaster. With knowledge of this potential problem area, an investigation could be undertaken by the marketing department to establish whether difficulties in achieving a selling price of £85.00 are likely. If so, then despite the initially favourable NPV, the project is not acceptable on economic grounds. This, of course, assumes there to be no sales volume/selling price relationship such that a reduction in price to £77.27 might well be associated with an increase in sales volume. This is one other area of investigation readily considered by using a computerised model.

In summary, such analysis permits project proposals to be evaluated and the analysis can be used to identify sensitive variables without having to input any additional data. In practice, the analysis would be extended much further than in the example so as to explore changes in a number of variables and any interrelationships between them.

10.7 Putting Together a Business Case for a Project

In seeking the approval of a project most organisations require a business case to be put together. The purpose of the business plan may be thought of with reference to a quote from one of *Rudyard Kiplings* verses:

'I keep six honest serving men (they taught me all I know) Their names are What and Why and When and How and Where and Who'

In other words the business plan should answer six questions posed by this verse;

❑ What is this project about?

❑ Why do it? i.e. rationale.

❑ When is it to be done? i.e. timings.

❑ How will it be done? i.e. implementation plan.

❑ Where in the organisation will it be done?

❑ Who will do it? i.e. who is responsible and accountable.

Table 10.16 Typical Structure for a Business Project

Summary	❏ Statement of the objectives that the project aims to achieve.
	❏ The rationale for why undertake the project and why now.
	❏ How it fits with the company's vision and mission.
	❏ A resume of the key risks & uncertainties impacting the project.
Definition and Scope of project	Description of the project from the perspective of:
	❏ Strategy: How it fits with the company's strategy, what the strategic rationale is in terms of the scope of the company's business activities.
	❏ Finance: Key headlines from the financial evaluation.
	❏ Operations: Key resources required to enable this project to be undertaken including people and their skills, critical business processes etc.
Alternative options	Discussion of the options open to management in terms of the timing of the investment, scaling it up or down, the flexibility that is built into the project to enable management to respond to changing circumstances.
Underpinning assumptions	List of critical internal and external assumptions that underpin the project, together with the interdependencies between them plus identification of the key risks and uncertainties and their potential financial impact.
Implementation plans	A high level implementation plan showing key milestone dates for:
	❏ commitment of resource;
	❏ critical decision points;
	❏ impact on other projects and the rest of the business;
	❏ possible contingency options.
Evaluation	Details of the financial evaluation techniques used plus their appropriateness together with a list of the relevant qualitative/ non-financial factors used to reach a decision.

CHAPTER ELEVEN

FINANCIAL MANAGEMENT

When you have finished studying this chapter you should be able to:

❑ Assess whether the size and composition of a company's asset structure is appropriate.

❑ Discuss methods to determine the size and composition of a company's future asset structure.

❑ Determine the volume of funds likely to be required to finance future asset structures.

❑ Assess the present and future capital structure.

❑ Understand the factors that shape a company's dividend policy.

❑ Describe the different methods of calculating the cost of capital.

❑ Understand the linkage between the company's Business plan and its Financial plan together with the associated key business decisions.

11.1   Introduction

Financial management requires a forward looking view to be undertaken of the business as a whole. This view typically has to take account of a good deal of future uncertainty and is reliant upon the discounted cash flow principles encountered in the last chapter, in addition to many other principles and techniques encountered in earlier chapters.

In this chapter we will provide an overview rather than a detailed insight of important areas of financial management, some of which were encountered in earlier chapters. For example, we considered return on equity and associated ratios instrumental in gauging the ability of the business to generate profit for future growth. We also had a brief encounter with one other important aspect of financial management in terms of the rate of return to be used in discounting cash flows for calculating the net present value from an investment opportunity.

Good financial management is vital to the success of the business. Just as production management is concerned with handling physical resources at its disposal to increase corporate profitability and value, so financial management is concerned with improving the use of financial resources for the same objective. Financial resources represent the funds available to the business for which financial management is required to plan and control both their supply to and their use within, the business.

In this chapter we will draw together the various components of financial management by considering the following key questions:

❏   Is the size and the composition of the present asset structure appropriate?

❏   What should be the size and composition of the future asset structure?

❏   What volume of funds is likely to be required to finance the future asset structure?

❏   What should be the composition of the capital structure both now and in the future?

❏   Is there any other action that should be taken to enhance the long-term growth in market value of the equity holders' investment?

11.2   Present Asset Structure

Concern with the present asset structure focuses upon one key question, *'Is the volume and composition of the assets currently employed justified by the value of sales activity being achieved?'* You will recognise this question from our discussion of the sales generation ratio in *Chapter 4*. We saw there that the sales generation ratio is calculated from:

$$\text{Sales Generation Ratio} \quad = \quad \frac{\text{Sales Revenue}}{\text{Total Assets}}$$

This ratio, which shows how many £ of sales are generated per £ of total assets, can be subdivided into a number of interrelated component ratios to identify the success or otherwise of particular areas of the business such as:

❏   Stock control, to ensure that stocks and work-in-progress are no higher than is necessary to service the volume of activity achieved.

❏   Credit control, to ensure that sales effort is channelled into areas of low credit risk and that outstanding debtors (accounts receivable) are collected and banked with the minimum of delay.

❏   The control of cash and near cash funds to prevent them from lying idle, and therefore not generating any return.

❏   The existing fixed asset base. Would it be worthwhile realising the value from certain assets and subcontracting outside?

In considering the present asset structure, aspects of short-term decision analysis discussed separately earlier in *Chapter 8* can be seen to be relevant. In fact, within financial management you will see a number of the principles and techniques discussed earlier being used in an integrated fashion. For example, ratio analysis covered in *Chapter 4* can be used to identify the relationship between certain assets and the sales value they generate, but the benefit of the assets can only be gauged by asking the type of searching questions raised in *Chapter 8* on short-term decision making. We now turn our attention to the measurement and management of working capital.

1.   Working Capital Measurement and Management

Working capital is the life blood of all businesses and has to be managed carefully to ensure that money and stocks are available when required. Poor working capital management is a sure way of threatening profitability and survival.

The main components of working capital for a manufacturing or trading organisation are stock (from suppliers), debtors (money due from customers), cash and creditors (money owed to suppliers). These are all linked by the cycle of events shown in *Figure 11.1*. Stock is acquired, very often on credit from creditors, and then sold as goods to debtors, who eventually pay cash used to pay creditors and so on. For a service business there may be no stock, in which case a service is provided to a client (now a debtor) who pays cash eventually which in turn is used to pay creditors for goods and/or services and so the cycle goes on.

Figure 11.1   Cash Conversion Cycle

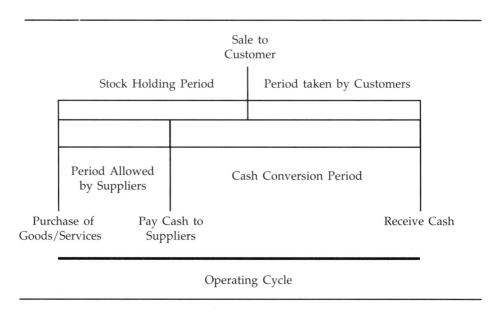

In *Figure 11.1* above there are two key time periods. The first is the **operating cycle,** which is the period of time between receiving/buying the goods from suppliers and receiving the cash from customers. This operating cycle reflects the normal day to day activities of a business.

The second is the **cash conversion period,** which is the time period between paying suppliers and receiving cash from customers. In other words the cash conversion period is the period of time that cash is tied up in the business.

It is important to control working capital. Too little or too much can be a severe disadvantage, so how can control be achieved? We will now consider the main issues involved in controlling three of the parts of a business' working capital – stock, debtors and cash. The management of creditors is largely a mirror image of debtor management.

a. Stock Control

The financial objective of stock control is to minimise the overall costs of holding stock while taking into account the various objectives of other functions within a company. For example, marketing might want to maintain a full range of merchandise, purchasing might want to concentrate on a reduced range but in greater volumes because they can obtain better prices and finance might want to minimise the amount of working capital tied up in stocks. An effective system of stock control seeks to optimise the needs of these various users.

Stock control is achieved through implementing the following system which involves:

❏ Setting stock levels;

❏ Monitoring movements against stock levels;

❏ Taking corrective action.

Calculating Stock Levels

A company should set maximum, minimum and reorder levels. Stock levels should take account of historic and forecast volumes, lead times, cost of holding and reorder size.

Monitor Movements Against Stock Levels and Corrective Action

Once levels have been calculated for all stock items it is important to monitor movements and take the necessary corrective action. For example, if following a receipt of goods the stock goes above the maximum level, any outstanding purchase orders should be cancelled. If it is forecast that the usage will reduce, then the company might consider a special offer or sale.

Similarly, following an issue of goods, if stock reaches the reorder level, this should automatically trigger the preparation of a purchase order, where it would be anticipated that the goods would be received before stocks reached the minimum level. Should an issue of goods cause the stock level to fall below minimum then outstanding purchase orders should be referred to the supplier to obtain a delivery date.

b. Credit Control

The main objective of credit control is to minimise bad debts. This requires that a balance is achieved between the risk of granting credit to a customer and the loss of profits through not trading with that customer.

It is not uncommon when discussing credit control with a group of managers for the first thoughts to be 'how quickly can we collect monies owed from customers'? What needs to be borne in mind is that this is a control system and will require the following:

❑ The establishment of a credit control policy

❑ The vetting of new customers

❑ The monitoring of the ageing of debts

❑ The taking of corrective action

Establishing a Credit Control Policy

A credit control policy sets the general terms by which a company will offer credit. This will include the period of credit, for example 'net 30 days', and the timings and actions which will take place should the credit period be extended by the customer. A good example of the actions taken is provided by the (UK) electricity, telephone, and gas companies. First there is a reminder, then usually two weeks later a final reminder, followed by a polite letter advising that your supply will be 'cut-off' if payment is not made within say, seven days. This is often followed up by a further letter advising that supply will be 'cut-off' from a specified date unless payment is received.

When a company establishes its credit period it is important to take into account the competitive environment. For example, if other companies in the same industry are granting 60 days credit, a company offering 30 days would tend to lose customers to its competitors.

Vetting New Customers

All new customers should be vetted to determine their creditworthiness and establish credit limits. This process takes many different forms but attempts to determine customers':

❑ *Ability to pay.* This should be relatively simple, requiring a review of a customers' financial position. This could be achieved through bank references, analysing the annual accounts, or by using a credit bureau.

❑ *Willingness to pay.* Assessing a company's willingness to pay by assessing their track record. For example, if individuals pay their household bills within the accepted time limits they would be deemed as showing a willingness to pay.

Establishing credit limits can take the form of making an allowance for an initial sum with regular reviews to increase the credit limit if required. Other systems involve complex models that take into account a number of variables or the use of a credit bureau.

Monitoring the Ageing of Debts

On the receipt of an order from an existing customer the credit department should check that:

❑ the new order would not make their balance outstanding exceed their credit limit; and,

❑ there are no outstanding debts on the account.

When the order has been fulfilled and an invoice sent to the customer there should be a continuous monitoring of the account. Regular reports should be produced to show the age of all outstanding amounts, for example between one month to two months, two months to three months, and over three months. An ageing report can take the following format:

Table 11.1   Age Classification of Debtors

Invoice	Amount £	1 to 2 Months	2 to 3 Months	Over 3 Months	Remarks
MR 201	30,000			30,000	Court action
MR 209	15,000			15,000	Receiver
MR 245	60,000		60,000		Letter sent
MR 246	25,000		25,000		Cheque promised
MR 247	100,000	100,000			
MR 260	40,000	40,000			
	270,000	140,000	85,000	45,000	

Corrective Action

It is important that corrective action is taken in accordance with the credit control policies of the company. If customers know that they can extend their credit periods without losing their rating then the marginally good 'payer' may move to being a marginally bad 'payer'. The forms of corrective action should include:

❏ A review of the credit limit of a customer.

❏ Reject orders due to poor creditworthiness. For example, when a customer attempts to extend the credit limit, or a potential customer fails the creditworthiness checks.

❏ Send out regular statements, final reminder and, if necessary, final offer.

❏ Start court proceedings. This will often mean a lengthy procedure of claim and counter claim taking at least six months. If successful with a court action, there is no guarantee that the debt will be paid. A small company will often have to rely on the courts to recover the debt.

How to Improve Collection

One of the simplest methods of reducing the overall credit is to ensure that customers are invoiced promptly. In many cases this can reduce the payment period by anything up to two weeks.

Offering cash discounts for earlier payment can result in a significant improvement of cash flow. For example, if a company's credit terms were net 30 days it might offer a cash discount of two percent for payment within 10 days.

Many small companies charge interest of up to 10% on overdue accounts in an effort to encourage prompt payment despite the competitive risk involved.

Some companies factor the collection from debtors to a debt collection agency. Depending upon the terms agreed, the agency will normally advance between 80 to 90 percent of the debts, the balance being paid less a percentage when they recover the debts. This is particularly useful to companies who cannot afford to set up and run their own credit control department.

c. Cash Control

The main objective of a system of cash control is to plan the expected operations of a company over a future period of time. Such a plan requires forecasts of future sales and cash expenditure covering purchases of materials, wages, equipment etc. Assumptions will also have to be made concerning the time delays from sales to receipts and from purchases to payments. The following example shows the three main components of a cash budget:

i.   Forecast of sales and cash receipts

ii. Forecast of cash expenditure

iii. Monthly net cash flow and cash balance

i.   Forecast of Sales and Cash Receipts

Sales forecast for the six month period July to December, together with a forecast of 75% being credit sales.

Credit periods are expected to be 80% collected after one month and the remaining 20% after two months.

Table 11.2   Components of a Cash Budget

i. Forecast Sales and Cash Receipts

	May	Jun	Jul	Aug	Sept	Oct	Nov	Dec
	£m	£m	£m	£m	£m	£m	£m	£m
Forecast Sales	40.0	44.0	68.0	80.0	64.0	32.0	24.0	44.0
Credit sales	*30.0*	*33.0*	*51.0*	*60.0*	*48.0*	*24.0*	*18.0*	*33.0*
Credit receipts								
1 month (80%)		*24.0*	*26.4*	*40.8*	*48.0*	*38.4*	*19.2*	*14.4*
2 months (20%)			*6.0*	*6.6*	*10.2*	*12.0*	*9.6*	*4.8*
Total credit receipts			*32.4*	*47.4*	*58.2*	*50.4*	*28.8*	*19.2*
Cash Sales	10.0	11.0	17.0	20.0	16.0	8.0	6.0	11.0
Total Cash Receipts			49.4	67.4	74.2	58.4	34.8	30.2

Note: The above calculations show the variation in forecast sales and the expected total cash receipts. For example, in October the forecast sales are £32 million with expected total cash receipts of £58.4 million. In practice, a company would not prepare a forecast without making adjustments for bad debts.

ii.   Forecast of Cash Expenditure

	Jun	Jul	Aug	Sept	Oct	Nov	Dec
	£m	£m	£m	£m	£m	£m	£m
Forecast Purchases	26.4	40.8	48.0	38.4	19.2	14.4	26.4
Cash Payments for Purchases		26.4	40.8	48.0	38.4	19.2	14.4
Wages paid		5.6	5.6	5.6	5.6	5.6	5.6
Overheads and Expenses Paid		9.0	9.0	9.0	9.0	9.0	9.0
Capital Expenditure		15.0	15.0	0	0	15.0	0
Total Cash Expenditure		56.0	70.4	62.6	53.0	48.8	29.0

iii. Monthly Net Cash Flow and Cash Balance

	Jul £m	Aug £m	Sept £m	Oct £m	Nov £m	Dec £m
Total Cash Receipts	49.4	67.4	74.2	58.4	34.8	30.2
Total Cash Expenditure	56.0	70.4	62.6	53.0	48.8	29.0
Net Cash Flow	−6.6	−3.0	11.6	5.4	−14.0	1.2
Opening Cash Balance	3.0	−3.6	−6.6	5.0	10.4	−3.6
Closing Cash Balance	−3.6	−6.6	5.0	10.4	−3.6	−2.4

2.   Investment in Working Capital

The ratio analysis used in *Chapter 4* allows us to obtain an estimate of the cash conversion period as follows:

Stock holding period	X
plus: Debtor days	X
less: Creditor days	-X
Cash Conversion period	X

The example below shows how this principle can be applied to calculate the investment required in working capital:

200X–1 figures

Stock inventory days	= 60 days
Trade Debtors days	= 30 days
Creditors days	= 30 days

200X Forecasts

Revenue	= £100m
Costs of Sales	= £60m

Calculation of Working Capital for 200X

Stock   =   £60m x 60 ÷ 365   =   £9.9m
Debtors   =   £100m x 30 ÷ 365   =   £8.2m
Creditors =   £60m x 30 ÷ 365   =   £4.9m

The amount of capital tied up in working capital is:

Stock	£9.9m
plus Debtors	£8.2m
less Creditors	£4.9m
Total Working Capital	£13.2m

What this means is that an investment in working capital of £13.2m is required in terms of cash, hence there will have to be a cash outflow from the business in the sum of £13.2m.

In terms of the operating cycle from purchase to production to selling the level of investment increases over the period of the cycle. See *Figure 11.2*.

Figure 11.2   Investment in Working Capital

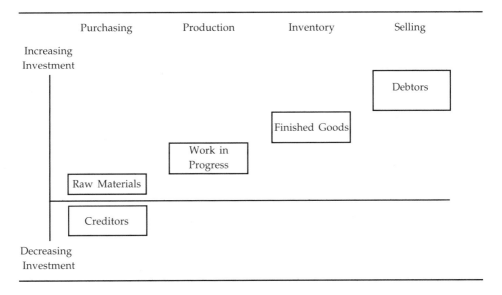

When carrying out these working capital ratio calculations the implicit assumption is that the relationships remain constant over time, i.e. stock turnover period, debtors days and creditors days remain constant. As a check it is recommended that one consider whether the future will resemble the past.

Factors Affecting Investment in Working Capital

There are a number of factors that affect these ratios and the underlying relationships:

❑   **Industry**: In terms of the external environment every industry has its own particular structure in terms of customers, suppliers, competitors, regulation and technology. Similarly each industry may be at a different stage of the life cycle and have correspondingly varying strategic intents. Thus working capital can vary enormously across industries.

❏ **Attitude to risk**. At the level of the economy one of the key influences on working capital is the health of the economy and hence the stage of the business cycle the economy is in. At the company level, the strategy of the business and the management's team aversion to risk plays an important role on working capital levels. In essence what we have here is a trade-off between risk and return, that is, the risk avoided by having working capital versus the costs associated with investment in working capital.

We should also not ignore that different working capital practices may exist between countries. This in part results from cultural and social factors and partly from the efficiency and effectiveness of the distribution infrastructure within the country.

The table below highlights the trade-offs that exist in managing working capital.

Table 11.3   Working Capital Trade-Offs

	Risk avoided	Costs incurred
Stock	Lack of stock and loss of customer who cannot wait.	Cash tied up in stock and cost of physically holding stock.
Debtors	Loss of customers who finds attractive opportunities elsewhere.	Cash tied up in debtors and more possible bad debts.
Creditors	Reliance on alternative forms of financing e.g. bank overdraft.	Damage to market reputation and being charged higher prices.

11.3   Future Asset Structure

Future assets required by a business are usually the result of business plans which project business activities into the future, taking account of product/market strategies and their impact on growth and diversification. Sound financial management requires that those future assets acquired as part of the plan are indeed worthwhile to the business. We illustrated in Chapter 8 how analytical techniques can be used to appraise projects, but there is the overriding requirement that particular attention should be paid to the quality of the input data. In our opinion too much attention can be and has been given to the techniques which can only be as good as the user's judgement in selecting appropriate input data.

The most theoretically preferred appraisal technique is that requiring the calculation of a project's net present value. In calculating a project's net present value, there appear to be two discernible issues concerning cash flow estimation which form the data input:

❏ How are initial estimates to be generated as accurately as possible?

❏ How can the importance of the various components within the estimates be judged?

With regard to the first of these, forecasting methods can be used reliant upon one or more of the following; subjective managerial judgement, sensitivity analysis, consensus of expert opinion, and computer simulations. The evidence available suggests that most large companies use two or more of these and, where larger capital expenditures are involved, more quantitatively orientated methods reliant upon probability theory may well be used.

Further, and related to the second issue, the initial estimates should be broken down as far as possible. For example, in discussing the basic principles we used information about only annual cash flows from a project, which alone would be unsatisfactory for larger and therefore riskier projects. In their case, such information should be broken down into key factors and as will be illustrated later in this chapter such a break down can be powerful when using a computer spreadsheet package to investigate the importance of each factor to the end result.

Just exactly what are the factors that should be used in cash flow estimation? It is difficult to be entirely prescriptive because some factors will vary from project to project, but a useful way of considering them is within the following three groupings:

1. **Financial Factors**

   ❏ Inflation

   ❏ Risk

   ❏ Working Capital Requirements

   ❏ Taxation

   ❏ Residual Value

2. **Marketing factors**

- ❏ Sales Forecast
- ❏ Product Life
- ❏ Discount Policy
- ❏ Promotional Costs
- ❏ Selling Costs
- ❏ Market Test Costs
- ❏ Competitive Advantages and Disadvantages
- ❏ Transportation Costs

3. **Operating factors**

- ❏ Operating Costs
- ❏ Material and Supply Costs
- ❏ Start-up costs
- ❏ Shutdown Costs
- ❏ Maintenance Costs
- ❏ Repair Costs
- ❏ Capacity Utilisation

The Effects of the Business Life-Cycle

It has been widely observed that businesses, and the industries that they form a part of, typically go through a life cycle comprising four stages; start-up, growth, maturity and decline. *Table 11.4* shows how various characteristics of a business, grouped under three categories, typically evolve over the life-cycle and will impact the future asset structure of the business

Table 11.4 Business Life Cycle

	Start-up	**Growth**	**Maturity**	**Decline**
Operational and Strategic Aspects				
Growth Prospects	Very High	High	Medium	Lower
Business Risks	Very High	High	Medium	Lower
Revenue	Often None or Small	Some and Growing rapidly	Significant and steady	Significant and declining
Profits	Often none or negative	None or small	Significant	Significant
Investment Needs	High	High	Replacement only	Minimal
Cash Flow	Negative	Neutral to slightly positive	Significantly positive	Positive to neutral
Financing Aspects				
Financing Type	Entirely equity	Largely equity	Debt and equity	Largely debt
Financial Risk	Lower	Low	Medium	High
Dividend payout				
Dividend Payout	Nil	Minimal	High	Medium

During the start-up phase, a business is typically making heavy investment expenditures to grow its product/service and its market. As a result the business may have little revenue, small or no profits and hence negative cash flow. Such a business is often funded by capital providers who are willing to take high risks for a period of time, taking a deferred return in the form of a capital gain at the end of their investment period. Given the fact that the start-up phase is cash negative it makes no sense to pay dividends or borrow debt which can't be serviced as all cash is needed to grow the business.

Moving into the growth phase, sales are growing rapidly and the business is still making significant marketing building expenditures and capital investments to grow the market. As a result, cash flow is likely to be at best small or neutral and the most appropriate source of funding is still equity. As the market is growing rapidly, investors will want the business to invest to take advantage of the growth opportunities that exist rather than return cash in the form of dividends. During this phase the venture capitalists will want to realise their capital gain, at the same time new investors need to be attracted to the business with an offering of a small dividend. However most of the return to new investors will be in the form of a capital gain in the value of their shares.

As market growth slows and expenditures and investments are curtailed, both profits and cash flow become significantly positive. At this stage business risks are receding and its makes sense to change the funding policy of the business by introducing debt capital which can now be serviced more easily – this change in capital structure introduces financial risk into the business. In addition, a change to the dividend policy is appropriate in that as growth slows there are unlikely to be the same level of growth opportunities for the business to invest in and hence surplus cash should be returned to the shareholders. The growth investors who want their return in the form of capital gain will have started to exit and be replaced by investors wanting steady returns in the form of annual dividends.

As one would expect the strong profits levels and positive cash flow will fade as the business moves into the decline phase. As the growth prospects for the business are minimal it makes sense to curtail significantly all investment and expenditure to that required to sustain the business for as long as is possible to squeeze out returns. The resultant cash flow freed up is best returned to shareholders in a high dividend payout. Given business risks are lower it makes sense to replace expensive equity funding with cheaper debt, which has the benefit of disciplining the business to focus on cash flow generation to service it.

In summary, what is important to notice is the changing picture of investment needs, capital structure and dividend policy over the life cycle as the profile of business and financial risks change over time. What also changes is the profile of investor, both equity and debt, and the nature of their risks and returns.

11.4 Future Requirement for Funds

One important area of financial management usually assumed not to be relevant in the appraisal of capital projects is how they are to be funded. Not only is it important to ensure that there is a supply of appropriate future projects which, when taken on balance, will generate adequate return for shareholders, there is also the need to predict the future profile of cash flows to avoid unexpected cash deficits. One of the most frequent causes of bankruptcy is the inability to forecast future requirements for funds and taking on large monolithic projects.

The form that a forecast of future requirements for funds might take depends largely on the purpose for which it is needed. If concern is with a general indication of average future requirements, then a forecast funds flow statement will be sufficient. However, the problem with this is that the forecast will only illustrate the final financial position. We have reproduced the cash flow forecast from (*Chapter 1, Table 1.1*) where an equilibrium cash position was achieved at the end of the 6 month forecast but significant cash deficits were incurred at the end of some individual months, to provide an example which highlights the importance of forecasting at frequent time intervals.

Table 11.5 Cash Flow Forecast (reproduced from Chapter 1, Table 1.1)

Part A							
Receipts £'000	July	Aug	Sept	Oct	Nov	Dec	Total
Sales	430	600	600	800	1,300	1,600	5,330
5 year Loan	250					250	
Share Capital		150				150	
Sub Total A	830	600	600	800	1,300	1,600	5,730
Part B							
Payments £'000 (unchanged)							
Sub Total B	1,430	1,180	780	780	780	780	5,730
Part C							
Balance A – B	–600	–580	–180	20	520	820	
Part D							
Balance c/f,							
Cumulative							
Cash Position		–600	–1,180	–1,360	–1,340	–820	0

For this reason, you will find it usual practice for cash flow forecasting as described in *Chapter 1* and *Chapter 7* to be used. In fact, you will find that many large organisations forecast their cash flows daily in recognition of their importance. The benefits of such a procedure in planning future cash flows are considerable and may be summarised as the following:

❏ Future requirements for funds can be planned both with respect to volume and timing. The advantages will be that time will be available to negotiate acceptable terms in advance with any prospective lender, and such a demonstration of effective management planning will assist by building confidence in the business.

❏ Future surpluses will be evident and early steps can be taken to ensure that any available are utilised adequately.

❏ The future shape of any funds required will be revealed. Such an early warning system will prevent following a course of action which is ultimately destined for disaster.

Of course, even with the best possible forecasting there will always be a chance that unexpected funds will be required not only because of poor conditions, but maybe because of good opportunities. Contingency planning is an important part of financial management and can be assisted by:

❑ Attempting to develop an awareness of the nature of the likely future contingencies and quantifying them with respect to the sensitivity of their impact upon financial resources.

❑ Developing a stock of resources that can be called upon in case of need, indicating in each case the speed by which they can be realised in cash.

❑ Formulating a strategy which can be implemented immediately to deal with emergencies that might arise.

Understanding Cash Flow

When we refer to cash flow in conversation it is imperative that we are clear as to what cash flows we are referring to as there are several possible definitions depending upon the purpose for which the cash flow is being calculated.

❑ In a day to day business context, an example of which we saw in *Table 11.5,* we looked at the cash flows associated with the receipts and payments associated with customers paying for goods and services and suppliers being paid for their goods and services.

❑ In a financial management context there are a number of specific cash flow terms which are relevant to different audiences as we will highlight shortly.

Starting with the latter point above, consider selected data in Table 11.6, for the 1998 Profit and Loss account and Balance Sheet for our example company *Meunier plc,* from which we will derive the various cash flows used in financial management. (For full details refer to *Appendix B*)

Table 11.6   Meunier plc – Selected Data

Profit and Loss Account		Balance Sheet		
All figures in £m	**1998**		**1997**	**1998**
Gross Margin	108.8	Fixed Assets	76.2	86.7
less Operating Expenses [1]	96.7	Current Assets		86.4 105.6
Operating profit (PBIT)	12.1	Current Liabilities		69.6 96.3
less Interest	3.4	Creditors: after one year		27.0 20.1
Profit Before Tax (PBT)	8.7	**Increase/Decrease**	**1998 less 1997**	
less Taxation	2.4	Fixed Assets (86.7 – 76.2)		10.5
Profit After Tax (PAT)	6.3	Current Assets (105.6 – 86.4)		19.2
less Dividends	5.5	Current Liabilities (96.3 – 69.6)		26.7
Retained Earnings	0.8	Creditors: after one year		
		(20.1 – 27.0)		(6.9)

[1] Includes depreciation of £5.9m

Operating Cash flow (OCF)

This refers to the cash flow generated by the underlying operations of the business, whether they be manufacturing a product and/or supplying a service. Such cash flows ignore any cash flows associated with the financing of the business in the form of interest payments made on debt capital and dividends payments made on the equity capital of the business.

Operating cash flow can be calculated on either a pre or post tax basis by taking the difference between receipts from customers and payments made to suppliers, employees and others providing services to the business, for example rent on premises, lease cost of cars etc. An expedient short cut is to take operating profit and add back the depreciation figure that was deducted in arriving at the operating figure. Note that interest is always excluded as we are looking at the operating performance of the business and do not want financing effects distorting the picture.

Operating cash flow = Operating profit (pre or post tax) plus Depreciation

For *Meunier plc* the pre tax operating cash flow is:

$$= \quad £12.1m + £5.9m = £18.0m$$

On a post tax basis operating cash flow is:

$$= \quad £12.1m - (£2.4+1.1m)^* + £5.9m = £14.5$$

* For ease of calculation taxation payable is taken as a proxy for the cash tax paid such that timing differences and the deductibility of interest on debt are ignored

Depreciation is not a cash flow item as it is an accounting adjustment designed to try and reflect the consumption of an asset with use in the business or the effluxion in its value over time.

Free Cash Flow to the Firm as a Whole (FCFF)

Free cash flow to the firm represents the cash flow that is freely available to the providers of capital to a business, both the debt-holders and equity-holders. The cash flows that debt-holders receive are in the form of interest and debt repaid/raised whilst the cash flows to equity-holders are in the form of dividends and equity brought back/raised. Typically it is calculated on an after tax basis. The calculation of free cash flow to firm is shown in *Table 11.7*.

Table 11.7 Meunier plc – Calculation of Free Cash Flows for 1998

	£m
Operating Cash Flow (OCF) after tax	14.5
less Investment in Fixed Assets [1]	–16.4
add (Investment)/Divestment in Working Capital [2]	7.5
Free Cash flow to Firm (FCFF)	5.6

[1]   Calculated as change in net book value of fixed assets plus depreciation (see Table 11.6), i.e. £86.7 – £76.2m + £5.9m = £16.4m.   The figure of £16.4m represents an increase in fixed assets therefore a reduction in cash flow.

[2]   For ease of calculation calculated as current assets less current liabilities (see Table 11.6), i.e. (£105.6 – £86.4m) – (£96.3m – £69.6m) = £7.5m.   The figure of £7.5m comprises of an increase of £19.2m in current assets and an increase of £26.7m in current liabilities.   This represents an overall increase in cash flow to the firm i.e. an additional £7.5m from current liabilities.

If FCFF shows a surplus, the question arises of what to do with the surplus? Invest in the future of the business or repay the capital providers of the firm. In the case of a deficit of FCFF the question arises as to how to finance the deficit: from debt or equity holders? This topic is considered in a little more detail in *Section 11.5* on Capital Structure.

Free Cash Flow to Equity holders (FCFE)

Free cash flow to equity holders represents the cash flow that is attributable to equity holders which may take the form of dividend payments, equity bought back or equity raised. FCFE is for the most part calculated on a post tax basis by taking the FCFF and removing all the cash flows associated with the debt holders i.e. after tax interest costs and any debt repaid or raised. The calculation of free cash flow to equity is shown in *Table 11.8.*

Table 11.8   Meunier plc – Calculation of Free Cash Flow to Equity for 1998

	£m
Free Cash Flow to Firm (after tax basis)	5.6
less After Tax Interest Costs at 33% [1]	
Marginal Tax Rate i.e. £3.4m x 67%	2.3
less Debt Repaid/(Debt Raised) [2]	6.9
Free Cash Flow to Equity	–3.6

1   Interest payable is £3.4m (see *Table 11.6*). Assume taxation at 33%. Therefore the after tax interest costs = £3.4m x 67% = £2.3m.

2   For ease of calculation, calculated from creditors: amounts falling due after one year which are assumed to consist entirely of debt.

If the FCFE is positive the surplus may be used in one of two ways, first, to pay cash to equity holders either in the form of dividends or by buying back their shares or second, retaining the surplus within the business for future reinvestment. This topic is considered in a little more detail in *Section 11.6* on Dividend policy. If FCFE is negative the question arises as to whether the dividend is cut to finance such a deficit.

The Importance of Time Horizons

The focus on Planning, Cash flow and Working Capital really arises from the requirement to look at an extended time horizon when undertaking any sort of cash flow planning.

When examining an extended time horizon it may usefully be split up into a number of parts as shown in *Figure 11.3* below.

Figure 11.3   Extended Time Horizon

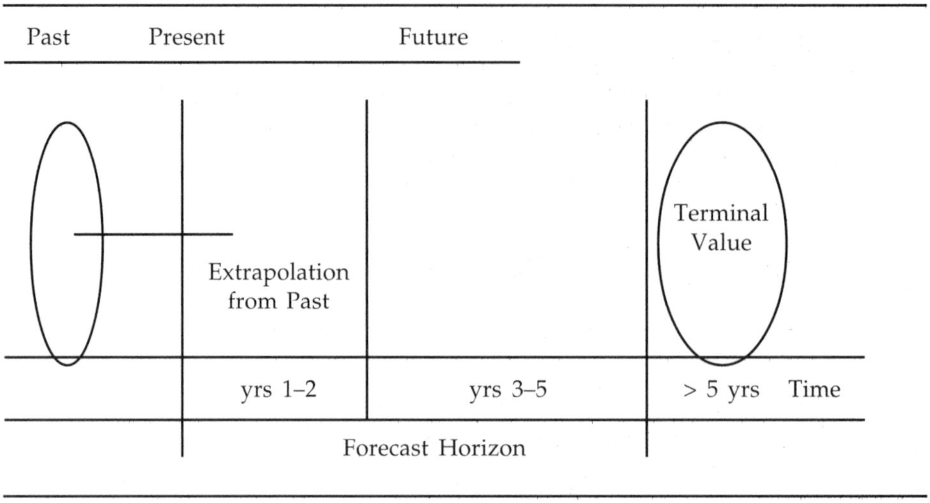

1. Years 1–2

Past historical information is often used as a guide to forecasting for years 1 and 2 provided one assumes that the past is a good guide to the future. In general most managers are comfortable with this type of forecasting for the first two years. If things are expected to change from the past they are typically able to make the appropriate allowances relatively easily.

2. Years 3–5

This period of time often does not get the attention it deserves. Typically the formulas in the spreadsheet for years 1 and 2 are copied across without any real interrogation of whether it is appropriate to do so. One needs to investigate whether the business environment and hence the firms strategy are likely to remain unchanged. In addition one of the things that gets missed when examining this time period is Working Capital.

The importance of focusing on this time period derives from the fact that what a business does during these years is often what gives it its competitive advantage. The sustainability of this competitive advantage enables the business to continue creating value into the period beyond five years.

3. Beyond 5 years

As mentioned above the sustainability of the businesses capital advantage is what underpins whether value is captured by a business beyond five years. The value captured is reflected in a terminal value which is the subject of *Chapter 12*.

11.5   Capital Structure and Gearing

We discussed capital structure briefly within the context of ratio analysis in *Chapter 4*. The key point about capital structure is that by raising a larger proportion of funds from debt than equity, it is quite possible to improve the return on capital employed. If debt capital can be raised and employed in the business to earn a rate which exceeds that rate being paid in fixed interest, then it must follow that a surplus will remain after payment of the interest. This surplus will clearly add to the profits available to the equity shareholder, which the following simple example demonstrates:

Example

Assume a company which presently has an all equity capital structure is to undertake an investment of £50 million which will earn incremental profit before interest and tax of £7 million. It may finance this investment either by additional equity or by a long-term loan carrying an interest of 10%. *Table 11.9* demonstrates that the use of further equity dilutes the return on equity, whereas the use of debt enhances it.

Table 11.9   ROE% – Effect of Equity v Debt Financing

		Before	After All Equity	After Debt and Equity
		£'m	£'m	£'m
Equity Capital	(A)	100.0	150.0	100.0
Debt		0.0	0.0	50.0
Profit Before Interest and Tax		20.0	27.0	27.0
less Interest Payable		0.0	0.0	5.0
Profit Before Tax		20.0	27.0	22.0
less Taxation (35%)		7.0	9.5	7.7
Profit After Tax	(B)	13.0	17.5	14.3
ROE %	(B ÷ A x 100)	13.0%	11.7%	14.3%

This example suggests a tremendous advantage in the use of significant amounts of debt. However, in practice, the following factors would be taken into consideration in determining the amount of debt to be used:

❏   The articles of association of a limited company normally restrict the volume of debt.

❑ The nature of the security which could be offered may detract from the acceptability of further debt.

❑ The anticipated level of future profits may provide an insufficient safety margin for future interest payments.

❑ The equity holders may not wish to accept any greater risk to dividends or share value caused by the creation of additional prior debt charge.

❑ The anticipated level of cash flow may be inadequate to service interest, debt repayment and equity dividend, thus the risk of insolvency presents itself.

Careful assessment of all of these factors enables a safe amount of debt that does not jeopardise the value of equity shareholders' investment, to be determined. The determination of the debt capacity of an organisation is an essential part of financial management, and organisations do monitor their debt position very carefully.

What is Gearing?

There are a number of methods used to determine the gearing of a company. For the purpose of this example we are using the components of the Borrowing Ratio i.e. total borrowings divided by equity.

An Example

Two identical companies. Run by twins; one twin owns Company A while the other twin owns Company B. The have similar premises – in the same street, manufacture the same products, to the same specification, using the same machinery. All costs and volumes are the same. The employ similar staff i.e. twins, each employing one twin. The only difference between the two companies is the way in which they are financed. Twin A financed Company A mainly from equity capital (shareholders) while Twin B financed Company B mainly from borrowings. Therefore the gearing would be shown as follows:

	A	**B**
Borrowings	20	80
Equity	80	20
GEARING	LOW	HIGH

It can be seen that the gearing for Company A is 20 ÷ 80 equals 0.25 to 1, while the gearing for Company B is 80 ÷ 20 equals 4.00 to 1. Why do we add back interest payable to the profit before taxation figure? The answer is to remove the effect of gearing when comparing the profitability of different companies.

In the *Table 11.10* we show both companies have achieved an operating profit of £1,000. We have also assumed that interest payable is in proportion to the company's borrowing, therefore, Company A has £200 of interest payable while Company B has £800.

Table 11.10   Profit and Loss Accounts for Company A and B

	A	B
Operating Profit	1,000	1,000
less Interest Payable	200	800
Profit Before Taxation	**800**	**200**
less Taxation at 25%	200	50
Profit After Taxation	600	150
less Dividend	300	75
Retained Profit	300	75
No. of Shares (assumed)	80	20
Retained Profit Per Share	3.75	3.75

From the above example it can be seen that if we took Profit before Taxation as our figure for profit, it would be after the payment of interest on borrowings but before the payment of dividends to shareholders for financing of the business. Therefore we take the profit figure before any financing of the business i.e. Operating Profit.

Why do Companies Move Towards Higher Gearing?

Quite simply, in good times it pays to finance a business by debt provided that the return is in excess of the cost of the debt.

	A	B
Borrowings	20	80
Equity	80	20
GEARING	LOW	HIGH
RETURN	LOW	HIGH

Companies that move towards higher gearing will provide a higher return to each individual share when the economic climate is good. If we take the previous example and add an extra £500 to the Operating Profit for both companies, the result is shown in *Table 11.11*.

Table 11.11 Profit and Loss Accounts – Increase in Operating Profit

	A	B
	£	£
Operating Profit	1,500	1,500
less Interest Payable	200	800
Profit Before Taxation	1,300	700
less Taxation at 25%	325	50
Profit After Taxation	975	650
less Dividend	300	75
Retained Profit	675	575
No. of Shares	80	20
Retained Profit Per Share	8.44	28.75

We can see from the above table that an incremental Operating Profit of £500 means that the Profit before Taxation is increased by £500 since the Interest Payable is covered from the initial £1,000 profit. Given that both companies pay the same rate of tax and pay the same amount of dividend, means that the Retained Profit is £675 for Company A and £575 for Company B. Extending the calculation we can produced a retained earnings per share of £8.44 for Company A and £28.75 for Company B. We can now see that Company B achieves a higher return (per share) given an increase in the profits earned by the company. Therefore, higher gearing produces a higher potential return to shareholders.

What Can Happen to Highly Geared Companies When There is an Economic Downturn?

Companies that move towards higher gearing should always keep a look out for the possibility of an economic downturn. Many companies fail to consider their financial structure and find that they are highly geared at the start of a recession. A substantial number of these companies will fail. The results of high gearing that produce a high return (per share) will place companies in a high risk category. Therefore:

	A	B
Borrowings	20	80
Equity	80	20
GEARING	LOW	HIGH
RETURN	LOW	HIGH
RISK	LOW	HIGH

Companies that move towards higher gearing will provide a higher return to each individual share when the economic climate is good. If we take the previous example and deduct £500 from the Operating Profit for both companies, the result is shown in *Table 11.12*.

Table 11.12 Profit and Loss Accounts – Decrease in Operating Profit

	A	B
Operating Profit	500	500
less Interest Payable	200	800
Profit/Loss Before Taxation	300	–300

Here we can see the risk involved. At times of recession, sales often decline. This will inevitably cause a decline in profits which in turn will cause a decline in the amount of funds coming into the business. The only thing which doesn't decline is the borrowings and the interest payments. In many cases interest rates will increase, therefore causing an even larger outflow of funds and an eventual, long-lasting cash crisis.

What is an Acceptable Level of Gearing?

The potential tax related benefits of debt capital and 'gearing up' on the one hand, and the disadvantages of increased risk on the other has given rise to the view of there being an optimal, or ideal, capital structure. That is, there is some mix of debt relative to equity at which the tax advantage can be maximised before the perception by debt and equity providers that the risk needs to be compensated for by a higher return.

The answer to the question is that it all depends upon the economic climate and the business itself. As for the economy, we know that perceptions and the reality of borrowing can change given different economic conditions. For instance, in times of recession a massive change typically occurs in views about what constitutes an acceptable level of borrowing. Individuals and corporations often see the upside of borrowing from boom-time turn into a very real downside as interest rates rise at a time when effective demand and confidence are falling. In addition to what is regarded as an acceptable level of gearing from a broad economic perspective, there is a need to consider specific business/industry characteristics since different types of business have different types of asset and repayment structure. Those with more to offer as security, or with more robust cash flows, should be able to gain most benefit from debt financing. The same is also the case for businesses with a good track record, even though their tangible sources of collateral may be limited.

Many believe that it is difficult to determine a single truly optimal capital structure in practice, but that it is more valuable to see it as corresponding with a limited range of possible debt and equity mixes.

Irrespective of the exact characteristics of the capital structure, the real challenge is to locate where it potentially lies when taking a forward-looking view. This is because in terms of undertaking a valuation, the real concern is typically to find the required rate of return or cost of capital to apply in valuing a potential opportunity from a series of estimated future cash flows. This means that the cost of capital should relate to the future, which is achieved by attempting to identify the most beneficial blend of debt and equity over the future planning period. Attention will have to be paid to the most appropriate debt structure, which will have to take into consideration conditions relating to both the economy and the business.

11.6 Dividend Policy

A substantial amount of research has been undertaken about the decision to retain profit, or whether to distribute it by way of dividend. The conclusion in practice suggests that dividend policy is a vital factor in enhancing the value of shareholders' equity. However, there is still inadequate empirical evidence to confirm exactly the importance of dividends in market value, and one source of difficulty is that different shareholders have different expectations from their individual investments. Whereas some investors look for dividends, others look for capital growth. Except for very closely controlled companies, it is very difficult to establish the attitude of shareholders with any precision, nevertheless, in determining a dividend policy, the following factors do appear to be of significance:

❑ A stable dividend rather than a fluctuating one is generally regarded as a sign of strength, and should have a favourable impact upon market value.

❑ Steady growth in dividend is generally desirable, even though such growth may lag slightly behind earnings growth. Such a conservative approach is preferable to a hasty response which may subsequently require a cut in dividend.

❑ Dividend cover, although questioned by some, does provide a crude indication of the amount of retained profit which should, in principle, result in a growth in market value in the future. However, this does assume that any such retained profit will be employed successfully within the business.

In determining dividend policy, the balance between how much to distribute and how much to retain is vital and there is a crucial link between the capital investment decision (*Chapters 9 and 10*) and the financing decision. This aspect is discussed later in this chapter.

Theoretically, the shareholders are no worse off (they may even be better off!) whether or not a dividend is paid. The proviso is that the cash flows from profits retained (rather than paid out as a dividend) are invested in projects which earn at least the corporate cost of capital.

In practice, dividends do matter. The theoretical arguments outlined above are not supported by experience in the real world. For the most part in finance, it can be assumed that investors are rational and that they would therefore accept the argument about dividend policy outlined above. But in this one case, investors do not appear to be rational. They prefer dividends now rather than in the future – even if the future dividends will be high enough to compensate. Thus, a company may miss profitable investment opportunities because the cash is not immediately available – because it has to be paid out as a dividend, to maintain the company's earlier dividend policy.

If a company has set a level of dividends in the past, they will be expected in the future. If the dividends have been so much per share, perhaps growing at the rate of inflation, then that dividend payment has set a precedent for the future. Company directors will deviate from that at their peril. If dividends are reduced, the share price will typically be most adversely affected. Conversely, directors will be reluctant to *increase* dividends much, because, once the dividend has been increased to a higher level, it will be expected that the new level will be maintained. So, corporate boards of directors tend to maintain a policy of steadily increasing dividends

Why should investors be irrational on this one point of policy? Over the years, analysts have come up with arguments and suggestions to provide logical reasons for investors attitude towards dividends and these, in summary, are as follows:

❏ dividends have an *information* content. This means that investors can be sure that the company really has made some money in the year. The cash is available to pay the dividend;

❏ uncertainty about the future prospects of the company means that investors prefer current dividends to distant dividends;

❏ shareholders do rely on cash income (from the dividends on their investments);

❏ maintenance of a steady dividend policy will mean that the share price is maintained and that it is not trading at a discount.

11.7 Cost of Capital

The one remaining area for consideration is the cost of capital which is a very contentious topic. This subject is supported by a substantial body of research and literature and the following discussion represents only a very brief review.

How can a business evaluate whether a potential investment is really worthwhile? In every day life it is common practice to answer this question with reference to the rate of return that will be earned on funds invested. If money needs to be borrowed to undertake such a potential investment then there will be a cost associated with it, typically expressed as the percentage return required by the lender. Common sense would dictate that the return required from an investment should at the very least cover the cost of funds needing to be raised to finance it. What applies in everyday life also applies in corporate life. Organisations have to ensure that the opportunities in which it invests are those that will at minimum satisfy the returns required by the providers of funds. In other words, the cost of capital should equate with the opportunity cost of the funds tied up; i.e. the return which would be achieved from their next best use.

The importance of understanding the role of the cost of capital in value creation may be simple, but in practice its estimation is far more problematic, as will be seen in this chapter. One source of complication is that the providers of funds to a company are not typically a homogeneous group with identical requirements and expectations from their investment. At one extreme they may comprise long-term debt-holders seeking a secure and fixed rate of interest, while at the other they may be ordinary shareholders who accept that the return received is most likely to be contingent on the company's performance. Somehow the requirements of all providers have to be captured. One commonly accepted way is via the Weighted Average Cost of Capital (WACC) in which the requirements of all providers of funds are expressed in one percentage rate of return.

Weighted Average Cost of Capital (WACC)

As indicated opinions differ about the size of the cost of capital. To understand the source of such differences we will review the cost of capital, which is often referred to as the weighted average cost of capital, or WACC for short, with reference to three steps involving estimation of the:

a. Cost of Equity.

b. Cost of Debt.

c. Capital Structure.

These three steps and the building blocks associated with them are illustrated in *Figure 11.4.*

Figure 11.4   Three Steps for Estimating WACC

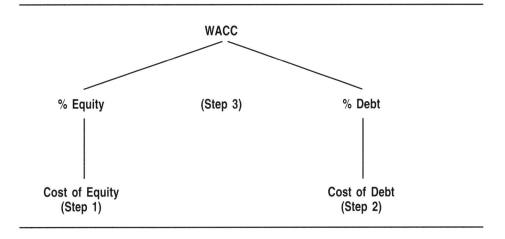

Of the three steps, the most difficult and controversial issue concerns the estimation of the cost of equity.

Step 1: Cost of equity

Among the approaches available for calculating the cost of equity are the

a.   Capital Asset Pricing Model,

b.   Arbitrage Pricing Theory,

c.   Dividend Valuation Model.

a.   Capital Asset Pricing Model (CAPM)

Modern financial theory suggests that the cost of equity can be estimated from analysing what return investors require when buying a share. Their requirement can be estimated using the Capital Asset Pricing Model, known as CAPM. The underlying premise of the approach is the more risk an investor is required to take on, the higher the rate of return that will be expected. It is in a class of market models called 'risk premium' models which rely on the assumption that every individual holding a risky security will demand a return in excess of the return they would receive from a risk-free security. This excess return is the premium to compensate the investor for risk that cannot be diversified away.

The CAPM cost of equity can be estimated using the following formula:

Cost of Equity = Risk-Free Rate + (Beta x Equity Risk Premium)

For example, *Meunier plc* has a WACC of 12 per cent which was calculated using the CAPM to determine a cost of equity of 14.03 per cent, assuming a risk-free rate of 6.94 per cent, a beta of 1.222, and an equity risk premium of 5.8 per cent. In terms of the CAPM cost of equity formula, this can be shown as:

Cost of Equity   =   6.94% + (1.222 x 5.8%)

      =   14.03%

Within the CAPM the variable specific to the type of business is the beta. Both the risk-free rate and the equity risk premium are assumed to apply to all companies within the market. Each of these three will now be examined in turn.

Beta

Beta is a relative measure of volatility that is determined by comparing the return on a share (stock) to the return on the stock market. In simple terms, the greater the volatility, the more risky the share, which will be reflected in a higher beta.

Risk-Free Rate

The risk-free rate represents the most secure return that can be achieved. From a UK perspective, anyone wishing to sleep soundly at night might invest all available funds in government bonds which are largely insensitive to what happens in the share market and, therefore, have a beta of nearly zero.

In developed economies, government securities tend to be the best candidates for the risk-free rate, since the government in many countries guarantees payment. However, government securities may have different maturity dates and different yields. Preference for a medium-term rate is not uncommon because it often comes close to matching the duration of the cash flow of a company being valued.

Equity Risk Premium

The equity risk premium, sometimes known as market risk premium, is the excess return above a risk-free rate that investors demand for holding risky securities. The risk premium in the CAPM is the premium above the risk-free rate on a portfolio assumed to have a beta equal to 1.0. If an individual security is more or less risky, then it will have a higher or lower risk premium.

Historical analysis is a popular way to estimate the risk premium, the rationale being that history is a good predictor of the future.

Until recently it seemed to be accepted practice in the UK to use an estimate of 8–9 per cent for the equity risk premium. However in recent regulatory rulings in the UK much lower figures have been used. The historical average of 8–9 per cent applies to a period that was by all accounts, on average, different to the current situation.

The Appropriateness of CAPM for Estimating the Cost of Equity

Like all models, CAPM abstracts from reality by making a series of simplifying assumptions. Many of the assumptions behind CAPM may not hold in the real world, but that does not necessarily mean that the model is not valuable. Even simple models can yield useful results with practical applications. For example, *Thomas Edison* understood very little of what we now know about electricity, yet he was able to harness it and produce the light bulb.

Criticism of the CAPM approach stems from doubt being expressed about the linear relationship between beta and expected returns. Research has shown only a weak relationship between average return and beta over the period 1941 and 1990, and virtually no relation over the shorter period 1963 to 1990. Firm size and market-to-book ratios were found to be far more important in explaining differences, although such findings are still the subject of considerable academic debate.

b. Arbitrage Pricing Theory (APT)

Concerns about the inadequacy of the CAPM resulted in the search for a better model. The result of this search is the approach known as arbitrage pricing theory (or APT). This model is based upon much the same logic as the CAPM. Company *specific risk*, which is diversifiable and idiosyncratic, is not priced by the market place because it can be eliminated at virtually no cost by spreading among a large number of assets in a portfolio. This is quite unlike the *systematic risk* which cannot be diversified away in a portfolio, thereby necessitating the payment of a risk premium in order to compensate investors for bearing it. Unlike CAPM, in which the measure of systematic risk is solely the return on the market portfolio, in the APT a number of the risks are identified and used. Empirical research so far has not demonstrated APT to be sufficiently superior to the CAPM to warrant the added complexity involved. Econometric research studies continue to strive to discover those fundamental characteristics, like the industry in which a company participates, its balance sheet characteristics (e.g. gearing) and earnings performance (e.g. earnings variability), that will provide a basis for estimating a company's exposure to general market or economy-wide developments. The result of such research will hopefully be the establishment of future related betas that are not too complex to apply in practice.

c. Dividend Valuation Model

The Dividend Valuation Model considers that the return shareholders require (hence the cost of equity to a business), can be determined with reference to the future dividend stream they demand. At its simplest, this approach takes the view that the cost of equity to a company is only the dividend it has to pay which is derived by assuming that a company's dividend per share grows at a constant rate and that the company's risk will remain unchanged. If we call K_e the cost of equity, the model is:

$$K_e \% = \frac{d\,(1 + g) + g}{P} \times 100$$

Where,

K_e	=	Cost of Equity;
d	=	Current Dividend;
P	=	Market Price;
g	=	Expected dividend or price growth rate provided that investors expect dividends to grow at a constant rate in perpetuity.

Thus, if a company had a current dividend per share of 4p, a market price of £1.00 and an expected growth rate of 10 per cent, its cost of equity would be:

$$K_e \% = \frac{4p\,(1 + 0.10) + 0.10}{100p} \times 100$$

$$= 14.4\%$$

However, for calculating the cost of equity relating to ordinary share capital the dividend valuation approach has to be used with care.

❏ First, the growth rate g is a long-run growth rate over an infinite horizon and as such is a difficult parameter to conceptualise. It relies on accurate estimates of growth rates that can be reliably projected into the future – a daunting task given that few businesses have a history of constant growth.

❏ Second, the long-run growth rate must, by definition, be strictly less than the cost of equity, K_e.

❏ Third, the parameters of the model are interdependent. It would seem that a higher growth rate implies a higher cost of equity. However, this is not true because the higher rate of growth will imply a higher current share value. The net effect will reduce the cost of equity but, if one estimates a higher growth rate, how much greater should P become? The answer is unclear.

❏ Finally, the model provides no obvious answer to the question – what cost of equity should be applied when the company is considering projects of different risk than its current operations? For this, approaches like CAPM are required.

Step 2: Cost of Debt

The second step in calculating the cost of capital is to calculate the cost of debt, which is the rate of return that debt-holders require to hold debt. To determine this rate the yield to maturity (YTM) has to be calculated, often by drawing on the principles of discounted cash flow analysis and particularly the internal rate of return. For example, consider a non-redeemable debenture with a nominal value of £100 that pays 10 per cent, or £10 per annum in perpetuity. What this represents as a return to the investor will depend on the value of the debenture in the stock market. If the value has fallen from £100 to £92, then the return or yield will be 10.87 per cent ([£10 ÷ £92] x 100). However, this may not tell the full story. First, the debenture may have a redemption date such that it may return £10 for a fixed number of years, at the end of which a sum of money will be paid by the company to redeem it. For example, if the debenture is to be redeemed after ten years at its face (par) value of £100, then the yield is the percentage that equates an annual interest payment of £10 up to the point of redemption together with £100 redemption payment in year ten, having its present value of £92. This percentage, represented by i in the following formula, is 11.38:

$$\frac{£10}{(1+i)} + \frac{£10}{(1+i)^2} + \frac{£10}{(1+i)^3} + \ldots + \frac{£110}{(1+i)^{10}} = £92$$

Second, the impact of taxation has to be taken into consideration as follows:

Cost of debt after tax = Cost of debt before tax x (100 – Marginal tax rate)

The marginal tax rate is the tax rate applied to the company's last earned pound of income, i.e. the rate that applies to the highest 'tax bracket' into which the company's income falls. Marginal tax rates can differ from the statutory tax rates due to different income thresholds and net operating loss carry-forwards, which act to reduce the tax rates.

The marginal tax rate should not be confused with the average tax rate, which is the company's total tax liability divided by its total taxable income. Because the tax rate changes with the amount of taxable income under current laws, the marginal tax rate is often different from the average tax rate. In any event, before the marginal tax rate for an unquoted business can be estimated, it is necessary to first estimate its taxable income. Once this is known the current tax schedule can be used to determine the appropriate tax rate.

The cost of debt generally increases with financial leverage. Therefore, a change in target capital structure will change the cost of debt. The cost of debt must also follow the matching principle in that it must match the risk of the cash flows being discounted.

One key point to recognise is that for purposes of estimation, reality checks should be used. For example, one invaluable cross-check is reference to the views of the commercial banker.

Dealing With More Than One Source of Debt

Typically businesses have more than one source of debt financing. In this case the overall cost of debt can be calculated by taking the weighted average of the individual instruments based on market values. This involves multiplying the yield to maturity of each instrument by the percentage of the total market value of the portfolio that each instrument represents, and summing the products. This is illustrated in *Table 11.13*, where the approach was used to find the cost of debt for a large US buy out:

Table 11.13   Calculation of Weighted Cost of Debt

Type of Debt	£m	Weight	Yield %	%
		A	B	A x B
Short-Term Debt	13,600	0.5199	11.27	5.86
Existing Long-Term Debt	5,262	0.2011	9.75	1.96
Subordinated Increasing-Rate Notes (Class I)	1,250	0.0478	13.00	0.62
Subordinated Increasing-Rate Notes (Class II)	3,750	0.1433	14.00	2.01
Convertible Debentures	1,800	0.0688	14.50	1.00
Partnership Debt Securities	500	0.0191	11.20	0.21
Total	£26,162	1.0000		11.66 %

Once the weighted cost for all debt has been estimated before tax, the effect of tax needs to be considered as follows:

Cost of Debt after Tax = Cost of Debt before Tax x (100 – Marginal Tax Rate)

= 11.66% (100 – 35.5) = 7.52%

It is important to note that it has been assumed there are tax advantages associated with debt. However, this may not always be the case. Where a business has large tax losses carried forward, the position may be much more complex; there is always a need to review each situation on a case by case basis and take specialist advice when necessary.

Step 3: Capital Structure

The third step in the WACC calculation involves the estimation of the capital structure and to understand the issues involved here, let us consider the following formula:

$$WACC = K_e + (E \div V) + K_d (1 - T_c)(D \div V)$$

Where,
V	=	debt (D) + equity (E);
D/V	=	the proportion of total value (V) claimed by debt (D);
E/V	=	the proportion of total value (V) claimed by equity (E);
K_d	=	the required rate of return on debt capital;
K_e	=	the required rate of return on equity capital;
T_c	=	the marginal corporate tax rate.

The calculation of WACC can be demonstrated by drawing on the example company, *Meunier plc*. In *Table 11.14* it can be seen that the cost of equity using the CAPM approach is 14.03 per cent and the cost of debt after tax is 8.4 per cent. These two, when weighted by the debt equity mix of 36:64 per cent produce a WACC of approximately 12 per cent that has been used in *Chapter 12*.

Table 11.14   WACC for Meunier plc

	£m	%
Cost of Equity (general)		14.03
Risk-Free Rate		6.94
Beta	1.222	
Equity Risk Premium		5.8
Cost of Debt		12.0
Marginal Rate of Corporation Tax		30.0
Cost of Debt (after tax @ 30%)		8.4
Equity (market value)	125.33	64
Debt (book value)	70.92	36
	196.25	100

$$WACC = \left[14.03\% \times \frac{125.33}{196.25} \right] + \left[8.4\% \times \frac{70.92}{196.25} \right]$$

$$= 12.00\%$$

As regards the D/E ratio used in the WACC calculation, there is the question of whether book (balance sheet) values or market values should be used. Market values are conceptually superior, despite their volatility, because the firm must yield competitive rates of return for debt-holders and shareholders based on the respective market values of debt and equity.

Despite the preference for market values, there are many difficulties associated with the determination of the market value of debt and equity. In very simple terms, the market value of equity can be determined for a quoted firm by multiplying the current stock price by the number of shares outstanding. For an unquoted business, the task is more difficult. In the case of the market value of debt, for a quoted company it is its price in the market multiplied by the volume of traded debt. In the case of an unquoted company it could be computed by discounting the future cash flows of each instrument at an estimated current yield to maturity, as described in the previous section on the cost of debt. If this information is not available, the book value of debt may have to be used as a proxy for the market value of debt. However, very often the difficulties associated with the estimation of actual market values for equity and debt encourages the use of a target capital structure, i.e. a target D/E ratio. This target will be either based on judgement or benchmarked against peer group companies.

Summary

Determining the cost of capital is a real challenge. This is for many reasons, not least because there are different views about the methods to be adopted for calculating the cost of equity.

Understanding the cost of capital is one of the major challenges for management. Those who understand it should be able to ensure that their organisations benefit. However, as will be seen from what follows, its estimation requires a good deal of tough analysis and the exercise of sound judgement. It is also important to recognise that it is all too easy to become side-tracked by some of the issues relating to the determination of the cost of individual components that make up a corporation's capital structure. Nowhere is this more the case than for the cost of equity for which a number of approaches have been developed to try and capture the rate of return required by shareholders. These approaches in themselves are challenging, but there is one important issue to acknowledge, any approach is only as good as the data on which it is based.

11.8   Linking the Business Plan and the Financing Plan

This section aims to provide a framework that brings together the two aspects of any firm; the business aspects or Business Plan and the financial aspects or the Financial Plan. The glue that ties these two parts together is cash flow as will be illustrated shortly.

The Business Plan

In essence, the Business Plan is all about the strategy of the firm and how it intends to create value, the investments it makes in deployment of that value creating strategy and its operations in execution of this strategy. The Business Plan both needs cash to execute the strategy in terms of its expenditures and investments and produces cash when the strategies are being realised. The cash flows that are important to the Business Plan are OCF and FCFF, the relationship between the two is shown in *Table 11.15* for our example company *Meunier plc*. In terms of cash flow, the Business Plan answers two questions; how much cash is required to fund the businesses strategy and how much cash will the businesses strategy eventually produce.

Table 11.15   Operating Cash Flow (OCF) to Free Cash Flow to Firm (FCFF) [1]

	£m
Operating Cash Flow (OCF)	14.5
less Investment in Fixed Capital (both replacement and incremental)	16.4
add Investment in Working Capital	7.5
Free Cash flow to Firm (FCFF)	5.6

[1]   Reproduced from *Table 11.7*.

The Financing Plan

In order to be able to undertake its strategy a business needs capital to do so. This is the reason d'être of the financing plan. It provides answers to the two questions; how will the business strategy be financed and what should be done with any surplus cash?

The following table helps us to answer these questions. Taking the FCFF as our starting point, if it is positive the cash flow may be used to service debt in the form of interest or repay principal leaving FCFE which may be returned to shareholders or retained within the firm for future reinvestment. Conversely, if FCFF is negative it may be funded through borrowing, raising equity, curtailing dividends or by using internally generated funds.

Table 11.16   Free Cash Flow to Firm (FCFF) to Net Cash Movement

	£m
Free Cash flow to Firm (FCFF) (after tax basis)	5.6
less After Tax Interest Costs	2.3
less Debt Repaid/(Debt Raised)	6.9
Free Cash Flow to Equity (FCFE) [1]	–3.6
less Dividends	5.5
add Equity Raised/(Bought Back) [2]	9.1
Net Cash Movement	0

[1]   This part of the table is reproduced from *Table 11.8*.

[2]   Calculated by taking the difference between the 1998 less 1997 figures for issued share capital plus share premium account. The basic data is taken from the balance sheets on page 415, i.e. (£13.9m + £38.7m) – (£13.2m + £30.3m) = £9.1m.

11.9   Framework for Business Decisions

When we look at *Tables 11.15 and 11.16* the common element is FCFF. For any one firm the FCFF in the Business Plan and the Financing Plan must be the same due to the self balancing nature of the double entry book keeping system of accounting that we saw in *Chapter 1*. Thus, we can write the following statement:

Business Plan = Financing plan

If we now expand on what is encompassed under each plan we can write the following expression *Figure 11.5*, which highlights the high level business decisions that any management team has to consider:

Figure 11.5   High Level Business Decisions

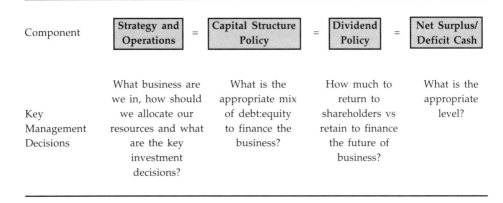

Component	Strategy and Operations	=	Capital Structure Policy	=	Dividend Policy	=	Net Surplus/ Deficit Cash
Key Management Decisions	What business are we in, how should we allocate our resources and what are the key investment decisions?		What is the appropriate mix of debt:equity to finance the business?		How much to return to shareholders vs retain to finance the future of business?		What is the appropriate level?

In summary, there are three key interrelated management decisions as shown in *Figure 11.6.*

Figure 11.6 Three Key Interrelated Management Decisions

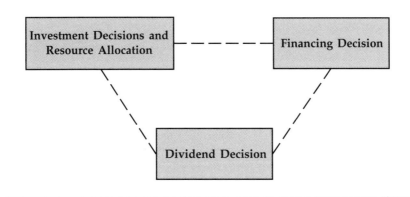

Some observers say that the Dividend decision should be a residual decision after the other two decisions. The rationale for this is that if there are investment opportunities to grow the business which create value then these should be undertaken and financed accordingly because this will generate returns to shareholders over the longer term. If there are no value creating investments in the medium term then it makes sense to return surplus capital to shareholders either in the form of dividends or in the form of share buy backs (legislation permitting). What this rationale ignores is that a company may already have an existing commitment to pay a certain level of dividends to its shareholders.

Although this commitment is not binding, shareholders may sell the shares if the dividend is cut which may depress the share price opening the company to a possible take-over.

STRATEGIC FINANCIAL MANAGEMENT

When you have finished studying this chapter you should be able to:

❏ Comment on the shortcomings of accounting based measures like earnings per share in evaluating financial strategy.

❏ Describe the relevance of discounted cash flow analysis to financial strategy.

❏ Describe the principles underpinning Shareholder Value Analysis (SVA).

❏ Identify the key value drivers required, and their interrelationship, as input data prior to shareholder value analysis.

❏ Calculate both the cash flows during the forecast period and the residual value in order to prepare a statement of shareholder value.

12.1   Introduction

The price placed by the market upon a public limited company's shares is an indicator of its perceived success. The competition for shareholders as well as customers, and hostile corporate raids that now span national barriers, requires that a company's share price performs well relative to the rest of the market and, in particular, within its own market sector.

What does a company have to do to be successful in the eyes of the market? *Peters and Waterman (1982)* in their book 'In Search of Excellence', considered this question in relation to a sample of US Corporations over a twenty-five year period. Long-term wealth creation was emphasised in the *Peters and Waterman* study as being a key contributor to excellence. Such wealth they measured using:

❑   Compound asset growth.

❑   Compound equity growth.

❑   Ratio of market value to book value.

❑   Average return on total capital.

❑   Average return on equity.

❑   Average return on sales.

To qualify for excellence a company was required by *Peters and Waterman* to have been in the top half of its industry in at least four of these six measures over a twenty-year period. Those companies that qualified were then examined in more depth to find the distinguishing attributes of excellent companies.

You will recognise some of the six qualifying measures of long-term wealth from our discussions in earlier chapters. A number of them we discussed as financial measures of performance and were shown to draw heavily upon accounting principles for the measurement of profit and financial position. That they are reliant upon accounting rather than economic principles can be appreciated with reference to first three of them which require balance sheet data for their calculation, whilst the other three require profit data from the profit and loss account.

We have considered some of the limitations of accounting measures in relation to short and long-term decision making. For example, the theoretical benefits of discounted cash flows measures particularly net present value were illustrated in *Chapter 9*, and compared with accounting based measures such as the rate of return. The relevance of accounting measures can also be questioned for purposes of making decisions associated with financial strategy as we will illustrate in the next section.

12.2   Shortcomings of Accounting Measures for Financial Strategy.

Why are accounting measures like profit and earnings per share inappropriate to financial strategy? The simple answer is that they have the following important shortcomings:

❑   Earnings can be calculated using alternative and equally acceptable accounting methods. A good illustration of this was provided in *Chapter 3* with reference to the profit and earnings per share provided for *Cray Electronics* plc before and after an independent review of the performance of the company.

❑   Business and financial risk are excluded. A business evaluating two alternative strategies with a mean earnings growth rate of 10% might at first sight find them equally acceptable, even though the variability in their return because of financial or business risk was significantly different.

With regard to financial risk the effect of changes in the level of gearing is the important consideration. A company can improve earnings per share by using debt rather than equity financing, because of the tax shield associated with debt. Does this improvement in earnings per share necessarily improve economic value? The simple answer is no. Increases in the level of debt may increase financial risk because of the danger of insolvency. Shareholders may therefore demand higher rates of return as a consequence. The simplest way to view this is to remember that one measure of value is:

$$\text{Value} \quad = \quad \frac{\text{Earnings}}{\text{Required Rate of Return}}$$

Unless any added earnings are sufficiently large to offset the rise in the required rate of return, value may decline.

With accounting measures it is important to realise that:

❑   The timing of the impact of investment is ignored. Investments in working capital and fixed capital needed to sustain and make a company grow are excluded from the earnings calculations. It is therefore possible for a company to achieve high earnings even though the associated cash flow figure is much lower. For example, a company might report a net profit of £1 million but only generate £50,000 cash, the difference between the two figures being because of significant cash outflows for, working capital and replacement capital expenditures, with only a small proportion being reflected in the profit reported via the depreciation charge. Thus, the net profit figure conceals the real position of a company in such a replacement programme. A relatively good net profit may not always be associated with increases in economic value which might at first sight be expected.

❑ The time value of money is ignored. Consider our earlier company evaluating two alternative strategies with a mean earnings growth rate of 10%. Both strategies might appear to be equally acceptable using an earnings criterion even though the annual cash flows associated with each may be very different. From our discussions in *Chapters 9 and 10* we know that on economic grounds the preferred strategy would, other things equal, be that yielding cash flows earlier rather than later.

Our review of the shortcomings of accounting measures has focused upon earnings and earnings per share, but caution is also necessary in using the other alternatives that are available. Accounting measures, like return on capital employed (total assets) are sometimes compared to the company's cost of capital. The difference between the return on capital employed and the company's cost of capital is referred to by some authors as the 'spread'. Successful corporate performance is usually considered to correspond with a positive spread, that is where:

Return on Capital Employed is *GREATER THAN* Cost of Capital

For example, if the company's return on capital employed and the cost of capital have been calculated as 15% and 10%, respectively, then the spread is 5% and should, in principle, add to the value of the business. The problem with such 'spread' approaches is their reliance upon accounting numbers and, according to evidence available, the best of them leaves more than 60% of the variation in share prices unexplained. Why is this so? In effect, the return on capital employed is really adopted as a substitute for the internal rate return, but, unfortunately, it is not an accurate or reliable estimate. Furthermore, there is no systematic pattern enabling a specific correction to be made to adjust a return on capital employed percentage to a percentage internal rate of return. With a given set of cash flows and therefore a known internal rate of return, a book value return on capital employed calculation will either over or understate the real rate because of such factors as the:

❑ Length of project life.

❑ Capitalisation of investments in a company's books.

❑ The depreciation policy.

❑ The lag between investment outlays and their recovery in the form of cash inflows.

These problems are exacerbated when total return on capital employed is measured rather than just the increment arising from a particular strategy. This is because the measure will incorporate not only prospective investment and cash flow, but also that from earlier periods. The implications of this are that two divisions or business units with identical strategies, but with different initial values of capital employed, would face different accounting returns during the forecast/planning period in spite of identical internal rates of return!

It should also not be ignored that accounting-based measures of return typically only measure the benefits to be gained during the forecast period of the strategy and by themselves ignore key information about the value of the business after the forecast period has elapsed. In many cases, the real benefit of a strategy can only be properly evaluated with reference to the total economic return that results. This total economic return comprises not only that return provided during the forecast period of the strategy, but also the estimated value of the business at the end of the period. We will provide a numerical example with will cover this aspect in more detail later in this chapter.

Some strategies require substantial investment during the forecast period in order to grow the business and to achieve benefits beyond the forecast period. The logic of measuring the total return comprising the return associated with the plan and increases in value in the post-planning period can be likened to the increase in economic value sought by shareholders in the form of both dividends and capital gains. In fact, as we will illustrate, increases in return from a planning period may be associated with different residual values for different types of strategy, thereby making reference to a measure related to the planning period alone wholly inadequate.

However, while accounting-based numbers such as earnings per share and return on capital employed are not reliable indicators of long-term strategy and shareholder value, accounting should not be viewed as having no purpose. It may be inappropriate for evaluating financial strategy, but it is essential for assessing past performance. Performance for the most recent year cannot be properly evaluated without recognising that investments made during this and previous years may not be recouped until later years.

Accounting-based numbers do deal with this time lag and the uncertainty surrounding the amounts and timing of prospective cash flow by assigning costs systematically to a set of future time periods.

The conclusion to be drawn from this review of accounting measures is that shareholders may not be satisfied with only excellent financial performance as conveyed by accounting numbers, particularly when it has been illustrated that such numbers can be influenced significantly within the principles of accounting and by individual company policy, for example *Cray Electronics plc* in *Chapter 3*. At the end of the day the concern of shareholders is most likely to be with the total return they receive on their shareholding from dividends plus share appreciation.

In this chapter we consider financial strategy within the context of the economic orientated discounted cash flow approach discussed in *Chapters 9 and 10*. Before we consider the applications and implications of discounted cash flow analysis within strategy, we offer the same word of caution mentioned earlier with reference to project appraisal. It is all too easy to become immersed in the apparent precision of numbers relating to uncertain future financial data and lose sight of less tangible but equally important issues.

12.3 Discounted Cash Flow Analysis and Financial Strategy

The use of discounted cash flow analysis in financial strategy has been popularised in the US where the approach has come to be known as Shareholder Value Analysis (SVA). Shareholder value in SVA, is the NPV generated by the firm for its shareholders after all obligations have been met.

In the UK a similar approach to SVA has developed under the name of Strategic Financial Management, (SFM). For both SVA and SFM the quest for management is to maximise the cash generating potential from the business (or part of the business) as portrayed by the net present value of projected cash flows discounted at the cost of capital. By adopting this approach top management and the board of directors should be better equipped to answer the following basic questions:

❑   Will the current strategy as conveyed within the corporate plan create value for its shareholders and, if so, how much?

❑   Which business units below the corporate level are creating value and which are not?

❑   How would alternative strategic plans effect shareholder value?

In principle, the approach, can be applied throughout a company and be translated into a language, for, all levels of management and managerial functions. This means that alternative future courses of action may be compared and their desirability can be assessed by the process of discounting cash flows at the relevant cost of capital. The returns obtained from these alternatives can be converted into conventional accounting performance indicators, making the approach relevant and usable by all managerial levels. Of course, as we will demonstrate, the principles involved are not without their difficulties in terms of their application.

We will illustrate that one major advantage of adopting a discounted cash flow rather than an accounting approach is that life after the end of the current financial year is taken into consideration. In contrast to the accounting approach, where a loss in a particular activity this year may be regarded as unacceptable, that reliant upon discounted cash flow analysis takes a longer term perspective and recognises that it may well be desirable to accept such a loss in a year, if there will be a substantial profit in future years.

12.4   The Principles Underpinning Shareholder Value Analysis (SVA)

In what follows we will direct our discussion of discounted cash flow analysis for financial strategy towards SVA and the measurement of shareholder value. In common with our discussion in *Chapter 9* on project appraisal we require the measurement of forecast cash flows and the cost of capital in order to compute the net present value of the business according to alternative strategies. Those strategies that create positive net present values should, depending upon the quality of the assumptions made, increase shareholder value, whereas those with negative net present values are likely to reduce such value. The logic of the approach is straightforward if you have a good understanding of the material covered in *Chapters 9 and 10* but, as we will identify, there are some practical difficulties.

In order to apply the net present value approach to business strategy a number of stages need to be followed:

❏   A projection is required of annual operating cash flows for the planning period in question for each business defined as being in the corporate portfolio. The difficulty of their estimation discussed with reference to project appraisal is equally applicable within the context of a financial strategy model.

❏   The cash flows, once estimated, must be discounted at the cost of capital relevant to the company during the planning period and summed to give the present value of projected cash flows.

❏   The final stage, and often the most difficult in practice, is the estimation of the residual or terminal value of the individual businesses at the end of the planning period, discounted to its present value.

❏   The total present value for any particular strategy is the sum of the present values of annual operating cash flows and the residual value. As indicated earlier, there are parallels between the net present value approach and the measurement of value derived from holding a share. Just as a shareholder will usually be concerned with both dividend and capital growth potential, a company will be concerned with annual operating cash flows and the residual value.

As indicated, however, one significant problem in practice is the calculation of the residual or terminal value for the business at the end of the planning period. Whereas for capital projects terminal values are not usually a significant influence, and can usually be estimated with reference to realisable value sources, it is far more difficult for businesses which will still be going concerns at the end of the planning period.

Various approaches have been proposed for establishing residual values. Realisable values from disposal may be appealing but are not relevant if the business is to be viewed as a going concern. Two alternative traditional methods are to use the price earning (PE) multiple method and the market to book (MB) ratio method, which we have discussed in *Chapter 4*. Using the PE ratio method, residual value is the product of some measure of after tax earnings at the end of the forecast period and the projected PE at the end of the forecast period. A claimed advantage of this approach is that the PE is widely used and readily available from for example, the *Financial Times*. Against this must be weighed the assumption implied by its use that price is driven by earnings, and the difficulty of predicting future PE multiples.

The problem of earnings and other accounting-based measures have been discussed at length! To the concerns we have expressed about the use of earnings we need to recognise that PE ratios move over the course of time, and no reliable models exist for forecasting their future value accurately.

With the MB ratio method, the residual value is the product of the book value of equity, and the projected MB ratio at the end of the forecast period. Similar to the PE ratio, the MB is relatively easy to calculate but it has all of its shortcomings.

An alternative to both of these, is to capitalise cash flow in the last planning period. This approach treats the cash flow in the last planning period as a perpetuity in the same way as a fixed income security. For example, consider a £1,000 security offering a £100 per annum. The interest rate for one year is calculated by:

$$£100 ÷ £1,000 \text{ x } £100 = 10\%$$

Alternatively, if we know the fixed income from the security and the interest rate, the capital value of the security can be calculated by rearranging the formula:

$$£100 ÷ 10\% = £1,000$$

Using such an approach the value of a fixed income security can be readily calculated in the event of a change in the interest rate. Thus, at a rate of 12.5 percent the value of the security would be:

$$£100 ÷ 12.5\% = £800$$

For the calculation of the residual value from a strategy, a perpetuity cash flow is taken to represent the fixed income, which is then divided by the company's cost of capital, i.e.

$$\text{Residual Value} = \frac{\text{Perpetuity Cash Flow}}{\text{Cost of Capital}}$$

The support for the perpetuity method for estimating residual value is that it is argued as corresponding broadly with the realities of business. Value creating strategies are those that yield positive net present values as a result of producing returns over the cost of capital demanded by the market. By the end of the planning period corresponding with a value creating strategy, there are likely to have been additional entrants to the market who will have identified opportunities for themselves, such that any company is not expected on average to be able to produce positive net present values

The perpetuity cash flow assumption can of course be relaxed and modified using tailor-made computer software that is available. Commercial software is available which can be used to provide residual values involving growth rates and returns beyond the planning horizon.

12.5   Calculating Shareholder Value

1.   Estimating Free Cash Flow Using the Seven Value Drivers

A shareholder value calculation is reliant upon cash flow data with many of the attributes required for the type of NPV calculation discussed in *Chapter 9*. However, in addition to this data other inputs are required like details of fixed and working capital investment requirements. These inputs to a shareholder value calculation have collectively been labelled *value drivers*. They take their name from being key elements that drive the value of the business and to shareholders and comprise:

❏ Sales Growth

❏ Operating Margin

❏ Cash Income Taxes

❏ Working Capital Investment

❏ Fixed Capital Investment

❏ Life of Projected Strategy

❏ Cost of Capital

The first five of these value drivers are critical in determining the size of the annual cash flows generated. As we will illustrate with the aid of an example, the annual cash flow can be easily calculated using summarised data relating to each driver. This approach which has been referred to as a *scratchpad* valuation can be readily applied manually or using a computer spreadsheet or programmable calculator. For greater accuracy a more detailed valuation can be undertaken by broadening the calculation to include the elements which make up each of these five value drivers. However, such a detailed approach really warrants the use of bespoke valuation software.

So, we can generate a free cash flow forecast using the first five of the seven value drivers. Given these five cash flow drivers, how do we establish values for them in any particular case? Quite simply, they may be estimated by looking at a mix of past experience, management judgement about what is likely to happen in the future, and observations about the marketplace.

It is vital not to underestimate the importance of the cash flow data in measuring business value. We have already referred to Garbage In, Garbage Out (GIGO) which is very apt for issues relating to business valuation – the quality of any business valuation can only be as good as the input data upon which it is based. With this in mind let us review the issues associated with estimating the cash flow drivers.

Sales Growth Forecasts

Estimated future sales can be projected from market information to produce forecasts about the markets for goods or services. Such market forecasts should be based upon an analysis of market opportunities and product strategies should be developed to supply those markets discovered from such analysis. A pricing policy will also have to be established in each sector in order to put a monetary value on the forecast sales quantities. Obviously, prices (in most markets) affect the quantity sold, so there will be an interactive process to estimate the sales volume at the most appropriate prices to provide what is thought to be the optimal level of planned sales value.

The current level of sales (for each product at current prices) is very much the starting point for sales growth analysis. Any expected growth in sales volume from, for example, prior investment in fixed and working capital must be added. There may also be some adverse influences upon sales value, for example, as a result of a decrease in sales volume, or even a lowering of prices.

It is quite logical to think of the first driver of business value as being sales growth. If the enterprise does not sell anything, then it cannot really be said to be in business! In a sense, this also applies to not-for-profit organisations. Perhaps one does not think of their activities as "sales" but the level of activity in which they expect to be involved, or level of service they expect to provide, sets the scene for the facilities required to support that level of performance.

Operating Profit Margin

Once sales forecasts and more concrete sales plans are agreed, managers will need to consider the means of ensuring the supply of those sales to customers, and the costs of doing so. Such costs will relate to:

❑ the sourcing and costs of raw materials;

❑ employing and training an adequate labour force;

❑ establishing sufficient sales and distribution facilities;

❑ ensuring adequate production facilities;

❑ creating a management team able to manage the business.

In a not-for-profit organisation, activities will also generate costs that have to be charged against sales. However, in some not-for-profit concerns, the income may not be linked to the service in quite the same way that costs are linked to sales in a commercial enterprise. For example, a charity where the income from donations and grants is unrelated to the 'output' or activity of the charity. In this case, the not-for-profit undertaking has to ensure that the best use is made of its income by providing a cost effective service. It is arguably more difficult to manage this – where one is measuring benefits against costs – than in the commercial world where the amount of profit is a measure of the degree of success.

What this illustration also flags up is that very different approaches may need to be adopted in generating forecast cash flows depending upon circumstances. What drives cash flow is by no mean common to all types of business operations, an issue that has to be considered in forecasting future cash flows. A sequence of events starting with sales growth may be difficult to apply in all circumstances.

It is important to realise that the profit margin on sales depends on the type of business. Generally, the principle is that the greater the need for investment in fixed assets and working capital, the higher the profit margin has to be on sales. For example, food retailers in the UK have relatively low amounts tied up in fixed assets and working capital. They may own some of their stores, but also rent others, and have very little tied up in working capital by way of stocks and debtors. Such companies work on a sales margin of 5–6%. By comparison, heavy goods companies like those supplying plant and equipment to industry, have to plan for much higher margins on sales value. Such companies have large factories to pay for and the net profit on each sale has proportionately to be much higher than the retailer – something in the order of 12–15% or more.

Cash Tax Flows

Once operating profit has been estimated, a forecast amount of tax to be paid on those profits will have to be taken into account. However, tax is more difficult to consider from a general managerial perspective than the other cash flow drivers because it is very much a specialist area. For this reason you may often find general assumptions about the cash tax rate being used in running a business. Nevertheless, there are one or two issues that are important for you to understand.

Tax payable upon profits is an income tax paid by a venture on its income (or net profit) in just the same way that individuals have to pay income tax on their income. Companies in many countries must also pay capital gains tax on any gain made from holding an asset or investment over time. Thus, if an office building were sold for £10m which had originally cost £4m, there would be tax to pay on the capital appreciation of £6m. In many countries though the capital gains tax is not levied on the full capital gain – an allowance is made for the general rate of inflation. In this example, the £4m original cost would be indexed to a higher figure and the resultant gain would be lower. Furthermore, companies actually accrue capital gains tax, as time goes by. So a charge, for what has become known as deferred tax, is made in each year's accounts for the amount of capital gains tax that would have to be paid if the asset were sold at the date the accounts were drawn up.

The point about deferred tax is that it is irrelevant as far as free cash flow is concerned. Our concern is with the amount of tax actually payable and, more particularly, when, that is the year during which it is payable. The tax on capital gains is not payable, however, until an asset is sold and the gain realised, thus the date of payment of the tax may be many years hence. Thus, although the deferred tax calculated on the basis of the potential capital gain is charged against profit over the years, the tax is not paid until the asset is sold. The tax payment date, however, is important when budgeting for free cash flow many years ahead.

Operating Cash Flow

What we have discussed above with reference to sales forecasts, operating profit margin and tax cash flows enables operating profit to be estimated. However, it is important to recognise the potential complexity that may be involved in deriving operating profit in reality. First, many businesses produce multiple products and/or provide multiple services, so that the future overall operating profit may be most meaningfully and accurately calculated by undertaking a number of computations which are then aggregated to form a total view. Second, in so doing, constraints upon the business have to be recognised. These constraints are often referred to as 'limiting factors' in accounting/finance. One has to recognise that, for example, the market conditions may constrain the potential sales growth and/or the operating profit margin. One such factor will often predominate and has to be taken into consideration in ensuring realism in developing forecasts.

Operating profit may often not be the same as operating cash flow. Accounting attempts to report a 'true and fair' view of the affairs of a business, and there are several accruals and apportionments which have to be made which often make operating profit very different from operating cash flow. A major difference between the two is because of the apportionment against 'cash income' for depreciation of assets.

Depreciation can be thought of as being an apportionment of the sum paid for a fixed asset over its useful economic life. The simplest way to understand this is with reference to an illustration. Imagine a piece of machinery bought today for £100,000, which is expected to last for five years, and to be worth nothing at the end of this time period. If paid for by cash then there would be a cash outflow of £100,000 at the time of purchase. However, for accounting purposes it would be written off over the five year period, such that only a proportion, say one fifth or £20,000, would be charged against profit each year.

Operating cash flow may be considerably more than operating profit. This is illustrated in *Table 12.1* with reference to *Meunier plc*. Information contained in the annual accounts and notes (see Appendix at the end of this chapter) have been used to calculate the operating cash flow.

Table 12.1   Operating Cash Flow for Meunier Plc

	1997	1998
Operating Profit	14.7	12.1
add Depreciation (see *Table 12.5*)	5.2	5.9
Operating Cash Flow before tax	19.9	18.0
less Taxation	2.7	2.4
Operating Cash Flow after tax	17.2	15.6

Fixed and Working Capital Investment

The distinction between operating cash flow and free cash flow is that investment necessary to support future cash flows is taken into consideration in deriving free cash flow. Such investment will be concerned with:

1. Replacement Fixed Capital Investment (RFCI), that is investment in the replacement of fixed assets to maintain the level of productive facilities currently in place.

2. Incremental Fixed Capital Investment (IFCI), that is investment in new assets to provide additional facilities to enable intended sales growth to occur.

3. Incremental Working Capital Investment (IWCI), that is investment in additional working capital, such as stocks of materials.

Estimating these can be difficult in practice, and for which many different approaches can be adopted. For replacement capital expenditure, a frequent assumption is that depreciation is a good estimate. What is added back to operating profit as depreciation to calculate operating cash flow, will be deducted from operating cash flow to derive free cash flow. For the other two investments, which represent additional or incremental expenditure necessary to support the intended sales growth, there are many different forecasting approaches. A popular approach that we illustrated earlier is to estimate the relationship between increased sales and increased fixed and working capital expenditure using historical data.

2. Producing a Free Cash Flow Estimate

To see how these value drivers can be used to provide a free cash flow estimate, let us consider the following example:

Assume a business with sales revenue today of £100m and sales growth rate expectations of 5% in the first year, 10% in the second and third years, and 15% for the remaining years. With knowledge of this information the sales receipts would be as indicated by the figures in italics in *Table 12.2*.

Table 12.2   Forecasting Future Sales Revenue

Now	Year 1	Year 2	Year 3	Year 4	Year 5	Year 6
£100m	x 1.05					
	= £105m	x 1.10				
		= £115.5m	x 1.10			
			= £127.05m	x 1.15		
				= £146.11m	x 1.15	
					= £168.03m	x 1.15
						= £193.23m
£100m	*£105m*	*£115.5m*	*£127.05m*	*£146.11m*	*£168.03m*	*£193.23m*

The values of the operating profit margin and the cash tax rate for these years have been estimated as follows:

Year	1	2	3	4	5	6
Operating Profit Margin	10%	10%	12%	12%	14%	10%
Cash Tax Rate	30%	30%	30%	30%	30%	30%

Applying these two percentages to the projected sales revenue calculated in *Table 12.2*, results in the after tax operating profit shown in *Table 12.3*.

Table 12.3   From Forecast Sales Revenue to Operating Profit after tax

Year	1	2	3	4	5	6
	£m	£m	£m	£m	£m	£m
Forecast Sales Revenue	105.00	115.50	127.05	146.11	168.03	193.23
Operating Profit Margin	x10%	x10%	x12%	x12%	x14%	x10%
Operating Profit	10.50	11.55	15.25	17.53	23.52	19.32
Cash Tax Rate	–30%	–30%	–30%	–30%	–30%	–30%
Operating Profit after tax	7.35	8.09	10.68	12.27	16.46	13.52

What is required is cash flow and not profit. As we indicated earlier, the main difference between the two is the apportionment against 'cash income' for depreciation of assets. In addition, the normal process of accounting adopted by businesses, known as *accrual accounting*, means that there will be other deductions from income, known as provisions (for anticipated costs which have not yet come to fruition), such as provisions for possible bad debts. To be prudent (conservative), businesses make a provision for doubtful debts against current income based upon past experience. This will further depress accounting profit but not necessarily actual cash earned because the basis for the provision is only an expectation.

For our example company, for the sake of simplicity let us assume that the depreciation for each of the six years has been estimated as £5m. This means that the after tax operating cash flow is £5m higher than the operating profit for each year:

Year	1	2	3	4	5	6
	£m	£m	£m	£m	£m	£m
Operating Cash Flow	12.35	13.09	15.68	17.27	21.46	18.52

However, operating cash flow does not take account of important cash outflows that will need to be incurred to support the intended sales growth. In order to achieve the intended sales growth rates, fixed and working capital investment may need to be incurred.

Fixed capital investment is made up of two components, replacement and incremental. Replacement fixed capital investment (RFCI) is required to maintain the existing capital stock. Without maintenance and replacement the ability to meet current levels of demand let alone increases will prove impossible.

What about incremental fixed capital investment? Quite simply an estimate has to be made of the amount of incremental fixed capital that will be required to support incremental sales. One way to build this in is to assume that for every £1 of sales to be generated some fixed capital investment will need to be incurred, albeit that it may not occur in even increments but may be incurred in 'lumps'.

Typically, there will also need to be an investment in working capital since additional sales will be difficult to sustain without incurring incremental working capital. More stock may be required and it may only be possible to achieve a growth in sales by extending credit and increasing debtors.

In common with incremental fixed capital it can be assumed that for every additional £1 of sales to be generated, some working capital investment will be required. In other words, any increase in sales can only incur by taking on more stocks of raw materials and, possibly, by increasing accounts receivable (debtors). For purposes of our earlier example we will assume incremental fixed capital investment (IFCI) and incremental working capital investment (IWCI) to be:

Year	1	2	3	4	5	6
IFCI	4%	6%	3%	2%	2%	2%
IWCI	3%	3%	3%	4%	4%	4%

To find IFCI and IWCI in money terms, these percentages are applied to the change in sales receipts from year to year. Therefore, in Year 1:

$$\text{IFCI} = (£105m - £100m) \times 4\% = £0.2m$$

and

$$\text{IWCI} = (£105m - £100m) \times 3\% = £0.15m$$

Let us now pull all of this together to estimate prospective free cash flows. These are illustrated in *Table 12.4*.

Table 12.4   Operating Profit after tax to Free Cash Flow

Year	1	2	3	4	5	6
	£m	£m	£m	£m	£m	£m
Operating Profit after tax	7.35	8.09	10.68	12.27	16.46	13.52
add Depreciation	5.00	5.00	5.00	5.00	5.00	5.00
Operating Cash Flow	12.35	13.09	15.68	17.27	21.46	18.52
RFCI	–5.00	–5.00	–5.00	–5.00	–5.00	–5.00
IFCI	–0.20	–0.63	–0.35	–0.38	–0.44	–0.50
IWCI	–0.15	–0.32	–0.35	–0.76	–0.88	–1.01
Free Cash Flow	7.00	7.14	9.98	11.13	15.14	12.01

As a result of having estimates for sales revenue today and knowledge of the five cash flow drivers we have shown how future free cash flows can be estimated. But how can the values for the cash flow drivers be estimated in real life? Let us now consider this with reference to *Meunier plc*.

3.   Estimating Values for Cash Flow Drivers – *Meunier plc*

The usual starting point for estimating values for cash flow drivers, particularly when working with publicly quoted companies, is the information contained in the annual report and accounts. As an illustration we will draw upon the information contained in *Appendix A* relating to extracts from the annual report and accounts of *Meunier plc*.

In *Table 12.5* we have extracted key items relating to *Meunier plc* for the last three years. Further information is also provided about the depreciation for the year and RFCI.

Table 12.5   Historical Data Relating to Meunier plc

	1996 £m	1997 £m	1998 £m
Turnover	187.4	199.6	210.6
Profit Before Interest and Taxation	20.2	14.7	12.1
Taxation	5.0	2.7	2.4
Tangible Fixed Assets	66.9	76.2	86.7
Depreciation for year	4.4	5.2	5.9
RFCI	6.1	6.9	7.9
Working Capital	20.5	16.8	9.3

Using this information we can calculate the five cash flow drivers for 1997 and 1998 as illustrated in *Table 12.6*:

Table 12.6   Calculating Value Drivers for 1997 and 1998

Cash Flow Driver	1997 %	Calculation	1998 %	Calculation
Sales Growth Rate	6.5	$\dfrac{(199.6-187.4) \times 100}{187.4}$	5.5	$\dfrac{(210.6-199.6) \times 100}{199.6}$
Operating Profit Margin	7.4	$\dfrac{14.7 \times 100}{199.6}$	5.7	$\dfrac{12.1 \times 100}{210.6}$
Tax Rate	18.4	$\dfrac{2.7 \times 100}{14.7}$	19.8	$\dfrac{2.4 \times 100}{12.1}$
IFCI *	62.3	See below	77.3	See below
IWCI	30.3	$\dfrac{(20.5-16.8) \times 100}{(199.6-187.4)}$	68.2	$\dfrac{(16.8-9.3) \times 100}{(210.6-199.6)}$

*   The calculation of the percentages for IFCI is often more complicated because depreciation and RFCI can differ. They should be calculated as shown in *Table 12.7*, because this will accommodate situations where RFCI and depreciation values differ.

Table 12.7 Calculating Incremental Fixed Capital Investment (IFCI) for 1997 and 1998

		1997	1998
		£m	£m
Net Tangible Fixed Assets at end of year		76.2	86.7
add Depreciation for the year		5.2	5.9
Tangible Assets before depreciation		81.4	92.6
less Net Tangible Assets at beginning of year		66.9	76.2
Increase/(Decrease) in Tangible Assets		14.5	16.4
less Asset Replacement (RFCI)		6.9	7.9
Increase in Tangible Fixed Assets	(a)	7.6	8.5
Increase in Sales	(b)	12.2	11.0
IFCI	(a ÷ b x 100)	62.3%	77.3%

These values for the cash flow drivers, based upon an historical review, represent just the starting point. As we indicated earlier when we reviewed each of the cash flow drivers, a good deal of research is required to ensure meaningful forward looking free cash flow estimates.

Let us assume that research has been undertaken for *Meunier* which has been used to produce the cash flow driver estimates for 1997 to 2001 shown in *Table 12.8.*

Table 12.8 Cash Flow Drivers

	1997	1998	1999, 2000 and 2001
Sales Growth Rate	6.5%	5.5%	9.0% – Best estimate
Operating Profit Margin	7.4%	5.7%	9.0% – Improved cost control
Cash Tax Rate	18.4%	19.8%	20% – Conservative estimate (in need of review)
IFCI	62.7%	77.3%	20% – Minimum necessary to satisfy growth targets
IWCI	30.3%	68.2%	20% – Best estimate

With a knowledge of these cash flow drivers and estimates of depreciation and RFCI, we can produce free cash flow estimates by following a similar procedure as the earlier illustration. The result is as shown in *Table 12.9.*

Table 12.9   Free Cash Flow Estimates

	1998 £m	1999 £m	2000 £m	2001 £m
Sales	210.6	229.6	250.3	272.8
Operating Profit Before Interest and Tax		20.7	22.5	24.6
Taxation		–4.1	–4.5	–4.9
Operating Profit After Tax		16.6	18.0	19.7
Depreciation		7.0	7.0	7.0
Operating Cash Flow		23.6	25.0	26.7
RFCI		–8.0	–8.0	–8.0
IFCI		–3.8	–4.1	–4.5
IWCI		–3.8	–4.1	–4.5
Free Cash Flow		8.0	8.8	9.7

Once the cash flows have been calculated, and the life of the project strategy determined, the cost of capital is required for purposes of discounting the free cash flow to establish the present value. As with the other value drivers, the cost of capital can be applied as a *scratcbpad* discount factor, or if greater accuracy is required a more detailed approach can be adopted focusing upon components cost of equity, cost of debt, and the tax rate (please refer to the discussion on weighted average cost of capital in *Chapter 11*).

To express these future cash flows in present value terms we need to discount them at the required rate of return (cost of capital). Let us assume that the cost of capital of *Meunier* after tax and when appropriately adjusted for inflation is 12%. With knowledge of this cost of capital we can calculate the present value of the cash flows of *Meunier plc* for the three-year planning period as being £21.06m:

Table 12.10   Present Value of Free Cash Flows

	1999	2000	2001	
Free Cash Flow £m	8.0	8.8	9.7	
Multiply by: 12% Discount Factor	0.893	0.797	0.712	
Present Value £m	7.14	7.01	6.91	
Total Present Value				21.06

4.   Calculating shareholder value

Continuing our example, *Meunier plc* a planning period of three years was selected consisting of 1999 to 2001 inclusive and, given this, we can assume that 2002 and beyond corresponds with the continuing period. A breakdown of the components of free cash flow for both the planning period and the years comprising the continuing period are shown in the *Table 12.11.*

Table 12.11. Free cash flows for the planning and continuing periods

	1998	PLANNING PERIOD			CONTINUING PERIOD		
		1999	2000	2001	2002	2003	2004
	£m	£m	£m	£m	£m	£m	£m
Sales	210.6	229.6	250.3	272.8	272.8	272.8	272.8
Operating Profit Before Interest and Tax		20.7	22.5	24.6	24.6	24.6	24.6
Taxation		−4.1	−4.5	−4.9	−4.9	−4.9	−4.9
Operating Profit After Tax		16.6	18.0	19.7	19.7	19.7	19.7
Depreciation		7.0	7.0	7.0	7.0	7.0	7.0
Operating Cash Flow		23.6	25.0	26.7	26.7	26.7	26.7
RFCI		−8.0	−8.0	−8.0	−8.0	−8.0	−8.0
IFCI		−3.8	−4.1	−4.5	0	0	0
IWCI		−3.8	−4.1	−4.5	0	0	0
Free Cash Flow		8.0	8.8	9.7	18.7	18.7	18.7

Because sales growth is assumed to cease at the end of the planning period, sales and hence operating profit remain the same in each year of the continuing period as in 2001. Similarly, with depreciation assumed to be unchanged, operating cash flow remains the same in 2001 as in each year of the continuing period. However, where there is a noteworthy change is in the level of investment. Whilst RFCI remains unchanged because such investment will need to be undertaken to maintain the quality of existing assets, IFCI and IWCI fall off to zero. These you will remember were forecast upon the basis of sales growth – no sales growth, no IFCI or IWCI!

The result is that the free cash flow for 2002 and beyond is greater than that for 2001 by £9m, the value of IFCI and IWCI in 2001. We know how to put a value on the free cash flows for the planning period by discounting them by the cost of capital, but, how can we value the free cash flows for the continuing period which may be assumed in principle to be received indefinitely?

5.   Calculating the residual value

If we assume the 2002 free cash is received into perpetuity its value as we discussed earlier may be calculated as follows:

$$\text{Value of Perpetuity} \quad = \quad \text{Free Cash Flow} \div k$$

$$= \quad £18.7m \div 0.12$$

$$= \quad £155.83$$

However, this assumes that the perpetuity is measured at the end of the planning period in 2001. It is *not* the present value of the perpetuity i.e. its value in 1999. What its value is will depend on the cost of capital. Given that we know this to be 12% we can calculate the present value of the perpetuity by discounting it at the relevant discount factor, i.e. 12% at the end of year 3. Thus, the present value of such a perpetuity is calculated as follows:

$$\text{PV of Perpetuity} \quad = \quad (\text{Payment} \div k)\,(1 \div (1 + k))^{n}$$

$$= \quad (£18.7m \div 0.12)\,(1 \div (1 + 0.12))^{3}$$

$$= \quad £110.95m$$

Seen another way, £110.95m compounded for the next three years at 12% per annum produces £155.83m. To be more precise, £155.83m is the future value and £110.95m is its present value.

Now, the implication of this is that to calculate a business value where there is a given planning period, the present value of the planning period has to be combined with the present value to be derived from the business beyond it. In the case of *Meunier plc* assuming a three year planning period and a cost of capital of 12%, the result is a total business value of £132.01m (£21.06m + £110.95m).

The size of the value from the continuing period, often known as the *residual value*, is the largest contributor to total value. In fact, in this case the residual value represents 84% of the total value, hardly surprising when one considers that it represents a period of infinity, less the three years accounted for by the planning period.

The further into the future that the planning period extends the lower is the relative contribution made by the continuing period. But, does it make sense to value over such a long period? There is good reason when one considers the value of a share by way of dividends and capital appreciation. A crude, but effective, indication of the long-term nature of share valuation is provided by the PE ratio. For example on Tuesday 22 February the FTSE-A all share index had a PE ratio of 24.89, meaning that the average price might be simplistically viewed as reflecting 24.89 years' earnings.

In summary, there are three important points to appreciate about the perpetuity residual value:

❑ The value of the business is very dependent upon the cost of capital. This is because it is used in determining the perpetuity value which, together with the free cash flows for the planning period, are discounted to a present value using a present value factor itself derived from the cost of capital.

❑ In many cases most business value comes from the continuing period, and for this reason many practitioners of the approach also look to methods other than just the perpetuity.

❑ Related to the second point, the value is very dependent upon assumptions about the characteristics and length of the planning period.

6.   Business Value, Corporate Value and Shareholder Value

The value we have discussed so far and calculated for *Meunier* is what is known as *business value* and **not** shareholder value. Business value can be defined as the value generated by the free cash flows in which *all* providers of funds have a claim.

The concern within Shareholder Value Analysis is with the determination of that part of business value (and any other value) generated which is attributable to the shareholders. How do we find this?

To arrive at business value we discounted free cash flows at a cost of capital that took account of the benefit of borrowed funds. Now we need to remove the present value of any such funds in order to find the claim on the value of the business attributable to just the shareholders.

It may also be the case that investments are held in other businesses, the benefits of which are not captured in the business valuation process. Any such benefits have to be added to determine corporate rather than business value. In fact, two adjustments are required to calculate shareholder value which take the following form:

Business Value

add Marketable Securities or Investments

Corporate Value

less Market Value of Debt and Obligations

Shareholder Value

Number of Ordinary Shares

Shareholder Value Per Share

In terms of *Meunier plc* we have estimated a business value of £132m, there are no marketable securities (e.g. interest earning deposits), and the notes to the accounts for 1998 show creditors amounts falling due after one year of £20.1m. If we take such creditors as being a proxy for the market value of debt and obligations we can calculate shareholder value as follows:

	£m
Business Value	132.01
add Marketable Securities	0
Corporate Value	132.01
less Market Value of Debt and Obligations	20.10
Shareholder Value	111.91

In Note 4 of *Appendix B*, the number of shares for *Meunier plc* for 1998 is shown as 139 million. With knowledge of the number of shares this shareholder value can be converted into a shareholder value per share.

Shareholder Value	£111.91m
Number of Ordinary Shares	139m
Shareholder Value Per Share	81p

What does this shareholder value per share represent? It is the estimated value per share which is very dependent upon the assumptions made about the seven key value drivers. Change any of these seven and so too does the value. For example, changing only the cost of capital to 11% produces a business value of £145.72m, a shareholder value of £125.62m and a value per share of 90p.

Appendix A

Polly Ester Holdings plc

(December 1995 to December 1998)

This case study was prepared by John Robertson and Roger W Mills from published sources. It is intended as a basis for assignment/class discussion and not as an illustration of good or bad management.

1. BUSINESS EXPANSION

During the year 1996, 72 new shops were added to the portfolio, including three *Pencosmo* and two *Green and Gillies* and six shops in North America that related to a new venture which the chairperson believed was significant to the group's future direction. These were *Polly Ester* mother and daughter shops, selling a coordinated range of clothes and bedroom furnishing products for babies and daughters up to the age of 15, and dresses for their mothers.

In the year 1997, 76 new shops were added to the portfolio including 15 mother and daughter shops. The group envisage further expansion of the *Polly Ester* shops, particularly in North America, Europe and the Far East. Increasingly, however, the emphasis was to move towards the Mother and Daughter and Home concepts. Mother and Daughter was a growing success in North America and the group tended to capitalise on the achievement by a rapid build up of the chain. *Polly Ester* Home shops were launched in the UK in April 1998, in North America in January 1998 and opened in Europe and the Far East later in the year.

It appeared to be the groups' intention to build the Home Furnishings range to a point where they could offer a complete *Polly Ester* furnishings collection while the introduction of cabinet furniture was seen as a significant step in the realisation of this aim.

The group actively planned to extend the sales of their home furnishing ranges outside the retail shops and mail order. Their plans included department store shop-in-shops in the UK and North America, and wholesaling of home furnishing ranges in Germany, North America and the Far East.

In the year 1998 the group were committed to launch their new *Polly Ester* Home Collection in the UK at a time when escalating interest rates were dampening consumer demand in the sector. In relative terms, the new furniture range sold well but sales of wallcovering and fabrics suffered a sharp decline. This in turn, led to reduced demand for print production at their plants in the Belgium and in Ireland.

2.   ACQUISITIONS

In 1997 the group acquired two small businesses which enjoyed a strong brand identification.   These were *Green and Gillies*, a traditional outdoor clothing specialist wholesaler and retailer in the UK.   Also *Pencosmo* in the UK, a long established perfumery business with five shops in the Birmingham area.   It was intended to develop the product ranges of these two companies, and expand the shop outlets.   The company appears to be actively seeking other acquisitions of brand names which will sit comfortably alongside *Polly Ester*.

A new textile plant was opened during 1996 in Ireland which together with a vinyl wallcovering plant they were expected to provide substantial increases in volume and quality of products for the foreseeable future.

In February 1998, the group acquired *Nufurnishing Industries Inc.*, a company engaged in the sourcing and sale of designer bed linen mainly to department stores in North America and the Far East.   The group also signed a franchise agreement with *Styleright Corporation* of America, a retail company in the US trading as Units.   The agreement gave the group exclusive right to operate Units shops in the UK.   It was a new concept in female attire and is enjoying tremendous success in North America.

3.   DISPOSALS

During the year 1998 the group disposed of *Green and Gillies* an outdoor clothing venture in North America.   It was considered that the group resources would be better deployed supporting the *Polly Ester* brand business.

4.   EUROPE

Europe offers opportunities for UK business.   *Polly Ester* opened its first shop in Florence in 1975.   The group now has 65 shops in seven countries and expects to open in Portugal during the year 1999.   Europe is not an easy market to operate in, each country having different requirements and tastes, but the group is now well established and can look forward to the benefits of harmonisation.

5.   DECLINE IN PROFITS

In 1997 and 1998, the major reason for the decline in profits were a loss of margin in the overseas core business, a substantial start-up loss and subsequent venture in *Green and Gillies* and a sharp increase in interest charges.   Most of the reduction in margin can be attributed to the fact that, as sterling based manufacturers, the group has passed the point where they can raise prices to their customers to compensate for the effects of an overvalued pound, particularly in their most important market, North America.

6. CHANGE IN ORGANISATION STRUCTURE

The group have taken action to reduce the cost base of the business and improve margins. As a preliminary step in this process, the group now operates as a number of strategic business units, rather than on a divisional basis.

The product division has now been divided into Brand Management – the design, sourcing and supply are of the *Polly Ester* brand, and *Polly Ester* Manufacturing which is subdivided into four business units, Garment manufacturing businesses, Textiles and wallcovering, Soft furnishings manufacture, and Distribution.

The creation of strategic business units will give senior managers the freedom to take decisions within a framework which clearly defines their responsibilities. It will increase the level of financial awareness throughout the business and allow increased control over working capital and investment decisions.

7. REORGANISATION and QUALITY

In 1998 the reorganisation of the Garment division led to the loss of 89 staff. Major cost-cutting and quality improvement initiatives leading to the adoption of BS 5750 introduced in the Garment and Textile factories are already showing results and will produce further significant benefits for the group over the next two years.

8. OPERATIONS

The North America retail division is committed to improving operating systems to support business growth. During 1999 new wholesale, merchandising and point-of-sale systems are planned to be installed.

With an increasing proportion of the product range being sourced from outside the group, the brand management group has strengthened its international buying team, resulting in a more efficient and imaginative purchasing operation.

Improved quality assurance procedures have been introduced at the plants in Belgium and Ireland leading to the adoption of BS 5750.

9. BORROWINGS

Despite the considerable achievements which have served to enhance the value and prospects for growth in the *Polly Ester* brand, the Board recognised that the group's borrowing levels remained high and that specific measures were needed to reduce them. The board has implemented a further reduction in overheads and a rationalisation programme which might include the disposal of certain businesses or assets, the reduction of stock and restrictions of new shop openings. The benefits of this rationalisation programme should be seen during the course of 1999.

The chairman announced that the Group has recently signed new credit facilities with its bankers to meet funding requirements.

In view of the level of Group borrowings and the results for the year, the directors have decided not to recommend a final dividend in respect of the year ended December 1998 and are unlikely to declare an interim dividend during the current year.

10.   MOVEMENT OF DIRECTORS

Mr. R.J. Somers resigned on 8th July 1996.

Mr. Philip Peters who was the Group Finance Director resigned on 20th December 1997.

Mr. Adrian Moorhouse who was the Managing Director Industries, resigned on 28th July 1997.

Mr. Harold Waterman was appointed as Finance Director by the Board on the 15th April 1999.

During the year 1998, Mr. Michael Smythe who was Managing Director Retail, took over as Managing Director Industries.

POLLY ESTER HOLDINGS PLC

CONSOLIDATED PROFIT AND LOSS ACCOUNT

for the year ended 31st December

	1995	1996	1997	1998
	£'000	£'000	£'000	£'000
Turnover	170,892	201,477	252,431	296,608
Cost of Sales	65,624	78,214	108,044	138,042
Gross Profit	105,268	123,263	144,387	158,566
Other Operating Expenses	83,862	99,486	120,820	152,428
Operating Profit	21,406	23,777	23,567	6,138
Profit/(Loss) related companies	87	-45	42	-177
Royalty Income	1,563	1,709	1,610	1,091
Interest Receivable	711	85	60	28
Interest Payable	-1,317	-2,448	-5,023	-8,663
Profit Before Taxation	22,450	23,078	20,256	-1,583
Exceptional Items				-3,070
Taxation	-7,993	-8,511	-7,135	-2,096
Profit After Taxation	14,457	14,567	13,121	-6,749
Extraordinary Items				-1,391
Profit Attributable to Shareholders	14,457	14,567	13,121	-8,140
Dividends	-4,491	-4,691	-4,691	-1,697
Retained Profit for the year	9,966	9,876	8,430	-9,837
Earnings Per Share (pence)	7.24	7.3	6.57	-3.38

POLLY ESTER HOLDINGS PLC
CONSOLIDATED PROFIT AND LOSS ACCOUNT

for the year ended 31st December

	1995 £'000	1996 £'000	1997 £'000	1998 £'000
FIXED ASSETS				
Tangible Assets	57,292	70,241	79,734	80,784
Investments	505	468	460	682
CURRENT ASSETS				
Stock	45,521	66,824	75,790	104,804
Debtors	12,148	15,340	20,970	27,550
Short-Term Deposits and Cash	5,507	4,448	4,336	1,947
	63176	86,612	101,096	134,301
TOTAL ASSETS	120,973	157,321	181,290	215,767
CREDITORS, falling due within one year				
Borrowings	7,864	34,240	8,155	85,741
Bills of Exchange	745	1,128	2,326	0
Taxation and Social Security	11,014	12,133	5,048	978
Proposed Dividend	2,994	2,994	2,994	0
Trade and other Creditors	18,292	24,982	36,122	49,779
	40,909	75,477	54,635	136,498
CREDITORS, falling due after more than one year				
Borrowings	8,670	6,555	42,112	2,858
Taxation	1,394	545	949	6
Trade and other Creditors	1,053	2,062	1,636	534
Provisions	512	-1,119	2,172	2,853
	11,629	8,043	46,869	6,351
CAPITAL and RESERVES				
Called up Share Capital	9,980	9,980	9,980	9,980
Share Premium	21,440	21,440	21,440	21,440
Profit and Loss Account	37,015	42,381	48,366	41,498
Shareholders' Fund	68,435	73,801	79,786	72,918
TOTAL LIABILITIES	120,973	157,321	181,290	215,767

POLLY ESTER HOLDINGS PLC
NOTES TO THE ACCOUNTS

	1995 £'000	1996 £'000	1997 £'000	1998 £'000
1. GEOGRAPHIC ANALYSIS OF TURNOVER				
United Kingdom	77,244	94,247	125,931	136,412
North America	66,530	74,860	90,143	118,351
Continental Europe	21,606	26,142	28,509	30,578
Other	5,512	6,228	7,848	11,267
	170,892	201,477	252,431	296,608
2. GEOGRAPHIC ANALYSIS: RETAIL OPERATIONS				
Turnover:				
U.K. and Eire		95,000	125,900	135,400
North America		74,800	90,200	103,300
Europe		24,800	28,500	27,900
Number of Shops:				
U.K. and Eire		140	164	184
North America		140	172	185
Europe		61	66	65
Retail Space: (square feet)				
U.K. and Eire		302,700	344,200	393,700
North America		197,700	235,600	255,600
Europe		95,400	100,700	99,000
3. OTHER OPERATING EXPENSES				
Retail and Distribution Costs	56,122	67,858	85,306	103,285
Administrative Expenses	27,740	31,628	35,514	49,143
4. PROFIT BEFORE TAX is stated after charging				
Depreciation of Assets	7,142	11,447	13,708	16,382
Directors' Emoluments	922	1,104	1,093	1,039
Auditors' Remuneration	312	335	298	321
Operating Lease/Hire Charges	10,074	13,226	15,046	20,082
Interest Payable	1,317	2,448	5,023	8,663

POLLY ESTER HOLDINGS PLC
NOTES TO THE ACCOUNTS

	1995 £'000	1996 £'000	1997 £'000	1998 £'000
5. EARNINGS PER SHARE				
Profit Attributable to Shareholders	14,457	14,457	13,121	−6,749
Number of Ordinary Shares	199,600	199,600	199,600	199,600
Earnings Per Ordinary Share	7.24	7.30	6.57	−3.38
6. EMPLOYEES				
Average Weekly Number:				
Manufacturing	2,218	2,384	2,839	2,838
Retail	2,538	3,425	3,289	3,636
Administration	993	1,132	1,296	1,470
Employee Costs:				
Wages and Salaries	46,727	56,132	65,091	74,798
Social Security Costs	4,711	5,562	6,213	7,351
Other Pension Costs	684	1,472	1,551	2,478
Over £30,000: Number of employees				
30,001 – 35,000	4	2	10	2
35,001 – 40,000	6	7	7	7
40,001 – 45,000	7	6	9	4
45,001 – 50,000		2	2	13
50,001 – 55,000			2	3
55,001 – 60,000				1
60,001 – 65,000			2	2
75,001 – 80,000				1
80,001 – 85,000				1
7. DIRECTORS' EMOLUMENTS				
20,001 – 25,000	1			
30,001 – 35,000		1	1	1
45,001 – 50,000		1		1
50,001 – 55,000	1		1	
60,001 – 65,000			2	
65,001 – 70,000	1			
70,001 – 75,000	1			
75,001 – 80,000		2		
95,001 – 100,000	1		1	
100,001 – 105,000				1
115,001 – 120,000				1
150,001 – 155,000	1			
245,001 – 250,000			1	1
255,001 – 260,000		1		

POLLY ESTER HOLDINGS PLC
NOTES TO THE ACCOUNTS

	1995 £'000	1996 £'000	1997 £'000	1998 £'000
8. FIXED ASSETS				
Cost at beginning of year		80,393	101,345	121,956
Translation Difference		–3,450	–1,292	4,233
Additions		28,526	25,167	17,019
Disposals		–4,124	–3,264	–6,668
		101,345	121,956	136,540
Depreciation at beginning of year		23,101	31,104	42,222
Translation Difference		–997	–513	1,745
Depreciation Charge for year		11,447	13,708	16,382
Disposals		–2,447	–2,077	–4,593
		31,104	42,222	55,756
Net Book Value at end of year		70,241	79,734	80,784
Net Book Value at start of year		57,292	70,241	79,734
9. PROFIT AND LOSS ACCOUNT				
Balance at beginning of year		37,015	42,381	48,366
Exchange Differences		-2,990	–1,918	3,838
Profit Retained for the year		9,878	8,430	–9,837
Goodwill on Acquisitions		–1,520	–547	–869
Balance at end of year		42,381	48,366	41,498

Appendix B

Meunier plc

Consolidated Profit and Loss Account

for the years ended 31st December

	Notes	1996	1997	1998
		£m	£m	£m
Turnover		187.4	199.6	210.6
Cost of Sales		80.6	94.1	101.8
Gross Profit		106.8	105.5	108.8
Operating Expenses		86.6	90.8	96.7
Operating Profit		20.2	14.7	12.1
Interest Payable	(1)	3.9	5.3	3.4
Profit Before Tax		16.3	9.4	8.7
Taxation		5.0	2.7	2.4
Profit Attributable to Shareholders		11.3	6.7	6.3
Dividends		4.9	5.2	5.5
Transfer to Reserves		6.4	1.5	0.8
Earnings Per Share				4.53

Meunier plc
Consolidated Balance Sheet
as at 31st December

	Notes	1996 £m	1997 £m	1998 £m
Fixed Assets				
Tangible Fixed Assets		66.9	76.2	86.7
Current Assets				
Stocks		50.1	54.9	70.2
Debtors	(2)	28.6	31.2	35.1
Cash		0.2	0.3	0.3
		78.9	86.4	105.6
Creditors: amounts falling due within one year	(3)	58.4	69.6	96.3
Net Current Assets		20.5	16.8	9.3
Total Assets less Current Liabilities		87.4	93.0	96.0
Creditors: amounts falling due after more than one year	(3)	25.1	27.0	20.1
		62.3	66.0	75.9
Capital and Reserves				
Called up Share Capital (10p shares)	(4)	13.0	13.2	13.9
Share Premium Account		28.3	30.3	38.7
Revaluation Reserve		2.1	2.1	2.1
Profit and Loss Account		18.9	20.4	21.2
Shareholders' Funds		62.3	66.0	75.9

Meunier plc

Notes to the accounts

		1996	1997	1998
		£m	£m	£m
1.	**Interest Payable:**			
	Bank Borrowings and other loans			
	repayable within 5 years	3.3	4.2	2.6
	Finance Leases	0.3	0.5	0.6
	Hire Purchase and Sundry Loans	0.3	0.6	0.2
		3.9	3.3	3.4
2.	**Debtors:** amounts falling due within one year:			
	Trade Debtors	24.3	25.9	26.7
	Other Debtors, Prepayments and Accrued Income	4.3	5.3	8.4
		28.6	31.2	35.1
3.	**Creditors:** amounts falling due within one year:			
	Bank Borrowings	28.0	16.0	24.4
	Loan Notes	0.0	0.0	12.0
	Trade Creditors	16.4	24.3	26.7
	Bills of Exchange	0.9	0.2	3.2
	Taxation and Social Security	3.1	7.2	5.4
	Finance Leases	1.3	2.5	1.6
	Hire Purchase Creditors	1.8	3.6	4.2
	Other Creditors	0.8	2.4	7.5
	Accruals and Deferred Income	3.1	10.1	7.8
	Proposed Dividend	3.0	3.3	3.5
		58.4	69.6	96.3

Meunier plc

Notes to the accounts

	1996	1997	1998
	£m	£m	£m
Creditors: amounts falling due after more than one year:			
Loan Notes	12.0	12.0	0.0
Bank and Other Loans	3.6	2.2	5.6
Finance Leases	1.2	1.5	1.8
Hire Purchase Creditors	4.2	6.8	7.6
Other Creditors	4.0	4.3	4.9
Accruals Deferred Income	0.1	0.2	0.2
	25.1	27.0	20.1

4. **Called up Share Capital**

Ordinary Shares 10p each. 1998, 139 million (*1997, 132 million*)

%	1	2	3	4	5	6	7	8	9	10
Period										
1	0.990	0.980	0.971	0.962	0.952	0.943	0.935	0.926	0.917	0.909
2	0.980	0.961	0.943	0.925	0.907	0.890	0.873	0.857	0.842	0.826
3	0.971	0.942	0.915	0.889	0.864	0.840	0.816	0.794	0.772	0.751
4	0.961	0.924	0.888	0.855	0.823	0.792	0.763	0.735	0.708	0.683
5	0.951	0.906	0.863	0.822	0.784	0.747	0.713	0.681	0.650	0.621
6	0.942	0.888	0.837	0.790	0.746	0.705	0.666	0.630	0.596	0.564
7	0.933	0.871	0.813	0.760	0.711	0.665	0.623	0.583	0.547	0.513
8	0.923	0.853	0.789	0.731	0.677	0.627	0.582	0.540	0.502	0.467
9	0.914	0.837	0.766	0.703	0.645	0.592	0.544	0.500	0.460	0.424
10	0.905	0.820	0.744	0.676	0.614	0.558	0.508	0.463	0.422	0.386
11	0.896	0.804	0.722	0.650	0.585	0.527	0.475	0.429	0.388	0.350
12	0.887	0.788	0.701	0.625	0.557	0.497	0.444	0.397	0.356	0.319
13	0.879	0.773	0.681	0.601	0.530	0.469	0.415	0.368	0.326	0.290
14	0.870	0.758	0.661	0.577	0.505	0.442	0.388	0.340	0.299	0.263
15	0.861	0.743	0.642	0.555	0.481	0.417	0.362	0.315	0.275	0.239
16	0.853	0.728	0.623	0.534	0.458	0.394	0.339	0.292	0.252	0.218
17	0.844	0.714	0.605	0.513	0.436	0.371	0.317	0.270	0.231	0.198
18	0.836	0.700	0.587	0.494	0.416	0.350	0.296	0.250	0.212	0.180
19	0.828	0.686	0.570	0.475	0.396	0.331	0.277	0.232	0.194	0.164
20	0.820	0.673	0.554	0.456	0.377	0.312	0.258	0.215	0.178	0.149

%	11	12	13	14	15	16	17	18	19	20
Period										
1	0.901	0.893	0.885	0.877	0.870	0.862	0.855	0.847	0.840	0.833
2	0.812	0.797	0.783	0.769	0.756	0.743	0.731	0.718	0.706	0.694
3	0.731	0.712	0.693	0.675	0.658	0.641	0.624	0.609	0.593	0.579
4	0.659	0.636	0.613	0.592	0.572	0.552	0.534	0.516	0.499	0.482
5	0.593	0.567	0.543	0.519	0.497	0.476	0.456	0.437	0.419	0.402
6	0.535	0.507	0.480	0.456	0.432	0.410	0.390	0.370	0.352	0.335
7	0.482	0.452	0.425	0.400	0.376	0.354	0.333	0.314	0.296	0.279
8	0.434	0.404	0.376	0.351	0.327	0.305	0.285	0.266	0.249	0.233
9	0.391	0.361	0.333	0.308	0.284	0.263	0.243	0.225	0.209	0.194
10	0.352	0.322	0.295	0.270	0.247	0.227	0.208	0.191	0.176	0.162
11	0.317	0.287	0.261	0.237	0.215	0.195	0.178	0.162	0.148	0.135
12	0.286	0.257	0.231	0.208	0.187	0.168	0.152	0.137	0.124	0.112
13	0.258	0.229	0.204	0.182	0.163	0.145	0.130	0.116	0.104	0.093
14	0.232	0.205	0.181	0.160	0.141	0.125	0.111	0.099	0.088	0.078
15	0.209	0.183	0.160	0.140	0.123	0.108	0.095	0.084	0.074	0.065
16	0.188	0.163	0.141	0.123	0.107	0.093	0.081	0.071	0.062	0.054
17	0.170	0.146	0.125	0.108	0.093	0.080	0.069	0.060	0.052	0.045
18	0.153	0.130	0.111	0.095	0.081	0.069	0.059	0.051	0.044	0.038
19	0.138	0.116	0.098	0.083	0.070	0.060	0.051	0.043	0.037	0.031
20	0.124	0.104	0.087	0.073	0.061	0.051	0.043	0.037	0.031	0.026

% Period	21	22	23	24	25	26	27	28	29	30
1	0.826	0.820	0.813	0.806	0.800	0.794	0.787	0.781	0.775	0.769
2	0.683	0.672	0.661	0.650	0.640	0.630	0.620	0.610	0.601	0.592
3	0.564	0.551	0.537	0.524	0.512	0.500	0.488	0.477	0.466	0.455
4	0.467	0.451	0.437	0.423	0.410	0.397	0.384	0.373	0.361	0.350
5	0.386	0.370	0.355	0.341	0.328	0.315	0.303	0.291	0.280	0.269
6	0.319	0.303	0.289	0.275	0.262	0.250	0.238	0.227	0.217	0.207
7	0.263	0.249	0.235	0.222	0.210	0.198	0.188	0.178	0.168	0.159
8	0.218	0.204	0.191	0.179	0.168	0.157	0.148	0.139	0.130	0.123
9	0.180	0.167	0.155	0.144	0.134	0.125	0.116	0.108	0.101	0.094
10	0.149	0.137	0.126	0.116	0.107	0.099	0.092	0.085	0.078	0.073
11	0.123	0.112	0.103	0.094	0.086	0.079	0.072	0.066	0.061	0.056
12	0.102	0.092	0.083	0.076	0.069	0.062	0.057	0.052	0.047	0.043
13	0.084	0.075	0.068	0.061	0.055	0.050	0.045	0.040	0.037	0.033
14	0.069	0.062	0.055	0.049	0.044	0.039	0.035	0.032	0.028	0.025
15	0.057	0.051	0.045	0.040	0.035	0.031	0.028	0.025	0.022	0.020
16	0.047	0.042	0.036	0.032	0.028	0.025	0.022	0.019	0.017	0.015
17	0.039	0.034	0.030	0.026	0.023	0.020	0.017	0.015	0.013	0.012
18	0.032	0.028	0.024	0.021	0.018	0.016	0.014	0.012	0.010	0.009
19	0.027	0.023	0.020	0.017	0.014	0.012	0.011	0.009	0.008	0.007
20	0.022	0.019	0.016	0.014	0.012	0.010	0.008	0.007	0.006	0.005

% Period	31	32	33	34	35	36	37	38	39	40
1	0.763	0.758	0.752	0.746	0.741	0.735	0.730	0.725	0.719	0.714
2	0.583	0.574	0.565	0.557	0.549	0.541	0.533	0.525	0.518	0.510
3	0.445	0.435	0.425	0.416	0.406	0.398	0.389	0.381	0.372	0.364
4	0.340	0.329	0.320	0.310	0.301	0.292	0.284	0.276	0.268	0.260
5	0.259	0.250	0.240	0.231	0.223	0.215	0.207	0.200	0.193	0.186
6	0.198	0.189	0.181	0.173	0.165	0.158	0.151	0.145	0.139	0.133
7	0.151	0.143	0.136	0.129	0.122	0.116	0.110	0.105	0.100	0.095
8	0.115	0.108	0.102	0.096	0.091	0.085	0.081	0.076	0.072	0.068
9	0.088	0.082	0.077	0.072	0.067	0.063	0.059	0.055	0.052	0.048
10	0.067	0.062	0.058	0.054	0.050	0.046	0.043	0.040	0.037	0.035
11	0.051	0.047	0.043	0.040	0.037	0.034	0.031	0.029	0.027	0.025
12	0.039	0.036	0.033	0.030	0.027	0.025	0.023	0.021	0.019	0.018
13	0.030	0.027	0.025	0.022	0.020	0.018	0.017	0.015	0.014	0.013
14	0.023	0.021	0.018	0.017	0.015	0.014	0.012	0.011	0.010	0.009
15	0.017	0.016	0.014	0.012	0.011	0.010	0.009	0.008	0.007	0.006
16	0.013	0.012	0.010	0.009	0.008	0.007	0.006	0.006	0.005	0.005
17	0.010	0.009	0.008	0.007	0.006	0.005	0.005	0.004	0.004	0.003
18	0.008	0.007	0.006	0.005	0.005	0.004	0.003	0.003	0.003	0.002
19	0.006	0.005	0.004	0.004	0.003	0.003	0.003	0.002	0.002	0.002
20	0.005	0.004	0.003	0.003	0.002	0.002	0.002	0.002	0.001	0.001

%	1	2	3	4	5	6	7	8	9	10
Period										
1	0.990	0.980	0.971	0.962	0.952	0.943	0.935	0.926	0.917	0.909
2	1.970	1.942	1.913	1.886	1.859	1.833	1.808	1.783	1.759	1.736
3	2.941	2.884	2.829	2.775	2.723	2.673	2.624	2.577	2.531	2.487
4	3.902	3.808	3.717	3.630	3.546	3.465	3.387	3.312	3.240	3.170
5	4.853	4.713	4.580	4.452	4.329	4.212	4.100	3.993	3.890	3.791
6	5.795	5.601	5.417	5.242	5.076	4.917	4.767	4.623	4.486	4.355
7	6.728	6.472	6.230	6.002	5.786	5.582	5.389	5.206	5.033	4.868
8	7.652	7.325	7.020	6.733	6.463	6.210	5.971	5.747	5.535	5.335
9	8.566	8.162	7.786	7.435	7.108	6.802	6.515	6.247	5.995	5.759
10	9.471	8.983	8.530	8.111	7.722	7.360	7.024	6.710	6.418	6.145
11	10.368	9.787	9.253	8.760	8.306	7.887	7.499	7.139	6.805	6.495
12	11.255	10.575	9.954	9.385	8.863	8.384	7.943	7.536	7.161	6.814
13	12.134	11.348	10.635	9.986	9.394	8.853	8.358	7.904	7.487	7.103
14	13.004	12.106	11.296	10.563	9.899	9.295	8.745	8.244	7.786	7.367
15	13.865	12.849	11.938	11.118	10.380	9.712	9.108	8.559	8.061	7.606
16	14.718	13.578	12.561	11.652	10.838	10.106	9.447	8.851	8.313	7.824
17	15.562	14.292	13.166	12.166	11.274	10.477	9.763	9.122	8.544	8.022
18	16.398	14.992	13.754	12.659	11.690	10.828	10.059	9.372	8.756	8.201
19	17.226	15.678	14.324	13.134	12.085	11.158	10.336	9.604	8.950	8.365
20	18.046	16.351	14.877	13.590	12.462	11.470	10.594	9.818	9.129	8.514

%	11	12	13	14	15	16	17	18	19	20
Period										
1	0.901	0.893	0.885	0.877	0.870	0.862	0.855	0.847	0.840	0.833
2	1.713	1.690	1.668	1.647	1.626	1.605	1.585	1.566	1.547	1.528
3	2.444	2.402	2.361	2.322	2.283	2.246	2.210	2.174	2.140	2.106
4	3.102	3.037	2.974	2.914	2.855	2.798	2.743	2.690	2.639	2.589
5	3.696	3.605	3.517	3.433	3.352	3.274	3.199	3.127	3.058	2.991
6	4.231	4.111	3.998	3.889	3.784	3.685	3.589	3.498	3.410	3.326
7	4.712	4.564	4.423	4.288	4.160	4.039	3.922	3.812	3.706	3.605
8	5.146	4.968	4.799	4.639	4.487	4.344	4.207	4.078	3.954	3.837
9	5.537	5.328	5.132	4.946	4.772	4.607	4.451	4.303	4.163	4.031
10	5.889	5.650	5.426	5.216	5.019	4.833	4.659	4.494	4.339	4.192
11	6.207	5.938	5.687	5.453	5.234	5.029	4.836	4.656	4.487	4.327
12	6.492	6.194	5.918	5.660	5.421	5.197	4.988	4.793	4.611	4.439
13	6.750	6.424	6.122	5.842	5.583	5.342	5.118	4.910	4.715	4.533
14	6.982	6.628	6.302	6.002	5.724	5.468	5.229	5.008	4.802	4.611
15	7.191	6.811	6.462	6.142	5.847	5.575	5.324	5.092	4.876	4.675
16	7.379	6.974	6.604	6.265	5.954	5.668	5.405	5.162	4.938	4.730
17	7.549	7.120	6.729	6.373	6.047	5.749	5.475	5.222	4.990	4.775
18	7.702	7.250	6.840	6.467	6.128	5.818	5.534	5.273	5.033	4.812
19	7.839	7.366	6.938	6.550	6.198	5.877	5.584	5.316	5.070	4.843
20	7.963	7.469	7.025	6.623	6.259	5.929	5.628	5.353	5.101	4.870

% Period	21	22	23	24	25	26	27	28	29	30
1	0.826	0.820	0.813	0.806	0.800	0.794	0.787	0.781	0.775	0.769
2	1.509	1.492	1.474	1.457	1.440	1.424	1.407	1.392	1.376	1.361
3	2.074	2.042	2.011	1.981	1.952	1.923	1.896	1.868	1.842	1.816
4	2.540	2.494	2.448	2.404	2.362	2.320	2.280	2.241	2.203	2.166
5	2.926	2.864	2.803	2.745	2.689	2.635	2.583	2.532	2.483	2.436
6	3.245	3.167	3.092	3.020	2.951	2.885	2.821	2.759	2.700	2.643
7	3.508	3.416	3.327	3.242	3.161	3.083	3.009	2.937	2.868	2.802
8	3.726	3.619	3.518	3.421	3.329	3.241	3.156	3.076	2.999	2.925
9	3.905	3.786	3.673	3.566	3.463	3.366	3.273	3.184	3.100	3.019
10	4.054	3.923	3.799	3.682	3.571	3.465	3.364	3.269	3.178	3.092
11	4.177	4.035	3.902	3.776	3.656	3.543	3.437	3.335	3.239	3.147
12	4.278	4.127	3.985	3.851	3.725	3.606	3.493	3.387	3.286	3.190
13	4.362	4.203	4.053	3.912	3.780	3.656	3.538	3.427	3.322	3.223
14	4.432	4.265	4.108	3.962	3.824	3.695	3.573	3.459	3.351	3.249
15	4.489	4.315	4.153	4.001	3.859	3.726	3.601	3.483	3.373	3.268
16	4.536	4.357	4.189	4.033	3.887	3.751	3.623	3.503	3.390	3.283
17	4.576	4.391	4.219	4.059	3.910	3.771	3.640	3.518	3.403	3.295
18	4.608	4.419	4.243	4.080	3.928	3.786	3.654	3.529	3.413	3.304
19	4.635	4.442	4.263	4.097	3.942	3.799	3.664	3.539	3.421	3.311
20	4.657	4.460	4.279	4.110	3.954	3.808	3.673	3.546	3.427	3.316

% Period	31	32	33	34	35	36	37	38	39	40
1	0.763	0.758	0.752	0.746	0.741	0.735	0.730	0.725	0.719	0.714
2	1.346	1.331	1.317	1.303	1.289	1.276	1.263	1.250	1.237	1.224
3	1.791	1.766	1.742	1.719	1.696	1.673	1.652	1.630	1.609	1.589
4	2.130	2.096	2.062	2.029	1.997	1.966	1.935	1.906	1.877	1.849
5	2.390	2.345	2.302	2.260	2.220	2.181	2.143	2.106	2.070	2.035
6	2.588	2.534	2.483	2.433	2.385	2.339	2.294	2.251	2.209	2.168
7	2.739	2.677	2.619	2.562	2.508	2.455	2.404	2.355	2.308	2.263
8	2.854	2.786	2.721	2.658	2.598	2.540	2.485	2.432	2.380	2.331
9	2.942	2.868	2.798	2.730	2.665	2.603	2.544	2.487	2.432	2.379
10	3.009	2.930	2.855	2.784	2.715	2.649	2.587	2.527	2.469	2.414
11	3.060	2.978	2.899	2.824	2.752	2.683	2.618	2.555	2.496	2.438
12	3.100	3.013	2.931	2.853	2.779	2.708	2.641	2.576	2.515	2.456
13	3.129	3.040	2.956	2.876	2.799	2.727	2.658	2.592	2.529	2.469
14	3.152	3.061	2.974	2.892	2.814	2.740	2.670	2.603	2.539	2.477
15	3.170	3.076	2.988	2.905	2.825	2.750	2.679	2.611	2.546	2.484
16	3.183	3.088	2.999	2.914	2.834	2.757	2.685	2.616	2.551	2.489
17	3.193	3.097	3.007	2.921	2.840	2.763	2.690	2.621	2.555	2.492
18	3.201	3.104	3.012	2.926	2.844	2.767	2.693	2.624	2.557	2.494
19	3.207	3.109	3.017	2.930	2.848	2.770	2.696	2.626	2.559	2.496
20	3.211	3.113	3.020	2.933	2.850	2.772	2.698	2.627	2.561	2.497

Glossary of Terms

Accounting Period
The period of time between two reporting dates.

Accounting Policies
These are disclosed in the annual reports published by quoted companies and represent the interpretation of accounting principles and requirements adopted by the board of directors.

Accounting Principles
A number of generally accepted accounting principles are used in preparing financial statements. They are only generally accepted and do not have the force of law. You should note that sometimes they are referred to as accounting concepts and conventions.

Accounting Rate of Return
A method used to evaluate an investment opportunity that ignores the time value of money. The return generated by an investment opportunity is expressed as a percentage of the capital outlay.

Acquisition
The process by which a company acquires a controlling interest in the voting shares of another company.

Amortisation
The writing-off of a fixed asset over a time period. It is often used in conjunction with intangible assets, e.g. goodwill.

Annual Report
A report issued to shareholders and other interested parties which normally includes a chairman's statement, report of the directors, review of operations, financial statements and associated notes.

Annuity
A series of payments of an equal, or constant, amount of money at fixed intervals for a specified number of periods.

Balance Sheet
A statement showing the financial position of a company in terms of its assets and liabilities at a specified point in time.

Bank Borrowings
Includes bank overdraft and bank loans.

Beta
A relative measure of volatility determined by comparing a shares returns to the markets returns. The greater the volatility, the higher the beta.

Business Value
The value generated by the free cash flows in which *all* providers of funds have a claim.

Capital Investment Appraisal
The evaluation of proposed capital projects. Sometimes referred to as project appraisal.

Capital Structure
The composition of a company's sources of long-term funds e.g. equity and debt.

Cash flow 'Drivers'
Means by which free cash flow estimates can be generated and consist of:

1. Sales growth rate
2. Operating profit margin
3. Cash tax rate
4. Fixed capital investment
5. Working capital investment

Cash flow statement
A statement that UK and US companies are required to include in their published accounts. Such statements analyse cash flows under three types of activity:

Investing activities

Financial activities

Operating activities.

Chairperson's Statement
A statement by the chairman of a company, normally included as part of the annual report, and which contains reference to important events.

Common-Size Analysis
A method of analysis by which data in the profit and loss account and the balance sheet are expressed as a percentage of some key figure.

Compounding
A technique for determining a future value given a present value, a time period and an interest rate.

Corporate Value
Where a business holds investments in other businesses, the benefits of which are not captured in the business valuation process, any such benefits have to be added to business value to determine corporate value.

Cost of Capital
The cost of long-term funds to a company.

Creative Accounting
The name given to a number of approaches by which companies could use (and have used) considerable judgement to produce results which put them in the best possible light, whilst staying within the letter of the law.

Creditors: amounts owing within one year
The amounts of money owed and payable by the business within one year.

Creditors: amounts owing after more than one year

Long-term loans and other liabilities payable after one year.

Current Assets

Those assets of a company that are reasonably expected to be realised in cash, or sold, or consumed during the normal operating cycle of the business. They include stock, debtors, short term investments, bank and cash balances.

Current Liabilities

Those liabilities which a company may rely upon to finance short-term activities. They include creditors, bank overdraft, proposed final dividend, and current taxation.

Current Ratio

A measure of short-term solvency. It is calculated as current assets divided by current liabilities. It gives an indication of a company's ability to pay its way within one year.

Debtors

Amounts owed to a company by its customers.

Depreciation

An accounting adjustment to take account of the diminution in value of a fixed asset over its economic life.

Discounted Cash Flow (DCF)

A technique for calculating whether a sum receivable at some time in the future is worthwhile in terms of value today. It involves discounting, or scaling-down, future cash flows.

Dividend

The proportion of the profits of a company distributed to shareholders.

Earnings Per Share

Profit before taxation divided by the weighted average number of ordinary shares in issue during the period. The calculation and result is shown by way of note in a company's annual report.

Equity

The sum of issued share capital, capital reserves and revenue reserves which is also known as shareholders' funds, or net worth.

Equity Risk Premium

The excess return above the risk-free rate that investors demand for holding risky securities.

Equity Share Capital

The share capital of a company attributable to ordinary shareholders.

Financial Risk

The risk that results from a significant dependency upon capital funded by debt and which typically requires to be serviced by non-discretionary interest payments.

Fixed Assets

Those assets which an organisation holds for use within the business and not for resale. They consist of tangible assets, like land and buildings, plant and machinery, vehicles, and fixtures and fittings; and intangible assets like goodwill.

Floating Charge

A charge against assets as security for a debt. It is a general claim against any available asset of the company.

Free Cash Flow

The cash available to the providers of finance.

Gearing

Expresses the relationship between some measure of interest-bearing capital and some measure of equity capital or the total capital employed.

Goodwill

The difference between the amount paid for a company as a whole and the net value of the assets and liabilities acquired.

Income Statement

An US term for the profit and loss account.

Incremental Fixed Capital Investment (IFCI)

Investment in new assets to enable intended sales growth to occur.

Incremental Working Capital Investment (IWCI)

Investment in additional working capital, such as stocks of materials, to enable intended sales growth to occur.

Intangible Assets

Assets the value of which does not relate to their physical properties, e.g. goodwill and brands.

Internal Rate of Return (IRR)

The rate of discount at which the present value of the future cash flows is equal to the initial outlay, i.e. at the IRR the net present value is zero.

Interest Payable

Money payable (but not necessary paid) on interest bearing debt.

Key Ratio

A term sometimes given to the profitability ratio. In the UK this is usually defined as profit before tax plus interest payable expressed as a percentage of net capital employed.

Liabilities

The financial obligations owed by a company, these can be to shareholders, other providers of debt, trade creditors and other creditors.

Liquid Assets

The difference between current assets and stock.

Liquid Ratio

Liquid assets divided by current liabilities. It attempts to show a company's ability to pay its way in the short term.

Loan Capital

Finance that has been borrowed and not obtained from the shareholders.

Long-Term Liabilities

Liabilities which are not due for repayment within one year.

Market Value of Equity

The product of the market value of shares and the number of shares issued. Often referred to as market capitalisation.

MB Ratio

The relationship between market value and shareholders' funds.

Minority Interest

The proportion of shares in subsidiary companies which is not held by a holding company. Profit attributable to minority interests and accumulated balances are shown in the consolidated financial statements.

Net Assets

Total assets minus Current Liabilities minus Creditors: amounts owing after one year.

Net Capital Employed

The sum of fixed assets, investments, current assets minus current liabilities.

Net Current Assets

See working capital.

Net Present Value (NPV)

The difference between the discounted value of future net cash inflows and the initial outlay..

Ordinary Shares

Shares which attract the remaining profits after all other claims, and, in liquidation, which attract the remaining assets of a company after creditors and other charges have been satisfied.

Payback Period

How long it will take to recover the outlay involved in a potential investment opportunity from net cash inflows.

Peer Group Analysis

An approach involving the analysis of peer group companies which can be used in conjunction with financial information relating to a company to estimate its value.

PE Ratio

One of the most significant indicators of corporate performance which it is widely quoted in the financial press. It is calculated by dividing the market price of a share by the earnings per share (or the total market value by the total profit attributable to shareholders), i.e.

$$\text{PE Ratio} \quad = \quad \frac{\text{Market Price of a Share}}{\text{Earnings Per Share}}$$

PE Relative

A means of comparing a company's PE ratio with the market as a whole:

$$PE \ relative \ = \ \frac{PE \ of \ the \ company}{PE \ of \ the \ market}$$

Perpetuity

A special case of an annuity in which the cash flows are assumed to be received in perpetuity.

Present Value Rule

A rule which explains why in a world of certainty accepting all projects with a positive NPV maximises the wealth of shareholders.

Profit and Loss Account

A statement showing what profit has been made over a period and the uses to which the profit has been put.

Quoted Investments

Investments in another company which has its shares quoted on a stock exchange..

Reducing Balance Depreciation

A method of depreciation whereby the periodic amount written off is a percentage of the reduced balance. (cost less accumulated depreciation).

Relevant Data

Relevant data for decision making is *future oriented* – that is *yet to be incurred.*

Replacement Fixed Capital Investment (RFCI)

Investment in fixed assets to maintain the level of productive facilities currently in place.

Residual Value

Value generated beyond the planning period

Risk-Free Rate

The most secure return that can be achieved.

Sales or Turnover

Income derived from the principal activities of a company, net of value added tax (VAT).

Sensitivity Analysis

A commonly used approach to assessing risk whereby input variables are changed to determine their effect upon financial results.

Share Capital (Issued)

The product of the total number of shares issued and the nominal value of the shares.

Shareholder's Funds

Another name for equity.

Shareholder Value

A measure of value calculated as follows:

Business Value

+ Marketable Securities or Investments

= Corporate Value

– Market Value of Debt and Obligations

= Shareholder Value

Shareholder Value Analysis

A valuation approach which considers in broad terms that the value of a business to a shareholder can be determined by discounting its future cash flows using an appropriate cost of capital.

Share Premium

The excess paid for a share, to a company, over its nominal value.

Short-Termism

A term associated with managing for today rather than tomorrow and beyond.

Straight Line Depreciation

A method of depreciation whereby an equal amount is written off the value of a fixed asset over its estimated economic life.

Tangible Assets

An asset having a physical identity such as land and buildings, plant and machinery, vehicles etc.

Time Value of Money

A concept which is an integral part of the discounted cash flow technique used in capital investment appraisal. It recognises that cash flows in the later years of an investment opportunity cannot be compared with cash flows in the earlier years.

Total Assets

The sum of fixed assets, investments and current assets.

Weighted Average Cost of Capital (WACC)

A term associated with the view that there is an optimal or ideal capital structure. It is calculated as follows:

Weighted Average Cost of Capital $=$ %Debt (K_d) + %Equity (K_e)

$$\text{where} \quad K_d \; = \; \text{Cost of debt}$$

$$K_e \; = \; \text{Cost of equity}$$

Working Capital

The excess of current assets (stock, debtors and cash) over current liabilities (creditors, bank overdraft etc.).

References

Altman, E.I., *Corporate Bankruptcy in America*, Heath Lexington Books, 1971.

Altman, E.I., 'Accounting implications of failure prediction models', *Journal of Accounting Auditing and Finance*, Fall, pp.4–19, 1982.

Altman, E.I., *Corporate financial distress: a complete guide to predicting and avoiding bankruptcy*, John Wiley, 1983.

Argenti, J., *Corporate Collapse*, McGraw Hill, 1976.

Argyris, C., 'Human problems with budgets', *Harvard Business Review*, 1953.

Barnes, P., 'The application of multiple discriminant analysis in the prediction of company failure – an example of an undesirable consequence of the information technology revolution', *Managerial Finance*, Vol.10, No.1, pp.11–14, 1984.

Bennett III, S.G., *The quest for value: a guide for senior managers*, Harper Collins, 1991.

Bliss, J.H., 'The operating and financial ratios characteristics of industries', *Management and Administration*, Vol.7, No.2, February, pp.155–160, 1924.

Cadbury Report, Financial Aspects of Corporate Governance, 1992.

Copeland, T., Koller, T. and Murrin, J., *Valuation, measuring and managing the value of companies*, Second Edition, McKinsey & Company Inc., John Wiley, 1995.

Dobson, R.W., 'Return on capital', *Management Accounting*, November, pp.438–447, 1967.

Goold, M., Campbell, A. and Alexander, M., *Corporate level strategy: Creating value in the multibusiness company*, John Wiley, 1994.

Horngren, C.T., *Accounting for management contol*, Second Edition, Prentice Hall, 1970.

Johnson, G. and Scholes, K., *Exploring Corporate Strategy*, Prentice Hall, Fifth Edition, 1998.

McConville, D.J., 'All about EVA', *Industry Week*, April 13–14, pp.1–3, 1994.

McTaggart, J.M., Kontes, P.W. and Mankins, M.C., *The value imperative*, Free Press, 1994.

Mills, R.W., DeBono, J., DeBono, V., Ewers, D., Parker, D. and Print, C., *The use of shareholder value analysis in acquisition and divestment decisions by large UK companies*, Henley Management College, 1996.

P.A. Consulting Group, *Managing for shareholder value*, Survey – UK and Ireland, 1997.

Parker, R.H., *Understanding company financial statements*, Pelican Books, 1975.

Peters, T.J. and Waterman, R.H., *In search of excellence*, Harper and Row, 1989.

Porter, M.E., *Competitive advantage: creating and sustaining superior performance*, Free Press, 1985.

Price Waterhouse, *CFO: Architect of the corporation's future*, Price Waterhouse Financial and Cost Management Team, John Wiley, 1997.

Rappaport, A., *Creating shareholder value, the new standard for business performance*, Free Press, 1986.

Rappaport, A., *Creating shareholder value: a guide for managers and investors*, Free Press, 1998.

Robertson, J., 'Company failure: measuring changes in financial health through ratio analysis', *Management Accounting*, November, pp.24–28, 1983.

Taffler, R.J. and Houston, W., 'How to identify failing companies before it is too late', *Professional Administration*, April, p.2, 1980.

Index

A

B

C